GUNPOINT CAPITALISM

COMPARATIVE POLITICS AND INTERNATIONAL STUDIES
SERIES

Series Editor: Christophe Jaffrelot

This series focuses on the transformation of politics and societies by international and domestic factors, including culture and religion. Analysing these changes in a sociological and historical perspective, it gives priority to trends from below as much as state interventions and the interaction of both. It also factors in dynamics at the interface of inter/transnational pressures and national tensions.

LAURENT GAYER

Gunpoint
Capitalism

Enforcing Industrial Order in Karachi

Translated by Laurent Gayer and Jane Roffe

OXFORD
UNIVERSITY PRESS

OXFORD

UNIVERSITY PRESS

Oxford University Press is a department of the
University of Oxford. It furthers the University's objective
of excellence in research, scholarship, and education
by publishing worldwide.

Oxford New York

Auckland   Cape Town   Dar es Salaam   Hong Kong   Karachi
Kuala Lumpur   Madrid   Melbourne   Mexico City   Nairobi
New Delhi   Shanghai   Taipei   Toronto

With offices in

Argentina   Austria   Brazil   Chile   Czech Republic   France   Greece
Guatemala   Hungary   Italy   Japan   Poland   Portugal   Singapore
South Korea   Switzerland   Thailand   Turkey   Ukraine   Vietnam

Oxford is a registered trade mark of Oxford University Press
in the UK and certain other countries.

Published in the United States of America by
Oxford University Press
198 Madison Avenue, New York, NY 10016

Library of Congress Cataloging-in-Publication Data is available

ISBN: 9780197813287

Printed in the United Kingdom by Bell & Bain Ltd, Glasgow

In memory of Talat 'Tito' Aslam (1955–2022)

CONTENTS

ACKNOWLEDGEMENTS

In his erudite critique of the mechanisms of debt, David Graeber concedes that while solitary pleasures do have some appeal, for most human beings, 'the most pleasurable activities almost always involve sharing something: music, food, liquor, drugs, gossip, drama, beds'.[1] Research is no exception to this rule. While it does offer a certain amount of personal satisfaction, it is above all a tremendous provider of shared joys. What I remember most from my successive stays in Karachi is not so much the debts accumulated towards all those with whom I had the chance to work, but rather the joys (and sometimes the sorrows) that brought us together. Zia Ur Rehman was a constant source of support and inspiration; his unrivalled knowledge of Karachi's society and politics will never cease to amaze me. Ali Arqam awakened me to the subtleties of *dera* culture in western Karachi, Waseem Yaqoob opened my eyes to the fate of Christian industrial workers, and Sartaj Khan was a fountain of knowledge on the history of Karachi's working-class politics. My analysis of the Baldia factory fire case was sketched out during a series of exchanges with Barrister Faisal Siddiqi on the resonance of E.P. Thompson's *Whigs and Hunters* in the Pakistani context, while those tireless defenders of workers' rights, Nasir Mansoor and Zehra Khan, introduced me to various labour struggles as they helped me gain access to the court records that proved crucial to my research.

Nida Kirmani, Zehra Abid, and Mahim Maher are also among these free spirits whose determination in the face of a hostile world is awe-inspiring. In addition to being the mentor who introduced me to the lyricism, struggles, and biting irony of the poets chronicling the woes of the times, Hidayat Hussain also introduced me to a number of executives and business leaders. I guaranteed their anonymity, but without their trust, this investigation could not have been carried out.

I am also grateful to Faiza Mushtaq, Khurram Husain, and Sohail Zuberi for their lasting friendship and for brightening Karachi's nights. Last but not least, my warmest thanks go to all those who assisted me on the field or in the transcription of my interviews: Fawad Hasan, Riaz Sohail, Imtiaz Ali, Abubakkar Yousafzai, G.M. Baloch, Raviya Mysorewala, Kaleemullah Bashir, and Sibtain Naqvi.

This personal work has also built upon a multitude of scientific collaborations and informal exchanges, which matured through the time spent (and sometimes wasted) together. Together with my colleagues Gilles Favarel-Garrigues, Laurent Fourchard, and Anthony Amicelle, I co-direct a research group on policing at the Center for International Studies (CERI) where we have more recently been joined by a cohort of inventive PhD and post-doctoral students (Romane Da Cunha Dupuy, Pierre Labrunie, Lucie Revilla, and Sophie Russo); this group has guided my thinking throughout the preparation of this book. My gratitude also goes to the students of the Master's in Political Science at Sciences Po, who were my first audience and contributed to each stage of my reflection.

The sensible and valuable advice of Laurent Bonelli, Quentin Deluermoz, Fabien Jobard, Emmanuel Blanchard, and Atreyee Sen encouraged me to widen the scope of my comparisons between policing experiences, while suggestions from Markus Daechsel, Nandini Gooptu, and Geert de Neve helped sharpen my arguments about the securitization of development and the organization of informality in Pakistan. Far beyond our shared passion for Pakistan, my informal conversations with Paul Rollier have also been an inexhaustible source of inspiration.

At CERI, Christophe Jaffrelot has worked alongside me at every stage of this project, enriching it with his intimate knowledge of comparable dynamics in India. And my collaboration with Gilles

Favarel-Garrigues has opened up a fruitful conversation between Russian and Pakistani experiences of capitalism.

The supervisor of my *Habilitation à diriger des recherches*, Gilles Dorronsoro, never stopped pushing me to broaden my argument by drawing connections between contemporary Karachi and seemingly distant cases. The transformation of my *Habilitation* thesis into a book has also benefited from constructive criticism from the members of my jury—Assia Boutaleb, Christophe Jaffrelot, Christian Lund, Dennis Rodgers, and Johanna Siméant. The finalization of the manuscript benefited from the meticulous and imaginative proofreading of Adam Baczko and Adèle Blazquez, while Jane Roffe not only helped me translate the book into English but significantly improved the text from its French original.

My successive missions to Karachi benefited from the financial support of Sciences Po and CERI, whose administrative team greatly facilitated my work.

My final thanks go to my family: my parents, Michel and Catherine Gayer, my children, Anju and Gabriel, and finally to my wife, Mayuka, who originally inspired me to compare the incomparable.

GLOSSARY

Akhara	Gymnasium
Banya	Hindu merchant/moneylender
Badmash	Thug/henchman
Basti	Working-class neighbourhood
Bhai	Brother
Bhatta	Extortion
Chamcha/Chamchi	Bootlicker
Charas	Hashish
Chela	Disciple
Chowkidar	Watchman
Dada	Neighbourhood boss
Dadagiri	Thuggery
Dera	Reception room/workers' quarters/lair of a criminal
Fauji	Soldier
Goonda	Thug
Goth	Urban village
Gutka	Chewing tobacco
Hartal	General strike
Hujra	Reception room
Jama'at	Among the Memons: associative structure based on the locality of origin in India

Jawan	Soldier/Trooper
Katchi abadi	Informal neighbourhood
Kirana	Gujarati term for spices, pulses and edible oils
Kunda	Illegal connection to the electricity grid
Lathi	Bamboo cane used by the police
Maal	Merchandise
Malik	Owner/employer
Malang	Itinerant Sufi
Mazdoor	Manual worker
Paan	Betel-based chewing paste
Phadda	Scuffle
Mistri	Mason/recruiting agent (in high value industries)
Muhajir	Urdu-speaking migrant from northern India and Deccan
Mohajir	Descendant of these migrants
Parchi	Extortion letter
Pehelwan	Wrestler
Reki	Reconnaissance
Sahab	Sir
Sardar	'Lord'/recruiting agent (on the docks)
Serang	Boatswain
Shalwar-Kamiz	Unisex garment traditionally worn in Pakistan and Afghanistan, consisting of loose trousers and a long shirt
Seth	Boss/owner of capital from the Gujarati merchant castes. In Karachi, refers mainly to the Memons active in the textile industry
Thekedar	Contractor
Zakat	Almsgiving
Zulm	Tyranny/oppression

LIST OF ACRONYMS

AHRC	Asian Human Rights Commission
ANP	Awami National Party
APCOL	All Pakistan Confederation of Labour
ATA	Anti-Terrorism Act
CIO	Congress of Industrial Organizations
CDU	Calcutta Dockers' Union
CFT	Confédération française du travail
CGSI	Confédération générale des syndicats indépendants
CNIC	Computerised National Identity Card
CPEC	China-Pakistan Economic Corridor
CPLC	Citizens-Police Liaison Committee
CPP	Communist Party of Pakistan
CSP	Civil Service of Pakistan
DHA	Defence Housing Authority
EOBI	Employees' Old-Age Benefits Institution
FATA	Federally Administered Tribal Areas
FC	Frontier Constabulary
FIA	Federal Investigation Agency
FIR	First Information Report
FNJ	Fédération nationale des Jaunes de France
GHQ	General Headquarters (Pakistan Army)

LIST OF ACRONYMS

GM	General Motors
IB	Intelligence Bureau
IO	Investigation Officer
IR	Industrial Relations
ISI	Inter-Services Intelligence
IWW	Industrial Workers of the World
JI	Jama'at-e-Islami
JIT	Joint Investigation Team
JUD	Jama'at-ud-Dawa
KATI	Korangi Association of Trade and Industry
KCCI	Karachi Chamber of Commerce and Industry
KKF	Khidmat-e-Khalq Foundation
KP	Khyber Pakhtunkhwa
LFP	Labour Federation of Pakistan
MQM	Mohajir Qaumi Movement (1984-1997) / Muttahida Qaumi Movement (since 1997)
NADRA	National Database and Registration Authority
NLF	National Labour Federation
NTUF	National Trade Union Federation
ILO	International Labour Organization
PAC	People's Amn Committee
PECHS	Pakistan Employees Cooperative Housing Society
PIDC	Pakistan Industrial Development Corporation
PILER	Pakistan Institute of Labour Education and Research
PPP	Pakistan People's Party
PRGMEA	Pakistan Readymade Garments Manufacturers and Exporters Association
RSG	Rangers Security Guards
SAC	Service d'action civique
SESSI	Sindh Employees' Social Security Institution
SHO	Station House Officer
SITE	Sindh Industrial Trading Estate

SSP	Sipah-e-Sahaba Pakistan
ST	Sunni Tehrik
TTP	Tehrik-e-Taliban Pakistan
UAW	United Automobile Workers
VPF	Volunteer Police Force

LIST OF ILLUSTRATIONS

Geographies of Capital

INTRODUCTION

In the Sindh Industrial Trading Estate (SITE), Karachi's oldest industrial area, factory architecture has long since given up on modernist experiments, settling for variations on the prison form. With their concrete facades punctuated by barred windows, the Ali Enterprises buildings are typical of the garment factories that dot the battered landscape of this urban periphery, where a precarious, tightly supervised workforce toils away for the benefit of the biggest global brands.

On this particular day—11 September 2012—this factory located on the edge of the working-class district of Baldia Town is bustling with activity. It is payday, so in addition to people at work on the shop floor, there are others who have come to collect their monthly pay—the equivalent of about a hundred dollars. As night falls, nearly a thousand people are still in the building. More than half of them are gathered on the second floor, where the payment operations are taking place.

These paydays are synonymous with increased company security—especially given that Ali Enterprises has no perimeter wall and is therefore directly exposed to the dangers of the city. The factory's emergency exits are sealed off and the windows fitted with bars and grills, or even bricked up. This has more to do with discouraging the theft of fabric and materials by the company's own employees than it does with deterring burglars. By restricting workers' mobility, these security measures also serve to extend the

1

working day so that order deadlines are met at all costs. Today, the factory is almost hermetically sealed; the only possible exits are the door to the first floor and the entrance to the ground floor (which serves as a warehouse and is constantly clogged with bales of cotton).

When a burning smell starts to spread in the upper floors of the building, the workers are not overly alarmed. Fires are commonplace at Ali Enterprises, as in every textile factory in Karachi. On this occasion, however, by the time the flames appear, it is too late. With no accessible emergency exit and no functioning fire extinguishers, many employees are trapped. The fire spreads from the ground floor to the second floor, where the employees number several hundred, via a wooden mezzanine built in violation of safety regulations.

Arriving at the scene half an hour after being informed of the disaster, firefighters are visibly taken aback by its magnitude. The first team deployed on site has just two fire engines, whose water supply

The Ali Enterprises building devastated by fire on 11 September 2012. This photograph, taken a few days after the disaster, was featured in a group exhibition at the Arts Council in Karachi in February 2013, aimed at mobilizing public opinion for structural reform of the manufacturing sector.

quickly runs out. This obvious lack of preparedness exasperates the families of the workers caught in the flames, and altercations break out. Meanwhile, rescue vehicles from the Edhi Foundation (Karachi's main philanthropic organization, which manages the city's largest fleet of ambulances) are blocked from entering the site by gun-toting militants of the Muttahida Qaumi Movement (MQM)—the party that has dominated the local political scene since the second half of the 1980s. The MQM's philanthropic wing, the Khidmat-e-Khalq Foundation (KKF), is already onsite, and the party leadership intends to keep control of the rescue operation. Taking advantage of the general confusion, the owners of the factory—Abdul Aziz Bhaila and his two sons, Shahid and Arshad—manage to slip away.

Sixteen hours later, when the fire is finally brought under control and firefighters manage to get inside the factory, they find dozens of charred bodies, which are added to the corpses already pulled from the flames during the night. This is not the first time the Edhi Foundation morgues have been called upon in such emergency situations, but they are soon beyond capacity. By the end of the day, the city's hospitals announce 249 victims—an estimate destined to rise higher still over the coming weeks.[1]

Chains of predation

Though official statistics scarcely reflect this reality for want of reporting, accidents are part and parcel of the routine functioning of Pakistani industry. Yet the Baldia Town disaster differed from these ordinary tragedies from the outset; it was the deadliest industrial fire ever, worldwide (the final death toll was over 250), and the legal proceedings that began in the following months in Pakistan were widely publicized—both nationally and internationally.

The investigators and judges in charge of the various civil and criminal proceedings pointed to criminal negligence on the part of factory owners, but the scope of the accusations soon became more general. Because Ali Enterprises was mainly producing jeans for the German discount retailer KiK and had just been awarded an SA 8000 certificate by the Italian company RINA, the trial risked drawing in global value chains and their regulatory regime.[2]

The Ali Enterprises fire thus positioned a certain global capitalism model in the dock—one based simultaneously on worldwide economic integration and the formation of niches, each trying to assert its own competitive advantages in the international division of labour. This competitiveness concerns more than just wages; the existence of a 'business-friendly' environment, free of regulatory burdens and hostile to collective action, is equally decisive.

Both nationally and internationally, the current vogue for outsourcing is not just about cutting costs. It is also about externalizing illegalities by transferring legal and reputational risk to subcontractors.[3] By reproducing binary opposition between the centre and the periphery, the relocation theme tends to obscure what is at stake here: the advent of a global productive order based on the circumvention of regulatory constraints, the neutralization of trade union bargaining power and the dismantling of insurance mechanisms once guaranteed by the social state.

While this has yet to lead to a general state of anomie, this global offensive is nonetheless a strong signal of the revival of *predation* as the mainspring of capitalist accumulation. As anthropologist Michel Naepels has suggested, this notion deserves to be revisited in order to 'get to grips with capitalism's destructive power', as close as possible to the forms of vulnerability caused by the over-exploitation of man and nature.[4]

This proposal is in line with the concerns of heterodox economists who, starting with James Galbraith, argue for a re-reading of Thorstein Veblen's work in the light of recent transformations of the state and capitalism. For the founder of economic institutionalism, historically predation is the mark of warriors and hunters, those who 'reap where they have not sown' and defend their status by force or fraud. With the advent of industrial capitalism, Veblen believes, this predatory instinct has been rehabilitated, with bells on. In the late nineteenth century, its most uninhibited manifestations were found in the American 'robber barons', who went on to establish their own transgressions as vectors of economic progress.[5] In the twentieth century, the regulations of the 'new industrial state' theorized by John Galbraith sought to tame capitalism by imposing a series of restrictions on individual appetites.[6] Defending his father's intellectual legacy while following in Veblen's footsteps, James Galbraith noted that the crisis of this regulatory model, which began in the 1980s, has resulted in a predatory relapse that has been particularly evident in the United States, but also exists in Europe.[7]

This regression accelerated during the 2000s under the effect of a series of cumulative phenomena including: the retreat of national and international regulatory bodies; the advent of international conflicts that, while ruinous for states, benefited a small coalition of large companies (as was the case during the Iraqi conflict—a decisive moment in the consolidation of a 'corporate republic' in the United States); the impunity granted to delinquent elites, whether in the financial markets, at the head of big business, or in government circles; and the systematic attacks on workers' rights in the name of the doctrine of flexibility.[8]

In this sense, the notion of predation cannot be reduced to either the capture of rents (as in 'booty capitalism', of Weberian inspiration[9]) or a phenomenon of spoliation that is reminiscent of primitive accumulation (as in the neo-Marxist concept of 'accumulation by dispossession').[10] Rather, it is a concerted effort to neutralize (or even dismantle) regulatory mechanisms, on the part of those companies least willing to be held accountable.[11] These new predators may combat the power of prohibition that, in the eyes of entrepreneurs, is the most obvious manifestation of the state.[12] Yet, their aim is not to neutralize state power altogether. The convertibility of economic capital into political influence is characteristic of the capitalist societies in which they operate, and they use this to open up significant prospects for enrichment via the private appropriation of public resources.

In this rereading of Veblen, predation thus also points to the contemporary ways in which wealth is being transformed into political clout—as well as the uses of public authority as a wealth multiplier. In the United States, the arrival of George W. Bush in 2001 marked a turning point, with the establishment of an administration closely linked to the regulated sectors, starting with extractive industries. Throughout its mandate, this administration consistently redirected public wealth to the companies in question, while at the same time neutralizing control bodies by appointing notorious opponents of regulation to positions of power.[13]

The longest-established companies tend to exert excessive political influence—either through pressure groups, or due to their mastery of the bureaucratic game, or because of their embeddedness in the economic and social life of certain constituencies. These are also the companies for whom the costs of compliance with new regulatory measures are highest. Regulatory schemes tend to be better accepted by emerging companies; not so much because they are more virtuous or more concerned with the common good, but because compliance costs eliminate competition from less innovative segments of the business community.[14]

The criminal practices of the pharmaceutical sector (fraud, corruption, falsification of products and clinical tests, etc.) serve as a reminder that the most advanced industries are in no way immune to corporate crime.[15] As it is understood here, predation goes well beyond irregular practices, however. At its most ambitious, it consists of shaping the state to suit one's own ends, appropriating its material and symbolic resources, while paralyzing it in the exercise of its regulatory functions.

Though this discussion has thus far remained very US-centric, the Pakistani textile and garment industry demonstrates that the phenomenon is not confined to the oldest industrialized societies. As the most powerful national lobby, the companies dominating this sector are masterful in capturing state subsidies while containing the state's attempts at control—if necessary, neutralizing its reforms.[16] The successful insertion of this industry into the globalized circuits of fast fashion also demonstrates that predatory logics, far from being archaic, embody a very contemporary modality of capitalist control and accumulation.

Making order out of disorder

In the weeks following the Ali Enterprises fire, this predatory capitalism and its global relays were put in the dock—yet the judicial process soon took a completely different direction. While doubts persisted as to the exact origin of the fire (largely due to the lack of resources of the investigators, as they themselves admitted) what Pakistanis refer to as the 'deep state' (*bari sarkar*, lit. 'big government', i.e. the army and its intelligence agencies) soon joined the fray, giving the controversy a political twist. By relaying the confessions of a former hit man in the service of the MQM, the army designated a new culprit, paving the way for a different interpretation of the tragedy. The MQM now stood accused of being behind the factory fire in a racketeering case and paid the price for its past abuses; the former ruling party's extortion practices and criminal affiliations rendered these accusations plausible to broad sections of the media, public opinion, and the judiciary. In Pakistan at least, the trial of global value chains thus gave way to the trial of the mafia-esque methods of the political parties, accused of having bled the country's economic and financial capital dry.[17]

While exonerating both the owners of Ali Enterprises and the production system in which they participated, this reclassification of the industrial disaster as a terrorist act led the investigators to uncover a vast network of collusion between Karachi's employers, the city's underworld, and its militarized political parties.[18] The exact causes of the tragedy may remain mired in controversy, but successive investigations have exposed a myriad of violent specialists in the service of *industrial order*—a notion which here encompasses the organization of production processes and the control of workers (in the workplace and beyond) at the behest of the owners of capital.

What the Baldia Town disaster and its judicial aftermath revealed, then, was not only the extent of the irregularities inherent to this production model but, more fundamentally, a coercive organization of industrial work and related modes of existence. Transcending the boundaries between the factory world and neighbourhood life, these forms of control have the specificity of making intensive use of extra-economic coercion—either directly (through the recruitment of henchmen) or indirectly (through the instrumentalization of everyday social violence).

Precipitated by the militarization of society and the advent of a new criminal economy in the wake of the Afghan jihad (1979–1989),[19] the proliferation of violent actors in Karachi has exposed the industry's employers and managers to new risks (kidnappings,

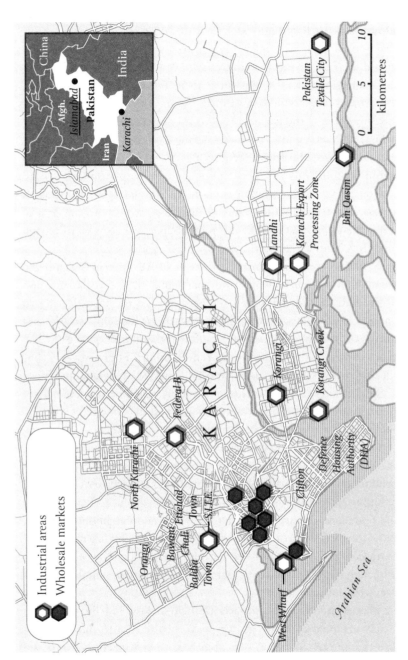

Main zones of economic activity in Karachi (2022)

racketeering, renewed conflict within the workshops, etc.). Faced with these security risks and, more structurally, with the disruption of the factory order by new urban disorders, industrialists first tried to sanitize their production sites.

These prophylactic measures, which aimed to insulate industrial firms from their troubled surroundings, were not, however, the employers' only form of engagement with the protagonists of violence. Over the years, industrialists have learned both to protect themselves from armed groups and to use the latter's coercive resources to strengthen their own control over workers, to cut production costs, and to secure their supplies.

The absence of massive capital flight to safer locations tends to confirm this acclimatization to urban turmoil. Despite competition from the region's manufacturing industries (India, China, and Bangladesh for the textile sector), poor infrastructure, and chronic insecurity, the local industrial sector has continued to attract investment[20] and still employs nearly 30% of the city's working population (approximately three million people, mainly concentrated around the industrial zones of Landhi and Korangi in the east and SITE in the west).[21]

The urban conflicts that have characterized Karachi since the 1980s may have granted free rein to some industrialists—but their case is far from isolated; on the contrary, it is part of a long trend in the history of capitalism that extends well beyond the phase of primitive accumulation. As a reinforcement or substitute for professional law enforcement agencies, large corporations have always relied on controversial auxiliaries. Indeed, while being instrumental in the emergence of private security, they have been drawing on the human and logistical resources of the mob, of paramilitary organizations, and of armed militias in a bid to 'make order out of disorder' (as Marc Caussidière, former French Prefect of Police, once put it).[22] Putting their muscle power in the service of employers, these specialists in violence were particularly active both in the United States and in Europe in periods of social unrest, such as during the late nineteenth century, the Great Depression of the 1930s, or the late 1960s/early 1970s.

Far from being consigned to history, these henchmen of capital have continued to reinvent themselves alongside the productive and extractive practices of capitalism itself. Thus, while Colombian paramilitaries have been working since the 1990s to dismantle the institutions of industrial citizenship (labour law, trade unions),[23] further north in the Mexican region of the Isthmus of Tehuantepec, the Zapotec Indians (who have mobilized against the construction of gigantic wind farms) are facing joint repression by the armed forces as well as local and federal police. Also involving death squads financed by industrialists and large landowners, along with mercenaries from the rest of Mexico (and even from abroad),[24] this repressive configuration illustrates the capacity of so-called 'green' capitalism to generate its own share of violent enterprises against a backdrop of massive dispossession and the commercial militarization of nature.[25]

Productive though it is, this intertwining of capital and coercion rarely results in a stable system. As the tensions around the securing of Karachi's manufacturing economy show, this process of securitization is negotiated through an unstable balance of forces, feeding its own economy of suspicion. *Gunpoint Capitalism* is devoted to examining this relationship of suspicious intimacy between a fearful capitalist class and its fearsome guardians.

* * *

Drawing on fieldwork conducted from 2015 to 2022, this book traces the anxiety-laden formation of this industrial order. Spread over seven non-consecutive months in Karachi and extended by several archival trips to the United States and the United Kingdom, my investigation has made it possible to cross-reference a wide variety of primary sources and documentary corpuses. Approximately 160 interviews were conducted (mostly in Urdu and on the condition of anonymity) with workers, supervisors, and senior managers, as well as with trade union activists, lawyers, labour inspectors, members of law enforcement agencies, and private security personnel.[26] This research has focused on the textile and clothing industry, but I have also taken an interest in the pharmaceutical industry, in order to account for the variations in the control practices prevailing in two sectors of activity that seem opposed to one another—whether as a result of their historical trajectories, their respective places in the economy, or their organization of work. Pakistan's industrialization was founded on textiles. It is also the sector most prone to illegalities and most attached to the patriarchal, family-based managerial model that is associated with the figure of the *seth*.[27] In Karachi as in the north-eastern province of Punjab, this industry took off in the 1950s, and its golden age came in the decade that followed. Historically specialized in the production of low value-added yarn and fabric, it suffered from competition from synthetic textiles and the global recession that followed the oil shocks of the 1970s. The obsolescence of this economic model, combined with the political uncertainty generated by the arrival in power of Zulfikar Ali Bhutto (1971–1977), led many industrialists to lay off large numbers of workers—and, in many cases, transfer their capital abroad. It was not until the 1990s that the textile industry in Karachi was granted a new lease of life, when companies began focusing on ready-made garments for the national and international market.

The pharmaceutical industry is newer, more regulated and more open to managerial innovation—although it has not abandoned tight control of workers and certain illicit practices, whether in the placement of its products or the management of its workforce. This sector began developing in the 1960s, and thanks to significant investments in technology and training, the Pakistani pharmaceutical industry has grown rapidly since the 2000s. It now covers a wide production spectrum, from simple tablets to high value-added generic components, biotechnology, and oncology. Despite this growth, the political influence of pharmaceutical manufacturers remains modest compared to that of their textile counterparts. As the largest employer in the secondary sector and the country's largest foreign exchange earner, the textile and garment industry occupies a special place in Pakistan's economy, and is seen as the nation's lifeline.[28]

My first points of entry into this industrial world were journalist friends who, through their participation in the survey, found an opportunity to trace the working-class history of their own families. Their family circles included many industrial workers, both active

11

and retired. In addition, these long-time friends introduced me to their neighbours—especially the *buzurgs* (the 'noble elders' who hold a neighbourhood's memory), the trade union activists who had been involved in the social struggles of the 1960s and 1970s, and the local working-class intellectuals who continue teaching the precepts of Marxism in their study circles.

Through these journalists, who grew up in the predominantly Pashtun working-class neighbourhoods of Landhi (in the east of the city) and Orangi (in the west), I also met a group of managers who had risen through the ranks. Although they embody the opportunities for social mobility offered by Karachi's large industrial enterprises, these production or finishing managers remain in a precarious position. The pressures of global value chains—with their ever-greater demands for quality, speed, and competitiveness[29]— are exerted most intensely on these mid-ranking departmental managers, making them valuable informants; these are the people who helped me complicate my approach to the precariousness of the industrial labour market.

My access to industrial circles was facilitated by a handful of trusted informants, whom I often approached in informal settings (family gatherings, social dinners, or evenings at local elite clubs). The bonds of trust forged with these gatekeepers allowed me to access the managers and security officers of their companies, as well as their recruiting agents.

The development of my ongoing relationship with this group of employers and managers led me to focus on a small sample of companies: two in the textile sector and two in the pharmaceutical sector. In parallel with the repeated interviews conducted as part of the longitudinal study of these four companies,[30] I interviewed a series of small- and medium-sized employers on a more ad hoc basis, approaching them through professional bodies (chambers of commerce, trading estate associations). Generally, these interviews were less dense and less conducive to observation than were the prolonged discussions in the workplace of my privileged informants. They did, however, provide additional insight, especially into the common grievances and concerns of middle-ranking business leaders actively involved in employers' bodies.

The publication of my previous book (which was devoted to the routinization of a situation of 'ordered disorder' in Karachi from the mid-1980s onward)[31] allowed me to gain access to actors previously out of reach, particularly within law enforcement agencies. The book received a great deal of media attention in Pakistan and aroused the curiosity of the police and the armed forces; I took advantage of this by requesting interviews on relations between the business community and law enforcement agencies. Those interviews proved extremely enlightening.

My fieldwork was supplemented by access to US and British diplomatic archives[32] as well as judicial sources, company documents, autobiographical writings (memoirs written by entrepreneurs, high ranking officials, or trade union actors), and literary texts (satirical compositions and militant hymns produced by Urdu-speaking poets).

Because they tend to focus on the most contentious cases, these sources probably reinforced the bias of my study towards the mechanics of conflict, at the expense of the production of consent. This bias is particularly pronounced in the 'awards' made by Industrial Courts (and later, by the Labour Courts), on which I have relied to uncover the authority structure of Karachi's industrial firms in the early decades of independence.[33] Since these judgements do not include the full exchanges between judges, lawyers, and plaintiffs during the hearings, they do not allow for work on trial proceedings. They do, however, contain long extracts from plaintiffs' statements and their lawyers' interventions, as well as from disciplinary procedures initiated within the companies—which have, over the years, led to a great many disputes being brought before the courts. Little used by the (few) historians and sociologists of Pakistani industry,[34] these judicial sources provide valuable insights into the functioning of its apparatus, the claims made by its employees, and their access to justice.

The overemphasis on conflictual relations within factories that is inherent to these documentary sources could have been compensated for by more in-depth ethnographic observations. Yet, other than for brief, closely supervised visits, the shopfloor remained beyond my reach. Direct observation of the production lines probably did not fit in with the vision my employer contacts had of academic research. In their eyes, such a practice would be more akin to the requirements of external auditors, labour inspectors, and other troublemakers—whose potential nuisances they are constantly and imaginatively trying to neutralize.

Faced with this employer resistance, I was quick to renounce traditional ethnographic work in favour of a synoptic perspective.[35] Drawing my inspiration from the figurational sociology of Norbert Elias, I sought to uncover the productive configuration operating at the scale of the city as a whole. To identify the 'game structure'[36] of this social formation, I moved from one neighbourhood, one factory, and one professional group to another, trying to make the most of the troubled situations I encountered in the course of my investigation. 'Starting from the sand in the gears', as Carlo Ginzburg invites us to do, means both pointing out the fragility of any apparatus of domination and taking the measure of its immune resources, which are revealed by the work of re-ordering that follows any disruption.[37] Suspending the ordinary course of things, the dysfunctions of varying intensity around which the plot unfolds—from the industrial disaster that constitutes its main thread to the more minor incidents we encounter along the way—allow us to observe the disorderly manufacture of industrial order at various scales.

While these intrigues may focus on the characters, objects, or architectural elements that create confusion, they also attempt to capture disorder as a sensory experience—a set of tactile, visual, sonic, or olfactory engagements with an unpredictable world, waiting to be deciphered. My particular attention to the visuality of this troubled world is strongly indebted to my practice of photography. I have been making extensive use of my camera ever since my very first investigations in Karachi, back in the early 2000s. In this elusive landscape where the existence of graffiti, flags, or fences is often ephemeral, for me the camera is first and foremost an archiving tool. My images also have a sharing value, and some were used to illustrate articles written by the journalist friends I accompanied on assignments when they were not supporting me in my own investigations.[38] This intensive use of photography has rubbed off on my writing practice. It has afforded me an attention to the setting of the scene, the costume of the protagonists, the language of the built environment—in short, to the striking detail in the larger picture.

When authorized to do so, I continued this documentation work at production sites (alongside those involved in industrial safety) and in the workers' quarters. I have come away with two series of images, each having a distinct status. Mixing my own pictures with those of photographer and artist Naila Mahmood, the first series accompanies the developments of the text, before taking the lead and directing the story towards its denouement. The second series, presented at the end of the book, explores an alternative narrative framework by giving voice to the industrial landscapes of Karachi and their geography of capital. Experimenting with a form of dialogue between researchers and their images that remains rare,[39] this photographic essay focuses on how Karachi's urban margins have been reshaped by the capitalist mode of production, on how its project of subjugation has been inscribed in the built environment, and on the breaches that have opened up in its architecture of domination.

* * *

In the spirit of the comparative monograph, this case study is committed to a dialogue with seemingly distant situations, both in time and space.[40] Indeed, it was often in the light of Indian, American, or Latin American experiences of capitalism that my understanding of the dynamics I observed in Pakistan was refined. With this perspective inspired by historian Paul Veyne, comparing is neither just about conversing across borders, nor a matter of pursuing the illusion of a general explanatory model through the simple accumulation of knowledge. On the contrary, it is all about beginning with determining 'invariants' that act as 'operators of individualization'—in other words, mobilizing the general abstractions that 'allow access to the diversity of phenomena'.[41]

Presenting the central object of the book, the first chapter seeks to restore the henchmen of capital to their rightful place in the general dynamics of capitalism. Indeed, well beyond the phases of primitive accumulation, the history of capitalism is intertwined

15

with that of specialists in violence who mobilize their knowledge, coercive skills, and relational networks in response to an employer's demand for order and security on production sites.

The manufacturing economy of Karachi is a prime terrain in which to study this nexus of productive and coercive actors. As shown in Chapters 2 and 3, this entanglement of capital and coercion takes root in the conditions of the emergence of local industrial capitalism during the 1950s and 1960s, at the initiative of non-native merchants who tried to mitigate their weak social anchorage by resorting to a myriad of coercive intermediaries.

These interdependencies between the owners of capital and the providers of security were further strengthened by the civil unrest that punctuated life in Karachi between 1985 and 2015. To fully immerse ourselves in this state of violent disruption, we follow the path of a threatening letter addressed to the director of a pharmaceutical company, which shows that the productive sphere was not spared by the crisis of evidence affecting the city at large (Chapter 4).

Taking as its starting point the lynching of a worker in a tannery of the Korangi industrial area, Chapter 5 shows that while urban conflict did disrupt productive processes and the authority structure of the factory world, it also provided Karachi's business elites with new opportunities for control and accumulation. Arrangements made with political parties and criminal groups to discipline and repress the labour force accelerated the reconfiguration of the industrial labour market, leading to increased casualization.

Chapter 6 is based on the analysis of a harshly repressed workers' mobilization, and suggests that the repressive arsenal with which the state equipped itself, in the name of restoring civil peace, constituted an additional resource for industrial companies—one that could be redeployed to repress union struggles. This blurring of the lines between the fight against terrorism and the defence of industrial peace paved the way for new assemblages of capital and coercion, confirming the topicality of Marx's theses on the 'secondary benefits' of crime for the ruling class.[42]

Chapter 7 is based on interviews and field observations, retracing the trajectory of the businessmen who came together in the Citizens-

Police Liaison Committee (CPLC)—an organization originally dedicated to citizen oversight of the police that has now become a centrepiece of industrial security in Karachi. Pioneering the use of geocriminology in Pakistan, CPLC members have mobilized cartographic reason to restore order and predictability to an urban landscape made threatening by its illegibility. Crime statistics and geo-physical information systems have also helped industrial elites to develop self-defence capabilities that, via an additional windfall effect of urban disorder, have helped impose a new surveillance regime on the working class.

Composed of successive layers, this security apparatus at the service of capital is characterized not only by its prolific character, but also by the fact that its operators are as ready to mobilize the weapon of the law as they are to resort to *extra-legal methods*—actions that do not merely violate the law but exceed it in scope or severity while claiming to serve a similar purpose.[43]

As plethoric and versatile as this coercive apparatus has been, it has not been enough to confer serenity upon Karachi's anxious elites. The last two chapters therefore look at the flaws in the new industrial order. Chapter 8 begins with an examination of the distrustful relationship between industrialists and their highly insecure guards, in particular through the study of a series of disciplinary proceedings brought against industrial guards accused of professional misconduct by their employers. Concluding the exploration of this predatory capitalism with a return to the catastrophic event that opens my questioning, Chapter 9 looks at the legal proceedings initiated after the Ali Enterprises fire and their successive reversals. The examination of these judicial sources offers a complementary look at the economic and social role played by the bosses' henchmen—who during the trial became the main means of clearing their employers of any wrongdoing.

By reading these sources, and through a dialogue with the lawyer for the civil parties, I am ultimately left wondering what remains of the defences of the Pakistani working class today, and what industrial workers are still entitled to expect from their state. Echoing E.P. Thompson's pioneering reflections on the double-edged sword of the law,[44] I question the ability of the most vulnerable to win their case in a society where the force of law seems constantly undermined—by the illegal acts of delinquent elites, by extra-legal forms of coercion, and by the ubiquity of unofficial practices. Yet Pakistan is far from having a monopoly on such irregular practices. Before we set sail for Karachi, an overview of these practices is in order. After all, what is really at stake in Karachi's industrial capitalism and its modes of control?

1

THE GUARDIANS OF INDUSTRIAL PEACE

*The business of strikebreaking has long been known to exist in
this country. [...] Invariably, you will observe that the use of
these industrial mercenaries was attended by violence, strife, and
bloodshed.*

Senator Robert M. La Follette, 1939.[1]

Several thousand auto workers, most of whom were unemployed as
a result of the Great Depression, braved the bitter cold to march on
the Ford River Rouge industrial complex on the outskirts of Detroit.
The demonstration got off to a quiet start, but the arbitrary use of tear
gas by the police soon sparked a firestorm. Armed with stones and
clods of frozen mud picked up in surrounding fields, the protesters
responded to police provocation with a shower of projectiles and
managed to advance as far as the factory gates. For this audacity, they
were greeted with a deluge of lead, and four protesters were killed
in the clashes, while a fifth died of his injuries shortly thereafter.

Referred to in the annals of the American labour movement as
the 'Ford Hunger March' or 'Ford Massacre', the demonstration of
7 March 1932 and its bloody repression are of course emblematic
of police brutality at that time. But they also reveal the collusion
between regular police forces and private auxiliaries in the United

19

States during the interwar period. On that day, the Dearborn police had not acted alone in their use of force: they had been backed up by the henchmen of Ford's Service Department—a private police force headed by Harry Bennett, a one-time boxer in the navy, who had become an industrial security officer. It seems that the escalation of police violence was triggered by Bennett's bravado. According to Ray Pillsbury, a *Detroit Mirror* photographer present at the scene, Henry Ford's favourite enforcer suddenly burst out of the plant in a company car and into the crowd. As he got out of the car to address the demonstrators, Bennett was greeted by a rain of projectiles, one of which cut his forehead. Convinced that their leader had been shot, his men opened fire, in concert with the police.[2]

Some accounts suggest that Bennett himself eventually joined the shooting and, when he was out of ammunition, turned to a police officer to borrow his service weapon and continue firing into the crowd.[3] Other (less 'heroic') versions suggest he was taken to hospital shortly after being wounded.[4] In any case, the incident served to enhance Bennett's standing with Henry Ford. As a reward for his 'personnel manager' (Bennett's official title at the Ford Motor Company), a brand new Lincoln was delivered to his home in Ypsilanti.[5] Some of the local press, starting with the *Detroit Times*, praised the courage of this 'born fighter' who, rather than supervising operations from his office, had not hesitated to 'charge [the] mob bare-handed'.[6]

Underlying this dramatic episode was a set of more routine practices of surveillance and repression, implemented by specialists in violence on behalf of large industrial groups. First spotted by Henry Ford in 1916, Bennett was Head of the Service Department by 1921. Over the next few years, he set up a vast network of informers and thugs who were responsible for spying on and intimidating both union activists and ordinary workers—even in the privacy of their own homes. Housed within this security service was a veritable militia, complete with pistols, whips, and hoses known to Bennett's men as the 'Persuaders'. By the end of the 1930s, Ford's Service Department had more than 8,000 members (including about 350 ex-military men and several hundred ex-convicts), plus thousands of informers recruited from among Ford employees. It was the world's most powerful private police force.[7]

Bennett's rise in power went hand in hand with a change in Henry Ford's managerial policy, which abandoned paternalism in favour of an aggressive strategy of cost reduction and downsizing[8]—the number of group employees fell from 170,502 in 1929 to 46,282 in 1932.[9] Though it did not overshadow the profound changes in the organization of work that were taking place in both the United States and Europe at the time, the coercive turn observed at Ford in the 1920s invites us to nuance the sometimes overly univocal approaches to managerial rationalization in so-called 'Taylorian' industrial organizations—of which the automobile industry is a paradigmatic case. Not content with having outlived the scientific organization of work, in this case the visible fist of management paid scant attention to formal hierarchies. Disregarding the company's organizational chart, the Service Department answered only to Henry Ford, and any of its members, regardless of rank, could sanction or even dismiss any company employee, including white-collar workers.[10]

In terms of numbers and longevity, the repressive apparatus Bennett put in place certainly stands out from the crowd. Yet it exemplifies the police forces of capital that, since the second half of the nineteenth century, have been mobilizing their violent skills and relational networks in response to a corporate demand for order and security. From the Pinkerton agency detectives who repressed the Homestead strikers at the end of the nineteenth century, to the Guatemalan *maras* or the Colombian paramilitaries who participate in casualizing labour in the factories of large contemporary multinationals, the history of industrial capitalism and its modes of domination is intimately linked to that of the specialists of coercion who put their skills at the service of factory discipline, the extraction of surplus value, and the protection of capital and its owners.[11] Over the course of industrial change and social struggles, this repertoire of action has been deployed in three main directions: for social control of the workforce by unofficial authorities; for spying on employees and union activists on production sites and in their private space; and for the physical intimidation of unionists and other disruptors of industrial order.

As brutal as it is controversial, this repressive repertoire sheds light not only on the history of capitalism, but also on processes of state formation. Based on the level of impunity guaranteed to snitches and strongmen, it highlights the volatile alliances between professional and unofficial enforcers, as well as the more structural connivances arising out of the entanglement of the defence of industrial order and the preservation of political order. This co-production of employer violence does not stop at covert support or de facto tolerance of private police forces. Rather, it feeds on a rich ideological production, structuring the legitimate problematic of the economy—that is (to extend Pierre Bourdieu's remarks about political representation), what is economically thinkable and speakable of, in a given power configuration.[12]

As Charles Tilly lamented in the late 1980s, historians and sociologists of work have tended to neglect the contribution made by private police forces to the development of industrial conflicts.[13] In recent years, however, there has been a renewed interest in global variations of the phenomenon, in both its national aspects and its transnational extensions.[14] This historiographical revival is primarily concerned with the United States, where the practices of worker surveillance and repression took on particularly elaborate forms in the early twentieth century.[15] However, recent works tend to relativize American exceptionalism by opening up the field of analysis to include European metropolises and their colonies.[16]

This renewed interest in employers' struggles is not confined to the field of history. A number of recent works in anthropology, sociology, and political science have contributed to placing both the exercise of coercion and its various forms of commodification at the heart of contemporary dynamics of capitalist accumulation.[17] The history of these employers' struggles is also a history of the present; far from having been eclipsed by managerial methods that seek workers' consent to their own domination, 'the employers' penchant for the stick rather than for social dialogue' remains relevant—even in the supposedly most pacified economies.[18] Bringing together captains of industry, yellow unions, conservative political elites, regular law enforcement agencies, and every kind of auxiliary, the defence of the right to work continues to fuel repressive configurations, notably by drawing on the fight against terrorism.

Violent entrepreneurs in the service of corporate violence

It was an ordinary street fight that propelled Harry Bennett into the heart of the American business world. The 24-year-old sailor got into a brawl with customs officials while on leave in New York City, and was only saved from arrest by a journalist from William Randolph Hearst's newspaper group, Arthur Brisbane. In the navy, which he had joined at the age of 17, Bennett had made a name for himself fighting in the featherweight division under the name 'Sailor Reese'. Brisbane was so impressed with the young man's boxing skills that he offered to introduce him to Henry Ford, whom he was about to meet for an interview. Receiving the two men in his hotel room, Ford listened intently to Brisbane's account of the brawl. After satisfying himself that Bennett knew how to use a firearm, he offered him a job at the River Rouge complex. The workers employed in the construction of this new factory were known for being 'a pretty tough lot', as Ford put it, and the patriarch was looking for a man he could trust to keep order on the site.

This story, as recounted in Bennett's autobiography (published a few years after his early retirement),[19] has left a lasting impression— even on opponents of the fighter-turned-anti-union-mercenary.[20] Indeed, it is difficult to avoid succumbing to the evocative power of this scene, which remains one of the most famous statements of the laws of attraction between capital and coercion. And yet, as Bennett himself admits, his rise within the group was far from instant. He found himself up against the hostility of the executives mandated by Henry Ford to corral him, themselves every bit as exasperated by this favouritism as they were by the fact that this impetuous young man was a flagrantly poor fit for the factory world. After leaving for Detroit, Bennett failed to get back in touch with the industrialist, and it was his pencil, rather than his fists, that got him his first job at Ford, as a draughtsman in the group's art department.[21] It was not until 1921, when Bennett had proved himself on the construction site of the Eagle-class patrol boats, that Ford finally entrusted him with security at the River Rouge plant.[22]

Capitalist business leaders do not have a monopoly on the use of thugs to contain social protest and impose their domination. Similar tendencies can be observed among large landowners confronted with peasant mobilizations, in contexts as diverse as nineteenth-century Sicily (where the mafia was first and foremost an enterprise of violence in the service of the owners), 1950s Colombia (where the *pájaros*, militias in the service of the conservative party and landed elites, hunted down liberal and communist activists, peasant leaders, and trade unionists), or the present-day Pakistani province of Sindh (where the heavily armed brigands known as *dacoits* terrorize the small peasantry on behalf of 'feudals').[23]

Because these repressive strategies are integral to the reproduction of many dominant groups, they are not specific to industrial capitalism—or even to capitalism itself. Industrial firms do, however, provide fertile ground for such hybridizations of capital and coercion. This is particularly true in labour-intensive sectors (such as textiles and clothing, or mining), where cost-cutting is traditionally achieved by reducing the wage bill, although capital-intensive sectors are not immune. This can be seen in the case of the car industry, where employers have historically favoured the use of strong-arm tactics to maintain order on the shop floor and stifle workers' attempts to organize.[24] On the supply side, as Marx and Engels pointed out, the disruptions engendered by industrialization have generated a venal and 'absolutely brazen crew' of *lumpen* elements, composed of 'the decaying elements of all classes'.[25] In turn, Michel Foucault has shown the importance of these 'extra-proletarian plebs', in terms of both the division of the working class and the formation of capitalist societies of control.[26]

To write the history or sociology of industrial capitalism (as a social order and as a mode of production, equally) is thus inevitably to invite confrontation with a myriad of *violent entrepreneurs*. Introduced by Anton Blok and later revived by Vadim Volkov, this notion refers to public or private actors with access to recognized skills in both the use of force and the commercial exploitation of their coercive resources.[27] Within the context of industrial capitalism, it is possible to identify two ideal types of henchmen in the service of employers. In the first case, the defence of corporate order is entrusted either to the local 'boss' or to labour contractors who deploy their authority at the point where the factory world meets neighbourhood life. Such authority figures bear some resemblance to the violent entrepreneurs depicted by Anton Blok in his classic study of the Sicilian mafia. Inspired by the figurational sociology of Norbert Elias, Blok sees the historical *mafioso* as a 'broker of a violent type', who produces social bonds by 'forming specific configurations between interdependent individuals'.[28] This status of 'broker', acting as a link between distant worlds, is common to most violent entrepreneurs in the service of employers, with the figure of the labour boss distinctive in both his local anchorage and his ability to root himself in everyday working-class life. In addition to physical prowess and a reputation for intransigence, the authority of these middlemen derives from their social standing and their ability to control access to certain essential services (not just employment, but also housing, credit, etc.).

While labour bosses and their agents are often involved (via the surveillance of workers at their workplace) in anti-union struggles, the spying and intimidation of trade union activists has gradually become more professional. These surveillance and repression activities constitute the core business of anti-union mercenaries, who have formed the shock troops of industrial order. Acting as providers of a repressive service, the leaders of agencies specialized in spying on workers or union-busting have more in common with the type of violent entrepreneurs studied by Vadim Volkov, in his work on the turbulent genesis of Russian capitalism. Blok's violent broker emerged from an agrarian society and is intimately linked to the social world of the latifundia, whereas Volkov's virtuosos of coercion are the product of a nascent capitalist economy in which property rights and compliance with contractual commitments are still far from guaranteed. In this context, those trading in force (whether they hail from the criminal world or certain state services) are better described as specialists in 'the skilful use of force and information on a commercial basis', than as intermediary figures between dominant and subaltern classes.[29]

However voracious and brutal these actors may have been, in the case of post-Soviet Russia, they did help restore a certain predictability to the economic field, and in so doing, they promoted a favourable business climate by reducing transaction costs for numerous firms. Dusting off neo-institutionalist theories, Volkov thus comes to conceive of these coercive service providers (collectively) as an institution in their own right, or rather, as 'one of the possible institutional arrangements for the protection of property rights'.[30] Within industrial capitalism, the violent entrepreneurs most in line with this process of commodification of coercion are detective agencies, 'armies' of strike-breakers, and, since the 1970s, security companies and union-busting agencies—major auxiliaries of employer domination and key protagonists in the global history of anti-unionism.[31]

Not every anti-union mercenary necessarily reaches this degree of institutionalization, however, and thugs recruited from the local underworld continue to be widely used in contemporary industrial disputes. And while this recruitment can sometimes be intentional on the part of employers or managerial authorities, these 'arts of repression' can also be deployed more discreetly, by letting ordinary violence leak into the factory world.[32]

Violent brokers of industrial order

As historians of industrial capitalism on the Indian subcontinent (as elsewhere) have repeatedly emphasized, the coercive intermediaries that emerged in the wake of industrialization testify to the intertwining of the factory world and neighbourhood life.[33] These middlemen initially took the form of labour bosses from humble backgrounds, determined not to be downgraded. In nineteenth-century France, for example, *tâcherons* or *marchandeurs* relieved their employers of recruitment and managerial tasks by distributing work as well as, sometimes, supervising the workers.[34]

In Indonesia, the term *preman* is now synonymous with 'gangster'. It is derived, however, from the Dutch *vrijman* (lit. a 'free man'), which in Batavia in the early 1700s referred to a commercial agent licensed by the East India Company, and thus under its jurisdiction (though not employed by it). The term was subsequently used to refer to mid-level plantation supervisors, who maintained discipline with an iron fist, inflicting humiliation and corporal punishment on unruly workers.[35] In the early twentieth century, the figure of the *preman* came to be confused with that of the labour boss, providing migrant workers with shelter and employment in exchange for a commission. These recruiting agents were often surrounded by strongmen—responsible for disciplining workers and reminding employers of their duties, while keeping their competitors at bay. These coercive resources were often also used to provide more unsavoury services such as prostitution, pickpocketing, burglary, extortion, etc.[36]

In India and Pakistan, contractors (also known by the Hindi/ Urdu terms *sardar* and *thekedar*) have often been criticized for their propensity to exploit the most vulnerable workers. Omnipresent in the early industries of the Indian subcontinent—coal, textiles, and jute—these recruiting agents are now centre stage again, thanks to the transformations of the industrial labour market since the 1980s. Their patronage is not, however, limited to their powers of recruitment.

By dint of being part of neighbourhood life, they have accrued additional coercive resources through their control of credit, housing, and essential urban services such as water and electricity.[37] Yet the fact that they are embedded in neighbourhood life makes them accountable to shared ethical principles[38] and exposes them to certain social expectations in terms of job allowances, dispute resolution, or the funding of social and cultural activities.[39] At the same time, it leaves them vulnerable to the expression of worker discontent, which can easily turn against them or their properties.

When enlisted to the cause of maintaining industrial order, local underworld figures are not immune to such mutual dependencies. During the colonial period in India, one example of such a figure was the *dada*—a Hindi/Urdu term which, in its idiomatic sense, refers to an 'elder brother'. While occasionally committing his forces to the employers, this neighbourhood boss was obliged to comply with a redistributive requirement: he was expected to finance religious festivals, workers' pensions, or the *akharas* (wrestling clubs from which he recruited many of his followers). And when these 'elder brothers' took on repressive tasks on behalf of the bosses too openly, they exposed themselves to reprisals. In Bombay, in December 1928, after Keshav Borkar's men attacked the trade unionists of the Girni Kamgar Union, several thousand workers stormed the *dada*'s residence. He managed to escape, but his house and one of his gymnasiums were ransacked by the attackers.[40]

As rooted in shared ethical principles as they are in the ordinary constraints of neighbourly relations, these interdependencies also frame the authority of the Indonesian *premans*. While asserting themselves as criminal figures, they have reinforced their collaboration with economic and political elites—particularly under the New Order regime (1966–1998).[41] In addition to executing repressive practices on behalf of the authorities, these 'free men' provide a link between the *kampung*s (working-class districts) and the surrounding factories. It is not only their imposing physique, virtuosity in the martial arts, and reputation for violence that create the aura around these criminal figures. In charge of 'external security' at certain industrial complexes, they are responsible for ensuring that the company's operations remain unaffected by any conflicts or grievances arising within the local population, and their authority is based on their good deeds and their management of certain local facilities, such as workers' pensions. *Kampung* residents will thus think twice before engaging in any action that disrupts the industrial order—not only out of fear of physical reprisals, but also because they feel a moral obligation to these local bosses.[42]

Anti-union mercenaries

These middlemen often coexist with another type of violent entrepreneur in the service of capital—this time less involved in neighbourhood life and productive activity. As major consumers of coercive services, large-scale industrialists were behind the spectacular development of anti-union mercenaries in the early twentieth century, and it was the factory cop, as much as the private detective, who began to professionalize commercial security agencies around this time.[43] Following the example of more conventional firms, these specialists in union-busting developed their own marketing strategies—as exemplified by one of Germany's most famous strike-breakers of the 1910s, Karl Katzmarek. He distributed brochures attesting to his ability to provide personnel, weapons, and stewardship to employers facing labour disputes.[44]

It was in the United States, around the turn of the century, that this anti-union mercenaryism found its most accomplished form. As the historical matrix of this 'private army of capital', the Pinkerton agency was at the forefront of employers' efforts.[45] Founded in 1850 by a British immigrant who would distinguish himself during the Civil War by foiling a plot against Abraham Lincoln, then setting up a network to spy on the South, the agency began serving employers in 1877. It deployed its detectives to monitor workers, infiltrate unions, and, on occasion, confront strikers. These crackdowns culminated in the 1892 Battle of Homestead. To crush a strike by the Amalgamated Association of Iron and Steel Workers (at the time, the most powerful union organization in the United States), the President of the Carnegie group, Henry Clay Frick, called on Pinkerton, which promptly sent 300 Winchester-armed guards to the small Pennsylvania town in question. The attempted landing of the 'Pinks', who had arrived by boat, kicked off a pitched battle that resulted in the death of at least three mercenaries and a dozen strikers.[46]

Despite the anti-Pinkerton legislation passed in the wake of this fiasco, the strike-breaking industry continued to grow in the United States in the early twentieth century.[47] Dubbed 'King of the Strikebreakers' by the muckrakers of the day, James Farley claims to have started his career in 1895 after a toothache led him to take a bit too much cocaine.[48] Proving his worth under fire, he built a solid reputation as a fighter before opening his own agency in New York in 1902. A few years later, he boasted of being able to mobilize 35,000 'scabs' across the country.[49] His successor at the head of this booming industry, Pearl Louis Bergoff, embarked on a process of bureaucratization and professionalization. The brawlers who commanded gangs of scruffy thugs were succeeded by labour control specialists, whose operations were as formal as those of any other subcontractor in the industry.[50]

As demonstrated by the career path and methods of Harry Bennett (another central figure in interwar labour struggles in the United States), the use of physical force (whether potential or actual) was nonetheless inherent to these repressive tactics. In the early 1930s, Service Department heavyweights not only assisted the police in dealing with strikers and demonstrators, but also more routinely maintained industrial order by intimidating (and even punishing) unruly workers. Their use of force was sometimes inspired by the methods of the underworld, with which Harry Bennett had close links. He also drew on the repertoire of vigilantism that, since the end of the nineteenth century, has constantly drip-fed employers' repressive endeavours in the United States.[51]

The myth of an entrepreneurial class defending its property at gunpoint in the Wild West provided those promoting industrial policing with a powerful register of legitimization. Beyond the inner circle of the great captains of industry, it was propagated by successful writers like Owen Wister, who celebrated the violent defence of property against the threat of the dangerous classes.[52] The affinities with vigilantism were more than just rhetorical. Drawing an analogy between the private police of the moment and the vigilantes of yesteryear, they extended to actual practice. Strikers and trade unionists found themselves lumped in with ordinary delinquents in terms of the punishments inflicted upon them, which were historically associated with the summary justice of vigilantes and lynch mobs. The wave of counter-revolutionary violence that hit the Industrial Workers of the World (IWW) from 1909 to 1919 was a high point of these hybridizations and many 'Wobblies' (IWW militants) were subjected to torture inspired by 'frontier justice' or the lynch mobs of the South.[53]

Over the following decades, the infatuation of capital's henchmen with these spectacular and symbolic punishments showed no sign of waning. In 1937, the trade unionist Herbert Harris was kidnapped by the men of 'Fats' Perry, a former wrestler who now ran the Dallas branch of Ford's Service Department. Taken to a remote location where Perry and his men routinely dragged their victims to be whipped, Harris was stripped naked and tarred and feathered before being driven back to downtown Dallas. In this pitiful state, he was left outside the offices of a local newspaper only once his captors had enlisted a professional photographer to capture and publicize his humiliation.[54]

In addition to its heroic register and its distinctive punitive repertoire, vigilantism provided a framework for mobilization, mutualizing the exercise of coercion and diluting the defence of private interests into collective causes (the right to work, the defence of property, the preservation of public order). From the 1880s to the 1940s, few industrial regions of the United States escaped the grip and exactions of 'citizens' committees',[55] which confused the defence of capital with the 'right to self-preservation'—which is, according to the expression used by historical vigilante movements, the 'first law of nature'.[56]

In the late 1930s, the La Follette Commission confirmed the extent of these spying and repression activities. Established by Republican Senator Robert M. La Follette Jr., the commission met from 1936 to 1941 to investigate the unsavoury methods used by some employers to avoid collective bargaining with trade unions. Alongside the subpoenas served on hundreds of detective agencies and industry executives, its field investigations confirmed the massive use of espionage by large American companies.

General Motors (GM), Pinkerton's main industrial client, was most prominent in this respect. According to the La Follette commission, it was at this manufacturer that the 'craving for spy information' reached its climax. Each plant manager, as well as the personnel managers of Chevrolet and Fisher Body, independently contracted the services of detective agencies, while Pinkerton agents were tasked with spying on those of the Corporations Auxiliary Company—another agency serving GM. In the end, the commission notes, 'A weird framework of spies among spies was created that bewildered even the Pinkerton officials'.[57]

In addition to these spying practices, the La Follette Commission also confirmed the systematic use of strike-breakers and private police by large American corporations.[58] Some industrial groups, such as GM, preferred to offload their dirty work to auxiliaries recruited on an ad hoc basis—even if it did mean corralling them behind the scenes, as GM executives did with the Citizens League

31

for Industrial Security (a group of vigilantes based in Anderson, Indiana). Although the group's spokesman Homer Lambert was a real estate agent, the decision-making power was in the hands of GM management—which was very active in the league. When vigilantes ransacked the offices of the United Automobile Workers (UAW-CIO) and threatened to lynch its leader, Hugh Thompson, in 1937, two GM plant managers were present.[59] In some states, such as Pennsylvania, the industrial groups most hostile to unionism took full advantage of the police powers granted to them by local authorities. They founded armed militias along the lines of the security forces set up by the railway and mining companies in the second half of the nineteenth century.[60]

Thus, Ford was not the only industrial group of the time to have set up its own private police force. In the steel industry, while the giant US Steel Corporation accepted the principle of collective bargaining, 'smaller' companies like Republic Steel invested in the surveillance and repression of union activists. In times of strike, such as at the Berger plant in Canton, Ohio in 1935, the company's armed guards secured production sites and imposed a reign of terror throughout the city, not hesitating to open fire on picket lines, demonstrators, or even passers-by.[61] The 'flying squad' of tyre manufacturer Goodyear was notable for its American football tactics: when scuffles broke out, its recruits formed a block around the 'gas man' responsible for spraying the crowd with tear gas.[62] Indeed, this weapon figured prominently in the arsenal of large corporations; during the interwar period, they spent millions of dollars on sickening and toxic gases (such as chloropicrin), as well as on firearms.[63]

Having extensively documented these practices, which they considered unrepresentative of American democracy, the members of the commission sought to prohibit them by preparing a bill: the *Oppressive Labor Practices Act*. It targeted the use of 'labor spies', strike-breakers, and private police, as well as the possession by individuals of certain weapons (machine guns, sawn-off shotguns, and tear gas). However, the bill was met with strong resistance in both the Senate and the House of Representatives, where some Republicans accused it of playing into the hands of external enemies—both Nazi and Soviet. The law was never passed, and, at the end of the Second

World War, the Taft-Hartley Act marked a clear step backwards in trade union freedoms.

Nevertheless, the process of institutionalization of capital-labour relations initiated by the Wagner Act of 1935 continued. While it did not put an end to the anti-union practices of large corporations, it did force them to adopt more subtle methods of coercion. This period saw the rise of labour relations consultants who, over the following decades, tended to mobilize the law as a weapon, while using the tools of social psychology to break down both collective initiatives and individual impulses.[64] In return for their acceptance of institutionalization and their participation in collective bargaining, American trade unions became an integral part of the control apparatus—so that they were less involved in challenging industrial order than they were in reproducing it.[65]

Though the paramilitary resources deployed by large American corporations in the early twentieth century were remarkable for their scale and diversity, those in European countries and their colonies were no less impressive. In response to the hardening of social struggles and the rise of workers' internationalism, counter-internationalist groups (themselves strongly interconnected across borders) spread across the industrialized regions of the continent. Nationalist by persuasion and transnationalist in practice, this yellow movement had its headquarters in Paris and was institutionalized through the Fédération Nationale des Jaunes de France (FNJF, formed in 1902).[66] These cross-border connections were particularly intense in Central Europe, where German, Austro-Hungarian, and Swiss employers joined forces against the strikes, relying on recruitment agents whose networks extended as far as Italy. Some of these strike-breakers were armed, and the most organized groups—such as those run by Friedrich Hintze in Hamburg and Karl Katzmarek in Berlin (whose activities covered every German-speaking region of Central Europe) were compared by the contemporary German press to the Pinkertons.[67] On the eve of the First World War, the activities of these anti-union mercenaries were so well publicized that the Berlin press noted that the city's children were playing 'scabs and workers' rather than 'cops and robbers'.[68]

In the UK, self-proclaimed 'King of Scabs' William Collison set up 'free employment agencies' (often run by retired police officers) to meet the needs of industrialists,[69] and the most virulent employers' unions, such as the Shipping Federation, threatened to form vigilante forces along the lines of the 'Pinkerton police'.[70] These same employers also offered financial support to the Volunteer Police Force (VPF), whose members aspired to become auxiliaries to the forces of law and order in the face of strikers, but found themselves up against the mistrust of the Labour government.[71] The Economic League was more discreet and had a more lasting influence. It was founded in 1919 by Conservative MP (and former Director of Naval Intelligence) Sir Reginald Hall, with the support of a group of far-right industrialists and financiers, and was officially dedicated to pro-capitalist propaganda. But it also engaged in espionage against left-wing organizations, producing blacklists that circulated in UK business circles at least until the organization was dismantled in 1994—and perhaps beyond.[72]

Such repressive tactics sometimes also circulated between the UK (as a colonial metropole) and its colonies. While the leaders of the VPF would have liked to recruit colonial police and army officers on home leave within the metropolis, the first industrial groups in colonial India reproduced some of the anti-union practices developed in Europe and North America.[73] The trade in anti-unionism was never as well organized in India as it was in the United States or Central Europe. In the 1930s, however, some Indian political leaders (well known for their collusion with the underworld) organized 'yellow' unions that tried to resist communist organizations— even by force. Husain Shaheed Suhrawardy in Calcutta was one such leader who (thanks to his links with the criminal world of the Kidderpore district) controlled recruitment on the docks and was able to impose the pro-business Calcutta Dockers' Union (which was supported by shipping companies and colonial authorities alike) as a leading political force.[74]

While mobilizing these 'yellow' unions, Indian industrialists also used agents specializing in labour espionage. The Sassoon group, for example, was founded by a family of Iraqi Jews who settled in Bombay around 1830. It relied on its 'Watch and Ward' department to collect information and transcribe the content of political discussions between its workers. At the head of this network of informers was an Anglo-Indian ex-boxer, Milton Kubes, whose trajectory bore striking similarities to that of Harry Bennett.[75]

Despite attempts made by successive governments to rein in private policing, France was no exception to this trend; private police forces emerged in the country's main industrial areas as early as the end of the nineteenth century, in response to the subversive activities of the anarchist movement.[76] The 'Bande à Patin' was a corporate police force formed around repentant anarchists, and was led by an ex-employee who became executor of the dirty work of the Compagnie des Mines de Blanzy. This private police force spied on the miners in their private lives, recording their political and religious opinions. The group was also known as the *gang à palis* (palings gang), in reference to the lengths of wood torn from fencing and used as clubs against unruly workers or strikers.[77] Between 1900 and 1910, the self-designated 'yellow' trade union movement (whose primary vocation was to break strikes at mines and metal works) experienced a spectacular rise, and sought to federate counter-internationalist forces Europe-wide.[78]

In the 1930s, some French industrial groups also set up their own *police maison* (in-house police). This was the case, for instance, at Renault, where a White Russian (and former member of the Wrangel army) was responsible for maintaining order at Billancourt.[79] In the years of social turmoil that followed the end of the Second World War in France, the underworld sometimes played a supporting role in the repression of strikes—as in Marseille, where brothers Antoine and Barthélémy Guérini were responsible for breaking the dockers' strike via the harassment of pickets and CGT union leaders.[80] The history of post-war pro-employers' unions, which began with the foundation of the Confédération générale des syndicats indépendants (CGSI) in 1949, is equally unsavoury. This was an organization that crossed paths with former Nazi collaborators, the mob, and mercenaries who had gravitated towards the Service d'Action Civique (SAC).[81] In addition to everyday threats and intimidation by 'yellow' unions such as the

Confédération française du travail (CFT), private 'commandos' were, from time to time, mobilized against strikers.

In the 1970s, when a certain number of employers were worried about challenges to the productive order,[82] this repression increased in intensity, becoming more and more organized, to the point that the press would actually refer to *milices patronales* (corporate militias).[83] Pro-employers' union harassment of Confédération générale du travail (CGT) activists and supporters was an everyday reality, and several people fell victim to thugs working for employers.[84] In 1972, the Maoist activist Pierre Overney was shot dead by Jean-Antoine Tramoni, a security guard at Renault, during an altercation in front of the Boulogne-Billancourt factory. Five years later, in Reims, worker and CGT activist Pierre Maître was shot dead by a CFT commando as he stood on a picket line at the entrance to his factory, the Verreries Mécaniques Champenoises (VMC).

The dirty work carried out by this pro-business unionism came to light only after one repentant gangster handed CGT activist Marcel Caille the notebook in which he had methodically recorded his own activities—a precious source that set Caille on the trail of the pro-business unions and their victims, about which he wrote two outstanding books.[85] The commission of enquiry into the activities of the SAC was formed shortly after François Mitterrand came to power in 1981, and also confirmed 'the existence of commandos specialising in attacks on workers'. These violent groups, which were more than willing to storm factories and kidnap strikers (as happened at the Peugeot factory in Saint-Etienne in April 1973), were often structured around private security companies, which had the wind in their sails and were still poorly regulated by the state.

As members of the commission noted, these companies relied on the SAC's 'pool of henchmen'. Generally from modest backgrounds, these strike-breakers were relatively well paid, earning between 1,000 and 2,000 francs per working day (at a time when the average monthly income for workers was 2,200 francs). However, as the commission reported:

> They are rarely employed for more than three months by the same company for fear that they will overshadow their bosses.

> Among them are permanently unemployed and small-time mobsters who have recently switched trade and who sometimes play the detective, having no other ambition than to join the official police force.[86]

Given that their mandate was to restore industrial order at minimal cost, the performance of anti-union mercenaries left much to be desired. In the United States, the Pinkertons and their successors have more often been a burden than an asset; because capital's henchmen tend to be poorly trained and lacking in motivation, when they are confronted with crowds determined to put up a fight, their amateurism actually contributes to stirring up disorder.[87] Moreover, strike-breakers tend to come from the same working-class backgrounds as their adversaries, and it is by no means unusual for them to discover feelings of solidarity with strikers. In Bombay in the late 1920s, one ex-policeman recruited by Milton Kubes to infiltrate Girni Kamgar Union meetings was dismissed after becoming convinced that the communist union was 'an excellent union'.[88] Three decades later, one of the legionnaires recruited by the Bennes Marel company in Saint-Etienne to break up a series of cork strikes, 'seeing the workers fighting and struggling for something', decided he would rally to their cause, and joined the CGT.[89]

Such volatile loyalties are compounded by the propensity of these private enforcers to go rogue. Their violent enterprises are rarely confined to what is legal, and many end up compromised in various forms of trafficking. The hostility towards Harry Bennett among Henry Ford's entourage was not only because of his influence over the patriarch, but also because of his trade in spare parts—which were stolen from the group's factories before being sold on the black market. When they weren't fraternizing with the strikers, the French anti-union mercenaries of the 1970s relieved their boredom by organizing both rowdy get-togethers, and robberies, on their own account.[90] While such events were bound to (and did) irritate law enforcement officials, they were not serious enough to break the ties between the repressive services and the employers' thugs.

In the shadow of the state

Because they remain associated, particularly in the United States, with a phase of notoriously unbridled economic accumulation, the very existence of capital's henchmen seems to mark the triumph of private violence over public attempts to regulate the use of force.[91] But it would be reductive to see them as excesses peculiar to a supposedly 'wilder' brand of capitalism. In the United States, as elsewhere, the shock troops of industrial order have been able to flourish only with the benevolent blessing of the state apparatus—granted either because its ruling elites and field agents have openly endorsed the project of pacifying the working class, or because they have chosen to turn a blind eye to extra-legal responses to social struggles. In the field of repression—as in that of trade and production—laissez-faire was planned.[92]

The weaponization of industrial peace

As a response to the spectre of class warfare, the notion of 'industrial peace' provided the ideological framework for a programme of action outlined from the end of the nineteenth century in industrialized metropolises, as well as in their respective colonies. Originally—and particularly in the writings of economists such as Arnold Toynbee (1852–1883)—the notion of industrial peace was the bearer of a reformist project, sensitive to the fate of workers and quite favourable to the unions. By calling for the triumph of reason (mainly among workers, as though they were the only people exposed to the transport of passions), these early writings tended to also reject as 'barbaric' those worker mobilizations that were less inclined to a philosophy of consensus.[93] Around the turn of the century, the commitment to industrial peace highlighted the benevolence (towards the 'reasonable' demands of workers) of the European and American industrialists who adopted it.[94] However, by invoking an apocalyptic imagining of social struggles, it also contributed to the containment of trade unionism precisely because of the contrast between this imagining and the desire for peace and prosperity supposedly shared by the overwhelming majority of employers and their employees.

Industrial peace is thus inseparable from the spectre of war. The war register is invoked here at an analogical, rather than metaphorical level; like conflicts between nations, industrial conflict 'leaves behind feelings of bitterness, and does by its very nature prevent the growth of friendly and harmonious and amicable relations'.[95] These writings thus emphasize 'the analogy between a strike and a war': the notification of a redundancy plan being akin to a declaration of war, followed by an assessment by each party of the resources at its disposal, which will determine the outcome of the battle.[96]

This notion, which is indigenous to the industrial capitalism of the late nineteenth and early twentieth centuries, is thus irreducible to the social reformism of its early theorists. It also outlines a programme of action more concerned with the neutralization of troublemakers than the search for dialogue. The enemies of peace must be neutralized in the general interest, and it is only natural to resort to strong-arm tactics against such spoilers—either by calling on the official police, or by contracting the services of henchmen. Over time, the coercive measures taken to ensure industrial peace have become more subtle. Through judicial or administrative retaliatory measures, intense media propaganda, and surveillance practices that sometimes intruded into the private lives of workers and trade unionists, this enterprise of pacification led to a taming of worker mobilizations.[97]

By enlisting reason and progress under the banner of anti-union struggles, the notion of industrial peace had considerable success and imposed itself in official speeches and legislative provisions well beyond its birthplace. At the same time as it developed in Europe and the United States, it made its way into certain colonial states, where it was more of an invitation to delay and rule out the most radical solutions in the 'spirit of cooperation and mutual understanding' than an accompaniment to the institutionalization of collective bargaining.[98] This was the case in India, for instance, where—in the context of the growing social tensions of the 1920s and 1930s—the preservation of industrial peace was made an imperative for labour-capital relations. At the same time, social measures were discredited because they were deemed too constraining for employers.

In its 1931 report, the Royal Commission on Labour in India invoked this imperative to social harmony as a way of dissuading the legislator from imposing a legal and institutional framework that would result in transferring the resolution of labour disputes outside the enterprises.[99]

By setting moral and institutional limitations on worker mobilizations, the conception of industrial peace promoted in employers' circles and endorsed by liberal democracies (and by a certain number of (post-)colonial states) has always included an implicit repressive dimension. From this perspective, actors who go beyond the legitimate framework of expression of worker discontent are doing far more than just breaking labour laws; they are challenging the rules of coexistence and the very foundations of the rule of law. This is the reason for the recurrent reference by the promoters of industrial peace to the catastrophic horizons of poorly managed worker mobilizations. In an article published in 1978 in the journal of the Federation of Pakistan Chambers of Commerce and Industry, a lecturer at Karachi University warned: 'Industrial peace is the backbone of economic development. Failure to realise the importance of maintaining good industrial relations often results in chaos and confusion.'[100] In the face of such threats to economic and social order, anything goes—as long as state authorities are prepared to close their eyes to employers' most unsavoury practices.

The mixed economy of repression

Prior to becoming Henry Ford's eyes and ears at the River Rouge plant, Harry Bennett had been a discreet intermediary between the great carmaker and the intelligence apparatus that had emerged in the US following the First World War. During his years in the navy, he made contacts within the Navy Intelligence, and it was in collaboration with its agents that he was tasked with preventing sabotage at the Highland Park factory, where the prototypes of Eagle patrol boats were designed.[101] Bennett made the most of this opportunity to extend his network of contacts and join the 'social world of surveillance' that was in the making by means of connivance between the military, local and federal police forces, private detectives, journalists, and corporate backrooms.[102]

Proving that neighbourhood bosses do not have a monopoly over violent brokerage practices, Bennett continued to cultivate this middleman role even after being promoted to head of Ford's security department. As a frequent visitor to the Detroit gangsters (who had enriched themselves during Prohibition by smuggling in liquor from neighbouring Canada), Bennett both awarded contracts and business licences (automobile concessions, supply of factory canteens, etc.) to local underworld figures and offered them legal assistance. In return, he benefited from privileged access to their workforce—as well as information that he used to protect his employer against kidnappings and attacks. His possession of this confidential information added to his social utility, as it enabled him to help the police solve high-profile crimes.[103]

Bennett was boastful of these connections, and most of those gathered around his table in Ford's administration building were professional sportsmen and notorious mobsters. Such dubious associations did not, however, stand in the way of maintaining cordial relations with police, which were further strengthened following the 1929 appointment of former Service Department member Carl Brooks at the head of the Dearborn police force—the very Detroit suburb in which the River Rouge factory was located, and whose mayor was none other than Henry Ford's cousin.[104]

This network of relationships blurred the boundaries between the mob, law enforcement professionals, and the corporate world, which proved very useful when the Service Department heavyweights—or Bennett himself—became overzealous. The complicity between Carl Brooks and his former boss was fuelled both by their past collaboration and by various subsequent schemes (such as the allocation of jobs at the River Rouge plant in exchange for a $50 commission),[105] ensuring that Bennett could count on police cooperation in times of need—such as during the 1932 Hunger March and the (no less controversial) 'Battle of the Overpass' in 1937.[106] The Service Department's thugs and their boss were guaranteed impunity, and this connivance intimidated workers and managers alike, further reinforcing Bennett's authority at Ford.

The tolerance shown by American law enforcement agencies towards Bennett and the Service Department was no aberration; on the contrary, it pertained to a long-standing trend in liberal democracies—namely a tolerance of private policing and other extra-legal responses to social unrest, especially in times of chronic turmoil and challenges to economic order.[107] This was already the case in the United States in the 1890s, with the Pinkertons acting as 'the shock troops of industrial order' even as they were also the manifestation of state power—that is, a 'powerful but pragmatic state that demanded order but delegated its authority'.[108] The Great Depression marked a new high point in these employer counter-mobilizations that were not unlike those of the 1970s in France. In both cases, challenges to the productive order, against the backdrop of an economic and social crisis, opened up new margins of impunity for employers.

The reformulation of social issues through the prism of national security also plays right into the hands of capital's henchmen. In the United States, the First World War was marked by a resurgence of vigilantism and private policing in response to social upheaval. Although a number of political leaders questioned their legitimacy, vigilantes of all stripes enjoyed the goodwill of the authorities when they claimed to be working against subversive practices that endangered the war effort. In Bisbee (Arizona) in 1917, several thousand vigilantes were commissioned by the local sheriff to break a strike in the Copper Queen mine that was jeopardizing the supply of ammunition to the US army. As a result of this counter-mobilization, 1,200 'Wobblies' were forced to board special trains and 'deported' to New Mexico.[109] The federal authorities also played their part: in that same year, the American Protective League (APL) set up a formidable auxiliary security force, with the full support of the Department of Justice. Its 250,000 members enthusiastically participated in raids on the IWW and the Socialist Party, and, by the time the group was disbanded in 1918, its leaders boasted that they had brought three million disloyal citizens and illegal aliens to justice.[110]

The advent of universal suffrage and mass media has only served to encourage liberal democracies to offload their repressive dirty work—even in the most routine situations. The use of extra-legal violence has thus become a way of defending the 'productive classes' at a lower economic and political cost.[111] The professional careers of violent entrepreneurs in the service of corporate interests (who have often moved between the repressive services of the state and private security) have contributed to their impunity while at the same time granting them access to public resources and coercive know-how. The trajectory of Harry Bennett is a prime example of this, and the same is true of the security directors of many large contemporary firms, who often rely on their police contacts for access to supposedly confidential legal files—sometimes for a modest fee.[112]

These instances of collusion between official law enforcers and corporate security have led some researchers to conclude that the authority exercised by capital's henchmen is fundamentally state-based.[113] Far from being limited to the defence of 'private' interests, in this scenario they are an integral part of the state apparatus, in the sense of Louis Althusser and Nicos Poulantzas: i.e. a repressive apparatus at the service of the ruling class.[114]

In the field of capital-labour relations (as in other sectors of social life), laissez-faire and subcontracting are forms of indirect government that accord pride of place to private intermediaries.[115] Within the context of social struggles, the impunity granted to both henchmen and more institutionalized security specialists allows the dirty work of repression to be offloaded and the myth of state neutrality to be preserved.

The attachment of democratic states to this façade of legality and impartiality is, however, fairly relative, and ordinary police forces can act as enforcers of industrial order—notably when they protect strike-breakers, or brutally repress the labour movement, in clear demonstrations of partiality. Thus, when mobilized against the Bethlehem Steel strikers in 1910, the men of Pennsylvania's first professional police force displayed such brutality that the workers dubbed them 'Cossacks'.[116] Such repressive configurations can be extended to trade unions when they assume (in collaboration with employers) a role of social control or corporatist regulation. In this case, the unions themselves are taking on the coercive functions that are characteristic of capital's henchmen.[117] This model flourished in the United States from the 1940s onwards, and was introduced at

Ford early in that decade, which was marked by the rise in power of the United Auto Workers (UAW) and, thence, by the exclusion of 'communist obstructionists' from its ranks.[118]

These social formations dedicated to the surveillance and repression of unruly workers are, like any configuration, fluid and criss-crossed by multiple lines of conflict. The Marxist thesis of a 'historic inter-operability [...]' of corporate and government security', which postulates the unicity of bourgeois and state violence, reaches its limits here.[119] Far from stabilizing in a single coercive apparatus that encompasses state and social violence, these repressive configurations hinge on a 'tensile equilibrium'[120] that is prone to frequent—and often spectacular—reversals of alliances.

There is no better illustration of this than the fall of Harry Bennett, which was precipitated by the betrayal of his presumed-successor-turned-nemesis, former FBI agent John Bugas.[121] After trying to secure a position at the head of Ford, Bennett was forced to resign by Henry Ford II in 1945. In the years that followed, a new managerial era took hold at the top of the group: that of the 'Whiz Kids'— young veterans trained by the air force in 'scientific' management. After demobilization, these men applied their knowledge to the rationalization of both production chains and administration at Ford. Meanwhile, Harry Bennett retired to his luxury estate in Desert Springs, California, where he took up painting again, gaining some notoriety for his desert art.[122] Of his last day at Ford, the most abiding memory of those around him is of the acrid smell of smoke as three decades of archives went up in flames.[123]

* * *

Since their emergence in the wake of industrial capitalism in the nineteenth century, capital's henchmen have undergone a series of mutations, attesting to the margins of impunity negotiated by the dominant classes to defend themselves against social struggles. The advent of states governed by law and claiming a monopoly over the use of force absolutely did not put an end to employer violence, because it was accompanied by a multitude of compromises with private specialists in coercion. Two ideal types of violent entrepreneurs in the service of employers were identified: the violent broker, who sits at the interface of the factory world and neighbourhood life, and the anti-union mercenary, who is less locally rooted and therefore less accountable to ethical principles shared with workers. The boundaries between these seemingly distinct custodians of industrial order can get fuzzy, though, so that in the course of the controversies in which they inevitably become embroiled, they often merge in the eyes of the parties involved. On the Indian subcontinent, this merging is demonstrated in the tense pairing of the *dada* and the *goonda*, and the conflicts of labelling around them (see Chapters 3 and 5).

The defence of 'industrial peace' has provided the ideological framework for these conservative mobilizations. Although this cause does invoke the general interest, it has often merged with the defence of employer domination in its claim to control production processes as much as worker behaviour, both in the factory and beyond. Relativizing the alleged aspiration of modern states to monopolize the use of force, these employers' struggles have fed the repressive pluralism of industrial societies—especially as they tend to intermingle with other movements, in defence of the established order (vigilantism, paramilitarism, etc.).

The persistent violence of the industrial firm and the trade in force that feeds on it contradict a central hypothesis in Marxist theories, namely that there is a tendency in capitalist societies for 'extra-economic' forms of surplus extraction to decline, yielding to the 'mute compulsion of economic relations'.[124] The endurance of the repressive tactics outlined in this chapter also invites us to qualify univocal accounts of the Taylorian revolution by suggesting that technical and managerial knowledge has never constituted more than one possible source of authority in large-scale industry, including laboratories of the scientific organization of work, such as the Ford group. The enduring nature of these henchmen of capital suggests there is nothing inevitable about the transition from a 'despotic' to a 'hegemonic' regime of labour control that seeks to obtain workers' acquiescence to their own domination.[125]

The 'private' nature of these coercive services is extremely relative, and in many ways a sham. This is not to say that corporate violence and state violence are interchangeable—to do so would deny autonomy to both, by relegating law enforcement agents to 'custodians of business interests' and elevating capital's henchmen to 'special state apparatuses'.[126] What is at stake here is better understood as an unstable equilibrium of repressive forces oriented towards productive ends—a configuration that generates not only profit but also distinctive power relations and morally loaded representations of achievement and authority. In the next two chapters, we explore the formation of one constellation of productive and repressive forces that is specific to Karachi's industrial capitalism—a configuration riddled with tensions around its regulatory framework, its network of alliances, and its figures of authority.

2

NATIONAL SECURITY TRUMPS SOCIAL SECURITY

> *Labour must remember that the interest and welfare of Pakistan*
> *comes before the interest of any individual or class of individuals*
> *and it must not do anything which in any way weakens Pakistan.*
> Liaquat Ali Khan, Prime Minister of Pakistan, 1949.[1]

In January 1959, an international conference was held at the Institute
of Development Economics (IDE) in Karachi, one of Pakistan's oldest
and most influential think tanks in public policy and economics. The
meeting, which focused on the industrialization process and labour
relations, brought together senior Pakistani officials, economists,
industrialists, and trade unionists, as well as several distinguished
guests from the United States. Among those making the trip to
Karachi (which was to remain the federal capital of Pakistan for a
few more months) were Ford Foundation Vice President Thomas
H. Carroll and University of California President Clark Kerr—
along with several professors from MIT, Harvard, and Princeton.
For the American participants, this meeting offered an opportunity
to reiterate certain general principles of economic development,
while the Pakistani speakers presented the broad outlines of the
industrialization programme promoted by Field Marshal Ayub Khan,

47

who had taken power three months earlier in a military coup—the first in the country's history.

It was a formal exercise, but one that soon strayed beyond its institutional boundaries. When it came to discussing development issues and their social implications, the Pakistani hosts were much bolder than their guests. The authoritarian nature of the country's emerging industrial capitalism allowed these Pakistani officials and experts a freedom of speech that clearly surprised (and sometimes embarrassed) their American counterparts. This awkwardness was particularly evident when it came to the issue of trade unions.

At the end of a long speech on the challenges facing Pakistan's emerging industry, one of the directors of the Pakistan Industrial Development Corporation (PIDC),[2] Muhammad Ayub, asked the American visitors about what trade unions might conceivably contribute to this industry: should Pakistani authorities 'encourage trade union movement or discourage it'? At this stage of its economic development, could the country afford the 'luxury' of a strong trade union movement and progressive labour laws?[3]

The question clearly caught Dr Kerr—who was in charge of this part of the debate on the American side—off guard. Perhaps afraid of making a faux pas, he asked for time to confer with his colleagues, suggesting that he answer this 'very serious question' the next day. This tactical retreat offered the representative of the All Pakistan Confederation of Labour (APCOL, a reformist trade union federation supported by the United States) a way into the discussion.

Muhammad Ayub had just speculated about an industrial configuration in which trade unions would be confined to a purely formal role, without any real ability to influence or block decisions. Without taking offence, Jamal Hasan Sherazi patiently explained to his American interlocutors that Pakistani trade union leaders faced outright hostility from local employers. The large industrial groups that had recently emerged were family-run businesses, he said, founded by merchants only recently converted to industry. Fresh from their transition from the cotton trade to the textile industry, these first-generation industrialists had no experience in industrial relations. Sherazi, with his constructive reformist mindset, was sensitive to the constraints faced by these young captains of industry and did not challenge their virulent anti-unionism: 'Naturally, when the trade unions started forming themselves in different plants, we were faced with the problem that the industrialists would not reconcile themselves to the existence of trade unions.'[4]

This diagnosis, by one of the great figures of reformist trade unionism of the day, identified migrant groups historically specialized in trade as the spearheads of the industrialization process, while attributing their virulent anti-unionism to their persistent mercantile ethos. Beneath the veneer of this naturalized economic order, however, there were glimpses of early friction. Conversely, by bringing the state back in, M. Ayub's plea for unfettered development served to relativize the contribution made by trading communities. This speaks volumes about the authoritarian ideology of development that guided the economic policy of Ayub Khan's regime and was to flourish in the following decades—so much so that it has outlived the developmental state itself.

In terms of industrial policy for the years to come, this ideology of development (and the underlying economy of insecurity) established the rules of the game, the costs of transgression, and the limits of what was conceivable. More fundamentally, the Pakistani state was now set on a formative path in which warfare took precedence over welfare. And while the emerging industrial bourgeoisie favoured the use of coercive intermediaries to bridge the social and linguistic gap between it and the working population (see Chapter 3), the warfare state was an obstacle to negotiating a Fordist compromise that might have rebalanced labour relations and offered a minimum of protection to workers. Momentarily challenged by Zulfikar Ali Bhutto's reforms in the early 1970s, these dominant strategies have combined to sideline more hegemonic arrangements seeking workers' consent to their own domination.

Blame it on the merchants?

In a report dated 11 June 1955, the British Labour Attaché in Karachi, J. J. Keane, noted that the Pakistani capital was teeming with labour experts of one kind or another:

Hopler and Lyman of the ILO [International Labour Organization] were passing through on their way to Geneva; Whittaker and Wyne-Roberts, also of the ILO, are engaged in trying to raise productivity in industry; Ogden is concerned with training schemes; while Mason has taken over the manpower survey from Hepler.[5]

The IDE conference participated in both these proliferations of experts and in the controversies that—since its infancy in the 1950s—have surrounded Karachi's industrial capitalism, particularly insofar as the role of trading communities in its genesis and (mal-) practices were concerned.

At the time of its inception, Pakistan had only about 30 large factories. Most local production units were dedicated to the export of raw materials, alongside which were a handful of light engineering and agricultural processing enterprises.[6]

Despite having inherited a quarter of undivided India's population, the two wings of Pakistan were allocated just 9% of its industrial base and 7% of its labour force.[7] Karachi itself remained weakly industrialized. Founded in 1729 by a group of *banyas* (Hindu merchants/usurers) from the interior of Sindh, the port city was primarily a warehouse at the crossroads of the maritime routes that connected the Indian subcontinent to Africa, China, and the Middle East.[8] The Dalmia Cement Factory was the first production unit to be built there; it opened in 1925 and remained, up until independence, the city's only industrial unit of its kind.[9]

The city's rail connections and port facilities were however strategic assets—a point constantly reiterated, from the late 1940s onwards, by advocates of industrial development within the indigenous business community.[10] Colonial officers tasked with assessing the prospects for industrialization in Sindh province also argued for efforts to be concentrated on Karachi, taking the government trading estates developed in the UK in the 1930s as their model. This was a public-private partnership prototype based on public development of infrastructure, provision of turnkey factories, and management of the area's administrative affairs by a limited liability company by guarantee, without share capital.[11] It

Location quotient of major employment sectors in Karachi (2011) was these proposals that inspired the large industrial parks around which the industrialization and urbanization of Karachi's peripheral districts unfolded in the 1950s and 1960s.[12]

Most major Indian trading houses already had branches in Karachi prior to Partition; the city was home to one of the region's main cotton markets, supplying the major centres of the Indian (Bombay, Ahmedabad) and European textile industries. Combined with the decision by Pakistani authorities to make Karachi the country's capital (a status it retained until 1959, and which facilitated the access of its economic elite to both the political class and the bureaucracy), this extraversion contributed to its appeal for Muslim merchant groups driven into exile by Partition. Sometimes assimilated to 'castes',[13] these endogamous groups were, alongside the large landowners of Sindh and Punjab, the main holders of capital in the country. When the landed elites (with their limited penchant for internationalization and reputation for risk aversion) seemed reluctant to embark on an industrial adventure, the authorities turned to large merchant groups as drivers of the country's economic modernization.

The merchants who had converted to industry quickly caused controversy. The first reports on working conditions in Karachi's factories (whether by the foreign experts who crowded into the city or by their Pakistani counterparts) denounced exploitative practices towards the working population as unacceptable from a state subscribing to International Labour Organization (ILO) conventions. In line with J. H. Sherazi's analysis at the IDE seminar (though less prone to absolving these youthful sins), early Pakistani labour economists, ILO investigators, and Labour Advisers commissioned by the British and American governments shared a conviction that factory owners' eagerness to enrich themselves was only moderately (some would say disingenuously) tempered by their ostentatious piety.

The Labour Adviser to the British Embassy in India, James S. P. Mackenzie, who covered Pakistani industrial affairs and the trade union movement from Delhi, wrote in his replies to a 1958 questionnaire on working conditions in the Pakistani textile industry (then still concentrated in Karachi):

There are very few mills in Pakistan which date from earlier than 1947, and even the oldest opened as late as 1934. The owners of the older mills, being industrialists of comparatively long standing, are responsible in their attitude towards their workers, and follow this legislation more carefully than the newer employers. Thus, the older mills are well up to the average in spite of out-of-date lay-out and equipment. The new factories are owned by a new industrial class made up of former merchants, who tend to be very corrupt, ready to ride roughshod over legislation in their drive to get rich quickly. Fairly frequently, however, they provide good welfare facilities out of their huge newly-won fortunes, partly for prestige reasons and partly to satisfy their superstitious devotion to the Holy Koran.[14]

Such criticism was not confined to foreign observers, who feared that the accumulative spree of Pakistan's first industrialists would give rise to social unrest and serve the nefarious designs of communist agitators. In a slightly different mode, this critique could also be found in the writings of a young Pakistani economist, Iftikhar Ahmed Mukhtar, also present at the IDE conference. In 1958, he defended his thesis at Columbia University. His research was devoted to capital-labour relations in emerging Pakistani industry, and contained a section on 'the attitude of employers towards workers' that was decidedly critical:

Employers, with the exception of foreign firms operating in Pakistan, and a very few national industrial establishments, regard labour as a commodity-factor and not a human factor. This attitude is partly encouraged by the grinding poverty that prevails among the masses and throws the working class almost completely at the mercy of employers. Another factor which contributes substantially to the present attitude of employers is the lack of proper realisation on the part of the Government, that in its enthusiasm for industrialising the country it should not let employers exploit workers.

But the major factor underlying employers' existing attitude is that they are new entrants in the industrial field and lack both knowledge and experience in dealing with their employees. In the

British India, Muslims as a community were the least associated with industrial ownership and management. In the upper and middle classes, they were mostly landlords or government officials. Two small sub-communities among them were fairly successfully engaged in retail and wholesale trade. These were the Memons and Bohras. After Partition these people migrated to Pakistan to fill the vacuum created by the mass exodus of the non-Muslim traders and businessmen.

To begin with, the area of their operations was the import-export trade, which was extremely profitable on account of the acute shortage of consumer goods which had arisen precisely because the new state of Pakistan had little industry of its own. Later, many of them entered the field of industry, particularly because the importation of goods was restricted by the Government. They now control and manage a substantially large part of factory-industry in Pakistan. They are generally poorly educated and therefore ill-prepared; and from this point-of-view they are ill-equipped for the role they are playing in the new state of Pakistan. The lack of education is the hallmark of other industrialists too, besides the Memons and Bohras.

On account of the commercial background of the new industrialist class, its sole concern today is with immediate and quick profits. And since profits in trade and commerce in Pakistan have been phenomenally high, these new industrialists are accustomed to high profits.[15]

The idea that the first Pakistani industrialists, who came from merchant groups, were lacking in experience is repeated here. However, the critique of Pakistan's pioneers of industry takes a more elaborate form, by positioning the beginnings of Pakistani industry in the continuity of colonial India's ethnic division of labour while also clarifying the contours of this capitalist class in the making. Though the over-representation of merchant groups from Gujarat (the Memons and the Bohras) at the head of the first industrial groups is noted, this critique diverges from the British experts' indictment of the new Pakistani oligarchy, whose references were drawn from the dark side of the English industrial revolution.[16]

Even though this cultural substratum remains implicit, Iftikhar Ahmed Mukhtar's discourse bears the imprint of vernacular diatribes against merchants and trading groups more generally. In its popular variant, this critique is conveyed by a multitude of proverbs denouncing the propensity of the *banya* to fudge his scales, adulterate his products, and make up his accounts.[17] In Pakistan, this criticism could be found as early as the 1950s in the writings of the great Urdu-speaking satirists, such as Majeed Lahori (1913–1957). His poem '*Amir bachche ki du'a*' (The prayer of rich children) parodies the famous verses of the national poet Muhammad Iqbal:

> Prayer rises to my lips.
> May my life be like that of the *seth*.[18]
> May Lyari[19] be plunged into darkness thanks to me.
> Let my office, on the other hand, light up.
> Let my club shine because of me,
> Just as the moon illuminates the night.
> May my life be modelled on Qaroon's.[20]
> May I be forever in love with the National Bank.
> Let my mission be to side with the rich and to be the
>   sworn enemy of the poor.
> My God, preserve me from good deeds
> And may I never deviate from the wrong path.[21]

The imprint of mercantile practices on industrial illegalities must be nuanced by bringing the state back in—and with it the interdependencies between business circles and political elites. Among Pakistani and foreign experts of the 1950s and 1960s, however, there was a broad consensus around this legacy. Besides, the idea that the commercial practices and community organization of merchant groups predisposed them to unbridled forms of accumulation was not always seen as a problem requiring a solution. For some foreign experts commissioned by Pakistani authorities, the greed of these merchants, freshly converted to industry, appeared to guarantee an accelerated economic take-off, while their willingness to circumvent the law signalled an entrepreneurial spirit worthy of the American robber barons of the Gilded Age.[22]

The main proponent of this thesis was an Austrian-American economist, Gustav Papanek. Born in Vienna in 1926, he obtained his PhD from Harvard University in 1951. He was recruited by USAID as an economist but lost his position during the McCarthy era due to his socialist leanings. So when his alma mater asked him to participate in an aid programme in Pakistan, funded by the Ford Foundation, Papanek jumped at the opportunity. In 1954, he flew to Pakistan with his sociologist wife, Hanna, and they stayed in Karachi until 1958. Having taken up residence in the Drigh Road area, where *muhajir* (Urdu-speaking migrants from northern India) families were concentrated while awaiting relocation, Papanek and his wife had front-row seats to the upheaval generated by Partition.[23]

It was in this context (as well as through contact with his American colleagues and the Pakistani Planning Commission members who welcomed them) that Gustav Papanek was converted, signing up to a model of economic growth focused on industry, with an assumption of high social inequality.

This doctrine of 'functional inequality' inspired the second five-year plan (1960–1965) and is the subject of impassioned sections in the writings of both Papanek and Mahbub ul Haq (Chief Economist at the Planning Commission). In a book published in 1963, Haq encouraged developing countries to adopt a 'philosophy of growth' rather than a 'philosophy of distribution'; echoing Muhammad Ayub's words at the IDE conference, he considered that developing countries could not afford the luxury of welfare schemes and would be better advised, for the time being, to abandon any idea of equitable distribution.[24]

In his early writings, Haq was inspired by Rostow's growth theories (his *Stages of Economic Growth* had been published a few years earlier), while Papanek took a Schumpeterian perspective.[25] For him, the 'industrial entrepreneur' is a 'distinct personality type' in possession of qualities that are unevenly distributed in every society; these enterprising figures are not motivated by financial motives alone, but also seek a form of social recognition that is denied to them outside of the economic sphere—from this perspective, the developmental state is, above all, an incubator of social change, enabling the development of this new type of human being.[26]

For Papanek, the most remarkable feature of the Pakistani industrialization process at the turn of the 1960s was the speed with which this type of man (and the entrepreneurial ethos associated with him) took hold in the country. In a bid to explain this social transformation, he undertook a comprehensive study of the Pakistani manufacturing sector—the very first of its kind.

Conducted in 1959–1960, it was based on in-depth interviews with a sample of over 250 industrialists from the main manufacturing sectors.[27] The survey focused on large-scale industry and only covered establishments employing more than 20 people. Although this sample covered just 10% of the country's industrial companies, these few controlled as much as 50% of industrial capital. This was an early indication of the extent to which economic and financial resources were concentrated around a small number of family conglomerates—a trend that continued to increase during the so-called 'decade of development' (1958–1968).

Papanek's study confirms the prominent role played by erstwhile merchants (and more specifically, by the Memons of Karachi) in the early development of Pakistani industry. Like other merchant groups from western India (the Bohras and the Khojas, in particular), the Memons had had a presence in Karachi since the 1930s, when Bombay firms first began expanding into the city. This merchant community, historically specialized in the kirana[28] trade and the commercialization of textiles (yarn and cloth), only migrated en masse to Karachi after Partition. The violence of 1947, and the opportunities that opened up for these traders and entrepreneurs in Pakistan, fuelled an exodus of Memons—especially from their strongholds in the Kathiawar peninsula, Bantva, and Jetpur. Wealthier families did lose land, orchards, and houses in Partition, but most of their wealth comprised movable assets, which they were able to transfer to Pakistan.

By the end of the 1950s, there were an estimated 100,000 Memons in Pakistan, most of whom were in Karachi. For these merchants, the city's appeal was further enhanced by its port infrastructure and the departure of the Hindu trading elites (the *banyas*) in the months following Partition.

The first Memon immigrants may have been reluctant to invest in industry, but the waning of the Korean War trade boom, coupled with the introduction of state controls on imports, led a number of them to reconsider their options. As Papanek points out (with a measure of admiration), in this increasingly restrictive regulatory environment, 'only the more energetic and ruthless were in a position to become industrialists or to expand industrial holdings'.[29] He does also acknowledge that some of the money invested by these merchants in industry was the product of illicit commercial activities (smuggling, speculation, a thriving black market, etc.).

The most prominent trading families (the Bawanis, Haroons, Dawoods, Adamjees, Pakolawalas, etc.) had a further advantage over their competitors: they had access to a powerful distribution network, which allowed them not only to sell their products but also to evade price controls and taxation, since undeclared income could be hidden in the form of transfers between production and sales units.[30] Indeed, tax evasion was so widespread among these pioneers of industry that they were said to keep three books of accounts: one for the tax authorities, one for their partners/relatives, and one for themselves. Sometimes a fourth was added, destined to be handed over to the taxman on his second visit—when he insisted on being shown the 'real' accounts.[31]

This industry was characterized from the outset by strong community spirit, strict control of labour costs, and an entrepreneurial spirit that had scant regard for the law. These characteristics of the companies founded by the Memons (especially in the textile industry) tended to reinforce one another; their familial nature was conducive to an economy governed by secrecy, one that minimized transaction costs and maximized profits. For Papanek, higher profit margins would, for these Pakistani industry pioneers, outweigh any other consideration 'since the returns from increased efficiency were likely to be less than from the promotion of new enterprises and from coping with, and trying to evade, government regulations'.[32]

Karachi's Memon industrialists tended to recruit senior management and administrative staff (especially accountants) from within their own community, and this contributed to the widespread depiction in the late 1960s of a monolithic and hermetic business environment whose success could be explained by forms of tontine, arcane mathematical methods, and occult accounting techniques.[33] This communal *entre-soi* seems to have provided resources to Memon industrialists—allowing them, no doubt, to both circumvent certain regulations and, more generally, to build confidence in an uncertain world. In this regard, it is worth recalling that many of the newly settled Memon entrepreneurs in Pakistan had a poor command of Urdu, making it difficult for them to interact with either the working population or the bureaucracy—both of which were dominated by Urdu-speaking *muhajirs* until the early 1970s. Mocked by the *muhajir* intelligentsia for their broken Urdu,[34] some leading Memon industrialists sought to compensate for this lack of cultural capital by investing in organizations that promoted Urdu language and literature—starting with the Anjuman Taraqqi-i-Urdu (Association for the Promotion of Urdu).[35]

The social and linguistic distance between the working-class population and merchants only recently converted to industry certainly favoured the development of a 'despotic' production regime[36] in Karachi factories. Early on, recruitment to and control of the workforce was subcontracted to various coercive intermediaries (see Chapter 3). In the province of Punjab (where workers and management came from the same ethnic stock and shared a language), this kind of managerial domination may have been mitigated through paternalism or clientelism. By contrast, in Karachi, because management and workers belonged to distinct ethno-linguistic communities, such mitigating factors would not have been present.[37]

This hypothesis should probably be qualified, especially in view of the terror some Punjabi employers inspired in their workers—such as the founders of the Ittefaq group, who were reputed to get rid of unruly workers by throwing them into the furnace.[38] Nevertheless, in terms of managerial style, the differences between the country's two major centres of industrialization are well documented; the ILO's first in-depth report on productivity in the Pakistani textile industry is instructive in this regard. Based on observations made between 1955 and 1958 in factories across the two parts of Pakistan, it found that

Punjabi factories had become more professional, management-wise, than those in Karachi—where worker discontent had been fuelled by erratic personnel management and arbitrary dismissals.[39] Moreover, a 1960 study (conducted by a young Pakistani economist affiliated with the Ford Foundation) suggests that Karachi's industrialists were concerned with the ethnic (and to a lesser extent, religious) identity of their workers early on. Some companies conducted in-depth surveys on employees' geographical origin and community background, with the results posted in the office of the Head of Staff.[40] While this practice was not in itself coercive, it was indicative of early efforts to profile the working population for the purpose of control. Surveys like this led to adjustments to recruitment policies that were designed to maintain a balanced representation of ethnic groups. More generally, they helped employers and managers to keep a grip on a working environment that, for those freshly arrived from India, may initially have seemed difficult to decipher.

The economy of insecurity

Neither the mercantile origins of this industrial bourgeoisie, nor the forms of its social anchorage in Pakistan, can fully account for its hurried formation, its propensity for unbridled accumulation, or its penchant for authoritarianism. These also resulted from an economic policy that was underpinned by a catastrophist strategic perspective. The military-bureaucratic coalition governing Pakistan in the 1950s and 1960s justified its plans for unfettered development by raising the spectre of impending disaster. This economy of insecurity, haunted by the idea of imminent collapse, provided the foundations for authoritarian developmentalism. Its promoters were keen to unleash entrepreneurial zeal and demand sacrifices from workers—especially in terms of wages and social rights. References to industrial peace were omnipresent in official speeches, and played a central role in this project. By invoking a horizon of concord, conducive to the maximization of productive forces and linking economic development with national security, it also provided a powerful instrument for the vilification of labour struggles.

The securitization of development

Because of the chaotic conditions in which Pakistan emerged and the conflict with its Indian neighbour that had begun in the early months of independence, industrial development was both vital and urgent. Like other Asian states that were industrialized late (South Korea, Taiwan, Singapore, etc.), the Pakistani developmental state was formed in a context of 'systemic vulnerability'.[41] For the civilian and military elites of these states, whose survival was far from guaranteed at the time of their creation, the promotion of industry was more of an expedient on the road to national security than a conversion to the 'religion' of progress. In a context of budgetary shortages, the development of an efficient industrial sector was meant to generate the foreign currency essential to consolidate the defence apparatus. Indeed, none of these late-industrialized states were able to rely on mining or oil rents, and foreign aid offered only gradual compensation for limited tax revenues.[42]

India's industrial policy originally had a strong ideological undertone, but the same cannot be said of Pakistan. Industrialization, to Pakistan's civilian and military elites of the 1950s and 1960s, was primarily a means of maintaining a strategic balance with India.[43] By inciting Pakistani elites to prioritize 'the fastest route to capital accumulation',[44] this economy of insecurity played a crucial role in the social pact made with the merchant world. From the outset, this was a pact based on concessions and privileges, which structured both employer domination and the state's relationship to industrialists.

On 8 September 1949, in his inaugural address to the Pakistan Council of Industries, Prime Minister Liaquat Ali Khan declared that 'no country can have really modern and properly equipped army for purposes of defence and a high standard of living, without developing its resources'.[45] When invited to lay the foundation stone for a textile factory in Karachi a few months later, the Federal Minister of Industry concurred. On this occasion, Nazir Ahmad Khan invited potential investors to put aside their own interests in favour of those of the nation under threat. He argued that, for the government of Pakistan, industrialization was 'as important as defence', and that industrialists could count on the full support of the authorities.[46]

A reluctance among capital owners to embark on industrial ventures sometimes earned them rebukes from the authorities, and in October 1948, the country's first Finance Minister, Ghulam Muhammad, admonished the wealthier sections of the population, saying that they 'must give—and give with an open hand—to strengthen the defences of the country. It should not be necessary to appeal to them for contributions. Our industrialists instead of throwing their weight about and talking big, should get on with the work of setting up industries'.[47] The first industrial policy, announced in April 1948, placed the development of agriculture and small-scale industry at the top of the state's priorities, while also stating that 'the development of large-scale industries *essential to the security of the state*, or its general prosperity, will also receive the utmost attention and encouragement'.[48]

In the following years, more than half of the state budget was devoted to defence spending, while the challenges posed by the formation of a functional bureaucracy and the rehabilitation of refugees from India used up a large part of the remaining resources.[49] The Pakistani government's room for manoeuvre was all the more limited by its reluctance to impose a constraining system of taxation. In this context, if the state made war, the reverse was less obvious; consolidation of the defence apparatus translated into neither the development of a tax administration covering the national territory, nor concessions to society in the form of redistributive practices or social protection measures. From this point on, Pakistan asserted itself as a *warfare state*, having little interest in the welfare of its population. The defence effort took precedence over all other considerations, to the detriment of investments in health, education, and social protection. To finance this war effort and compensate for poor taxation, the civilian and military governments of the 1950s and 1960s turned to international aid and exports of low-value-added consumer goods, whose competitiveness was predicated on the compression of both workers' wages and agricultural prices.[50]

The social protection system that the country inherited at the time of its creation did not help. It operated on a discriminatory basis; rather than being a universal right, the protections on offer were akin to privileges reserved for certain categories of workers—

essentially those in the so-called 'organized' sector, who (in both Pakistan and India) represent barely 7–8% of the total working population. Yet these employees were (in theory at least) the only ones to benefit from permanent jobs protected by labour law across both the public and private sectors.[51] Access to social security and pensions had, for a handful of workers, been hard-won during the colonial period. In Karachi, this was the case for dockers and other employees of the Karachi Port Trust (KPT).[52] But it was not until 1967 that a federal law (the Provincial Employees Social Security Scheme) introduced social protection measures on a broader scale. And once again, this legislation covered only a tiny proportion of Pakistani workers—mainly those in the textile industry.

Two years later, the scope of this legislation (which notably provided for individual financial aid to complement access to medical care) was extended to all workers in the organized industrial sector, prior to its 1970 reorganization on a provincial basis, under the name of the Employees Social Security Institutions (ESSIs). The final essential component of this embryonic social protection system— the Employees Old-Age Benefits Institutions (EOBIs)—was created in 1976, on the initiative of the socialist-inspired government of Zulfikar Ali Bhutto. EOBIs manage retirement, disability, and survivor pensions, and are jointly financed by the federal government and employers (up to 5% of the gross salary of insured workers). However, because of low wages and employer contributions (and employers' reluctance to even pay their contributions), these welfare schemes have been chronically underfunded. In any case, many categories of workers are excluded from such schemes, especially in agriculture and the informal parts of the service and industrial sectors.

Combined with the low tax burden and budgetary trade-offs in favour of national defence, the failures of these insurance mechanisms have hindered the formation of a social state in Pakistan, leading the country on a trajectory similar to that of those intensely coercive and highly extroverted states that, as Charles Tilly notes, came to proliferate during the Cold War, including South Korea, Bolivia, and Nigeria. These states have managed to compensate for their low levels of tax revenue by using foreign exchange generated by their exports, and foreign aid (received because of their status as 'pivotal states' pre-9/11, or 'frontline states' in the 'war on terror'). With little dependence on taxation to finance their defence apparatus, these states are free of the constraints associated with maintaining an efficient tax administration, and the military elites of these praetorian states have managed to resist attempts made by civilians to control them—but by the same token, have avoided any real social contract with their taxpayers. Even though it is fundamental in the trajectory of these states, this last point is only briefly mentioned by Tilly.[53] Far from forcing the Pakistani state to make concessions to society, then, the military conflicts that have punctuated the country's history (1948, 1965, 1971, 1999) have led its rulers to sacrifice social welfare at the altar of national security.

As a structural component of state formation in Pakistan, the securitization of development thus has several facets:

1. It impacts budget decisions through the *strategic management of scarcity*, prioritizing national defence in the allocation of the state's limited resources—a scarcity which, as we have seen, has been sustained by a long-standing policy of state financing that chooses extraversion over taxation.

2. It also has a repressive aspect, which manifests in the *expansion of the domain of war* to social struggles—leading to a blurring of the enemy, the indeterminacy of the battlefield, measures of exception, and the confusion of genres insofar as instruments and agents of repression are concerned.[54] By refusing to submit to the requirements of development, workers asking for wage increases, uncompromising union leaders, and environmental activists are branded traitors and threats to national security. From this perspective, it is unsurprising that Pakistan's first emergency laws (known as the Public Safety Acts) were used in the early 1950s to incarcerate left-leaning trade union leaders such as Mirza Ibrahim.[55] Following implementation of this economic programme with security overtones, the defence of industrial peace became strategic in scope, becoming assimilated to the defence of national interests in the face of both internal enemies and external threats. Established as an official doctrine,

this commitment is at the heart of successive labour policies (1955, 1959, 1969, 1972, and 2002).

3. Ultimately, it was sustained through a *mixed economy of security*, associating capital owners and specialists in coercion with public funds and private capital. During the 1950s and 1960s, a new industrial policy emerged that was driven by the head of state, regulated by the bureaucracy, and financed by the agricultural sector and the emerging working class for the benefit of a handful of large industrial houses; this was achieved by means of price control policy on agricultural products (especially cotton) and the compression of workers' wages.

The business ventures of several prominent members of Ayub Khan's entourage further blurred the boundaries between the public and private realms, as well as between capital and coercion, while fuelling social criticism of this crony capitalism—criticism that inspired Z.A. Bhutto's attempts at reform in the early 1970s. These socialist-inspired reforms set the scene for a social state in Pakistan, though they remained incomplete and were soon unravelled by a new military regime. Moreover, while Bhutto's reforms were a significant step towards social democracy, this controversial experiment in 'Islamic socialism' failed to challenge either the security-based approach to development of previous regimes, or their commitment to industrial peace, with all its implications for labour movements.

As social struggles intensified under the aegis of a new generation of working-class union leaders, Bhutto appealed to the patriotism of workers and union leaders in a bid to dissuade them from resorting to strike action: 'an attitude that is not only detrimental to their own interests but suicidal for the nation'.[56] And when workers refused to comply with these injunctions, Bhutto responded to 'the strength of the street' with 'the strength of the state', brutally crushing demonstrations.[57] The military coup of 5 July 1977 brought General Muhammad Zia-ul-Haq to power—who was destined, over the following decade, to sign the death certificate of the developmental state. The tarnishing of social struggles through the invocation of national security, for its part, remained a common repressive tactic. Moreover, labour union repression found new resources in the anti-terrorist regime that emerged during the 1990s and expanded considerably in the course of the following decade (see Chapter 6).

The taming of the trade union movement

The fact that APCOL's representative at the IDE conference, Jamal Hasan Sherazi, showed such understanding towards employers was not only out of ideological conviction—but also as a result of his professional habitus. Born in Bihar in 1919, this *muhajir* became Joint Secretary of the West Pakistan Federation of Labour in 1951, while holding leadership positions in a variety of trade union organizations—this was common practice among early professional trade unionists in Karachi. In a memo to the British Labour Ministry tracing the career of this figure (whom he considered emblematic of the 'small group of union leaders who appear at the centre of activities in Karachi'), British Labour Adviser T. Hoskison estimated that in 1956, Sherazi was Secretary of two trade unions and President of nine others.[58] Four years later (as recorded in the 'Who's Who' of the Pakistani trade union world compiled by the US Embassy), he was chairing some fifteen of them while pursuing a parallel career as a lawyer—again, this was common practice among early professional trade unionists in Karachi.[59]

Trade union activities and judicial practice overlapped in his career as a lawyer, and from 1952 Sherazi began defending unions at Industrial Tribunals, ultimately becoming the official representative of workers at the Central Industrial Court in 1960. His twin careers thus progressed in line with the judicialization of labour disputes, which turned the Industrial Tribunals, and then the Labour Courts, into the legitimate forum for the adjudication of workplace conflicts. This process of judicialization was an essential instrument for the taming of social struggles; it transferred the expression of workers' discontent from the streets to the courts, under the watchful eye of the bureaucracy.[60] Professional trade unionists like Sherazi (who also often happened to be lawyers) were both products and agents of this legal subjugation of the trade union movement. They derived their social utility (and most of their income) from it. These material and symbolic rewards made them reluctant to challenge a bureaucratic system that hindered trade union activity by cutting its claws. Thus, the right to strike—not recognized as a constitutional right in Pakistan—was subjected to restrictions that made it almost unenforceable in practice.

This judicialization of labour disputes contributed to the development of an expert trade unionism dominated by lawyers with no personal experience of industrial work. While this legal framework heavily constrained the trade union movement, it did not impose much of a burden on employers, who faced only small fines for labour law violations. A more combative trade union movement developed in the wake of the great opposition movement to Ayub Khan (1968–1969), and then in response to the socialist discourse of Zulfikar Ali Bhutto (in power from 1971 to 1977). However, from 1972 onwards this movement waned, following repression by the combined forces of the police, the army, and the employers' henchmen, who were recruited both from among the *goonda*s (thugs) and from pro-employer unions, such as those founded by the Islamists of the Jama'at-e-Islami (JI)—namely the Labour Federation of Pakistan (LFP) and later on the National Labour Federation (NLF), both of which were established in the textile factories of Karachi during the 1950s, though their presence in the industrial sector remained marginal until the early 1970s.[61]

From the 1980s onwards, the casualization of the industrial labour market further discouraged unionization by making it easier to sack rebellious workers. As a result of these structural obstacles, trade unions have never managed to establish themselves as a negotiating force within companies. And (with the notable exception of the late 1960s and early 1970s) their ability to take to the streets has generally remained limited.

This chronic weakness of the trade union movement (further accentuated since the late 1980s by the liberalization of the economy and the casualization of industrial labour) has left the field open to a cost-cutting policy based on force and fraud. However, industrial illegalities could flourish only with the acquiescence of both civilian and military political leaders, and the level of their indulgence has kept pace with the thickening of interdependencies between these elites.

Labour conflicts in Pakistan, 1949–2005

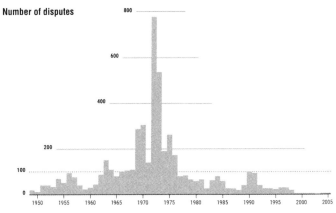

Number of disputes

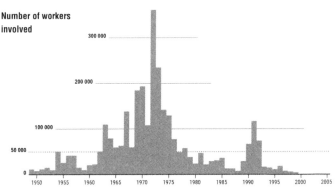

Number of workers involved

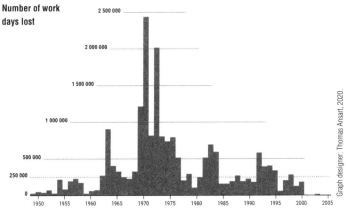

Number of work days lost

Sources: Pakistan Statistical Yearbook, 1948–2007.

Graph designer: Thomas Ansart, 2020.

The state manufacturing of industrial illegalisms

Qurratulain Hyder—a giant of the twentieth-century South Asian literary world—was a keen observer of social life in Karachi in the early 1950s. In her short story 'Housing Society' (originally published in Urdu in 1963), she paints a vivid picture of the urban environment that was so conducive to the formation of a composite power elite.[62] Indeed, until the end of the 1950s, Karachi's status as a federal capital favoured the emergence of a crony capitalism that thrived on the nightly libations of its intermingled elites.

The story traces the career of an unscrupulous *muhajir* merchant, Jamshed Ali Syed, and closes with the recollection of a party held at his luxurious residence in PECHS—a residential area originally reserved for senior officials of the new Pakistani state. For the occasion, the garden of Jamshed House (which had been designed by an Italian architect) was decorated with multicoloured Japanese lanterns and baskets of flowers. Luxury cigarettes and fine food awaited the guests, and the wine was stored in ice buckets, to protect it from the heat of the day. Through the bay window of the lounge (lit by chandeliers imported from Belgium), the well-manicured lawn 'looked like a technicolor scene on a cinemascope screen'. In air scented by Chanel N° 5, the garden saw the whole of Karachi's high society pass through: 'Cabinet ministers, secretaries and other senior officers, ambassadors. Press and Commercial Attaches. Big name industrialists. Packs of journalists busily taking notes. Photographers strolling around flashing bulbs. Pakistani ladies dressed in alluring "Indian" saris, foreign women in evening gowns and cocktail dresses'.[63] In this exclusive setting, as hips swayed to the beat of rock 'n' roll, 'African rhythms', or even 'the latest Latin dance', more business-focused guests finalized important contracts—occasionally coming to blows with partners they suspected of fraud.[64]

Beyond the plush villas of PECHS, the privileged setting for these elite sociabilities were the highly exclusive clubs inherited from the colonial period, one of which was the Sindh Club, built in 1871 in an Indo-Italian style, and forbidden—until independence—to women and non-whites. But one of the most popular places among local elites was the Beach Luxury—a hotel built in a tropical setting in

1948, offering an unobstructed view of the creek leading to Karachi harbour. These elite sociabilities were crucial to the formation and reproduction of the local industrial bourgeoisie.[65] Indeed, as Gustav Papanek points out, 'At least, until [the] 1960s, industrialists' ability to deal with government was more important for their success than any other management function'. Among politicians, bureaucrats, and law enforcement agencies alike, there was a tendency to turn a blind eye to certain illegal practices. In so doing, they opened up margins of impunity for industry, and this may have been even more decisive than their direct interventions (for example, through the issuing of permits or the provision of financial aid).[66]

As the aforementioned accounting manipulations show, some of the illicit practices of the first captains of industry were part of a long history of commercial illegalities that continues to this day.[67] This legacy must however be qualified by placing the fraudulent practices of industry in their political context. From 1952 onwards, a number of merchant families were persuaded to convert to industry in light of two factors: the introduction of a licensing policy restricting imports of consumer goods, and reduced demand for Pakistani agricultural products abroad (mainly due to a post-Korean War contraction of the international cotton market). The Pakistani developmental state ensured that these merchants received a return on investment comparable to what they had become accustomed to in their commercial activities. As the Assistant Labour Adviser of the British High Commission noted during a mission to West Pakistan in 1958:

> Stories of huge fortunes made since partition are common and the millowners make no attempt to hide their wealth. (At a recent tripartite labour conference talk of 500% net profit went unchallenged).[68]

These colossal profits (which were to decline steadily during the 1960s) owed much to a multiplication of tax exemption measures over the years, as well as to the compression of wage costs and the failures of the factory inspection regime—which allowed manufacturers to evade the health, environmental, and safety regulations introduced by the Factories Act (1934). Inherent to this authoritarian developmentalism is what Michel Foucault calls the 'differential management of illegalisms'—that is, the differentiated treatment of offences according to their nature and the social identity of the perpetrators.[69] The concept of *illégalisme* (which has long been mistranslated in English as 'illegalities') cannot be reduced to a failure of enforcement; rather, it is part of a system of power in which the non-enforcement of certain laws opens up margins of impunity for certain categories of the population. This selective application of the law was key to the formation of Pakistan's delinquent elites and their co-optation by the developmental state, while providing ruling elites with retaliatory measures against wayward businessmen.

Although some sectors (e.g. textiles) were more reluctant to comply with prevailing norms than others (e.g. pharmaceuticals, which emerged later on), none were completely immune to corporate crime, which (unlike crimes committed for the purpose of personal gain) refers to offences committed with the support, and in the interest, of a particular company.[70] Unlike what has been observed in other contexts (in the United States especially), it was not necessarily the least efficient companies that were most likely to break the law.[71] When it comes to illicit and coercive practices, the most prominent, most politically connected companies—whether through personal networks of influence or the most powerful business organizations—were no match for small, struggling companies. And as the mobilization of Karachi's business community following the 2012 Ali Enterprises fire showed (see Chapter 9), far from dissociating themselves from any smaller companies being held to account, industry heavyweights tended to rally round these companies to resist regulatory pushes collectively.

In some ways, Pakistani political elites have 'sold' the law to industrialists. Either by 'silent consent'[72] or by failing to invest in control bodies, successive civilian and military governments since the 1950s have deprived themselves of any effective ability to enforce the law and punish violations. While contributing to the attractiveness of industry among trading communities, this climate of impunity and non-compliance has had major consequences not only for working conditions in the manufacturing sector, but also for the process of state formation. The scale of tax evasion among merchant groups, and later by industrialists, has weighed heavily on public finances while lending credibility to the thesis that Pakistani society is resistant to taxation—a thesis used by Ayub Khan to justify his decision to abandon a system of universal taxation in favour of other sources of funding, starting with international aid.[73]

The ruling elites, both civilian and military, did more than just turn a blind eye to the illicit practices of industrialists. They also actively collaborated in a form of crony capitalism whose keystone was the Pakistan Industrial Development Corporation (PIDC). To compensate for the shortcomings of an embryonic financial system that hampered the development of capital-intensive industrial projects, this institution (represented by Muhammad Ayub at the IDE conference) entered into a series of joint ventures with the private sector, and also set up industrial ventures on its own before going on to sell them to private buyers at cost price. This policy of divestment primarily benefited a handful of large family-owned industrial houses and reinforced the dynamics of concentration of the national economy.

The PIDC, founded in 1950, was emblematic of the crony capitalism that crystallized under Ayub Khan's regime, and two of its first three directors (S. Amjad Ali and Mirza Ahmad Ispahani) were representatives of the business community. The controversial nature of this choice did not escape the authorities' attention. These prominent businessmen thus had to settle for a 'symbolic' annual revenue of a single rupee, and agree to relinquish their management positions at many private companies.[74] In the following years, four representatives of the major industrial groups—Ispahani, Colony, Adamjee, and Wazir Ali—joined the PIDC Board of Directors.[75] Throughout this period, the policy of divestment of PIDC to the private sector contributed to the consolidation of a handful of conglomerates—including the Adamjees, the Dawoods, and the Sheikhs of the Fancy group, which emerged as the country's largest industrial groups in the late 1950s.

Having become a campaign slogan with populist overtones, the theme of the '22 families', which were accused of exploiting the people and ruining the country, helped put the nationalization of key sectors of the economy on opposition party agendas. Building on the now widespread perception among the middle and working classes that 'monopolists' and 'millionaires' had bled the country dry, Zulfikar Ali Bhutto, who became President in December 1971, had the businessmen that compromised with the previous regime arrested.[76] He also announced a series of nationalizations and reforms that, to this day, remain the most ambitious attempt ever to reform Pakistani industrial capitalism. Combined with the devastating effects of East Pakistan's secession,[77] these reforms dealt a fatal blow to the big houses that had dominated the national economy, initiating a process of de-concentration and rebalancing in favour of the Punjab-based business community.

Although some families have weathered these successive shocks better than others, the degree of cartelization of the Pakistani economy has never returned to the levels of the late 1960s. In the textiles sector, which remains the flagship of Pakistani industry, a number of leading companies are direct heirs to the great houses of the 1950s and 1960s—such as the Crescent, Colony, Kohinoor, Gul Ahmed, and Nishat groups. However, most companies now active in this sector were established after 1970.[78] The main losers in this reconfiguration were the prominent business families of Karachi, especially the Memons. At national level, those who benefited were mainly Punjabi entrepreneurs (such as the Saigol and Nishat groups, dominated by Chiniotis).[79] In Karachi, the Memons have retained a dominant position in some sectors (textiles, clothing, real estate, and the stock market), but have had to face the pressure of the Chiniotis and the Punjabi Saudagaran-e-Delhi—an Urdu-speaking group historically originating from Sargodha in Punjab, which dominates the pharmaceutical industry, amongst others.

These reconfigurations of Pakistan's industrial capitalism were outlined as early as the 1980s—a decade marked by the military's return to power in Pakistan and by the regional shockwave of the Afghan Jihad (1979–1989), which precipitated a major political and social upheaval in Karachi. At this point, let us just note that the 1980s saw a strong reactionary backlash that stretched across the economic, moral, and democratic realms. Under the military dictatorship of Muhammad Zia-ul-Haq (1977–1988), strikes were banned, while companies nationalized under Bhutto started being privatized, and labour was casualized. Zia's authoritarian turn went hand in hand with the liberalization of the economy and the Islamization of society. Pakistani workers were thus invited by General Zia to 'shun politics and propagation of class differences, and instead work for the higher national and Islamic goals'.[80]

On the whole, the business community welcomed this authoritarian takeover, accompanied as it was by the beginnings of economic liberalization. However, not everything in the garden was rosy. Bhutto's reform of the civil service (which culminated in the dissolution of the CSP, in 1973) led to the politicization of the bureaucracy. Under General Zia's regime, a 10% quota for military personnel in new government recruitments was introduced, and this fragmentation was exacerbated. Besides, the reforms pushed in the direction of 'local democracy'—first by Zia-ul-Haq, and later on by Pervez Musharraf (1989–2008)—contributed to the emergence of a new political elite, which constituted an additional level of decision-making.

By the 1980s, Pakistan's crony capitalism bore little resemblance to that of the 1960s. It was no longer based on an alliance between a few dozen industrial houses and a few hundred all-powerful bureaucrats to control the allocation of financial and industrial capital, the distribution of business licences, or the terms of trade. Not only were the big houses weakened and facing competition from new entrants—they now had to deal with a myriad of bureaucratic, political, and military players.[81] This reconfiguration of Pakistan's crony capitalism, in a much more fluid mode than in previous decades, increased the sense of vulnerability among industrialists. Those who chose to remain in Pakistan in the wake of Bhutto's nationalizations had to learn to cope with an increasingly fragmented state.

* * *

During the 1970s and 1980s, alongside the major changes in the composition of Karachi's business world and its place in the national economy, important managerial transformations began to be implemented within large industrial companies. Gustav Papanek had already spotted early signs of a transition from a patriarchal, family model of management to a more bureaucratic model back in the 1960s, and this became clearer over the following decades. In the biggest groups, it became increasingly common for family heirs to receive formal education at business schools (either in Pakistan or, preferably, in the United States). Meanwhile, senior managers were no longer recruited primarily from a single ethnic group—a shift which was to the benefit of highly skilled professionals. Lastly, there was a cautious opening up of the shareholding and boards of these companies to people beyond the owning family.[82] In most companies, however, both the capital and the main decision-making positions remained in the hands of the founder's family, with the idea that 'loyalty only comes with blood'.[83]

These transformations, which remain to be precisely quantified (using the same model as was used for Indian business),[84] have not put an end to coercive practices and illegalisms within Karachi's large industrial firms. To varying degrees, these companies have jointly participated in the reproduction of a productive order that rests on three pillars:

1. *An ambivalent relationship with the law* among those industrialists who have mastered the art of navigating choppy waters on both sides of legality. Karachi's industrial capitalism is not entirely immune to the influence of legal norms, the regulatory action of the courts or the networks of police and military surveillance; these are institutional constraints that are not only imposed on the elites of this sector but can also, depending on the circumstances, be taken advantage of by economic elites to establish their domination.

2. *A phobic view of the social world and professional relations*, which equates workers with political and criminal risks that appear to be multiplied by the ethnic and religious diversity of the working population.

3. *A partial externalization of control*, conducive to the widespread exercise of coercion by countless violent actors who are external to the corporate world (law enforcement agencies, political party representatives, religious militias, criminal groups).

This entanglement of capital and coercion has been greatly exacerbated by the urban conflicts of recent decades. Nevertheless, the history of capital's henchmen stretches back a long way in Karachi, a city where authority comes in many shapes and sizes.

3

CAPITAL'S HENCHMEN

To the poor, I am the dada *(boss) of poverty. To the unfortunate, I am
the* dada *of new beginnings. To the thugs, I am the* dada *of thuggery.*
Dharma 'Dada' (played by actor Dharmendra),
in the film *Dadagiri* (Thuggery, Deepak Shivdasani, 1987).[1]

Habibullah's physique was impressive, with his colossal build and
long, jet-black mane. Wearing a military-style uniform with a baton
in hand, he could almost pass for an officer, and deliberately sowed
confusion. But even if no one was fooled, he was a respected figure,
and his authority was beyond question. In his own neighbourhood, he
is remembered as a 'powerful' (*taqatwar*) and 'unusual' (*khaas admi*)
man.[2] Originally from the Dir region (a Pashtun principality on the
border with Afghanistan that became a major centre of emigration in
the second half of the nineteenth century), Habibullah was educated
in Bombay in the pre-Partition years. There he met a young Memon
seth, Husein Ebrahim Jamal, who employed him as a bodyguard.
When the Jamal family left for Karachi, Ebrahim invited his trusted
employee to accompany him.

Ebrahim initially tasked Habibullah with caretaking duties at
the school he opened in Kharadar—a district of Karachi's old town
that was the epicentre of the Memon community's commercial and

philanthropic activities. By the late 1950s, Habibullah had risen to the top and was put in charge of the Watch and Ward department at Husein Mills, a textile factory that the Jamal family had recently built in Landhi. Housing 25,000 spindles and 500 looms, it was one of the ten biggest mills in this new industrial area.[3] Over the following years, this family experienced remarkable growth, extending its activities into the sugar industry. Even though it was not as big in Karachi as the Dawoods, Adamjees, Habibs, or Valibhais, the family was very well established. By the mid-1960s, Husein's older brother Latif Ebrahim Jamal was one of the undisputed leaders of the city's business community.[4]

As Chief Security Officer at the company (which employed more than 6,000 workers in the early 1970s), Habibullah was responsible for his *hawaldars* (sergeants), who in turn supervised 75 *chowkidars* (guards). From this position of authority, Habibullah enjoyed a power of patronage that exemplified the intertwining of neighbourhood life and relations of production in Karachi's working-class neighbourhoods during the early decades of the industrialization process. Newcomers—generally young, single men unfamiliar with the urban world—turned to him in search of employment. His reputation travelled as far as the 'Frontier',[5] and jobseekers often came to him with a letter of recommendation from a *khan* or *malik* (traditional elders) from their village. In an emergency, when it was necessary to inquire about the health of a sick relative or inform parents of an unforeseen event, Habibullah's office was the first port of call for residents of the Huseini Chowrangi neighbourhood, which had grown up organically around the Husein Mills. The company's head of security was equipped with one of the few telephones available to workers isolated from their families.

While Habibullah served as both a henchman to Karachi's burgeoning capitalist class and a community protector to freshly settled migrant workers, he also had a more transgressive side; he embodied the figure of the *dada* ('boss') imported from Bombay—a strongman, always ready to defend his neighbourhood with his bare hands, but also occasionally putting both his muscles and his underworld connections at the disposal of employers.[6] The *dada* was not necessarily a class traitor, and was also capable of mobilizing financial and coercive resources in support of strikers—such as the *pehelwans* (wrestlers) of the Punjab, who played a key role in the social struggles of the 1930s and were hailed by trade union leaders such as Bashir Ahmed Bakhtiar.[7]

The figure of the *dada* is a versatile one, and can also describe an agent of disorder. The Hindi/Urdu word denoting his range of action, *dadagiri*, is commonly translated as 'thuggery'—though at risk of considerable semantic impoverishment. Referring to a mode of economic accumulation, a form of authority as much as a transgressive lifestyle, it is better understood as the 'art of bossism'— to borrow from a recent book on *mafia raj* (the criminalization of the state) in South Asia.[8]

Infused with aesthetic preoccupations, moral claims, and political aspirations, the daily enactment of this art of domination involves a meticulous staging of the self, punctuated with performances of authority featuring various levels of brutality. The making of these neighbourhood bosses reminds us that power, in addition to being diffuse, also coagulates in certain places and around certain figures of authority.[9]

These active agents of power rely on resources and know-how in the field of coercion, and also require intermediation skills. Indeed, it is in their dual status as brokers and henchmen that these violent entrepreneurs are able to assert themselves as enforcers of the political and/or economic order.

In its ubiquity, this art of domination is an invitation to qualify the supposed claim laid by modern sovereign powers to a monopoly of legitimate physical violence. However attached they may be to the *qualification* of violent acts, the majority of modern states have never sought to completely disarm their society. Their agents have learned to coexist with various private wielders of force, whether these take the form of tribes, vigilantes, criminal organizations, or private security agencies.[10] Acting as auxiliaries to political domination, some of these actors have also put their violent know-how at the service of economic elites and productive or extractive processes. As much a mode of economic accumulation as it is an art of domination, 'bossism', or the exercise of authority by strongmen, can be found in various configurations of power and wealth.[11] Despite its varying manifestations, the very ubiquity of strongmen points to the enduring role of violence and coercion in the construction of economic and social order, both in South Asia and beyond.[12]

Enforcers of Industrial Order

However coercive Karachi's factory world may be, it is a place where the organization of work departs from the principle of uniform, rationalized, and impersonal obedience with which Max Weber associated discipline.[13] The authority structure of local industries has historically been characterized by its profuse, unstable and highly personalized character—not to mention the fact that ethnic or partisan affiliations frequently interfere with hierarchical relations. Control of the workforce also contrasts with factory discipline as envisaged by Michel Foucault in the European context;[14] it is less a matter of assigning a precise place to each worker, than it is one of governing through vagueness. Not only is the code of conduct with which workers are expected to comply rarely formalized, but the perimeter of action and competence of shop floor supervisors overlaps with that of managers and security guards.

This confusion was not dispelled by the managerial shift that began in the late 1960s, despite the fact that the task of security departments (still called 'Watch and Ward' until the 1980s) was theoretically limited to monitoring access to the factory—it was the administration and human resources department that was responsible for maintaining order within the premises.[15] This contested division of work echoes the one between internal and external security which (in industry as in so many other areas) has become increasingly blurred in Pakistan over the years.

Jobbers and supervisors: the disciplinary apparatus of workshops

In the early decades of the industrialization process, the maintenance of order in Karachi's factories was primarily the work of the jobber. In its original context (nineteenth-century Lancashire in the UK), this term referred to a worker specializing in the repair or maintenance of machinery.[16] In Bombay, the term seems to have emerged in the early twentieth century and then spread to the region's main industrial centres. Some historians believe that these middlemen originally acted as interpreters and mediators for those technicians and managers who struggled to communicate with the (mostly Marathi) workforce.[17] Recruited from the docks, the railways, and the cotton trade, these brokers seem to have quickly taken on the complementary tasks of recruitment, training, and management of the workforce.[18] However, because these jobbers were responsible for allocating tasks, evaluating each worker's productiveness, and keeping track of their attendance, they were also endowed with repressive power. And while the enforcement of penalties was, in theory, the prerogative of department heads, jobbers often imposed fines on negligent or disobedient workers, and could even dismiss them summarily. The documentation-based disciplinary apparatus introduced by colonial authorities did more to reinforce the jobber's authority than it did to regulate it. The power of these labour bosses was thus both restated and reinforced by their ability to bend rules and falsify documents.[19]

In Karachi, during the early decades of the industrialization process, a jobber would usually supervise a dozen workers; these would be people he had personally recruited and trained, and who were thus subservient to him. He was supposed to report to a head jobber, a supervisor, and ultimately to the Factory Manager.[20] In practice, however, the term covered a wide variety of statuses and functions, sometimes synonymous with foreman, other times with contractor—the difference being that the jobber was not responsible for paying the workers placed under his authority.

The figure of the jobber was intimately linked to a non-stabilized labour market in which responsiveness and flexibility were important requirements, because of fluctuations in production and seasonal labour migration.[21] Drawing on existing networks in their own village, family, or community to provide labour to the factories, jobbers also used these relationships to put pressure on workers and ensure that they kept their employers happy.

Within the textile industry, the jobbers responsible for the preparatory operations of the spinning process (blending, carding, and combing) were of considerably lower status than the head jobbers at the mills, yet often exercised tighter control over their subordinates. As the Indian working class historian Rajnarayan Chandavarkar suggests, this paradox stems from the 'weak bargaining position of the unskilled workers in the preparatory departments, both in the workplace, where they could not effectively resist the jobber's authority, and outside, where their uncertain conditions of employment meant that they needed his influence most'.[22] The power dynamics that prevailed in the Bombay textile industry in the first half of the twentieth century were, by and large, transposed to Karachi after Partition. It does seem, however, that the diffuse nature of authority became even more pronounced in Karachi.

Thus, neither the authority level, nor the respective responsibilities of shop floor supervisors were indexed to their position in the company hierarchy. The status of these supervisors was derived from their relational network and/or political affiliation, both of which were more important, in terms of the daily exercise of their authority, than their hierarchical position. In the Bombay of the 1920s and 1930s, the jobber's ascendancy was primarily based on his power of recruitment and dismissal. But it was also derived from the influence he exerted in his *chawl* (working-class neighbourhood), where he was often engaged in credit, counselling, and dispute settlement. Sometimes he collected rents, helped organize *khanavalis* (worker pensions), ran wine shops, or managed the local *akhara* (wrestling club). In addition, he often financed religious ceremonies and festivals. His workplace authority conferred upon him a certain prestige in his neighbourhood—as attested to by his participation in community and political life—and in return, this social integration was essential to his managerial role. It was only in the mid-1930s, amid the rise of labour activism and the growing intervention of the colonial state in labour disputes, that his authoritative polish was tarnished.[23]

A similar process is described in the few works addressing the subject of Karachi jobbers during the early decades of industrialization. Until the 1970s, these recruitment agents played a central role in the organization of both factory work and neighbourhood life. By levying a tax on each worker at recruitment and collecting rents from migrant worker hostels, jobbers were often able to build up a cash nest egg. Many went into business, in sectors that were either legal (transport, real estate, petty trade, etc.) or illegal (gambling, alcohol and drug trafficking, prostitution).[24] These recruiting agents sometimes doubled up as community bosses. And as in Bombay, it seems that their authority was eroded by growing worker militancy.[25]

Short-lived though it may have been, the rise of trade unions in the early 1970s weakened the controversial figure of the jobber. Jobbers did indeed provide both jobs and roofs over heads, but their brutal ways, coupled with their voracity, soon aroused the hostility of the working-class population.[26] The older workers I met with confirmed this: as emblematic figures of employers' tyranny, jobbers were frequently perceived as 'bootlickers' (*chamchas*) for their loyalty to employers, as well as reputed for their harshness. It is no coincidence that the term 'jobber' was pronounced *'jabir'* by the workers—a word which in Urdu refers to a cruel and tyrannical character. Until Zulfikar Ali Bhutto came to power, these petty tyrants would not hesitate to 'throw you out by the ears', says Shah Zarin Khan—a former Pashtun worker who arrived from the Swat Valley in the early 1960s and was hired as a laboratory assistant by the US-Pakistani company General Tyre in 1964.[27]

Several disputes brought before the Labour Courts during the 1950s and 1960s also confirm the brutality of the power dynamics at work in Karachi's factories.[28] Plaintiffs often mentioned insults and even physical altercations, which did occur on both sides, since workers could be quick, on occasion, to retaliate. We might well wonder, then, whether the verbal and physical aggressiveness of shop floor supervisors could be a reflection of the precarious nature of their authority, which was contested both vertically (by the workers) and horizontally (by rivals for authority).

One dispute at the Saifee Development Corporation in 1961 offers an excellent illustration of this. Shah Nimroze was employed as a labourer at this factory, which mainly manufactured jerry cans. On several occasions, he allegedly threatened his supervisors, to the point that the company's Labour Officer decided to provide them with a company car and driver to ensure their safety outside the factory. Although Shah Nimroze was quite clearly resistant to factory discipline, his misdemeanours (and the tensions to which they gave rise) took place within the context of a company whose organizational hierarchy seems to have been less than crystal clear. In response to each new instruction from his supervisors, Shah Nimroze retorted that it was not up to these petty bosses of uncertain status to assign him tasks, but to the Factory Manager himself—the only member of the management staff whose authority he recognized. This selective sense of discipline was not to the liking of the judge in charge of examining the dispute, who confirmed the dismissal of this worker who dreamt of choosing his own boss.[29]

The diffuse exercise of authority within Karachi's factory world thus seems to have encouraged its contestation and, in response, its reiteration through disciplinary sanctions as well as verbal (and even physical) violence—demonstrations of force that revealed the flaws in this apparatus of domination while simultaneously sustaining grievances among the working population.

Dadas and chowkidars: the security guards

The dissemination of authority within Karachi's factories was also due to the coexistence of management staff with the security agents of the Watch and Ward department. Workers had to contend not only with the daily pressure applied by tyrannical supervisors, but also with that coming from the Chief Security Officer (sometimes called *jamadar* in Urdu) who supervised the *hawaldar*s (sergeants) and *chowkidar*s (guards). He was supposed to prevent petty theft, and was also in charge of overseeing the factory's firefighting system. These responsibilities made him a man of high stature—both feared and respected.[30]

In the early stages of industrialization, use of the *chowkidari nizam* (a guarding system inherited from medieval India) became widespread in South Asia. Until professional police forces were formed in India in the 1860s, security in the country's major cities was largely provided by guards or militiamen paid by the inhabitants, who were charged with patrolling at night. In Mughal India, this task fell to the *chowkidar*s; these were guards funded by residents who acted as auxiliaries to the imperial forces, under the authority of the Kotwal (police lieutenant).[31] These guards outlived the Mughal Empire, and continue to guard the entrances to the residential areas of India's major cities, patrolling them at night. In Bombay in the early 1900s, merchants used local strongmen to secure their shops, while factory owners relied on *akharas* (wrestling clubs) and *dadas* to break strikes.

Another region from which Muslim merchants emigrated to Pakistan, the present-day Indian province of Gujarat, also has a long history of private policing. In Ahmedabad, for example, the increase in violence between Hindus and Muslims during the Maratha and Moghul reigns (1738–1753) led to the formation of *pols*. These were groups of dwellings bringing together inhabitants united by ties of family, caste, or religion; at night, their doors were locked, and security was provided by a guard (*polio*) paid by the inhabitants—a community security model that persisted until the 1950s.[32]

When they settled in Karachi in the months or years following Partition, the Memon, Chinioti, and Punjabi Saudagaran merchant communities (hailing from Gujarat, Punjab, and Delhi, respectively) were familiar with these private enforcers. Some of them would collaborate with these violent entrepreneurs—who, for a fee, provided protection to businesses and industries. This was particularly true of the Memons who had in the early decades of the nineteenth century established a strong foothold in Bombay, where a private security market had developed around the Pathans.[33] Working under a 'Head Pathan', groups of up to fifteen security guards would patrol the shops—whose owners would rather employ these potential troublemakers than have them attack their properties.[34] As Husein Ebrahim Jamal's relationship with Habibullah shows, the relations forged between Memon merchants and Pathan henchmen during the colonial era sometimes extended to post-colonial Karachi, whose industrial capitalism and modes of control were heavily influenced by those already tried and tested in Bombay.

This long-term relationship demonstrates that the inter-ethnic alliance between Memon capital and Pashtun coercion was sometimes directly transposed to Karachi's new industrial environment. This last was nonetheless fertile ground for innovation in the field of industrial security—as evidenced by the institutional mimicry of Husein Mills' Watch and Ward department with the Pakistani army. Ghulam Haji,* another Pashtun from the Dir region, was recruited in 1970 as a *chowkidar* at Husein Mills before being promoted to

Ghulam Haji, * *now retired, in his* hawaldar *uniform at Husein Mills, c. 1980.*

L. Gayer, 2018

hawaldar; he remembers that Habibullah not only always wore military style dress (using a peaked cap, khaki jumpers, boots, and an officer's baton), but also demanded that his subordinates do likewise.

This imitation of the military was not systematic, but most industrial groups maintained this confusion between their security guards and the regular security forces as a way of intimidating the workforce and commanding its respect. By the 1960s, many *chowkidar*s were given army-inspired khaki uniforms; others wore a *shalwar kamiz*[35] using black cotton finely stitched with white dots that was nicknamed '*militia*' by analogy with the uniform of the Frontier Constabulary (FC)—a paramilitary force left over from the colonial period, whose historical mission was to contain incursions by Pashtun tribal militias into the settled areas of the North West Frontier Province (NWFP).

This sartorial emulation, which sometimes went as far as the epaulettes sewn onto the uniform, was aimed in particular at Pashtun workers, who were, by the early 1970s, the majority at most of Karachi's textile factories.[36] Most of these workers were originally

A private security company employee posted outside a SITE textile factory wearing a Frontier Constabulary-inspired uniform.

L. Gayer, 2022

from the Swat district, though some were from the Buner, Dir, and Charsada districts of what is now Khyber Pakhtunkhwa (KP).

These migrant workers were less familiar with the FC than were residents of the Federally Administered Tribal Areas (FATA), where policing tasks were undertaken by these paramilitaries until the 'tribal areas' were merged with KP province in 2018. Among these Pashtun workers, however, the FC (itself referred to as the 'militia') maintained a reputation for intransigence; its leniency was said to be less easily bought than that of the police.[37]

As these sartorial experiments demonstrate, military and law enforcement personnel had a strong influence on social representations of authority in Karachi in the first decades of independence.[38] However, public security was not the sole source of authority summoned by the guardians of industrial peace. This security syncretism was exemplified by Habibullah Khan. The chief security officer at Husein Mills primarily drew his authority from his appropriation of the *hexis* and material culture of the military. But he

87

also personified the figure of the *dada* imported from Bombay, which referred primarily to reputation rather than status—'a reputation for physical prowess or for getting things done'. Despite their links to the underworld or indeed their own criminal activities, *dada*s acted as 'informal guardians of public order and morality'. In addition to their skills in the exercise and organization of violence, this claim to local authority was attractive to employers, particularly in times of social upheaval.[39]

Habibullah did not involve himself directly in the repression of strikes, but through his power of patronage (which was also a power of sanction) he was complicit in the defence of employer domination. His brokering services positioned him at the intersection of the factory world, neighbourhood life and village sociability networks. In this ability to stand at the crossroads of these worlds and connect them with one another, he can be likened to the coercive intermediaries introduced in Chapter 1. While Habibullah certainly did participate in the reproduction of the power relations specific to these interwoven social worlds, he also introduced a state of tension within them. At Husein Mills, his authority was not confined to the company's hierarchical system, and could challenge that of professional managers. In this respect, Habibullah was not so different from iconic union-buster Harry Bennett, who took his orders from Henry Ford and him alone. In the same way, Habibullah's direct link with *Seth* Husein Ebrahim bestowed a special aura of authority upon him, which he had no hesitation in using against the group's management staff. Thanks to the trust placed in him by the *seth*, he could afford to quarrel with the company's managers without incurring any repercussions.

The security syncretism of this department—its synthesis of institutional models and cultural repertoires of authority of different origins—was not embodied in its leader alone. It was also discernible in the antics of Habibullah's sidekick, Sheikh Mukamil Shah. He was a colourful guard, who watched over the comings and goings at the factory gate. With his long hair and finger rings,[40] his multi-coloured skullcap, his heavy consumption of *charas* (hashish), his regular visits to *dargah*s (the tombs of saints) and his hosting of musical evenings at his *dera*,[41] where he demonstrated his prowess on the sitar, this man had all the attributes of the *malang*.

Sometimes admired for their intense devotion to God and his saints, these transgressive religious figures are often feared; they are perceived to be prone to excess of every kind and have a reputation as impostors, thieves, and paedophiles. Subject to contrasting perceptions among working-class Pakistanis, these wandering Sufis are despised by orthodox clerics for their rejection of Sharia law and its codes of conduct.[42] Sheikh Mukamil Shah thus embodied yet another authority figure tinged with ambivalence, located at the frontiers of the licit and illicit, and attracted to excess. However distinct the cultural registers from which these two security agents sprang, their authority was comparable in its instability, drawing strength from unpredictability, a propensity to spill over and disregard established rules.

Chowkidars also occupied an ambiguous position in the hierarchical structure of companies—though, in their case, this ambiguity had more to do with the scope of their roles than with the nature of their authority. As a number of disputes before the Industrial Courts and then the Labour Courts have suggested, these guards were often used as jacks-of-all-trades, although their affiliation with the Watch and Ward departments of their respective companies theoretically confined them to surveillance and fire prevention duties.[43] Labour laws served to maintain this confusion: during the 1960s and 1970s, some Karachi-based trade unions tried to claim the status of 'workmen' for *chowkidars*, in order to protect them from unfair dismissal. However, this status was often denied them by the Labour Courts—at least when they upheld a limited interpretation of the term 'workman', reserving it for manual workers.

While this interpretation was not systematic, it did tend to prevail among judges assigned to employment courts, who often invoked Article 2 of the Industrial Disputes Ordinance of 1959.[44] Because this article defines a 'workman' as any employee in the industrial sector assigned to manual or administrative tasks, security guards (as well as management staff and commercial agents) were excluded from the option of joining a union—and thus from being represented by a trade union organization before the Labour Courts in order to challenge a possible dismissal.[45] With this important caveat (potentially decisive in the event of a dispute), *chowkidar*s enjoyed the same rights as workers in the so-called 'organized' sector. Even though labour law violations were frequent, most industry guards benefited (in theory at least) from permanent worker status, and this conferred upon them a number of social and employment rights (paid leave, severance pay, access to annual bonuses, a pension, etc.). However, following the adoption of the Industrial Relations Ordinance of 1969, which broadened the definition of a workman to include any employee in industry and opened up the possibility of unionization to any worker, the legal status of security guards was aligned with the general labour rights regime.[46]

In addition to the menial tasks assigned to them (gardening, loading and unloading lorries, relaying messages, etc.), *chowkidar*s were frequently asked to monitor the comings and goings of coolies and workers, to ensure that they did not leave their posts outside of official breaks. As Ghulam Haji explains,

> The number one rule for the *chowkidar* was to keep the workers under control, by preventing them from stealing or doing anything wrong. You had to keep them under constant surveillance to prevent them from doing anything stupid. [...] The workers tended to come and go as they pleased. So we kept an eye on them, saying, 'Come on, do your job'. We prevented them from leaving their posts before the scheduled time to go out to eat or drink.[47]

Besides fire prevention, the primary mission of Watch and Ward departments—like any security service—was to ensure the selective movement of goods and people. This assignment made them an integral part of the industrial coercive apparatus. These departments were superimposed on the hierarchy supervising workers in their daily tasks, which included jobbers, head jobbers, supervisors, foremen, etc. *Chowkidar*s seem to have been less prone to verbal and physical abuse than these bossyboots, though they were accused of being a little too trigger-happy during labour conflicts. For example, in the aftermath of a violent crackdown that left at least five workers dead in March 1963, strikers from the Pak Tobacco Company and several SITE textile mills accused local *chowkidar*s of adding to the death toll—the first such incident in the history of the Karachi labour movement. The crowd even called for a ban on *chowkidar*s in Karachi, arguing that the safety of the working-class population could not be guaranteed in their presence.[48]

In the following years, as social protests grew in Karachi and both wings of the country, the guards' authority was increasingly contested. These tensions culminated in the months following the coming to power of the Pakistan People's Party (PPP) in 1971. This was accompanied by strikes and factory occupations that often turned violent, during which *chowkidar*s were sometimes attacked by workers. The fear they inspired, of which they had been so proud, seemed to dissipate.[49] And following a decade of military dictatorship (1977–1988), a similar phenomenon was observed during the 1990s, a decade marked both by the rise of the Mohajir Qaumi Movement (MQM) and by a new, resolutely aggressive plebeian culture—which had repercussions on relations between workers, managers, and security agents.[50]

The *faujis*, at the interface of internal and external security

The use of retired military personnel for administrative, security, and law enforcement duties in Pakistani factories predates the Ayub Khan coup of 1958. An ILO mission (mandated to increase productivity in the textile industry and active in the country from 1955 to 1958) noted that 'where firms had a personnel officer he was often an ex-army officer whose principal duties were engagement and dismissal and ensuring security of the mills against possible unrest'.[51]

Although the authors of the report do not specify whether they were able to observe this practice in Karachi (the mission's investigators also visited Punjab, the North West Frontier, and East Pakistan), they tend to suggest that this practice had become ubiquitous even before Ayub's coup. Over the following years, these retired soldiers (who continue to be called by their rank) became commonplace in industry—including in positions for which they did not seem to have any particular predisposition. For example, former colonels have been appointed to the post of Labour Officer, mainly to contain trade union activities within the company—in collusion with the police.[52]

The term *fauji* refers to both serving and retired military personnel; it is a sign of the authority that remains attached to their person long after they have left the army. Little is known about how *fauji*s were perceived by Karachi's workers during the early decades of the industrialization process. Disputes arising from open conflicts between workers and retired servicemen seem to have been rare, but it would be wrong to conclude that *fauji*s commanded universal respect among the working population. Certainly, as the sartorial and organizational imitation of the Watch and Ward departments with the army or paramilitary forces tends to suggest, the *vardi* (military uniform) was supposed to inspire fear and awe among the working classes. Actual *fauji*s, on the other hand, could do without this fetish; more assured in their authority, they had no need to resort to public performance.

Under Ayub Khan's martial law in particular (1958–1962), an attack on a *fauji* could result in harsh criminal penalties. In 1961, Muhammad Nawaz and Ghulam Murtaza Khan, two workers at a cement factory in Daudkhel (Northern Punjab), were sentenced by a court martial to three years' imprisonment for assaulting the company's Administrative Officer, Colonel Amanullah Khan—possibly in connection with the anti-union activities of which he had been accused by union representatives.[53]

During General Zia's regime (1977–1988), industry was not spared the general militarization of society; under a system known as *subedari*, at certain factories, soldiers were posted to block trade unionists, with the volume of this military presence varying according to the size of the establishments.[54] The *fauji* presence in industry was greatly expanded in the 1990s alongside the emergence of a private security market dominated by retired military personnel (see Chapter 7).

Shadows of the underworld

In Karachi, as in Bombay before Partition, the underworld was sometimes called upon to assist in labour disputes. Initially, this contribution could take the form of mediation. Nayab Naqvi, the main leader of the 1963 strike at the Pak Tobacco Company, states that a few days after the strike began, 'in keeping with tradition, a gang of hoodlums from Sher Shah[55] offered to intercede in the dispute'.[56] The British management team of the Pak Tobacco Company seems, however, to have favoured legal means, fearing that any deviation from the law by a foreign company associated with the former colonizer would be exposed to public scrutiny. Indeed, most of the multinational companies active in Pakistan at the time seem to have kept their distance from these violent brokers. In 1968, on the occasion of unrest at the Bata factory in Tongi, a telegram sent from the British High Commission in Karachi to the British Embassy in Iran stated that 'non-Pakistan firms [...] are always more vulnerable to industrial action—take Excide batteries and Pakistan Tobacco Company for example in West Pakistan—and the expatriate firms cannot use the means which are open to many Pakistani employers, i.e. threats of physical violence, goondas etc'.[57]

The intensification of social conflict during the 1960s brought an illegitimate relative of the *dada* to the forefront; this was the *goonda* (goon, bully)—scorned by some as a criminal on the employers' payroll and disqualified by others as a rogue element fomenting trouble on behalf of the unions. As repression intensified, public authorities were also accused of criminalization. For labour movement actors, the '*dadagiri* of the state' (its recourse to thuggish methods in defence of capital) was all the more formidable as it took refuge behind the legal prerogatives of law enforcement agencies.[58]

Strongmen on the shopfloor

In 1965, Abdul Hakim Khan (then aged about fifteen) got a job at Shalimar Silk Mills—one of Karachi's very first silk factories, founded in the late 1950s by the Memon family of the Tabanis.[59] The young man's father was employed in the company as a controller, while his older brother worked as a weaver. For these Pashtuns from the Swat Valley, silk had been a family affair ever since one of Abdul Hakim's uncles had earned a solid reputation as a weaving master in Bombay in the pre-Partition years—a title that was key to his success

93

in Karachi, allowing him to train his male family members in the art of weaving.

Over the years, ordinary weavers often rose through the ranks to become supervisors or controllers—as had Abdul Hakim's father, brother, and cousin. The young man seemed destined to follow in their footsteps. But the movement (1968–1969) against President Ayub Khan was in full swing, and when you are just eighteen, the siren call of radicalism is not easily ignored, especially in this case, since the student and worker mobilization afoot in the country was filtering through to Shalimar Mills. In 1968, a trade union was created within the company for the first time, with the support of the Qaumi Mazdoor Mahaz (National Workers' Front, QMM), a Maoist movement led by Tufail Abbas.[60] One morning, then, Abdul Hakim decided to set foot in the office of these activists.

His visit did not go unnoticed, and that same day, Abdul Hakim's father was summoned by *Seth* Ashraf Tabani—one of Karachi's most prominent businessmen, and Latif Ebrahim Jamal's main competitor in the Karachi Chamber of Commerce and Industry (KCCI) and the Federation of Pakistan Chambers of Commerce and Industry (FPCCI).[61] Using a reproachful tone, the *seth* informed his controller that his son had been seen in the union office. For Abdul Hakim, this incident marked the beginning of violent arguments with his father, which plunged him into a deep depression. At one point he even considered suicide—though not without first shooting the *seth* and one of his particularly odious lackeys. Torn between his budding political convictions and his obligations towards a family that was siding with the employers, he ended up in exile in Swat, where he was able, finally, to give free rein to his activism.

In the meantime, tensions rose at Shalimar Mills. In 1969, a strike initiated by the union broke out. A pay rise was demanded, on the basis that wages at the company were the lowest in the entire sector even though Ashraf Tabani was its undisputed leader. Appalled by this provocation, the *seth* soon struck back. Shortly after the start of the strike, he sent his *chela* to pay a visit to the general secretary of the union. The literal meaning of *chela* is 'disciple', but in Karachi factory jargon the term refers to a henchman. This usage offers a further connection to the world of the *dada*, since in India's major pre-Partition industrial centres, the term *chela* referred to youths in the entourage of neighbourhood bosses, especially in the wrestling clubs (*akharas*).[62]

Like most of its top leadership, the general secretary of the Shalimar Mills union was Bengali—a community that, in the late 1960s, played a prominent role in labour struggles in both wings of Pakistan.[63] He lived in Chittagong Colony, a working-class neighbourhood not far from SITE, which had a majority of residents from the country's eastern wing. Iqbal, the *seth*'s henchman, was originally from the Hazara district of the NWFP but had grown up at the Tabani residence, where he and/or his parents were probably employed as servants. It fell to him to do the dirty work of his employer, and when he appeared before the union leader with a gun, a plane ticket, and a large sum of money in hand, it was hard to believe he had not been mandated by the *seth* himself. The trade unionist was told, at gunpoint, to accept these 'gifts' and take the first flight to Dhaka—some 1,250 miles away. A few weeks later, the same fate seems to have befallen his successor, also a Bengali.

While the exact circumstances of these nocturnal visits are open to question, the repeated departures of the union's leaders are beyond dispute. Clearly, these events have left their mark on people's minds, and not enough time has passed to soften them in Abdul Hakim's memory. During our conversation, he used the Urdu term *hashr* to relate this incident, which commonly means a 'commotion' but also refers to the Day of Judgement (*yaum-e-hashr*), when the dead will rise in an indescribable uproar to the sound of the angel Raphael's trumpet.

Like many of those who carry out dirty work on behalf of economic or political elites, Iqbal was quick to meet his maker. Shortly after carrying out these sensitive tasks, he died from an injury sustained in a fight with a worker. After the thug insulted him, this aggrieved worker grabbed a sharp piece of equipment and stuck it in Iqbal's stomach in a vindictive gesture, demonstrating that the chronic tension on which the authority of the employers' henchmen feeds is indeed a double-edged sword.

This repressive episode at the Shalimar Silk Mills speaks volumes about the auxiliary role played by local strongmen in the repression of labour struggles. The *goonda* has served as a supplementary force for the employers ever since the colonial period, and is the unworthy cousin of the *dada*. Unambiguously derogatory, historically the term *goonda* referred to the petty thugs from whom both the *dada* and virtuous workers sought to dissociate themselves.[64] The *goonda* embodies the figure of the venal and violent *lumpen*, less generously endowed with social capital than the neighbourhood 'boss'. Throughout the Indian subcontinent (India, Pakistan, Bangladesh), this term belongs to both the idiomatic and the judicial registers. It is in common use, and is also the subject of descriptions (as opposed to legal definitions) via specific laws or ordinances, such as the Goonda Acts.[65]

In Pakistan, it became a legal category in its own right with the passage of the Punjab Control of Goondas Ordinance, 1959, which was extended to the province of Sindh in 1972. This ordinance describes the *goonda*, highlighting the challenge it poses to the moral order (through its debauchery), to public order (through its criminal activities and riotous behaviour), and to the stability of society (through its propensity for fraud and forgery). Registered *goonda*s, labelled as such by the courts, could be subjected to judicial control and movement restrictions (designed to keep them away from schools, parks, cinemas, or political gathering places).[66] In Karachi, this notorious label (and the judicial control measures it was coupled with) seems to have mainly concerned Baloch delinquents from the Lyari district. These were people who had, during the 1970s, dominated the smuggling networks that supplied the wholesale markets of the neighbouring old city, ultimately taking control of gambling dens after they were banned in 1977. The repressive effects of the judicialization of the *goonda* were thus limited. While it may have played a role in placing this deviant figure at the heart of public debate, the rise of social protest undoubtedly also contributed, in its own way.

In the industrial world of Karachi, the term *goonda* is used to cast opponents as immoral, greedy, and duplicitous. In the eyes of labour activists, the moral flaws of these petty criminals predispose them to anti-unionism. As traitors to their class, they are seen as being predisposed to undertake employers' dirty work, whether by intimidating union activists, repressing strikes, or promoting yellow unions. In the early 1960s, *goonda*s were thought to be behind a pro-business union at the Mumtaz Ahmad Silk Mills—accused by the United Textile Workers Union of using coercive methods and deception to garner support among workers.[67] The *goonda*'s shadow also loomed over the Karim Silk Mills where, in May 1967, the union's general secretary and his deputy were set upon by knife-wielding thugs in an attack which, according to company management, was staged by the unionists themselves as a way of 'showing themselves as victims in order to gain popularity'.[68]

The *goonda* became omnipresent as the mobilization of workers and students against President Ayub Khan intensified, with each side accusing its rivals of colluding with the thugs—or even of being *goonda*s themselves. In September 1968, there was concern at the American Embassy when the Urdu daily newspaper *Tameer* (which because of its 'outrageous accusations against the United States' frequently caused conniptions among its American diplomat readership) published an article echoing the accusations of an up-and-coming female trade unionist named Kaniz Fatima.[69] According to her, CIA agents had infiltrated the Karachi Labour Department and, in collusion with local employers, recruited *goonda*s to impose a series of lock-outs and attack workers.[70]

Meanwhile trade unions themselves were not short of strongmen, and the recruitment of thugs by local employers sometimes gave rise to pitched battles within factories—even though, until the end of the 1970s, they were mainly fought with *lathi*s (bamboo canes, prized by the police, paramilitary organizations, and thugs in the Indian subcontinent since the colonial period).[71] Under the regime of Z. A. Bhutto, bladed weapons began to appear, and rivalries between left-wing and pro-employers' unions claimed their first victims. At SITE's Star Textile Mills in February 1972, a worker was stabbed to death in a brawl between two unions fighting for control of the factory. Star Textile Mills Workers Union leaders accused management of recruiting *goonda*s who were allegedly provided with access badges so that they could disrupt union meetings.[72]

During the same period, some union activists, tempted to exploit the prevailing tensions for personal gain, began developing criminal practices. For example, in 1974 the President of the Husein Industries Head Office Employees Union tried to extort a large sum of money from the company's management, in exchange for the signing of a memorandum of understanding that was favourable to employers' interests. When informed of this extortion attempt (which the accused did not deny), his comrades disowned him and promised to 'behave properly' in the future.[73] Despite attempts by some labour activists to dissociate themselves from these controversial practices, accusations of violence and corruption continued to surface in the following years, gradually lending credence to the idea that unions were more than just spoilers of industrial peace; they were also criminal organizations cynically exploiting the naivety of the working-class population.

Police thuggery

The police helped defend employers' interests through their use of legal violence against strikers, '*goondas*', and 'rioters', as well as through various extra-legal forms of coercion—such as the disproportionate and indiscriminate use of force against demonstrators and pickets, intimidation practices, false charges, arbitrary detentions, and the use of torture. This police propensity for circumventing the law in the service of private interests carried the legacy of repressive colonial tactics unconcerned with the legality of the means deployed. By breaking the law to maintain industrial order, police were placing their own *dadagiri* (thuggish methods) at the disposal of capital.

As early as the 1950s, police forces deployed in industrial areas were mandated to ensure the security of factories and the maintenance of social calm, for the benefit of the owners of capital. An official brochure from 1954, advertising SITE to potential investors, presents the scheme as follows:

> A Police Station, with sufficient staff, has been established on the Industrial Estate, to help the industrialists on [the] spot, in their day to day working and to maintain law and order at times of disputes. Regular patrolling is done, specially at night, for keeping a vigilant watch on untoward happenings.[74]

Relations between union activists and the police first became seriously strained in the early 1960s. For example, trade unionist Nayab Naqvi accused the police of continuously harassing the leaders of the mobilization at the Pak Tobacco Company by resorting to various intimidation tactics on behalf of the company. He claimed that the local police force, having been neutralized by corruption, had turned into a capitalist militia. Such indictments of law enforcement agencies, which denounced the formation of a government within the government, in the hands of big capital, would become a staple of labour activists' critics in later years.[75]

The following decade was marked by escalating confrontations between strikers and law enforcers, during which frequent recourse by the police to extra-legal methods gave more credence, within progressive circles, to this conspiracy theory. As a major site of these confrontations, the textile factories of the Dawood family and the Gul Ahmed group in Landhi saw ferocious police repression, which relied on the law and circumvented it in equal measure. At Dawood Mills, having won the referendum of 12 February 1970 with 92% of the votes, the local union raised its voice against the management and gave fresh strike notice. As the ultimatum expired, 2,000 workers were arrested and detained by the police on the factory premises. Some were tortured, and the union offices were looted and ransacked. In the month of April, police launched an offensive in the neighbouring workers' districts; three people were killed and 300 workers were arrested. As reported in *Pakistan Forum* (a leading journal of the Pakistani radical left, founded by Feroz Ahmed at Johns Hopkins University that same year), 'the Landhi-Korangi area looked like a police state for months'.[76]

Two years later, as strikes and factory occupations spread across Karachi, Dawood Mills and the neighbouring Gul Ahmed factory were once again at the centre of labour protests. Both companies turned to the Labour Courts to seek injunctions against the unions, which they claimed were disrupting industrial peace in Landhi. In response to this convergence of social struggles, the employers joined forces. A single lawyer defended both companies: this was Mahmood Abdul Ghani, a favourite among Pakistani employers. At Dawood Textile Mills, he accused trade unionists of inciting workers 'not to perform the duties, and also to cause damage to cloth, raise slogans, beat the drums, resort to go-slow and illegal Gherao [picketing]'.[77] At Gul Ahmed, he claimed that union activists had sought to intimidate management by stopping the machines, breaking window shutters, and piercing the ceiling of some rooms.[78]

The Labour Courts ruled in favour of the management of both companies—but its injunctions had no effect on the mobilization. Faced with an escalating protest, the Gul Ahmed management deserted the group's factory in Landhi. The workers managed to keep production going even as they prepared for a siege by the police. The police intervention on 18 October 1972 was one of the most brutal episodes of repression in a year that had already set the bar quite high in this regard. The following month, the *Pakistan Forum* published an account of the attack, highlighting its violence:

> On the morning of October 18 the Karachi police, assisted by the Rangers, smashed through the walls and gates of the Dawood Cotton Mills and Gul Ahmed Textile Mills in the Landhi-Korangi industrial area with the help of bulldozers and started beating and tear-gassing the workers who were busy eating *sehri* [the meal eaten before the start of fasting during Ramadan]. The workers, who had enclosed themselves in the mills in order to press for the acceptance of their demands, were evicted at gunpoint. The police then fired on the protesting workers and killed four persons, according to an official handout.[79]

Illegal behaviour by the police is not only a bone of contention during strikes and factory occupations, but also a matter of controversy in more ordinary social struggles. As trade unionists, employers' representatives, and the police traded mutual accusations of 'gangsterism' (*goonda gardi*), judges sought to restore some clarity to an increasingly blurred landscape. And as is often the case in such circumstances, judges tended to give the police the benefit of the doubt. This presumption of innocence is not specific to Pakistan and is due to the fact that while judges depend on the police institution for their cases, they lack any material means of challenging the retrospective definition of situations by police.[80]

One case brought before the National Industrial Relations Commission in Islamabad in 1978 illustrates this point well.[81] Two years earlier, a dispute had broken out at the Tariq Oil Mills (an oil factory in the working-class district of Lyari). The company's union representatives accused the owner and manager of closing down the factory and firing its 33 employees illegally, in part as a way of avoiding their profit-sharing obligations. The union activists accused the police of having falsely charged some 30 employees with the attempted murder of the Factory Manager. The owner and the manager, initially sentenced to three months' imprisonment and a fine of Rs. 1,000, argued that the police intervened only to ensure their physical protection and to clear the factory following its occupation.

The judge hearing the appeal eventually gave management the benefit of the doubt, pointing to a number of flaws in the prosecution's case while relying on two legal principles external to labour law. First, the judge put forward a:

> well-settled principle of criminal law, that when two constructions can be placed upon the evidence adduced in a case, one pointing to the guilt of the accused, and the other to their innocence, the construction favourable to the accused must be accepted, because there can be no presumption against the accused, and whenever two versions are probable, the version favourable to the accused must be accepted.

The second principle guiding the judgement invoked legal common sense by suggesting that the defence witnesses (including a local police officer and two officials from the Labour Directorate and Labour Court) were by nature 'independent and dis-interested persons', and could not in any way be said to be 'under the influence of the appellants'. After more than a decade of social struggles, in the course of which incriminating testimonies against the police had accumulated both in the press and in court, this uncritical belief in police neutrality was surprising, to say the least. However, insofar as it shows that the resolution of professional conflicts sometimes departed from the restrictive framework of labour law to enter into dialogue with criminal law, in the process becoming part of a broader

101

repressive configuration, it is in keeping with a general trend. Thus, beyond their role as arbitrators in labour disputes, judges were also key protagonists in the maintenance of industrial order by covering up the police illegalities that were integral to it.

* * *

Karachi's factory world has been characterized by a decidedly coercive atmosphere ever since the very beginning of the industrialization process. Multiple factors have contributed to this situation, including: the social distance between industrial elites and workers; the low attractiveness of the paternalistic model to employers; employers' distrust of collective bargaining and labour law; employers' visceral hostility to trade unions and their long-standing preference for a form of indirect domination that relied on a wide variety of actors specializing in physical coercion. However, the exercise of coercion is characterized here by its diffuse, contested, and precarious nature, which derives from an authority structure that is peculiar to local industries. Rather than using a transparent organizational hierarchy to achieve stability, this coercive apparatus relies on a multitude of authority figures whose spheres of competence can rarely be inferred from their official positions. Indeed, the jurisdiction of each of these contenders for authority varies from one factory to another, and sometimes within a single factory, from one department (or individual) to another.

The jobber, for instance, was no simple supplier of labour. He carried out various tasks relating to production processes (supervision of a group of workers, allocation of machines, distribution of materials), technical control (maintenance or repair of machines), or personnel management (recruitment, fines, granting of leave, dismissal). Sometimes, these tasks encroached on the responsibilities of his presumed hierarchical superiors, endowing him with an authority that extended beyond the workplace to the residential space of working-class neighbourhoods. This social embeddedness was in turn reflected in the workplace authority of these bossyboots—who were at once both essential cogs in the machine and weak links in the employers' domination. The chains of interdependence between jobbers and workers, which were formed at the intersection of the factory world and neighbourhood life, circumscribed the power of the former even as they participated in the exploitation of the latter.

In addition to this diffuse authority structure, Karachi's industries have been deeply impacted by their urban environment and its propensity for the mass production of specialists in coercion. Whether they are recruited from among the ranks of neighbourhood bosses, small-time thugs hungry for notoriety, or security professionals exiting the police or armed forces, a host of virtuosos of violence were on hand, offering their services to the highest bidder to help crush workers' attempts to organize. These specialists in coercion have been essential to the enforcement of employer domination— but they are also tricky allies, with divided loyalties and erratic behaviour. Above all, by participating in the intertwining of labour struggles and urban conflicts, they have reinforced the heteronomy of the factory world, hindering its chances of operating as an autonomous field insulated from its troubled surroundings. This permeability, and with it the amplification of the tremors of the city in the productive sphere, will be at the heart of the next chapters, which are devoted to the industrial world's adaptation to the armed conflicts that reshaped Karachi between 1985 and 2015.

4

THE TREMORS OF THE CITY

People say that all are losers in a hartal *(general strike). But we were about to reap the benefits.*
One of the protagonists of the film *Na Maloom Afraad*
(Unidentified People, Nabeel Qureshi, 2014).[1]

It was a curious bulge in the letter that immediately attracted the guard's attention. Like every guardian of industrial order in Karachi, Taj Muhammad* had learnt to make the most of his senses in general, and to 'think with his fingers'[2] in particular, so as to detect and decipher any sign of danger. A simple palpation of the envelope confirmed his suspicions; this was, in all likelihood, a *parchi*—a slip of paper used by racketeers to demand that their victims pay the *bhatta* (protection money), sometimes accompanied by a large-calibre bullet, by way of a reminder. Addressed to a manager of the pharmaceutical factory he worked at, Taj Muhammad believed the dubious-looking letter to contain such a bullet. Suspecting an extortion attempt, the security guard alerted the administration, which in turn informed the CEO. Keen to keep it to himself, the CEO made sure that he was in the privacy of his office before acquainting himself with the contents of the mysterious envelope.

Threatening letter to a pharmaceutical company executive (2016)

Rizvi,*

You inbred son of a dog, son of a bitch, son of a pimp. You Shiites are a plague on the Deobandis and the Ahl-e- Hadith.[3] Son of a bitch, we will fuck your mother. Your children are infidels, stop messing with Muslims [i.e. Sunnis]. We know where your house is and where you park your car [gives the vehicle registration number]. We will burn it down. You like to leave your house early in the morning, that is when we will shoot you. You fired Abdul Hanif* because he was a Muslim [i.e. Sunni]. But you are a Shiite infidel, your death will bring us a spiritual reward. We have passed all the details about you and your family to the Sipah-e-Sahaba and Jaish-e-Muhammad headquarters in Karachi.[4] Their people will screw your mother. For the last time, we ask you to show humanity. Stop oppressing people. Stop making up stories. If you fire anyone else, you and your people will pay the price. Rizvi, Akhtar Rizvi, you pimp, infidel, son of a dog, son of a whore.

Qudrat Pharma* is a leading player in the natural health products sector in Pakistan and a target of interest to criminals of all hues. Around 2011, during a particularly turbulent period in Karachi, the company was the victim of attempted extortion. It was foiled only by the intervention of the company's contractor—the recruiting agent providing Qudrat Pharma with most of its manpower, and whose ability to pierce the veil of appearances makes him a valuable ally in unravelling such situations. Over the years, the company's CEO,

Naeem Beg,* has learned to assess the seriousness of such threats himself. Faced with the odious letter addressed to Akhtar Rizvi,* he was nonetheless hesitant as to how he should proceed. The absence of financial claims and the nature of the target—a plant manager responsible for restructuring the company—immediately conferred a troubling character on the case.

Sensing that it did not fall within the contractor's usual field of intervention and anxious to avoid publicizing the incident, Naeem Beg decided to conduct his own investigation, as discreetly as possible. Although he quickly made up his mind about the instigators of this cabal, the authenticity of the threat—especially regarding the conspirators' proven links with terrorist organizations—was more difficult to establish. By becoming entangled with an urban environment rife with discord and suspicion, the productive world in turn threatened to become indecipherable—and thus uncontrollable.

This strange case offers a first glimpse of this entanglement. A variety of social, political, and religious conflicts became woven around the threatening letter addressed to Akhtar Rizvi. In following the path of this troubling and disturbing object, I seek to reflect on the reconfiguration of Karachi's industrial capitalism within a context of violent disruption that has fed into a 'crisis of evidence'. By this I mean one of those moments of turmoil in which the members of a community are no longer able to either agree on their interpretation of the world, or indeed hold on to their own judgements as to the substance of things, with any degree of certainty.[5]

The 'normality of the abnormal', from politics to the economy

In one of his most memorable texts, anthropologist Michael Taussig revisits Walter Benjamin's *Critique of Violence* in the light of Colombian experiences of terror. In order to apprehend 'the irregular rhythm of numbing and shock that constitutes the apparent normality of the abnormal instituted by the state of emergency', he preaches the virtues of the oxymoron.[6] For Taussig, this 'normality of the abnormal' corresponds better to a social condition than to a psychological state:

a state of doubleness of social being in which one moves in bursts between somehow accepting the situation as normal, only to be thrown into a panic or shocked into disorientation by an event, a rumour, a vision, a sight, something said, or not said—something that, even while it requires the normal in order to make its impact, destroys it.[7]

This tension lies at the heart of an emergent literature that, armed with the tools of anthropology, sociology, or history, questions the fragile invention of everyday life in those situations of chronic uncertainty in which it seems to slip away.[8]

In this literature, the consideration of economic activities is still in its infancy, yet some works have begun to investigate daily economic life in situations of war and chronic turmoil.[9] As Teresa Koloma Beck has shown, within these contexts of generalized disruption the reproduction of routine labour activities is essential to the preservation of a sense of personal equilibrium and social purpose.[10] Inspired by the pragmatic philosophy of John Dewey and the phenomenology of Maurice Merleau-Ponty, Beck suggests that the normalization of the Angolan civil war—that is, its gradual transformation into an everyday experience—took place through proactive forms of adaptation that allowed people to pursue their agricultural or commercial activities and thereby preserve a sense of continuity in everyday life. In the light of the Syrian conflict and its transnational extensions, other authors have revisited the famous distinction between the economy *of* war and the economy *in* war proposed by Roland Marchal, focusing in particular on the attempts made by industrial actors to adjust to the prevailing insecurity.[11]

While these works tend to emphasize the destructions of war and its disorderly effects on the productive economy, a handful of political scientists and anthropologists have begun to acknowledge the more fruitful links existing between armed conflict and the dynamics of capitalism—particularly in its agro-industrial and extractive variants. Both the Colombian palm oil industry and the Angolan oil sector are emblematic of the globalized economies that emerged amidst the tumult of armed conflict, and went on to acquire respectability.[12]

However, I am concerned with a significantly different case here: on the one hand, a 'civil war' analysis of the violent configuration that emerged in Karachi from the second half of the 1980s would be a stretch—in terms of both the intensity of the violence and (from a more sociological perspective) its disruptive effects on the political order.[13] On the other hand, while the violent entrepreneurs who emerged in the course of these conflicts were active participants in both the reproduction of the productive order and its disruption, none of these actors managed to turn their coercive resources into productive capital, as the Colombian paramilitaries involved in the cultivation and processing of palm oil had done.[14]

The economic and social cost of urban conflict

Although Karachi has experienced other violent episodes in its post-colonial history (including language riots between Sindhi and Urdu speakers in 1972), it was not until the mid-1980s that it entered a spiral of violence. In 1985–1986, the fires were ignited by a series of massacres and ethnic riots. Fuelled by the criminal economy that had developed in the wake of the Afghan jihad (1979–1989), and in particular by attempts made by Pashtun drug traffickers to enter the informal land market,[15] this cycle of violence brought the Mohajir Qaumi Movement (MQM)[16] to the forefront. This ethno-nationalist party claimed to defend—both at the ballot box and by the force of arms—the Urdu-speaking population of Mohajirs, who became a majority in Karachi as a result of post-Partition migration.

In addition to giving ethnicity a central role in political life for decades to come, this violence had a profound impact on the city's spatial organization, accelerating the regrouping of populations into communal enclaves controlled by militarized parties. In the course of the following three decades, opponents of the MQM would frequently switch personas, with the so-called Pashtun 'drug mafia' being succeeded by the Sindhi militants of the Pakistan People's Party (PPP) in the late 1980s, then by Haqiqi dissidents in the early 1990s, Islamist militias after 2001, Pashtun nationalists of the Awami National Party (ANP) from 2007 to 2011, and finally Baloch gangsters of the People's Amn Committee (PAC) from 2009 to 2013.

Despite their differences, all these actors contested the MQM's claim to political hegemony—even though its electoral success has been unbroken since the 1980s.

Evolution of political and police violence in Karachi

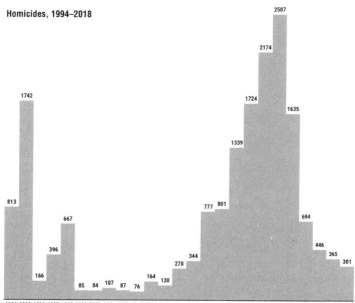

Homicides, 1994–2018

Source : Citizens-Police Liaison Committee (CPLC).

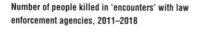

Number of people killed in 'encounters' with law enforcement agencies, 2011–2018

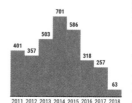

Sources: Sindh police; *Dawn*; *The News*.

Graph designer: Thomas Ansart, 2020.

Beyond the ballot box, the rivalry between these parties extended to the economic arena, relating to the control of lucrative markets, both licit and illicit (access to land, water, electricity, public jobs, protection money, etc.). The capricious nature of the army added to the complexity and volatility of these conflicts; having discreetly supported the MQM in the late 1980s as a way of weakening the PPP, from 1992 to 1994 the military carried out a 'clean-up' operation in the city, aiming to dismantle what was then perceived as a parallel MQM state. Under the regime of Pervez Musharraf (1999–2008), the party regained the support of the military institution only to once again suffer the wrath of the GHQ (army headquarters in Rawalpindi). The so-called 'Karachi Operation' launched in 2013 provided the army with an opportunity to disband the militant groups fighting for control of the city—and in particular the MQM, whose military apparatus was dismantled over the following years.

The armed conflicts that punctuated life in Karachi up until the mid-2010s varied in intensity, with an ebb and flow in the level of violence that closely followed the pattern of law enforcement agency interventions. Because commercial and industrial activities were directly targeted by the combatants, the local economy was strongly affected. From the late 1980s onward, the MQM systematically weaponized the *hartal* (a one-day general strike, often accompanied by violence) to impose its will on partners and opponents alike. The dominant party's propensity for 'bargaining by riot'[17] earned its leader Altaf Hussain the nickname '*Hartal Hussain*' (Hussain the strike).

Culminating in the mid-1990s (there were 30 *hartal* days in 1995 alone), these disorders raised the spectre of capital flight.[18] As always, poets chronicled the misfortunes of the times, relaying such concerns. For example, in one of his many laments for the city, Urdu-speaking poet Zeeshan Sahil addressed a plea to local investors tempted to withdraw in the face of the deteriorating security climate:

Ghair mehfuz sarmayakari
(A risky investment)

We have complete trust in you;
we believe
with all our heart
that come what may
you will not flee the city.
Unlike the foreign investors,

you will not
sell off all your shares in a single day.
You will not cart off
your investment to a branch of some foreign bank;
you will not take it abroad [...].[19]

Drawing inspiration from the troubled Karachi of the mid-1990s, the poet alludes to a decision made by the Hong Kong-based Hopewell Group to suspend a 7.5-billion-dollar investment project in the energy sector, following a sudden escalation in the level of violence in the city.[20] The resulting financial losses, which were widely reported in the local press (along with the macabre count of daily killings) served to sustain the image of a city in which 'disorder has become a permanent state', as another leading local literary figure, poet Fahmida Riaz, put it.[21]

While at the heart of the influence strategies of the warring parties, the industrial sector was also affected by criminal acts against both goods (pilfering, hijacking of cargo) and people (kidnappings of executives and factory owners). Besides, industrial companies ended up fuelling the protection economy, which became increasingly competitive over the years. This increased feelings of vulnerability among economic elites—whose confidence was also shaken by the insidious nature of protection rackets. Challenging the city/factory boundary, extortion involved a myriad of racketeers who—assisted by an invisible army of informers and infiltrators—sought to deny their victims one essential attribute of the dominant: the ability to see without being seen.

Disorder in protection

By the time this particular one found its way into the inquisitive hands of Qudrat Pharma security officer Taj Muhammad, lead-weighted threatening letters had become emblematic of the security crisis engulfing Karachi. These letters were regularly mentioned in the local press, leading to heated discussions between entrepreneurs and feeding their critique of state inaction. Their existence was key to a sense of insecurity (and of having been abandoned by the state) among economic elites. Such anxieties were widespread within business circles, and largely transcended distinctions of caste and rank. Even the foot soldiers of industrial order were affected—starting with the security guards who, in the face of urban strife, constituted the factory world's first line of defence.

The first *parchi*s appeared in the early 1990s, but the emergence of a city-wide protection market dates back to the previous decade.[22] *Bhatta* (an 'allowance') emerged at the intersection of two distinct sets of practices: fundraising (by student organizations, religious movements, and political parties), and criminal racketeering. *Bhatta* was thus a hybrid of the *chanda* (a donation, in cash or in kind) and the *goonda tax* (lit. the 'goon's tax') extorted from traders in the city's bazaars. Altaf Hussain, the founder of the MQM, writes at length in his autobiography about his first fundraising campaign among Urdu-speaking merchants and industrialists, in the late 1970s. It ended in outright failure: 'We went knocking on the door of every Mohajir big man (*bara admi*), but the only thing they were ready to share was advice'.[23] However, the doors to the city hall opened with the MQM's first electoral successes in the second half of the 1980s, when the party became a key partner in provincial and federal governments.

Even as it consolidated its institutional authority, the party armed itself, forming a formidable military branch. The accumulation of these administrative and coercive resources made the party's financial demands difficult to refuse and, by the early 1990s, every economic actor operating in neighbourhoods under MQM control was obliged to pay the *bhatta*, either through annual contributions under *zakat* (almsgiving), or in the form of smaller donations meant to finance political or cultural events. Closely controlled by the central party organs, this fundraising was fairly well accepted by economic actors. Because of the bureaucratic organization of this protection economy, the 'modest' nature of the party's funding demands (generally proportionate to business size and turnover, and very slightly amenable to negotiation)[24] and the effectiveness of the protection provided in return for these contributions, the MQM can been likened to the 'stationary bandits' discussed by Mancur Olson, who tend to rationalize their offer of protection as a way of maintaining the attractiveness of productive activities to their protégés.[25]

However, this balance was upset by the arrival of a series of competitors on the protection market who, to use Olson's categories, behaved more like 'roving bandits' and were focused on immediate accumulation. In a hurry to build up their loot and strengthen their military capabilities against more established organizations, these newcomers were further emboldened by the support of the military and its intelligence agencies. All of these factors, combined with their weak integration to local society, contributed to their voracity.

In 1992, a breakaway faction of the MQM, the MQM (Haqiqi), succeeded in expelling the dominant faction of the party from the industrial areas of Landhi and Korangi, as well as from surrounding working-class districts. For a decade, the Haqiqis reigned over this part of the city, where they imposed a heavy financial burden on industrialists. Few dared protest these extortion practices, for fear of reprisals. In 1995, Abdul Aziz Bombaywala,* the owner of Al Aziz Textile Mills,* fled Pakistan after receiving death threats. By standing up to the Haqiqis, this Memon industrialist had hoped to garner support from the business community, but he was soon disillusioned:

> We came in contact with the Haqiqis in 1994 when they gave a death threat to one of our office employees for being rude. The ensuing negotiation resulted in us paying Rs 50,000/- to free our employee. We had made a mistake, thereafter regular demands were made and some further payments were made. Then they asked for 3,000 meters of cloth, which we refused. They raided our fabric section and took away cloth on gunpoint. I then stopped all contacts with them and kept lodging complaints with CPLC, several PPP ministers, both in Federal and provincial governments, and Sindh's Chief Minister without any response. The collusion between PPP's Sindh government and Haqiqi became apparent to me. In retaliation the Haqiqi raided the factory's Cash office on pay day in May, 1995 and stole Rs 4 million, leaving a verbal message that if we do not pay this will be our fate. I tried to file an FIR with Afaq

[Ahmed]'s name as accused with the Police but they refused. Since I had no other recourse when my right to file an FIR was denied I decided to go to the media and make public the terror we went through. I expected to get some support from Karachi's industrialists when I went public in May, 1995, unfortunately not many supported [me] because of fear of opposing the government and violence of Haqiqis. Businessmen are feeble, they have much to lose.[26]

With the tacit support of civilian and military authorities, these perpetrators of violence continued to operate until General Musharraf's coup in 1999. In the following years, the Haqiqis' hold on the industrial areas in the east of the city was undermined by the MQM's main faction's return to favour with the military. In exchange for rallying to Pervez Musharraf's regime, the party was allowed to regain control of the former 'no-go areas' of Landhi and Korangi. The Haqiqis' unbridled looting was replaced by a system of fundraising that was both better supervised and more reasonable in its demands.

At the end of the decade, this fragile balance was upset afresh. Faced with competition from new entrants, namely the Pashtun nationalists of the ANP, the Baloch gangsters of the PAC, and the jihadists of the TTP (Tehrik-e-Taliban Pakistan), the MQM was no longer able to provide protection to economic actors. Traders and industrialists alike increasingly experienced *bhatta* as a form of illegitimate extortion, and greater competition in the protection market translated into increased violence. Not only did the addition of large-calibre bullets to threatening letters become commonplace, but attacks on recalcitrant merchants and industrialists were also on the rise throughout the city.

The deregulation of the protection market also benefited a myriad of impostors claiming affiliation to a particular group for purposes of intimidation. Until the late 2000s, *bhatta* was often collected by emissaries of political parties. In the event of doubt, economic actors had the option of ascertaining the origins of the request—for example, by contacting the MQM's Unit-in-charge or Sector-in-charge in the area concerned. The multiplication of *parchis* and telephone threats served to depersonalize these transactions,

Parchi *addressed to a shopkeeper in the Karachi bazaar. The racketeer, who gave his telephone number, demanded payment of 500,000 rupees and warned the victim: 'The fate of those who try to act clever is immediate death. We know your every move. Take this chance, there will be no other'.*

L. Gayer, 2014

rendering them less legible to entrepreneurs. In this increasingly troubled world, the visual economy of power relations seemed to have been reversed; the working classes and their criminal fringes became increasingly opaque to economic elites, while the activities of those in power no longer seemed to hold any secrets for those who tracked them down and spied on them, both at home and in the workplace. The language of threat standardized through the *parchi* was an art of transparency that claimed to subject patricians to the relentless surveillance normally reserved for the plebs. In response to this panopticon of the poor, new forms of knowledge emerged and were deployed by the 'operators of legibility'[27] acting on behalf of economic elites. With varying degrees of success, these watchful agents of industrialists tried to reintroduce clarity and predictability into an increasingly opaque world.

Contractors as operators of legibility

The proliferation of protection offers was met with new verification procedures, so that there was now a demand for specialists in identification. As the Qudrat Pharma example shows, these were not necessarily new actors emerging *ex nihilo* out of political turmoil. In large-scale industries, the rise of these perils was accompanied by increasing recourse to temporary workers (two phenomena that were, as we shall see, partly correlated), and industrial firms turned to their recruiters both to deal with difficult matters and try to see through a world of make-believe.

The contractor (or *thekedar* in Urdu) is a central figure in Indo-Pakistani industrial capitalism. In Karachi, as in the major industrial centres of colonial India (Bombay, Calcutta, Kanpur, or Ahmedabad), this middleman was, for a long time, known by different names: *sardar* (lord) and *jobber* in the textile and construction industries, *jamadar* (lieutenant) or *serang* (boatswain) on the docks, *mistri* (mason) in industries with higher added value. Historians of the Indian working class have highlighted the contribution made by these middlemen to the reproduction of employer domination.[28] Recourse to these middlemen was primarily intended as a means of mediation between management, engineers, and the working population.[29] It also allowed company managers to evade labour legislation (in such matters, for example, as the recruitment of women and children),[30] while absolving them from investing in more costly forms of labour control (housing, social protection, strict rules of conduct in workshops).[31]

In Pakistan, as in India, these services earned the contractor a controversial reputation. By subcontracting industrial illegalisms, he has been accused of exploiting village, caste, or neighbourhood ties to his own advantage. Beyond his tyrannical ways, he has been blamed for his greed, evidence of which can be found in the tax levied on the meagre emoluments of workers (the *dastoori*) and the fines he arbitrarily imposes. As early as the 1950s, some officials at the Pakistani Ministry of Labour became concerned about his malpractices. Though some recruiting agents did not pay their workers directly (this was true in particular of jobbers, who simply took commission on wages and bonuses), by reputation they were 'indifferent towards any orderly maintenance of accounts' and said to participate in the spread of irregular practices, even in the organized sector.[32]

With the liberalization of the region's economies in the 1990s, the contractor gained visibility, becoming the bête noire of global labour rights NGOs. They saw him as an obstacle to the regulation of global value chains, keeping their employees beyond the reach of international codes of conduct and local labour laws.[33] Yet, this figure is also characterized by a deep ambivalence. In his work on the textile industry of Tiruppur in South India, anthropologist Geert de Neve shows that the contractor occupies 'a highly ambivalent and unstable position within labour processes that are often marked by high levels of instability and unpredictability'.[34] Often, he is a former worker, whose social mobility remains fragile despite the fact that he has risen through the ranks, and is therefore at risk of relapsing into the proletariat. His room for manoeuvre is further limited by various networks of interdependence that are rooted in caste, kinship, or region of origin.[35] In his ethnography of contractors in Andra Pradesh, David Picherit comes to a similar conclusion, emphasizing the forms of mutual dependency that both link recruiters to their employees and minimize statutory boundaries between these seemingly polarized positions in the neoliberal division of labour.[36] A similar phenomenon can be observed in certain industrial sectors in Pakistan, starting with construction.[37]

The situation in Pakistan's large-scale industry is quite different. Some production managers are recruited along with their crews—a practice that remains common among textile workers from the Punjab, where an apprenticeship system has survived longer than anywhere else in the country. Until the 1990s, it was also common for contractors—like the jobbers of the past—to supply labour and monitor its performance in a specific department (e.g. spinning or weaving, in large factories integrating these different stages of the production process). However, such practices have been declining since the 2000s, and recent years have seen the emergence of genuine recruitment agencies that are more or less bureaucratized and employ thousands of workers. This new type of contractor tends to recruit well beyond his own ethnic group and to have a more distant relationship to his employees. This casualization of work, far from contributing to cultural norms of reciprocity as in the construction sector, is accompanied by a depersonalization of the relationship between employers and employees. These new labour relations do not however automatically lead to increased exploitation, any more than the sharing of a common ethnicity guarantees fair treatment.[38]

Many contractors began their careers as simple helpers in the industry, and they remain deeply embedded in the economic and social life of working-class neighbourhoods. Children learn to fear and respect them. One journalist friend, with whom I conducted some of my fieldwork, grew up in the working-class district of Landhi; he remembers that, during his teenage years, conflicts with his father ended with the threat of being 'sent to the contractor's house' to be disciplined. Today, the most successful of these labour bosses aspire to move away from working-class neighbourhoods to showcase their success—by which they demonstrate both the prospects for upward social mobility that are open to a handful of workers (generally those best connected, politically)[39] and the capacity of this highly coercive corporate order to produce consent among a segment of the working-class population.[40] However, partly to save themselves a long commute and partly out of concern about the cultural gap between themselves and the upper class, upwardly mobile contractors and managers tend to cluster in enclaves located on the edges of industrial areas (such as Metroville near SITE or Green Park City outside Landhi).

Ataullah Masood* is a contractor in the transport sector who began his career as a simple assistant helper in the packaging department of a garments company. During an interview in his *hujrah* (the vast ceremonial room in which he receives his guests, beneath an imposing portrait of Benazir Bhutto), he mentions the relaxation of the rules of *purdah* (physical segregation between the sexes) and the unbridled individualism of the residents of the city's most affluent neighbourhoods in explanation of his own decision to move to Green Park City. However, he also admits that he does not yet have the confidence to try to break into the high society of Clifton and Defence (the two most prestigious areas of Karachi, where the prohibitive cost of housing is in any case a disincentive for these new members of the upper middle class).[41] Even when they do manage to enter the middle class (or the 'second class', as Ataullah calls it), these big industry contractors are careful not to sever links with working-class neighbourhoods. They remain highly attentive to the needs of local elected officials, mullahs, and community elders, while weddings and funerals serve both to nurture these relationships and to keep them abreast of neighbourhood life. These newly self-made men are thus caught up in a dense network of interdependencies, leaving them still indebted to the surrounding populations. The closeness of these ties is reflected in the large number of visitors knocking at their doors.

These relational networks do not go to waste and are updated in the course of the investigations that contractors carry out for each new hire. Waseem Dehlvi,* Qudrat Pharma's main contractor, carries out a criminal background check on every candidate, prior to any new recruitment. He is particularly concerned about any history of activism within political parties or trade union organizations, and this extends beyond actual applicants, covering everyone in their family circle. It is not so much activism per se that poses a problem for recruiters, but the possible concealment of political engagement and its exploitation for purely personal ends—to the detriment of the company. Contractors and managers have political connections, but they are careful to present these as an asset to the company, whereas more discreet ties to political parties are perceived as a threat to the productive order. The vetting process (which includes inquiries being made within the applicant's own neighbourhood as well as in-depth questioning during the job interview) amounts to social prophylaxis: a defensive tactic aimed at preventing the infiltration of workshops by criminal elements while immunizing the productive space against the uncontrolled interference of party politics and community solidarity networks.

Anticipating loopholes in their vetting system, these profiling practices do not stop at recruitment, and sometimes equate the concealment of activism (even outside the workplace) to gross misconduct justifying immediate dismissal. This is exemplified in the code of conduct issued by Trading and Finance Consultants,* a consultancy firm that originally specialized in credit control but has now expanded into a range of outsourcing assignments (including the provision of labour) for large companies. Commissioned for one of Karachi's prominent pharmaceutical companies, the following form must be ratified by every one of the contractor's employees and replaces the employment contract with a one-sided moral commitment:

Trading and Finance Consultants

Here are the essential rules for Trading and Finance Consultants employees posted at Shahbaz Pharma:*

1. They must be punctual and refrain from taking unannounced leave.
2. It is strictly forbidden to keep food/drinks in the changing rooms and production area.
3. Workers in the production area are strictly prohibited from carrying food.
4. Workers in the production area are strictly prohibited from carrying ballpoint pens, pencils and markers inside the production area.
5. It is strictly forbidden for company employees to carry mobile phones.
6. Workers are encouraged to contact the Trading and Finance Consultants supervisor to request a day or half-day leave.
7. It is strictly forbidden to remove items from the factory without a pass.
8. Workers should feel respect and pride for their work clothes.
9. Female workers are strictly forbidden to wear jewellery.
10. Male workers should be clean-shaven and wear trousers, shirts and polished shoes, with neat hair and trimmed nails.
11. It is essential that workers keep a pleasant face and behave properly at work.
12. Workers are expected to follow the company's SOPs (Standard Operating Procedures) and disciplinary standards.
13. Smoking is strictly prohibited on company premises.

14. Workers are strictly prohibited from bringing weapons, tools, cigarettes, *paan*, *ghutka*, *chaliya*, *niswar*, chewing gum, *mainpuri*, etc. into the factory.[42]
15. I, [name], confirm that I am not associated with any religious, linguistic or political organization, that I am an employee of Trading and Finance Consultants, and that I will not claim to be an employee of Shahbaz Pharma, nor will I claim to be employed by Shahbaz Pharma.[43]

This attempt at social control via rendering political and religious affiliations transparent extends into surveillance practices in the workplace. Unlike the jobbers of the past, who often worked in the same workshops as their affiliates, the contractors of big industry now manage thousands of workers across different sectors. Waseem Dehlvi, for example, supplies recruits to the pharmaceutical, textile, chemical, and automotive industries. Because he lacks the time to monitor his employees in the workplace, he delegates this task to informers, referred to pejoratively by the workers as *chamcha*s (lit. 'spoons', a term suggesting that these boss/contractor spies have their snouts in every trough).

The forms of knowledge mobilized in these practices of profiling and surveillance are deeply embodied. The *hexis* of individuals—in particular the way they stand and how they look, but also their clothing—can betray the kind of self-confidence or a material affluence that could hint at an activist past or criminal affiliations. The behaviour of workers in the workplace can also be indicative of possible collusion with external predators:

> Knowledgeable people know how to interpret body language. Normal people don't ask questions left and right. That's how you spot those who have been put there [infiltrated by political and criminal groups]: their movements betray their purpose. That is why we must keep our eyes open.[44]

While contractors cannot be everywhere at once, they do visit the factories to which their workers are assigned, using paydays in particular to update their information. On those days, Waseem Dehlvi explains, 'it may look like I'm paying the wages, but in reality

I'm watching each and every one of them carefully, and I can guess their intentions by observing their body language'.[45] This vigilance, coupled with an unusual talent for physiognomy, is appreciated by the administrative managers at Qudrat Pharma. Trained in management at a local business school, the head of personnel is full of praise for this clairvoyant contractor, considered a master of detecting weak signals of collusion with outside forces of disorder:

> He is very good at exposing people. Once, we had a problem with an employee and before I knew it, he told me that the person had changed his attitude. He was one of my subordinates and I hadn't noticed. [...] He noticed it just by looking at his clothes. He was wearing very expensive shirts. I didn't notice. I thought someone must have gifted them to him. A few months later, we found out that he was dipping his fingers in the kitty. His [Waseem's] instincts are often right, he is rarely wrong about someone's nature, personality or behaviour. He can very easily guess whether someone is a good person or not.[46]

In the eyes of Naeem Beg, his contractor's ability to pierce the veil of appearances was confirmed by the extortion attempt targeting the company in 2011. This attempt was initially attributed to the MQM (Haqiqi), in whose name a *parchi* was sent to Qudrat Pharma's directors. At the end of his investigation, however, Waseem Dehlvi concluded that this was a sham: small-time criminals would have tried to hide behind this political party, known for its mafia-like practices, in a bid to intimidate the company management. The group's mole (a drug-addicted worker who was providing information to the racketeers to support his habit) was reported to the police and arrested.

For the directors and managers at Qudrat Pharma, the contractor's foresight is now beyond question. Nevertheless, in the case to hand, Naeem Beg chose to keep him out of the picture. Fearing that the hateful and foul content of the letter addressed to Akhtar Rizvi would be revealed and have the effect of panicking and humiliating the Factory Manager in question, he preferred to conduct the investigation in complete discretion. Certain clues led him to believe that, even though it looked a lot like a sectarian conflict, there was more to the case than met the eye. Naeem Beg's reticence points to the limitations of the forms of inter-subjectivity that, in other circumstances, made it possible to restore a semblance of legibility to this troubled world.[47]

Economies of violence and suspicion

The profiling techniques developed at Karachi's industrial firms over the years are not up to the task of dispelling suspicions among employers and the managerial class of the working population and the lower echelons of management.[48] Deregulation of the protection market has largely contributed to this crisis of confidence not only in the working population (which has once again become a dangerous class), but also in the factory world's ability to exist as an autonomous arena, insulated from outside disorder.

Contractor Waseem Dehlvi laments that, 'in Karachi, you come across a racketeer every two metres'.[49] Beyond those criminal actors specializing in extortion, here the term 'racketeer' (*bhattakhor*) refers to a whole range of violent entrepreneurs who use their coercive resources and their own interpretive skills to exert pressure on businesses for material or political gain.

This is the case of the Sunni extremist groups mentioned in the threatening letter to Qudrat Pharma in the summer of 2016. In previous years, the sectarian group Sipah-e-Sahaba Pakistan (the Army of the Companions of the Prophet, SSP) established itself in the working-class neighbourhood of Landhi.[50] From this stronghold, it extended its influence to the nearby Korangi industrial area— where Qudrat Pharma is based. In 2013, the party's candidate in the PS-128 provincial constituency Aurangzeb Farooqi lost to the MQM candidate following massive electoral fraud (this was confirmed to me by a party activist involved in the rigging).[51] SSP leaders in Karachi took this defeat badly, as attested to by the bullets shot at the residence of the aforementioned MQM activist in Landhi. Nevertheless, the SSP interpreted this electoral breakthrough as a sign of its taking root in the local working-class population, particularly among Pashtuns. Over the next year, the SSP—whose main social base had been the *madrasas*—worked to consolidate its image as a defender of the working class. In this spirit, the party set up a Labour Committee which, as graffiti on the walls of Landhi and Korangi proclaimed, was dedicated to 'the struggle for workers' rights' (*mazduron ke huqooq ki jang*, the Urdu term *jang* referring to both social struggles and war).[52]

SSP cadres used the party's violent history to break into this new battleground, playing on its reputation as a terrorist organization in order to intimidate local employers. The SSP and its armed wing, the Lashkar-e-Jhangvi (LeJ) have carried out hundreds of assassinations of Shiite figures across the country since the 1980s, and the fear instilled by these murders has always served as their calling card when approaching industrialists.[53] Very often, a phone call has been all it took to obtain the reinstatement or hiring of a worker. In addition to these occasional interventions, the committee was involved in labour conflicts, even (according to one of its executives, Mahmud

Election poster of SSP candidate Aurangzeb Farooqi in Landhi, in front of the entrance to the Alkaram Group textile factory. The poster presents Farooqi as the candidate of the 'oppressed' (mazlum) and the 'subdued' (mahkum). The children in the foreground carry a flag of a Pashtun nationalist party, the Awami National Party (ANP).

L. Gayer, 2018

125

Farooqi*) managing to reverse the dismissal of several hundred workers from a large pharmaceutical group and a prominent pipe company.

Despite the coercive resources at their disposal, the leaders of the SSP Labour Committee hailed from very modest backgrounds and were intimidated in the presence of corporate elites. Mahmud Farooqi remembers feeling uneasy ahead of his first meeting with the management of the abovementioned pharmaceutical group. Thus, intimidation can cut both ways in this type of coercive relationship— especially when violent entrepreneurs are as yet unaccustomed to the ways of the corporate world:

> They had given me an appointment at 9am and, although I am naturally punctual, I arrived at 10am. I arrived at 10am and sat on my motorbike, thinking, 'What the hell am I going to do? We have been told that Shiites must be killed and that all sorts of actions are needed [to reform/purify Pakistan]. But this is something else altogether (*ek ajib chiz hai*). What am I going to do by going there?' And then, finally, when I went there, I quickly got acquainted with the environment, sat with them, talked with them and understood what it was all about.[54]

This testimony confirms that the SSP, known for its violent methods, has taken root in the factory world of Landhi and Korangi. Even if their interventions were not limited to companies owned by Shiite industrialists, the party's cadres know that these entrepreneurs are more vulnerable to intimidation. Forged in the context of a sectarian rivalry that unfolded outside of the industrial world, the SSP's reputation for violence resonates forcefully with *some* entrepreneurs or managers. These pressure tactics show how violent entrepreneurs with political connections 'read' and interpret the industrial world, which is not always foreign to them. Prior to joining the SSP Labour Committee, Mahmud Farooqi, for example, held an administrative position at a large textile group in Landhi. Alongside his activities as an activist, this professional experience enabled him to identify certain business leaders as Shiites—and as such, particularly vulnerable to pressure from his party.

It was the fact that this sectarian party had taken root in the political and social landscape of industrial areas that made the threat to the manager of Qudrat Pharma credible. It opened up a range of worrying possibilities, in the face of which the limitations of the company's defensive mechanisms became clear. Like many other entrepreneurs in Karachi, the managers at Qudrat Pharma employed various prophylactic measures in a bid to defend their company—we have already had a first glimpse of these through the surveillance techniques used by Waseem Dehlvi. These measures were aimed in particular at tracking down infiltrators—those internal enemies threatening the integrity of the factory world and secretly working for the criminal groups, political parties, and religious organizations that covet the resources of industrial firms. With the proliferation of violent entrepreneurs, the multiplication of impostors, and workers' ability to use ethnic and sectarian divisions to advance certain labour demands, this social prophylaxis found itself up against its own limitations.

The ethnicization of politics and its impact on labour relations

Naeem Beg's investigation led him to probe a number of trusted employees, and in the end, he came to the conclusion that the threatening letter addressed to Plant Manager Akhtar Rizvi was most likely the result of a cabal orchestrated by a group of company employees. The tasks assigned to Rizvi (who had been recruited a few months earlier) were, according to his boss, 'delicate': 'control productivity, improve discipline, flush out superfluous workers and supervisors here and there'. The manager's abrupt manner and tendency to verbally abuse his subordinates did not help matters. One incident in particular seems to have ignited the fire: having detected an anomaly, Rizvi insulted a group of workers and supervisors very harshly. When informed of the incident, the CEO at Qudrat Pharma concluded that angry employees had retaliated: 'There was a reaction against him. Some people started to say: "He is a Shia, he is kicking us out to replace us with people from his community". But that was just a pretext.'[55]

Even if it was only a pretext, and even if the threats made in the letter were probably no more than bluff, Naeem Beg was not prepared to take any risks. He summoned his manager and, having shared selected highlights of the letter's content, asked him to rein in his overzealousness, saying something along the lines of: 'I received a letter. It mentions your Shiite identity, but I think it's just a reaction by some employees with whom you have lost your temper. They feel threatened. Take it easy, maintain discipline but don't shout at them. Try to work it out.'[56] This call to order seems to have borne fruit: Rizvi seemed to 'learn his lesson' and the situation calmed down. The way in which this call to order was made—by vindicating a group of employees at the expense of a senior manager—is, however, indicative of the way in which challenges to factory hierarchies are mediated by ethnic and sectarian conflicts.

Ethnic politics and workers' insubordination

'*Har admi ka ek sada maujood hai*': 'To each his own gang'. With this idiomatic—and multilingual[57]—phrase, contractor Waseem Dehlvi deplores the ethnicization of political and social life in Karachi, and its deleterious effects on labour relations. In his view,

> Karachi is a cosmopolitan city (*Karachi ho gaya international*). All ethnic groups live here and once people have settled in, they get involved in politics. Punjabi nationalism has no place in Sindh, just as Sindhi nationalism would have no place in Punjab, nor Mohajir nationalism in Balochistan. But in Karachi, everyone can defend their own identity. Karachi is an open city (*sab yahan khula hai*).[58]

What this labour boss deplores most is the factory world's heteronomy and the short-circuiting of its hierarchies by party politics; for him, the fragmentation of local society along ethnic lines is a lesser concern. Between the mid-1980s and the mid-2010s, Karachi's political life became structured around ethnically oriented parties: the MQM for the Mohajirs, the PPP for the Sindhis and the Baloch, the ANP for the Pashtuns, etc. This ethnicization of politics had a strong impact on labour-capital relations because it allowed workers to place themselves under the effective (or putative) protection of 'their' party. The demands of representative democracy (which require even the most coercive parties to be accountable to their electorate) were just as disruptive to hierarchical relations within large companies as the parties' reputation for violence. Supervisors and senior managers in contact with the working population had to control themselves if they were to avoid retaliation once they left the protective cocoon of the factory. Back in 2014, Ali Akbar,* General Manager at KFG Textile Mills,* a large textile and clothing group, explained to me:

> You see, people have become so politicized in Karachi that if you don't have control over the words you speak or the way you handle things, people down the line are so connected with any of the political parties, they'll catch you outside and it's an easy way to get back at you. Within the factory you can defend yourself, but outside they can put more pressure on you.[59]

The rise of sectarianism in Karachi's political life, coupled with the growing influence of Sunni extremist parties in the realm of social struggles, further complicated the situation for employers and their auxiliaries. Naeem Beg took this threat seriously enough to call his manager to order, lest his employees ended up reframing a banal labour dispute as a sectarian conflict that could have had repercussions far beyond the workshops. His concern was indicative of the pendulum swinging between micro-conflicts and regional or national identity causes, which have set the tempo for political and social life in Karachi ever since the 1980s.

Partisan conflicts indexed along ethno-linguistic lines have refracted into a myriad of hyper-localized confrontations in a process of 'particularization' that the anthropologist Stanley Tambiah has compared to the explosion of a cluster bomb.[60] Conversely, interpersonal frictions and confrontations can become generalized by being stripped of their singularity and aggregated into causes and interests that are less context-dependent.[61]

Tambiah himself has offered a detailed description of this two-fold process of particularization and polarization, which was at work in the clashes between Mohajirs and Pashtuns in Karachi of 1985–1986—clashes that profoundly changed the political landscape

129

by making ethno-linguistic affiliations the main referent of social struggles for decades to come.[62]

The echoes of these conflicts in the labour world remain under-studied. From the early 1990s onward, the struggles waged by the main political parties for the city were rooted both in the everyday life of working-class neighbourhoods and in the competition for control of resources (jobs, medical services, canteens, industrial waste, etc.) within the large manufacturing companies. This was particularly true within the public enterprises founded or nationalized under Bhutto, whose resources were coveted by political parties, sometimes fuelling deadly rivalries, as at the Pakistan Steel Mills.[63] The more discreet (and less organized) presence of political parties in the private sector can be explained both by the obstacles to unionization in this sector and by its reduced appeal from a clientelist perspective. Consequently, the nexus between professional micro-conflicts and identity-based macro-conflicts in the private sector takes more capillary forms, involving a multitude of personal initiatives whose actual connections with political parties are systematically disputed.

The central figure in these attempts at polarization is the partisan worker, who brandishes his party membership in negotiating privileges with his employers—a form of mobilization that is resolutely individualistic in nature, but which, by becoming routine, has significantly disrupted both the authority structure of industrial enterprises and their modus operandi. In large companies, this interference of party politics in industrial relations is usually dealt with by the industrial relations (IR) department. For more than three decades, Maqsood Ali* has been employed at Hamid Textiles,* a garment group based in Korangi. He currently occupies the position of Industrial Relations Officer:

> The responsibility [of the IR department] is to maintain order in case of an incident. If a worker takes legal action against us, it is our responsibility to deal with it. If someone misbehaves with a worker, it is up to us to initiate disciplinary proceedings. If political actors interfere in the company's affairs or if we receive a phone call asking us to hire this or that person, we deal with it. We know that if we respond positively to their request, we

will have problems. So we refuse, as courteously as possible (*pyar mohabbat se*, lit. 'with love'), by explaining that we don't have a vacancy at the moment, but that they should not hesitate to contact us again in the future.

Summing up a widely shared view among Karachi's industrial bosses and their administrators, Maqsood Ali deplores working-class dreams of grandeur: 'Here, every third worker thinks he is a leader (*har tisra banda to leader hai*)'. These mouthpieces for employer domination believe that the embedding of political parties in the daily life of working-class neighbourhoods would sustain such disorder. As proof, Maqsood Ali offers up this tale of a misguided young Mohajir worker, allegedly corrupted by his affiliation to the MQM:

> A few years ago we hired a young man. He was not affiliated to any group (*neutral tha*). But after a year he joined the MQM. From then on, he thought he would get support. Until then he was working seriously, but after that he started to argue, drawing sanctions on himself. We didn't understand why his behaviour had suddenly changed. He was behaving more and more like a thug. [...] For example, when he left the factory, he refused to stand in line [for the search] and bypassed everyone. No matter how much his comrades asked him to go back into the line, he continued to claim that he was a member of MQM.
>
> The guards at the factory gate were afraid and did not interfere. But one day one of our guards warned us that this boy had become a real thug (*bahut badmash hai*). So we called him in and asked him, 'What is this mess? Have you been appointed minister without our knowledge?' He replied, 'Brother, I am in the MQM'. So we asked him 'In which unit?' He told us his unit and we called them, saying that one of their members was causing trouble. The matter went up to the Sector-in-charge and we warned him that if he did not take action, we would contact Nine Zero [MQM headquarters in Karachi] directly. Here, you have to pay bribes to everybody. You have to give money to all the political parties.[64]

As this account suggests, the terror exercised by some political parties—starting with the MQM—and their entrenchment in ordinary power relations posed a challenge to factory order. A first solution, hinted at by Maqsood, was to neutralize these disturbances top-down, through agreements and negotiations with party leaders. At the same time, by adjusting their recruitment strategies, many industrial companies have tried to quell the unrest from the bottom up.

Restoring factory order by adjusting the ethnic division of labour

Masood Sheikh* is a director at Safar Textiles,* a company founded by Chinioti entrepreneurs. In 2013, he told me that he had recently begun employing migrant workers from southern Punjab (Seraikis) rather than Pashtuns and Mohajirs.[65] Newly settled in the city, the migrant workers still lacked the political protections other working-class populations had been able to avail themselves of:

> For the last ten years, things have changed with the Pashtuns of Karachi. Pashtuns used to be very reliable people. But now they are not considered very reliable, because of the Taliban factor and all these things... Now they have a stamp on them. Even if they're not... there is this perception that Pashtuns are not good [...] Also, in the last seven, eight years, a political party, the ANP, got some [provincial] seats in Karachi, and when they got some seats, the Pashtuns thought 'Now we are the [new] MQM of Karachi.' All of a sudden, the Pashtuns were doing the same things as the MQM *walas*. So now, people avoid keeping Pashtuns as well. There are still a lot of Pashtuns working in this field [weaving] but for the last two-three years, I have got some people from south Punjab, Seraikis. They are very reliable, they are not *badmash* like the others, they are cold-minded. With these people, we are working very nicely, the work goes very smoothly.[66]

As suggested by this textile industry executive, the political unrest and criminal violence associated with ethnic parties, alongside the emergence of a jihadist movement that replicated the extortionist practices of these parties, made candidates from certain communities unsuitable in the eyes of recruiters. Mohajirs and Pashtuns have been most affected by this discrimination, which worked in favour of new entrants to the industrial labour market. From the employers' perspective, the Seraikis' lack of political protections may have looked like a guarantee of docility and reliability. Urban disorder and the risk of its instrumentalization by the working population led to adjustments in the ethnic division of labour, and at the same time, ethnicity was reappraised as both a principle of intelligibility and a guarantee of predictability in an uncertain world.

Identity shadow plays

The shortcomings of this employer's strategy for restoring order to the factory world soon became clear, however. Here, as elsewhere, identity politics is a shadow play in which ethnicity or sectarian affiliation is only one of the possible frameworks within which social and political struggles play out, and through which power and production relations are negotiated.[67] And as the labour conflict discussed in this chapter shows, one false pretence can hide behind another. Indeed, lurking behind this professional dispute masquerading as sectarian rivalry, another conflict emerged—one that proved far more worrying for the company management. Some of the points put to me by Naeem Beg in the course of our initial exchanges in 2016 had alerted me to this possibility—but I was in thrall to the hypothesis of a worker's ruse, and failed to pay attention. Three years later, when I asked him to clarify certain points, Naeem *sahab* was categorical:

> I did not ask the contractor to intervene, because my suspicion fell on some individuals, who were not from the workers' grade. Those were rather supervisors of workers, who were not comfortable with the changes being brought by the Plant General Manager Akhtar Rizvi. They used the convenient route to target him because of his Shia faith and the threatening letter did not ask for some specific demand. They rather tried to scare him so that he leaves the job.[68]

Through this hateful and threatening letter, a double masquerade was thus played out: a labour dispute was dressed up as, and concealed behind, the threat of sectarian terrorism, while an internal power struggle within the company management was played out under the guise of a labour-management conflict. In his message of clarification (sent three years after the events), Naeem Beg sets out this point explicitly, linking the seemingly atypical incident to a more general set of facts:

> I thought that the letter was written by a worker, but dictated by a supervisor as the crude language used was meant to give the impression that the person is not very literate. But usually a Plant General Manager does not have any direct connection with workers. Normally his conflicts occur with his immediate subordinates.[69]

This irrefutable demonstration of 'interpretive relevance', which returned a troubling event to its typicality in light of Naeem Beg's past experiences, landed just as I was in the middle of writing this chapter.[70] It left me in a quandary. Had I allowed myself to be convinced of what I wanted to see—namely, a tactical use of urban disorder by rebellious and cunning workers? The incident raised many questions for me as to the limitations of my own investigation; based on a relationship of trust with Naeem Beg that had been forged through a series of meetings at the homes of mutual friends, my work was unable, from the outset, to accommodate a confrontation of points of view. Meeting with the Factory Manager targeted, or with the presumed conspirators, was out of the question, because this could have compromised Naeem Beg's efforts to hush up the affair and restore order to the factory at a lower cost. Thus, while the ins and outs of the matter seemed to have become clearer for my interlocutor over time, I experienced first-hand the difficulty for the researcher immersed in this world of pretence not to get lost in it, in search of a definitive truth that often eludes the actors themselves— at least for as long as they are caught up in the chaos of the situation.

The law—a blunt weapon?

While keeping his contractor out of this troubling affair, Naeem Beg showed himself to be deeply sceptical as to whether the law and its coercive apparatus would be capable of helping him. This is another structural effect of Karachi's urban disorder: the discrediting of law enforcement agencies (especially the police) in the eyes of economic elites. Each new kidnapping or act of aggression reinforced the industrialists' conviction that the state had abandoned them and that the law was no longer of any help. This crisis of confidence was due not only to a feeling of vulnerability to political and criminal violence, but also to renewed concern about so-called dangerous classes. As mentioned above, extortion and kidnapping involved not just the new specialists in violence, but also the working-class population at large, which was suspected of taking advantage of the prevailing disorder to pilfer, embezzle, extort—or simply yield to its own natural inclination for idleness.

Far from protecting industry from these perils, the law would only have increased its vulnerability. Criminal law (and more specifically the burden of proof imposed on plaintiffs) would only protect criminals, to the detriment of their victims. This criticism of the judicial system has been used to justify self-defence projects, or even rough justice, in the service of large industrial companies (see Chapter 7). While it appears to have played a more minor role in this security crisis, labour law was not completely unrelated to it. Industrialists have always had a distrustful relationship with this body of law, which they perceive as an obstacle to entrepreneurial freedom. With the escalation of political and religious violence, and the proliferation of criminal enterprises coveting the resources of the manufacturing world, the legislative and administrative staff responsible for regulating labour relations seemed, more than ever, to be in cahoots with the enemies of industrial peace.

The disqualification of labour law

In the eyes of Karachi's industrialists, labour law and its specialists have lost any regulatory function, and are now fuelling the prevailing disorder by supporting attempts at extortion and offering legal protection to troublemakers. Ashraf Siddiqui,* administrative director at Hamid Textiles and the hierarchical superior of Maqsood Ali (whom we met in the previous section), speaks disdainfully of

135

the rogue lawyers said to be prowling around factories in search of clients.[71] Maqsood Ali, who is on the front line in the group's legal battles, agrees: both labour law, and the entire judicial and administrative apparatus responsible for its implementation, are being hijacked—to the benefit of thugs and opportunists. To convince me of this, he conjures up the following fictional scenario:

> A worker is given a day off and extends his holiday by two days. He knows that he will not escape punishment, so he avoids returning to the factory. He goes directly to the Labour Department. There, he complains that he was dismissed without notice on such and such a date. After that, we are summoned [to the Labour Department]. There, we explain to them that this guy gave up his job without notice, forcing us to replace him. [Even though we are within our rights], they always end up asking us to settle with him, giving him satisfaction.[72]

Labour law is also accused of promoting the criminal activities of trade unions and those who have captured them for their own benefit. As we have seen, this figure of the criminalized trade unionist first emerged under the regime of Z. A. Bhutto, in response to an increasingly militant labour movement. It was consolidated during the 1990s, in a context of urban conflicts that threatened to spill over into the factory world. The equation of trade unionism with criminal enterprises is now widely shared, even among the most progressive sections of the economic and intellectual elite. This has important consequences: with rare exception, Karachi's employers are determined to contain the formation of unions within their companies.

In light of the fight against crime, this radicalization of anti-unionism among employers has only served to further restrict the legitimate channels of expression available to the working population. Naeem Beg himself agrees that the threatening letter that plunged him into an embarrassing situation also testifies to both this exhaustion and the enunciation of labour conflicts in a language (such as that of sectarian conflict) that is more audible to employers. However, the affair was not enough to convince him to change sides. Like his contractor, he remains convinced that all union organizations are virtual criminal enterprises, providing cover for unsavoury activities:

> Some of these labour leaders, or this labour aristocracy you could say, these blackmailers, they are not genuine labour leaders. They are here to get hold of certain factories and, using the workers, to create trouble and then negotiate with the management to blackmail them. These people change loyalties very quickly. Today they are affiliated to the ANP, tomorrow to the PPP, the day after tomorrow to the MQM, it doesn't matter, because the people behind it are criminals. Then they have contacts with Labour Department officials, who help them blackmail [industrialists]. Because genuine trade union activism has disappeared. The labour movement has been hijacked by these blackmailers.[73]

In the eyes of the employers, such misuse of labour law and the trade union movement by opportunists linked to political parties and criminal groups amounts to a complete reversal of legal normativity, one in which the law essentially becomes an instrument in the hands of deviants and criminals. Honest citizens, on the other hand, would prefer to stay away from the courts: 'If you decide to resolve a conflict through legal means, it's tedious', explains Naeem Beg. 'You have to take legal action, go to court... So you get discouraged quickly'. This distrust of the judiciary, the legal profession, and the law itself is common in Karachi's business community. Another industrialist, owner of a gum factory in SITE, ironically suggests that local entrepreneurs would turn to the courts only if they wanted to *prevent* a dispute from being resolved.[74]

According to Naeem Beg, when Karachi's industrialists find themselves in tricky situations, they would rather turn to the 'informal dispute resolution sector' than to legal solutions. Here, Naeem Beg is referring to the services provided by law enforcement agencies—which, far from being marginalized by this informalization process, act as one of its main propagators by proposing solutions based on compromise rather than on the strict application of the law.[75] Structurally biased in favour of economic elites, these offers of mediation are not enough to entirely appease relations between industrials and law enforcers, which remain tainted by mistrust.

What are the police doing?

Throughout this confusing case, Naeem Beg was reluctant to call in the police—who, as we have seen, have sometimes been involved in neutralizing racketeers that were threatening the pharmaceutical company. When Waseem Dehlvi reported to the Station House Officer (SHO) in Korangi the involvement of a company worker in an extortion attempt in 2011, the man was immediately arrested. But Naeem Beg has mixed memories of this episode. As is often the case in such circumstances, the investigation into the real perpetrators of the extortion attempt was dismissed. The Qudrat Pharma CEO keeps a tight hold of the bullet taped to the *parchi* addressed to Akhtar Rizvi, 'because we might be able to find fingerprints on it'. However, it seems destined to end its trajectory in his desk drawer.

Qudrat Pharma is by no means alone among employers in its distrust of the police. As threats to their lives, property, and business became more commonplace, Karachi's industrialists became convinced that the police were untrustworthy. This does not mean they won't turn to the police in certain critical situations such as theft or damage, where a complaint must be filed as part of a compensation procedure. Yet since it poses significant risk to the moral integrity of its 'clients', contact with local police is considered unworthy of the *faujis* (retired military officers), whose influence in the manufacturing sector has been growing steadily since the 1990s. These sensitive tasks are thus entrusted to conflict resolution specialists who take on the dirty work that is part and parcel of their job. An incident at Hamid Textiles in 2012, reported by its head of security, Major Qasim Balkhi,* speaks volumes about this division of work within the manufacturing world:

> One day I went to launch an FIR. We caught a thief red handed. He had jumped in from outside. He was taking things when we caught him. I asked Maqsood [Ali] *bhai* what I should do. He said: 'go to industrial area police station and lodge an FIR.' I went there and introduced myself as Major retired Qasim Balkhi: 'I am senior manager security at Hamid Textiles please lodge an FIR.' He said: 'no problem.' When I was about to leave, I asked him if there is anything else. If I am required to do any other

thing? I asked, '*koi khidmat?*' (what else can I do?) He said, '*ap ne khidmat kab ki hai abhi tak?*' (when do you think you did your *khidmat?*) [...] Then I rang up Mr Maqsood and I asked him 'what is he talking about? I'm a soldier and I don't understand anything about this.' He said 'just give the cell phone to him.' The police officer talked to Maqsood *bhai* on the phone and then said 'whatever, you can go now'. Maqsood *bhai* told him 'I will give you money, don't worry. You know me and I know you. Don't discuss this with Major *sahab*, he is not of this type and won't give you money'. So I left.[76]

This incident highlights the risks of moral contamination inherent to any transaction with the police, identified as such by enforcers of industrial order. As explained by Maqsood Ali, in the course of a discussion that also involved Major Balkhi,

Every honest man (*sharif admi*) is afraid to go to a police station or a court. But, by the grace of God, this is my job and I have to knock on every door.[77]

* * *

The employer's investigation that I have tried to follow here attests to the chronic state of uncertainty that gripped Karachi's industrial zones from the late 1980s. The brief career of this disconcerting letter, punctuated as it was by a series of hesitant interpretations and unresolved dilemmas, exemplifies the difficulties large industrial enterprises have faced in striving to exist as an autonomous domain, untouched by the struggles for the city. The ethnicization of politics, the proliferation of criminal enterprises, and the hold political parties and sectarian organizations have over productive activities have combined to create a new set of opportunities for the working population. Its effects have been particularly evident at the individual level, where they have opened up unprecedented opportunities to challenge and—to a certain extent—negotiate the terms of employers' domination.

However, it is important not to overestimate the emancipatory potential of urban strife—firstly because in this world of false pretences, one mobilization can hide another, as the web of entangled conflicts—or potential conflicts—revealed by Naeem Beg's investigation suggests, and secondly, because the knock-on effects of this troubled situation for the subaltern classes must be qualified. Its emancipatory effects remain modest, including at the individual level. The tactical use of outside disorder by certain workers and lower-ranking supervisors also encouraged the conflation of trade union activities, political activism, and criminal enterprises—a confusion that has served the repression of social struggles by strengthening links between the state security apparatus and the employers' community.

Lastly, the cost to the working classes of these situations of disorder and the ethnicization of political life must not be downplayed, whether in terms of residential and ethnic discrimination in hiring, or in terms of obstacles to collective mobilization. Despite the nagging feeling of insecurity among industrialists and the additional cost of these disturbances to economic activity, it is employers who have benefited most from urban conflict. These entrepreneurs' ability to compensate for the costs of urban turmoil (which is more the outcome of a long experience of irregularity than a matter of resilience) explains their decision not to succumb to the temptation to exit—in contrast to the many industrialists who did just that in response to Bhutto's economic reforms in the 1970s. It is to this creative management of disorder by Karachi's business community, and its consequences for the organization of work, that I now turn.

5

'THEY ATE OUR RIGHTS!'

They took away our rights at gunpoint. We used to have official working documents. Those don't exist anymore. It's all because of the political parties and 'security'.

Anwar Saeed,* former textile worker (2016).[1]

Jagdesh Kumar was in his early twenties when he left Mirpur Khas in central Sindh to try his luck in Karachi. Like most lower-caste Hindus fleeing poverty and rising religious intolerance in the rural areas of the province, he relied on fellow Hindus for shelter and employment in the sprawling city. Having found accommodation in a Hindu ghetto of Lyari, a working-class district at the centre of Karachi, his 'sources' directed him to a tannery in the Korangi industrial area.[2] NOVA Leathers was founded in 1986 by a Chinioti business family and employed 7,000 workers—around 60 of whom were Hindus. Pakistani Hindus (along with Christians) are traditionally assigned to the most arduous and degrading work, and have little recourse against exploitation: their status as a religious minority in a country that is 96% Muslim exposes the least docile among them to the vindictiveness of religious extremists, and this is sometimes instrumentalized by employers.

141

However, even for this overexploited proletariat, the factory is not synonymous only with alienation and violence. Across South Asia, for migrant workers having (at least partially) escaped familial pressures, factories and construction sites can also be places of emancipation from social constraints. This is true in particular of romantic relationships; in the interstices of corporate control, there can occasionally be room for the development of romantic liaisons that would be unthinkable in other circumstances.[3] This is not to say that the workplace is immune to the influence of social norms— or, for that matter, of 'moral entrepreneurs'[4] determined to enforce them. So when Jagdesh embarked on a romance with a young Muslim worker, he soon paid the price for this transgression.

At 10 am on 8 April 2008, Jagdesh was beaten by factory guards and a group of workers. They told him to stay away from female workers who were Muslim. Afterwards, his assailants dragged him to the head of the sewing department where he worked. There, Jagdesh was accused of blaspheming against the Prophet Muhammad, which he strongly denied. His manager, who had been informed of the love affair, slapped him before ordering him to return to his job. An hour later, he was again attacked and severely beaten—this time by a group of workers known for their affiliation to a sectarian Sunni group. Factory guards managed to pull him from his persecutors and lock him in a secure room with a metal door, for his own safety.

Before long, the company director and two managers arrived on the scene. Now convinced that they had the support of management, aggrieved workers forced the door open and seized the young man, then beat him with iron bars and hammers. All this took place under the impassive gaze of the factory's top management. The police had been alerted by an employee and sent a few officers along—but they refrained from intervening, even after backup arrived.

Several Hindu witnesses later told investigators from the Asian Human Rights Commission (AHRC)[5] that neither the management nor the police did anything to stop the lynching, even as the most rabid of the men were using screwdrivers to put out the victim's eyes.[6]

Having refused to register the complaint made by the victim's family, the Korangi police registered their own First Information

Report (FIR).[7] To mask their dismal performance, the police arrested three company employees who already had serious criminal records. NOVA's management claimed that the numerous surveillance cameras installed in the factory workshops were out of order, though this was not true. The police officer in charge of the investigation, who was deemed close to the company management, was in no hurry to indict other participants in the lynching. However, as the AHRC's thorough investigation showed, the massacre bore all the hallmarks of an Islamist organization known for its heavy-handed tactics and collusion with the underworld. Several hundred of its activists were said to be employed at NOVA, where they carried out their employers' dirty work while posing as defenders of the moral order.[8]

The following pages examine the integration of such strongmen (linked to political parties and Islamist groups) into the manufacturing economy. In the previous chapter, we saw how Karachi's industrialists have sought to protect their factories from urban strife by defending a certain idea of the company as an autonomous social arena. However, relations between local employers and those driving urban conflict also went beyond such pre-emptive safeguards. Continuing the relationship of connivance that had been established in the first decades of industrialization between the *seths* (large merchants converted to industry) and the *dadas* (neighbourhood 'bosses'), large industrial companies sought to contain the risk of resurgent labour mobilizations by calling on the services of the newer specialists in coercion, who had emerged in the second half of the 1980s.

More enterprisingly, entire sections of the manufacturing industry also negotiated access to the illicit rents controlled by the political parties and criminal groups, which had taken control of the parallel water market in particular. Regularly denounced in the press and sometimes sanctioned by judges, these collusions have nonetheless become routine. Far from being confined to a handful of deviant companies, these practices became widespread in large-scale industry and concerned the most prominent groups—especially those in the textile and garments sector, which was the main consumer of fresh water and had a historical penchant for strong-arm tactics.

Based on a series of interviews with manufacturing sector managers and workers, labour union activists, and police officers, cross-referenced with the AHRC survey, two forms of participation by the actors of urban disorder in the reproduction of industrial capitalism in Karachi will be discussed. The first is their role in enforcing industrial order by pushing the working population into chains of authority that straddled workshop and neighbourhood life, and the second is their logistical role connecting factories to a series of illicit distribution networks (the black markets in water and electricity), thus ensuring a secure supply of raw materials for industry (sometimes at lower cost).[9] These complementary roles have been embodied in two distinct types of violent entrepreneur: the political thug (*siyasi badmash*), who deploys his political connections in the service of factory discipline, and an updated version of the neighbourhood 'boss' (*dada*), now reinvented as a provider of urban services. At a more structural level, these new enforcers of industrial order both accompanied and accelerated profound changes in labour conditions.

'Eating' workers' rights

The enlistment of belligerent actors

At a time when armed conflicts in the city were becoming routine, the lynching of Jagdesh Kumar attests to the enlistment of Karachi's belligerent actors into the enforcement of industrial order. The young man's assailants were known for their close links with management at NOVA Leathers, and derived their authority from their affiliation to the Sunni Tehrik (ST). This is a sectarian group that was founded in 1990 by Saleem Qadri—a young Mohajir who started out as a rickshaw driver. The group is affiliated to the Barelwi strand of Hanafi Sunnism, which is characterized both by intense devotion to Prophet Muhammad and by its Sufi influences. The ST recruits mainly from the same social milieu as the MQM, namely the Urdu-speaking working class and lower middle class. Indeed, a number of MQM activists joined its ranks in the early 1990s, to escape the police and military crackdown on the party at the time.

As an adept of direct action, the ST first made its name through aggressive operations aimed at 'liberating' mosques occupied by rival groups (Deobandis in particular).[10] The ST was an important protagonist in the turf wars that bloodied Karachi between 2007 and 2015, and has been at the forefront of the battle against alleged 'blasphemers', systematically defending the so-called 'martyrs' who have fallen for this cause. Influenced by MQM methods, this politico-religious group, now turned party, has also been involved in various criminal enterprises (extortion, land grabbing, etc.).

The party has never made any real electoral inroads, even though it has a social base in some Mohajir-majority areas of Korangi and Landhi. However, with its military assets and its ability to mobilize around the explosive issue of blasphemy, it has certainly developed a strong capability to do harm, and several Korangi companies have had run-ins with its militants over the years.[11] NOVA's recruitment of so many party members could have been a way of neutralizing a potential troublemaker, but this sectarian party was also called in for its coercive resources. The profile of some of the activists enlisted by NOVA tends to confirm this: both Waqas and Usman (the two ST members arrested after the lynching of Jagdesh Kumar) had been involved in a series of murders and rapes in the past. Their criminal records seem to have been seen as assets (rather than shortcomings), and appear to have been put to good use by company management. According to witnesses interviewed by the AHRF, both men already had a reputation for violence, and the fear they exerted was enhanced by the protection they received from the company's General Manager.[12]

In some respects, the fruitful arrangements between these strongmen and Karachi's industrial employers in the field of labour discipline and anti-union struggles echo the situation observed in Russia in the early 1990s, where criminal groups initially imposed their services on legal economic actors, then created demand for these services that was itself conducive to more permanent forms of collaboration.[13] Karachi's industrialists have also been initially reluctant to enter into imposed partnerships. The senior executives I spoke to were unanimous on this point: in the ideal world of a peaceful city, they would have preferred to keep their distance from these unpredictable thugs. But in a city governed by violence, the best option was to neutralize potential troublemakers by means of an economy of favours based on: privileged access to certain markets (such as factory canteens or industrial waste), financial rewards (donations to political parties), and the sharing of redistributable resources (job quotas), divided between political organizations or between the small-time thugs claiming to represent them locally. These favours were meant to strengthen company security, the aim being to neutralize external threats (by dissuading parties and criminal groups from attacking goods and people or disrupting production processes) and to disarm community patronage networks (by creating distance between specialists in violence and workers who might be tempted to place themselves under their protection).

As Ali Akbar,* General Manager at KFG Textile Mills* (a prominent textile group) explains, 'Money is the easy solution. Other than money, it's a little complicated.'[14] The granting of less tangible favours (starting with the distribution of job quotas) to local political forces opens the door to interference, and the intrusion of *partibazi* (partisan quarrels) into the productive sphere is perceived as a threat to factory order. Over time, however, partnerships like these have sometimes led to a dense and complex network of interdependencies whose potential gradually became obvious to industrialists. During the 2000s, then, a circumstantial alliance took shape between industrial firms and violent entrepreneurs against the backdrop of structural transformations in the manufacturing sector.

The unofficial liberalization of large-scale industry

In recent decades, Pakistani industrialists as a whole have largely freed themselves from the (already light touch) constraints of labour law to impose their own conception of factory order. Back in the 1960s, the neutralization of legal constraints was achieved by means of derogatory measures aimed at protecting strategic industries considered to be 'in the public interest'—an exceptional status that certain employers continued to claim for their companies until the late 1970s. Since the early 1980s, some segments of manufacturing industry have been able to benefit from new exemptions in terms of taxation or legal status (mainly by joining export-oriented industrial estates such as the Karachi Export Processing Zone in Landhi). However, the companies choosing this status remain very much in the minority, and it is often only unofficially that manufacturing industry has become immune to the constraints and uncertainties of labour law.

Whatever their status, industrial workers are still theoretically protected by labour law, although World Bank experts have repeatedly deplored this state of affairs, arguing that these archaic protections undermine permanent employment by making it too expensive for employers.[15] Employers' obligations towards their employees are set out in a body of legislation largely unchanged since the 1960s. For example, the Industrial and Commercial Employment (Standing Orders) Ordinance of 1968 stipulates that any company employing more than twenty people is obliged to provide all staff with a proper contract, regardless of their status.[16] Employers are also required to make contributions to the Employees Old-Age Benefits Institution (EOBI) and the provincial social security institution (SESSI) for all their employees, and to provide each worker with an EOBI and social security card—possession of these documents is essential to claiming pension and health insurance rights. In practice, however, these legal constraints have been circumvented by increasing recourse to casual workers—the kind of worker who, as one textile industrialist noted in the early 1990s, has the dual advantage of 'getting paid only if he works satisfactorily and going the moment he does not do so'.[17]

Historically, the practice of subcontracting has mainly concerned the port sector, the construction sector, and seasonal industries (e.g. cotton ginning, jute pressing). It is by no means confined to the private sector—a survey conducted in the late 1950s testifies to its popularity among public works managers, on the basis that contractors were reputed to 'drive their crews harder than a government department would be allowed to do'.[18] Until the mid-1950s, however, the use of subcontracting was not very widespread in the 'large-scale' industry—that is, in industrial establishments employing more than 20 persons.[19] This was particularly true of the textile industry; one of the few quantitative studies available for this

147

period estimates that, in 1955, 93% of workers in this sector were permanent employees.[20]

From the mid-1950s onwards, the so-called 'contract system' began to spread across large-scale industry. In the textile and chemical industries (and later in pharmaceuticals), the use of casual work first became commonplace in the 1980s, under the dictatorship of General Zia-ul-Haq, before becoming widespread in the following decade.[21] Although there is a lack of reliable statistics on these informal practices, in the early 1990s it was estimated that almost 80% of the textile sector's workforce was made up of casual workers, compared to 45% in industry as a whole.[22] The pioneering role of textiles and clothing in this area can be explained by a competitiveness-driven strategy based on the reduction of wage costs as well as seasonal variations in demand and the historical pre-eminence of textiles workers in labour mobilizations.[23]

In other industries, although casual workers have in recent years come to greatly outnumber permanent workers, the status of 'contract worker' is by no means unequivocal, and can cover vastly different socio-economic realities from one company to another—or even within a single company. As Sébastien Chauvin and Nicolas Jounin point out with regard to the use of temporary workers in France and the United States, precariousness does not exclude forms of 'informal loyalty'.[24]

Although the pharmaceutical industry in Karachi makes extensive use of contract workers, employers in this sector tend to invest in their training, offering more attractive working conditions and remuneration than are available in the textile and garment industry. This 'informalization of loyalty' is aimed at minimizing staff turnover and securing investment in human capital (such as the training of skilled workers) while preserving employment flexibility and limiting the risks of unionization.[25]

The term *contract worker* might suggest the existence of an employment contract, yet these casual workers are not bound by any such thing. Recruited verbally by a contractor, they are generally paid cash on a piece-rate basis, and without any declaration of the sums paid. Strictly speaking, the use of temporary workers beyond a three-month period is illegal, but this law is rarely complied with, and most contract workers are rehired beyond this period (sometimes with a new employment card simply mentioning the name of the contractor), without ever being given permanent employment status. As a result, these workers are denied any documents that would allow them to claim their rights to social security, paid holidays or a share of the company's profits (bonus).

Casual workers like these now make up the majority of employees in Pakistan's manufacturing sector, and are also at a disadvantage in the event of any dispute with their employer. The pervasiveness of this precarious condition makes it almost impossible to form a trade union, which requires the support of at least 20% of all (documented) employees at the company. These casual workers are thus particularly vulnerable to arbitrary dismissal, and the fear of being ostracized by employers also tends to dissuade them from challenging employers' illegalisms, which—in addition to the abovementioned practices, include working days that can last up to 14 or even 16 hours,[26] the non-compensation of overtime in accordance with the law,[27] and non-payment of their SESSI and EOBI contributions (even though employee contributions to these institutions are often deducted from salaries).[28] And when some workers do try to assert their rights, companies offload their legal responsibilities onto contractors. In sum, at supplier level, this 'outsourcing of illegalities' process reproduces the logic of organized irresponsibility that guides buyers in global supply chains.[29]

The unofficial liberalization of Pakistan's industry, which has maintained the existing legal framework while simultaneously rendering it ineffective, proceeds by both action and omission. In Sindh, it was made possible only by the neutralization of the provincial control apparatus following the suspension of factory inspections from 2003 to 2018[30] and, more insidiously, the drying up of the human and financial resources of regulatory bodies (such as the Labour Department and inspection services).[31] On top of this neutralization of regulatory bodies, it is also important to account for the intimidation exerted by a myriad of coercion specialists. These violent entrepreneurs, whose profile varies from one province to another, have helped employers contain labour unrest in the wake of the casualization of work and the disenfranchisement of workers in the organized sectors of industry.

In Punjab, it is private security guards (often former police or military officers) who are at the forefront of this intimidation, and they go as far as incarcerating and torturing workers within factories.[32] In Karachi, particularly in the textile sector, representatives of political parties were awarded key positions—such as that of Labour Officer—from which they were able to monitor workers in an attempt to nip any social demands in the bud. Originally, the Labour Officer mediated between companies, the provincial administration, and, in the event of disputes, the Labour Courts. In principle, this position required a high level of qualification, and candidates were required to have a degree in law. But the politicization of this position has made it accessible to characters whose lack of educational capital was more than made up for by their coercive resources and local connections.

Within those companies engaged in such unofficial partnerships with political parties, the choice of Labour Officers has served a dual purpose: to access the disciplinary resources of the parties, and to co-opt neighbourhood 'bosses'. There has been no shortage of candidates in this field; large companies have even received a number of unsolicited applications. In the mid-2000s, the walls of industrial zones were covered with graffiti namechecking this or that kingpin (Sheroo Bangash in Landhi, for example), or 'signed' greetings to political leaders visiting the district—a common method of legitimation for aspiring notability. These were often shams executed by small-time hustlers looking for fame and a job in the industry. Managerial staff were sometimes fooled—especially when they were recent arrivals in post and still unfamiliar enough with the local political dynamic to believe that genuinely big men lay behind this flurry of inscriptions.[33] The specialists in detection mentioned in the previous chapter also imposed themselves by thwarting these attempts at deception. However, there is no better way of demonstrating local authority than through electoral contests. Municipal elections in particular serve to measure the mobilization capacity of political parties and their local representatives, who compete for both the control of working-class neighbourhoods and the resources provided by the factory world (both material and symbolic).

The mediating function of the Labour Officer has thus been redefined. Formerly a human resources manager at the interface between industrial companies and the Labour Courts, his role became that of a key player at the interface between the productive world and the political-criminal sphere. This redefinition took place during the 2000s, a period marked by the growing influence of political parties on economic and social life. It can be explained by the consolidation of these parties' 'military capital'—in other words, their ability to exercise organized violence via the mobilization of bureaucratic skills and economic resources, which has accompanied their move into urban life. [34]

In the final years of the military regime of Pervez Musharraf (1999–2008), who openly patronized the MQM, Altaf Hussain's party took over the municipality and its resources. [35] Armed with this tactical advantage, it was able to strengthen its authority over the Mohajir districts while remodelling the city through public works. The MQM's authoritarianism, as well as its aggressive development policy (which mainly benefited Urdu-speaking populations) alienated other ethnic groups. On the other hand, the MQM's armed clientelism was a source of inspiration for those political parties claiming to represent these different groups (such as the ANP for the Pashtuns, the PPP and PAC for the Sindhis and the Baloch, etc.).

These parties, which often transformed their strongholds into militarized ethnic enclaves, have taken control of both criminal markets and the various facets of daily life: access to housing, employment and medical care, water and electricity distribution, dispute resolution, and security. Combined with their military capabilities, access to these vital resources has been the basis of their authority, which both competed and intertwined with that of the state. This is also what made these parties so attractive to industrialists, as entities with considerable power to sanction.

At the peak of their influence, political parties derived their coercive resources from their power of intimidation and their status as gatekeepers for a multitude of urban services. They intimidated workers and dissuaded them from organizing or demanding better

151

working conditions. Some analyses claim that the emergence of the new precariat is no more than a reconfiguration of the labour sphere under the effect of neo-liberal reforms.[36] In Karachi, however, economic precariousness has been fashioned by social and political processes whose roots lay in both the political parties' modes of anchoring in their respective zones of influence, and in their ability to filter access to essential services—themselves largely informalized.

By stifling worker protest within a context of production cost reduction, labour casualization, and the dismantling of social protections, the enlistment of local strongmen has precipitated an increasingly unrestrained regime of accumulation, and this has in turn translated into a rapid deterioration in the living and working conditions of subaltern classes. As anthropologist Dina Makram-Ebeid points out in her ethnography of an Egyptian steel town, the insecurity generated by precarious work cannot be reduced to its economic roots alone. It has an existential dimension, linked to a feeling of loss of control over one's life and future. Drawing on Judith Butler's conception of precariousness as an inherent dimension of social life (in the sense that our existence is always at least partially in the hands of others),[37] Makram-Ebeid sees new forms of labour casualization as exacerbating this loss of control, leading to the deprivation of potential for self-realization.[38]

In a context closer to Karachi, sociologist Jan Breman has shown that the deindustrialization of Ahmedabad—capital of Gujarat, long nicknamed the 'Manchester of India'—has turned workers' relationship with time upside down. As a crucial element in the formation of the industrial proletariat and its exploitation, timed organization of the working day opened up access to leisure—that is, free time spent doing 'nothing' or devoted to keeping up with friends and family.[39] With the closure of factories and the spread of informal work, these opportunities disappeared—and with them, the sense, for these relatively skilled workers, of having control over their existence.[40]

In Karachi, this sense of disorientation had less to do with the closure of factories, and more to do with the unofficial deregulation of factory work, which has paved the way for new corporate irregularities. Workers in large-scale industry denounce not just the unpaid overtime, shorter rest breaks, and insults from management, but also, and above all, the opacity of factory rules and the erratic nature of their application. 'It is the reign of arbitrariness' (*andher nagri*, lit. 'of darkness') as one worker at a clothing company specializing in the production of jeans, told me.[41] Asif* concurred. He was involved in a protest movement within the Khaadi group that was precipitated in spring 2017 by the dismissal of 32 workers who had denounced their working conditions, and the generalization of precarious work in violation of existing laws:

> There must be rules at the factory, but there aren't. Whether you follow the rules or not, they tell you to buzz off and apologize. But what are we supposed to apologize for? If there are rules, tell us what they are. If there are house rules and we break them, we are prepared to accept it. But even when we do things right, you reproach us and ask us to leave the factory. There are no rules, there's no discipline. Or if there are rules, only the administration knows what they are. If there really are internal rules, they should be posted on the wall for everyone to see. [...] The managers, those who used to be workers, the administrative staff, those at the head office, they just do as they please.[42]

Governing worker conduct by means of regulatory vagueness and unpredictability has been characteristic of large-scale industry on the Indian subcontinent ever since the colonial period. Emerging forms of precariousness in Karachi confirm that (as in many other changing industrial economies) casualization of labour has at least as much to do with control as it does with cost.[43] For employers in Karachi, it is more than just a question of cutting down production costs; it is also about freeing themselves from regulatory constraints and protecting themselves against the risks of strikes and extortion that are induced by the presence of unions assimilated to mafia groups. It is in this context—at the interface of an increasingly informal industrial economy and a hyper-politicized neighbourhood life— that the Labour Officer has emerged as a violent broker in his own right, referred to by some of my respondents as a 'political thug' (*siyasi badmash*).

Asim,* who worked as an assistant to one of these strongmen at KFG Textile Mills, told me in 2014 that 'Retired soldiers deal with security issues, administrative matters, water and electricity problems... The political thugs, on the other hand, are hired only to do the dirty work.'[44] A few years later, Kamran Husain,* finishing director at a large garments company, reflected on this phenomenon—which was by then in decline. His perspective was that the representatives of political parties hired by factories in previous years tended to be a certain type of man in possession of neither honour nor morals, but with undeniable coercive resources: 'All he had to do was sit down, and his name would do the rest (*bas baith jatha bas uska naam chalta tha*)'.[45]

As a member of the ANP's Labour Committee suggested, these strongmen were primarily tasked with resolving ordinary conflicts between workers, as a way of lifting this burden from employers and senior managers.[46] In particular, they were expected to intervene in fights, which were frequent in the workshops. They were also expected to deter attempts at extortion, starting with those within their own ranks; even the MQM, which has undertaken bureaucratizing the collection of *bhatta*, has been unable to control the proliferation of its offer of 'protection'. Lastly, these henchmen were expected to prevent not only strikes but also legal proceedings being brought by workers after suffering workplace accidents or unfair dismissal— although these responsibilities were sometimes shared with retired military personnel who were employed in security departments, or in the administration of the same companies.

The trajectory of Riaz Ali is emblematic of the rise to power of these well-connected strongmen under Pervez Musharraf's regime. A Pashtun from Mardan (in the province of Khyber Pakhtunkhwa), Riaz began his career as a contractor by supplying labour to the textile industry in Landhi. In the early 2000s, he was recruited by the Alkaram Group as a Labour Officer, rising through the ranks over the following years to become the Director of Administration and Human Resources ('Admin') of this large garment group. Alongside this, he had also been pursuing a political career, and was elected as a municipal councillor in 2001. He joined a breakaway faction of the PPP led by Ginwa Bhutto, then shifted to the ANP after the

2007 elections, in which this Pashtun nationalist party won three provincial assembly seats.

Riaz's stature was reinforced by the influence he was said to wield over local police, with the main strands of his authority mutually reinforcing each other; thus, the patronage relations developed in the course of his activities as a contractor made him eligible for political roles, which contributed to his being co-opted by employers, and this in turn consolidated his position of authority in the eyes of the local police—who were always anxious to maintain cordial relations with industrialists, for fear of their political connections.

In accordance with the coercive model that has governed capital-labour relations since the 1950s, this authority both manifests, and finds its resources, in violence—both verbal and physical. It is the excessive nature of this violence—its unpredictability, its disregard for the normative framework intended to regulate ordinary productive relations—that disturbs workers, fuelling their resentment towards these impulsive characters. This resentment (reminiscent of the hostility of workers of the 1950s and 1960s towards jobbers) weakens their authority even as it encourages its frequent reiteration through more or less controlled performances of temper. Animosity amongst workers is further fuelled by both the ostensible idleness and the unbridled accumulation of these political thugs.

Anwar Saeed,* who spent forty years as a machine operator in the largest textile groups, does not mince his words when discussing these 'political thugs', whose brutality is matched only by their moral corruption:

> They come to the factory but they don't move their butts all day. Or they just go about their business. They have big salaries but they get paid to do nothing. They are thugs, you know, and the whole political system is on their side. If you talk to them or exchange a word with another worker, they slap you twice. Because of them, there are often fights. For them, work does not follow any rules (unke liye kaam ki koi qaid nahin). In each department you have five or six guys like that. They clock in in the morning and then they don't give a damn the rest of the

day. Even the managers and supervisors can't tell them anything. They come to the factory and then they grab a few pieces of cloth, make themselves a pillow and sleep the rest of the day. They have huge resources (*sari taqat ka istemal*, lit. 'they use all the power') and the system only applies to us, the poor, those who struggle.

Having worked under Riaz Ali for several years, Saeed's memories of him are damning:

He is a fraud. A fraud of the worst kind (*Voh do number admi. Do nahin, balke gyarah admi hai*, lit. 'He is a number two. No, not a number two but a number 11'). He took over the canteen and while the company was allowing us to have lunch at a subsidized rate, he raised the prices to the market price. He was getting his hands on all the fabric scraps and selling them outside. What are these ways of doing things? He is a Labour Officer: why does he sell fabric scraps? We were producing bed linen. Well, he would take roll after roll and sell them. And after that, the owners made us pay for the missing fabric.

This critique of 'political thugs' refers to a legal and moral normative order in factory work—one in which all wages require effort, the same rules apply to all, and supervisors are expected to earn their position by demonstrating exemplary behaviour. His verbal and physical violence were bad enough, but it was his attacks on worker morality that really earned Riaz Ali open hostility. This rancour is tinged with contempt: in using an idiomatic expression (*do number admi*) that implies fraud and is commonly used among the working-class people of Karachi to denounce the malpractice of industrialists and their henchmen, Anwar Saeed accuses his former supervisor of being the impostor incarnate—a false boss, but a true rogue.

This criticism is inextricably linked to a professional trajectory marked by increasing precariousness. Anwar Saeed, who began his career in the early 1970s, initially experienced stable employment. During a visit to his home, he showed me the business cards issued by his successive employers. On the early ones, the name of the company is clearly shown, indicating permanent employee status, protected by labour law. On the later ones, however, the company name and logo have been replaced by the contractor's name.

For him, the 'political thugs' elevated to the rank of Labour Officers have played a crucial role in rolling back workers' and social rights. He mentions Riaz's attack on the company canteen as an example. These canteens are a long-standing issue in workers' struggles, and feed the appetite for profit of many a contractor linked to political parties. The demand for cheap and healthy food, accessible to all, and in decent conditions, was one of the first demands of the trade union movement in Karachi. And while progress was made in this area (as in others) after the reforms initiated by Zulfikar Ali Bhutto in the early 1970s, subsequent decades were marked by significant setbacks. The poor-quality and unfairly priced food served in factory canteens is now again a focus of workers' discontent.

The undermining work of the 'political thugs' did not stop there. Far more systematic in character than in the earlier decades of the industrialization process, it targeted all of the collective rights fought for and won by the working class during the 1960s and 1970s. Anwar Saeed blames Riaz Ali and his predecessor for both the abolition of paid holidays and the ending of health insurance and pension rights for workers. He sums this up neatly: Labour Officers, who were originally responsible for enforcing labour law in factories, have ended up 'eating the rights' of workers.[47]

This subaltern critique of capital's new henchmen reveals industrialists' ability to co-opt the forces of disorder in order to reinforce their domination. More broadly, it also points to this productive order's ability to open up prospects for upward social mobility and thus to elicit a minimum level of consent—without which no apparatus of domination can perpetuate itself.[48] Of course, the constant pressure exerted by global value chains, coupled with employers' propensity for passing the buck down to managers and contractors in the event of an incident, means that workers who have risen through the ranks also complain about job insecurity. Kamran Husain (the Finishing Manager mentioned above), who has since been promoted to Production Manager, told me in May 2022 that: 'A manager is like a wife. If she does something wrong, you just say "*talaaq, talaaq, talaaq*" and she gets out of the way. It's the same in our business'.[49] Even if precariousness has crept into their success stories, the achievement of these men 'determined to make [their] mark' is, in the eyes of their subordinates, no less impressive.[50]

While the existence of these upwardly mobile individuals fosters both dreams of success and conformist tendencies among industrial workers, it does not prevent them from expressing a virulent critique of them as unprincipled thugs. Their very success is often attributed to their failings and compromises, rather than to any individual merit. In this respect, the condemnation of the voracity of employers and their henchmen refers to a symbolic and moral universe that is quite distinct from the one informing the 'politics of the belly' studied by Africanists.[51]

Derived from a locution of Cameroonian origin, this is a notion that brings into play a moral economy of power that establishes reciprocity and redistribution as cardinal principles of political legitimacy (the 'eaters' are expected not to fatten only themselves),[52] whereas the manducatory metaphors commonly used in Pakistan are part of a subaltern critique of predation, vilifying the rapacity of the dominant and their propensity for dispossessing the weak of both rights and belongings.[53] Power, here, is no floating signifier or disembodied microphysic: rather, it is embodied in well-identified figures denounced for their idleness and greed.

Echoing Veblen's developments on predatory societies based on force and fraud, this critique of the rapacious class and its lackeys is inseparable from another register used to 'call out' the powerful, namely in the form of accusations of fakery that reveal the dominant as what they are, behind the veil of appearances, i.e. as impostors unworthy of respect or loyalty.[54] Denouncing the fallacies of the dominant order, this indictment of false leaders as true thugs also points to the coercive element that is consubstantial with the exercise of domination: 'eating', here, also means assigning the dominated to a position of subalternity by means of plunder and illegitimate violence.

The only possible reason for the violence embodied in the excesses of tyrannical bosses, in the *lathi* (stick) carried by police officers and in the plethora of security guards at large companies, can be to contain the just anger of the cheated workers. 'If you eat my rights, I'll try to attack you, won't I?', Anwar Saeed asks rhetorically—and what he says next is still more explicit: 'That's why they [employers] keep security guards and give them Kalachnikovs: to intimidate us and deter us from attacking them'.

Like many workers of his generation, whose resignation is only a front, Anwar Saeed is acutely aware of the rights that have been snatched from him at gunpoint. And in his account of being downgraded from the relatively privileged status of a permanent worker to that of a casual worker and then to that of a pensionless pensioner, the consciousness he expresses is both legal and historical:

> Before 1985, 1986, the system was a bit better. Under Ayub Khan, labour laws were developed and workers had access to everything (*sab milta tha*). They were entitled to paid holidays, bonuses, new clothes on Eid day... Today, the working day has no limits. Whether you are fit to work or not, they don't let you out. 'Work!', they say. It is only through coercion that the system works (*zabardasti karte hain*, lit. 'they do coercion').

Along with that of other retired workers who joined the industry back in the 1970s, Anwar Saeed's testimony denounces the violent dismantling of social rights. These gradually disenfranchised workers are well aware that they are victims of a process of 'accumulation by dispossession'. And, as David Harvey and others have shown, it is a process that involves appropriation of both the tangible and the intangible resources of the dominated (land, raw materials, indigenous knowledge, etc.), alongside the dismantling of the defences of the working classes (social gains, labour rights, trade union freedoms, etc.).[55]

The lynching of Jagdesh Kumar must also be interpreted in the light of these structural transformations. The NOVA Leathers tanneries (in which the young man was employed) are emblematic of a general trend towards the casualization of employment. At the time of the murder, the company employed more than 7,000 workers, only 350 of whom were declared and thus entitled to health insurance, paid holidays, and pension rights, as well as a certain amount of job stability. Most of these casual workers were undocumented migrants from Bangladesh, who are even more vulnerable to exploitation than Pakistani workers.[56]

Bengali workers are, however, known for their propensity to organize and mobilize—sometimes violently. This reputation is not unfounded: until Bangladesh's independence in 1971, Bengalis played an active role in trade union life in Karachi, and the figure of Maulana Bhashani remains an inspiration to the radical left throughout the Indian subcontinent.[57] In the 1950s and 1960s, East Pakistan also experienced violent labour mobilizations. At the Karnaphuli paper mill and the Adamjee jute factories, clashes between Bengali- and Urdu-speaking workers resulted in hundreds of deaths in 1954. Portrayed by the authorities at the time as ethnic riots instigated by the communist movement and foreign agents, these industrial revolts—which were among the most violent the Indian subcontinent has ever seen—helped to cement in the minds of Pakistani employers the image of the Bengali worker as a troublemaker who needed to be kept under control.[58]

Although there is no evidence that these stereotypes reached the ears of the bosses at NOVA Leathers, it is clear that they set up an extremely coercive system within their factory. The Asian Human Rights Commission's investigation mentions the presence of 300 ST members within the company—a colossal figure which is, to my knowledge, without equivalent in the history of Karachi's manufacturing industry. The sheer scale of this presence implies that this sectarian organization, known for its propensity for violence, had thoroughly infiltrated the company's administrative apparatus. And it is difficult to avoid concluding that the punishment inflicted on Jagdesh Kumar (for violation of a sexual prohibition consubstantial with the domination of the Hindu minority by the Muslim majority) served as a lesson to other workers, especially Bengalis.

Both the accusation of blasphemy made against the young man and the punitive action that followed undoubtedly afforded the ST an opportunity to showcase its authority by means of a violent performance—one that was at best tolerated (and at worst encouraged) by the company's management. The passive attitude of NOVA's managers and directors may have been motivated by fear of being targeted in turn. However, given the absence of any management intervention (or even active complicity) during the first stages of the punitive sequence, a different interpretation is also possible: could it be that this lynching was able to be carried through to its conclusion precisely because it reaffirmed the hierarchical structure governing productive activities, in a brutal reassertion of the natural order of things?

In a paroxysmal but no less illustrative way, in terms of both its public nature and the chains of interdependence it revealed, this lynching demonstrated how the actors of urban conflicts were drawn into the routine mechanisms of factory policing. Certain armed groups are also occasionally mobilized to repress attempts at unionization. For example, in 2013, a large local pharmaceutical group used militants from the Jama'at-ud-Dawa (JuD, formerly Lashkar-e-Tayyeba, the jihadist group responsible for the 2008 Mumbai attacks) to intimidate a group of workers who were trying to set up a union in one of the group's factories, located in the heart of the SITE industrial zone. Using his affiliation with the Salafist strain that prevails in the JuD, the company's owner is said to have obtained the deployment of around 70 armed JuD militants in his factory. Generously paid, these henchmen were also awarded various privileges, as reported by a female worker at the group who was close to the trade unionists intimidated by the JuD:

> They [the factory owners] offered them salaries of 20,000 rupees [250 dollars]. There was really no need to bring them in. They should have distributed the money among the workers. They spend their days in the factory buildings with guns in their hands. What kind of behaviour is this? This is really nonsense! [...] Sometimes it's the people from the JuD, sometimes the police, who come and harass us. The atmosphere inside the factory is really terrifying (*khaufi khauf hai*). They take people away by force and threaten them with fourth-degree torture [*sic*]. They are constantly armed. And then they chew tobacco (*gutka*) and nobody says anything, even though in our company it is strictly forbidden to consume tobacco and *paan* [a betel-based preparation]. But they take *gutka* and are even allowed to carry mobile phones. The worst thing is that the administration prevents us from finding out about the [security] situation of the day, while our parents are worried sick [on days of unrest]. Despite this, women workers are not allowed to carry mobile

phones, except for the *chamchi*—those who are under their [the JuD activists'] thumb![59]

The anger expressed towards the employers' thugs here is symptomatic of the chronic state of tension in Karachi at the time—mobile phones had become a highly charged issue because they played a key role in social navigation practices, especially on days of unrest. This testimony is also indicative of how sex-based violence is entwined with anti-union repression. For women, who made up a significant proportion of the workforce at the factory in question, management's call to order was coupled with a reaffirmation of gender-based hierarchies. The presence of armed men in the workshops was all the more threatening because they were affiliated to a jihadist group determined to control women's bodies and behaviour.

As the proportion of women in the labour force, particularly in the clothing sector, continues to rise,[60] the sex-based aspects of repressive practices and organized forms of informality would merit more in-depth examination.[61] To date, the feminization of industrial work in Pakistan, which is bringing profound social transformations, remains relatively under-studied in comparison with similar dynamics observed elsewhere in South Asia, especially in Sri Lanka and Bangladesh.[62] Regrettably, my status as a male investigator was a constraint that proved difficult to overcome, limiting my access to female workers in the industry, or imposing mediation by their brothers or husbands. I did seek to correct this bias by hiring and training a research assistant, but her investigation of female garment workers, which had begun to produce promising results, remained unfinished after she left for the United States.[63] The growing interest among young Pakistani researchers in the worlds of labour does however give me hope that the sexual division of factory work could at last become a legitimate subject of enquiry in the near future.

Capturing the illicit rents of political parties

The fruitful relationship between Karachi's large industrial firms and the city's belligerent actors is not confined to the provision of coercive services. In a sign of their gradual acclimatization to the prevailing 'ordered disorder', a number of companies, especially those in the textile sector, have also benefited from the illicit rents controlled by political parties. These companies have negotiated access to the parallel water market (which is more reliable than the official supply network) through the ANP and the MQM. Ali Akbar,* the managing director of KFG Textile Mills we met earlier, who has been posted at SITE for eleven years and in Landhi for five years, explains how this system worked until political parties were cut down to size by the 'Karachi Operation' in the mid-2010s:

> At many intervals, people have punctured that line, taken out their own branches and they supply water to industries. Everybody needs water, so you don't have water coming from the official lines, so they will offer you your own water line, put your own meter... This is happening in almost every factory of SITE. [...] To run an industry, whether in SITE or elsewhere, you need to interact with a lot of political parties, in terms of security threats, in terms of hiring of people, in terms of firing of people. In SITE, there are three political parties. Because of the political situation, you need to have some affiliation with these gangs or political parties. [...] For water, which is one of the main resources for the textile industry, you need to rely on ANP, because there is this main water line which comes from Dhabeji, it's a pumping station close to the national highway [a territory at the time controlled by the PNA].[64]

In SITE, one of the main architects of this unofficial water supply network was a Pashtun *dada*, Lala Ajab Khan 'Bawani'. Originally from the village of Marghuz (in the Swabi district of Khyber Pakhtunkhwa province), he arrived in Karachi in the 1960s. It seems that he spent a few years working in the textile industry before being hired as a *chowkidar* at Eastern Film Studios—Karachi's only such facility, founded by the Haroon family in the mid-1950s.[65] As he became closer to Memon *seths*, he built his reputation as a *dada*. Living in the predominantly Pashtun working-class neighbourhood of Bawani Chali (named for its proximity to the Bawani family's textile factories), he developed close relations with local employers, for

163

whom he acted as a broker in various sensitive matters (repression of labour unrest, relations with the administration, etc.). According to a former activist of the Sindhi branch of the Pakhtun Students Federation (PkSF), who grew up in a neighbouring locality, 'he started dealing with [sensitive matters] in a few factories and became convinced that the Memons were cowards (*dar pok*)'.[66]

This testimony speaks volumes about how a kind of popular anthropology continues to underpin the ethnic division of work in Karachi. According to this common-sense view, Pashtuns and Memons are fundamentally and mutually complementary, in terms of mentality and professional skills. The figures of the *dada* and the *seth* constitute a balanced pair of opposite numbers, upon which rests one of the most enduring alliances between capital and coercion in Karachi's industrial history. The trajectory of Ajab Khan shows, however, that this alliance is not a functional mechanism in which the roles of each person are adjusted by the magic of inter-ethnic complementarity. Ajab Khan was an ambitious *dada* whose reputation and fortune were founded on intimidation and blackmail. By exploiting the numerous accidents that occur in the neighbourhood's factories, he extorted large sums of money from their owners in exchange for social peace; if they refused, he threatened to allow free rein to popular anger. By paying back part of these sums to victims or their relatives, he seems to have built up a large clientele in the neighbourhood, cleverly striking a balance between his penchant for brutality and his public display of generosity—a balancing act that has structured social representations of the *dada* and continues to underpin his ambiguous legitimacy.

Ajab Khan also relied on his coercive resources to get his relatives or protégés hired in surrounding factories. Like Habibullah, he imposed himself as a respected figure whose authority straddled, and bridged, the gap between neighbourhood life and the factory world. Like many other kingpins of his kind, he also enriched himself via the collection of industrial waste, which has fed one of Karachi's lucrative markets (that of Sher Shah, located on the edge of SITE). But his fortune was really built via the development of a parallel water supply network for SITE's textile industry, which made him a key figure. His admission to the ANP's central committee in the early 2000s formalized his authority.

Lala Ajab Khan was emblematic of a new generation of *dadas* navigating between the criminal economy and politics. He was much more than a racketeer imposing 'protection' through violence and intimidation; after all, he provided economic services that were essential to the smooth functioning and profitability of the textile industry. Karachi's chronic water shortage, artificially sustained by various public and private actors, has left the local industry dependent on the so-called 'water mafia'—a vernacular term encompassing a vast constellation of paramilitary, bureaucratic, and criminal actors. Karachi's main pumping station in Dhabeji gets 2.4 billion litres of water a day from the Keenjhar Lake reservoir, which is fed by the Indus River. According to the Karachi Water and Sewage Board (KWSB), the municipal department in charge of water and sanitation in the city, 42% of these resources are lost to leakage or diversion.[67] The most common method of diversion is to pierce the

Water pipeline running through a katchi abadi *(informal settlement) near Banaras Chowk, SITE.*

L. Gayer, 2018

main pipes and then open a water point from which tankers feed. In 2017, there were around 100 illegal supply points across the city, complete with a large fleet of tankers. Under Pervez Musharraf's regime, much of this trafficking was in the hands of the Rangers—a paramilitary force under the authority of the Ministry of Interior but commanded by an army general.[68] Following the revelation of these illicit practices in the local press, the Sindh Rangers have disengaged from this sector. It is now in the hands of private contractors—who are often in cahoots with KWSB officials, the police, and members of the provincial government.[69]

In the city's industrial areas, the public water supply system can only meet a negligible amount of fresh water demand. In 2015, the quota allocated to the city's five main industrial parks was 200 million litres per day, whereas the estimated requirement is 440–638 million litres. This official quota was rarely respected, and it was estimated that 90% of the industry's needs were actually met by tankers or, for the most water-intensive industries (textile, dyeing, bottling, or tanning), via illicit connections to the main public water supply, sometimes involving the underground pumping of water.[70]

In that same year, in SITE, KWSB officials overseeing the operations against water pilferage estimated that 154 of the 176 million litres consumed daily by local industries were supplied by unofficial operators.[71] Water is sometimes diverted at the expense of neighbouring slum areas such as Lyari in the city centre or Orangi in the north-west of SITE, causing severe shortages and forcing residents of these areas—some of the poorest in Karachi—to buy water from the parallel market.[72]

The quantities of water diverted are all the more considerable, feeding as they do a secondary market controlled by certain industrial groups. During the years of my fieldwork, one of SITE's most prominent industrialists, who was actively involved in the representative bodies of this industrial zone, developed his own redistribution network by supplying water to the surrounding factories. In 2018, the commission of enquiry mandated by the Supreme Court to examine the causes of water pollution in Karachi ordered SITE's industrialists to open their doors to inspectors from the Sindh Environmental Protection Agency (SEPA). Under normal

Waiting for the tanker in a neighbourhood of Orangi facing a severe water shortage.

L. Gayer, 2018

circumstances, according to a police officer involved in the operation, the inspectors would have been turned away and returned empty-handed, without their supervisory authority taking any notice. However, the judge chairing the commission, Hani Muslim, had the full support of the Supreme Court and was determined to call industrialists to order. After 75 of them refused to open the doors of their factories to SIPA inspectors, the judge threatened to take legal action against the offenders. Under pressure, the industrialists complied, leading police to discover that some of the biggest names in local industry were involved in the illegal sale of fresh water.[73]

Thanks not only to their connections in the administration, the 'water mafia', and the political class, but also to the inactivity of state regulators (environmental agencies, police, judiciary, etc.), large industrialists have not only benefited from secure access to this criminal rent—they have also become the providers of illicit services on behalf of their peers. And while the commission chaired by Judge Hani Muslim did momentarily disrupt these operations, its mandate—which ended in January 2019—has not been renewed. It

167

is true that the context was hardly favourable to a rethink of industrial practices. The health crisis of 2020–2021 and its economic and financial consequences in Pakistan generated new windfall effects; in textiles and clothing, in particular, the health crisis provided an opportunity to renegotiate margins of impunity, in the name of this industry's strategic nature.[74]

* * *

While disrupting productive activities, the protagonists of Karachi's armed conflicts have opened up new opportunities for the city's industrial elites in terms of both accumulation and social control. In exchange for financial rewards and contractual benefits, political parties and criminal groups have guaranteed businesses access to the urban services that are essential to their routine operations. This privileged access to illicit markets has often been supplemented by an offer of 'protection' that included both immunization against the violence of extortionists themselves, and repressive or disciplinary services that accelerated the casualization of work and undermined the social gains of previous decades. It is difficult to resist drawing a parallel here with the dynamics of 'armed neo-liberalism' observed in other societies facing endemic political and criminal violence, where warring actors have actively contributed to the dismantling of the insurance mechanisms and institutions of industrial citizenship (labour law, trade unions) that used to guarantee workers at least some relative security.[75]

One of the first laboratories in which this heavy-handed economic liberalization was tested out was the Philippines under Cory Aquino (1986–1992). Trade unionists affiliated to the Kilusang Mayo Uno (May First Movement—a left-wing trade union platform) opposed the Aquino government's policy of trade liberalization, as well as its close relationship with the United States and the increase in the Philippine defence budget. Because of this, they were systematically targeted by vigilantes backed by the army. These vigilante groups, which were also engaged in military operations against the communist rebels of the New People's Army (NPA), joined forces with corporate thugs to suppress strikes and intimidate union leaders.[76] By driving down land prices and labour costs, the use of intimidation and violence by employers' henchmen or local 'bosses' contributed to enhancing the attractiveness of certain regions in the eyes of investors.[77]

In the Guatemalan *maquiladoras* studied by Quentin Delpech, trade unionists were exposed to intimidation by local gangs (the *maras*) from their workplace to their homes, resulting in the maintenance of a feeling of permanent vulnerability that was highly detrimental to activism.[78] But these anti-union strategies have been taken furthest in Colombia, where right-wing paramilitaries have murdered several thousand labour rights activists since the 1990s. This violence accelerated both the destruction of social gains and the disintegration of organizations whose raison d'être was the mobilization of the working class. Trade unionists and workers in banana companies, the oil sector, and large foreign firms were most affected.[79] And by undermining 'working people's ability to establish control over their lives',[80] paramilitary violence prepared the ground for a reorganization of Colombian capitalism on an unequal, precarious, and authoritarian basis.[81]

Although political parties, criminal groups, and jihadist movements in Karachi have never been as openly violent towards trade unions as this, their enrolment in the liberalization process has created an intimidating climate, whose socio-economic effects have been supplemented by acute psychological disorders. After my meeting with Anwar Saeed, the retired worker whose career I have retraced here, his two sons confided that he was suffering from acute depression. Working respectively as a taxi driver and as a supervisor in a large textile company, both attributed their father's condition to his inability to claim his pension after a lifetime of hard work. Echoing the sense of dispossession of Colombian workers harassed by paramilitaries, Anwar Saeed's depression appeared to be intimately linked to the dismantling of social rights that had been hard won by Pakistani workers in the 1970s.[82] It is this neutralization of a historically contingent regime of industrial citizenship that justifies use of the term 'armed *neo*-liberalism', in contrast to the more structural tendencies of Pakistani industrialists towards coercive accumulation.

169

If the restructuring underway in Karachi bears a resemblance to the situation in the Philippines in the 1980s or Colombia in the 1990s, this is also because in each case, armed conflicts 'set the terms under which industrialization and other forms of "development" are proceeding today.'[83] In Karachi, this legacy was first manifested in the unofficial deregulation of the so-called 'organized' sector, in which all of the warring parties participated. As the next chapter will show, this was extended through new development and security arrangements; by putting the survival of the entire nation at stake, Karachi's urban conflicts justified the deployment of anti-terrorist legislation in the service of 'industrial peace'. This enterprise of pacification has created new interdependencies between the owners of capital and the professionals of violence, which have strengthened the repressive capacities of employers in both the legal and extra-legal domains. These state protections mobilize the weapon of law, even as they produce the conditions in which it can be circumvented, and it is to this terrible ambiguity that I now turn.

6

ANTI-TERRORISM TO THE RESCUE

*I told them that my father and grandfathers were also workers. And I
took it as my duty to side with the oppressed, but they kept accusing
me of taking money from other countries and blackmailing the
industrialists.*

Mohib Azad, lawyer and human rights activist
abducted by the police in September 2020.[1]

On the evening of 22 March 2012, seven weavers were arrested at
their home in Ettehad Town, west of Karachi. The men, who were
employed by a subcontractor of the garment giant Alkaram, were
accused of extortion—considered an act of terrorism under the
draconian laws in force in Pakistan since the 1990s. The Rangers
(a paramilitary force that has been supplementing the police in
Karachi's fight against terrorism since the 1990s) were leading the
raid on the suspected racketeers.

Over the next few days, as evidence of the mistreatment of
the defendants mounted, their supporters in Pakistan and within
international textile worker organizations tried to prove the men's
innocence. They claimed that the men had been punished for their
trade union activities—particularly after they had denounced not
only their employer's labour rights and safety standards violations,

but also the fact that they had been hacking into the electricity grid. The campaign was effective, and the suspects were released on bail in mid-May. Still, their trial dragged on, and, given that they had to attend more than a hundred hearings over the next two years, legal proceedings deprived them of any prospect of finding a stable job.

As exemplified by this repressive episode, which I will be returning to in detail later on, the imprint of Karachi's armed conflicts on its industries went beyond the plethora of coercive services they ordinarily generated for business elites. In Karachi and elsewhere in Pakistan, the repressive arsenal deployed by the state in its counter-terrorism operations has also had an impact on industrial relations, on access to the labour market, and on worker mobilizations. The fight against crime and terrorism has inspired new security measures which, in turn, have opened up new perspectives for the repression of social struggles. Echoing Marx's words on the contribution made by crime to the dynamics of capitalism, it is not out of place to speak here of the 'secondary benefits' to employers of Karachi's urban conflicts.

In a short text brimming with irony, Marx insists on the productivity of the criminal, who 'produces not only crime but also the criminal law' as well as 'the whole apparatus of the police and criminal justice, detectives, judges, executioners, juries, etc.' Thus, 'Crime, by its ceaseless development of new means of attacking property calls into existence new measures of defence, and its productive effects are as great as those of strikes in stimulating the invention of machines.'[2] This thesis resonates strongly in Karachi, where urban conflicts and associated criminal practices (notably extortion) have weaponized the critique and repression of social struggles over the past decade.

Beyond the derivative effects of the fight against terrorism and its repercussions on worker mobilizations, this chapter is also devoted to the state's reinvestment in the defence of industrial order. While the previous chapter considered the participation of armed groups in the enforcement of an economic order that was as precarious as it was authoritarian, the focus here will be on the repressive state apparatus itself—including the police, (para-)military forces, and the judiciary. Indeed, Pakistan's militarized state, in both its legal and extra-legal incarnations, has been central to the dynamics of industrial order in Karachi. As well as adding to the complexity and brutality of local conflicts over power, status, and wealth, these state interventions have refracted the struggles for the city—and control of its economy—through Pakistan's macropolitical dynamics.

Bringing law enforcers back in

Chief Justice Iftikhar Muhammad Chaudhry knew his classics. In October 2011—a period during which Karachi was facing renewed political and criminal violence—he invoked the spirit of the colossus of Heidelberg: 'Pakistan as a sovereign country as well as a nuclear power for all intents and purposes is a successful state because such a state, in the words of Max Weber, maintains a monopoly on the legitimate use of physical force within its borders.' The rest of his judgement, however, nuances this diagnosis, painting a picture of a city on the verge of chaos,

> where the lives and properties of the people of Karachi are not safe, frequent killings of innocent citizens have made their lives miserable; citizens are being abducted for ransom; beheaded dead bodies of innocent people with arms and legs tied and wrapped in sacks are being recovered in large numbers; street crimes are in abundance and different groups are involved in target killings.

Noting that this deleterious climate weighed heavily on business, threatening to result in massive capital flight, Justice Chaudhry called on the authorities in general, and law enforcement agencies in particular, to take action before the city dragged the entire country into ruin.[3]

The action taken (at its own instigation) by the Supreme Court ran until autumn 2013 and was a spectacular litmus test for the Pakistani state—one of those sequences in which public institutions become 'the object of collective uncertainty and scrutiny.'[4]

Galvanized by the success of the 2007–2008 lawyers' movement, the Supreme Court judges summoned the heads of law enforcement agencies to the bar, demanding that they uphold their responsibilities for the protection of people and property.[5] This show of force was part of a larger political tussle: Karachi's turf wars provided an embattled judiciary with an opportunity to reassert its autonomy against military and civilian elites. As in the 1990s, when the struggles for the city had determined the fate of governments in Islamabad, Karachi became a playground for the forces vying for supremacy at the national level.

As local conflicts were refracted through this nationwide battle for hegemony, law enforcement agencies sought to spruce up their image by multiplying raids against gunmen and racketeers of all kinds. The political elites in Islamabad were also drawn into this repressive spiral and in September 2013 the newly elected Pakistan Muslim League-Nawaz (PML-N) government, in alliance with a reinvigorated military, launched a vast anti-terrorist and anti-crime operation. The so-called 'Karachi Operation' was spearheaded by the Sindh Rangers, with the support of the Karachi police and intelligence agencies.[6] In the following years, it did restore relative calm to the city, though at a high price: between 2013 and 2015, more than a thousand suspected terrorists and criminals were killed by the police, without any investigation into the circumstances of these deaths.[7]

While pressure from the Supreme Court was embarrassing to law enforcement agencies, forcing them to react, paramilitary forces and the police also seized the opportunity to reposition themselves in the city. By depriving political parties of a large part of their coercive resources, these urban pacification operations have boosted the offer of protection by law enforcement professionals. These operations have, however, failed to lead to the restoration of a rational-legal state fitting the Weberian model invoked by Chief Justice Iftikhar Chaudhry; rather, they have induced further confusion regarding the roles and private uses of the repressive arsenal of the state. They also provided an opportunity for Pakistan's increasingly commercialized military to regain a foothold in the city, securing (and possibly expanding) its vast economic interests in the process.

'The Rangers are our nuclear weapon'

The arrest of the unionized workers of Ettehad Town by the Rangers on 22 March 2012 was indicative of the blurring of lines between the security tasks classically associated with the domain of war (or defence) and the domain of peace (or the police)—a distinction which has become increasingly fuzzy over the course of Karachi's armed conflicts. Pakistan has a number of 'paramilitary' forces—a term that, in the Pakistani context, refers to 'civil armed forces' commanded by senior police or military officers and placed under the authority of the federal government, rather than militia organizations acting as auxiliaries to law enforcement, or using illegitimate violence for private ends.

The 100,000 men of the Rangers are divided between the provinces of Punjab and Sindh. They are under the authority of the Ministry of the Interior, but commanded by senior army officers (the Director General of the Rangers, in Sindh as in Punjab, is always a Major General). This paramilitary force was initially tasked with defending the Indo-Pakistani border, although its mandate has since expanded to include policing duties within the country. Since the late 1980s, then, policing in Karachi has been divided between the police and the Sindh Rangers, of whom there were around 15,000 in the city in 2016 (about half of the police force).

This paramilitary force first intervened in Karachi in 1989, at the request of Sindh's provincial authorities and with the approval of the Corps Commander for the zone, to quell student union unrest on the city's campuses, and has never left.[8]

From 1992 to 1994, the Rangers assisted the army during 'Operation Clean-up', which primarily targeted the MQM. They later assisted the police in successive operations against armed militants associated with political parties (known locally as 'target killers'), as well as against jihadist groups and criminal organizations operating in the city.

As a result of these urban pacification operations, the paramilitaries have been granted ever-increasing police powers—a process that was only accelerated by the outbreak of violence in the summer of 2011. Under pressure from both traders and industrialists, provincial authorities gave the Rangers 'special powers' to arrest suspects and hold them in custody for 24 hours before handing them over to the police. These powers were granted under the Anti-Terrorism Act (ATA), which was the centrepiece of the anti-terrorism regime that emerged in the country in the late 1990s. In 2013, following the launch of the Karachi Operation, the Rangers were granted expanded police powers that allowed them to detain terror suspects for up to 90 days without charge or judicial interference. These powers were however temporary, and subject to renewal by provincial authorities every three months, which has sometimes led to tensions with these authorities.[9] In March 2016, the Supreme Court rejected a request by the Rangers for greater investigative powers and the ability to charge suspects without referring them to the police.

Alongside their law enforcement activities, the Rangers have been engaged in a variety of economic activities, both licit and illicit. During the 1990s, they took control of the water tanker business across the city, which relies on the supply of water to individuals and businesses through illegal hydrants.[10] In the early 2000s, they began to regulate the fishing market and have more recently entered cement production, while also running shooting galleries, petrol stations, printing shops, canteens, and schools.[11] In 2012, they established a private security company, the Rangers Security Guards (RSGs), which recruits mainly ex-military and paramilitary personnel and provides security for the SITE industrial zone.

This has both turned the Rangers into a violent enterprise and brought them into contact with employers—with whom their relationships range from contractual protection (as at SITE, through the RSGs) to informal collusion. In a sign of the persistent hold the ideology of national security has over industrialists, a former president of the Employers Federation of Pakistan uses the language of nuclear deterrence in speaking of this privileged relationship and the Rangers' contribution to securing the industrial zones of Karachi:

> We give more importance to them [the Rangers] than to ministers. Because they are a deterrent, they will protect the area from criminals. [...] So we can go to our industries in an atmosphere where there will not be a labour... a law and order

issue. Because a mob, a violent mob, or morons can attack our factories. The Rangers are a deterrent for us, like the nuclear bomb that we have. Otherwise, Indians and others would come and attack us. The same way, we [industrialists] have the Rangers.[12]

The collusion between industrialists and paramilitaries, coupled with the increasing police powers granted to the latter, have further restricted the room for manoeuvre available to workers and trade union activists challenging employer domination. The slightest hint of a threat to a supervisor (let alone collective protest action) can now result in a raid on one's home, or a summons to the barracks. Trade unionists who denounce industrial illegalisms are threatened with being labelled traitors to the country—a charge almost unchanged since the 1950s, and one that continues to equate disturbances of industrial peace with anti-national activities. This is what Abdur Rahman,* one of the leaders of the main trade union federation in Sindh, discovered in 2013. Following the dismissal of several hundred BP food group employees, he took part in a protest demonstration (*dharna*) in front of the group's factories in SITE. When informed of this mobilization, local Rangers officials summoned him:

> The Rangers called me. I went there. They told me that the employers might not want to keep their plant running and they accused me of forcing their hand. I told them that this [the employers' use of the *lock-out*] was coercion, not the other way round. But what does a colonel know about the law? [...] They threatened us, saying they were going to throw us in jail. They asked us if we were aware of the general situation in the country. I asked them why we should sacrifice our rights for the general situation of the country. A worker is a worker (*mazdoor bhi mazdoor hai*). [...] The right to form a union belongs to all workers, but this colonel did not know this, so what could we expect from him? [...] Even today, BP refuses to pay the legal minimum wage to its workers and if you fall ill, don't count on any help. None of their employees is entitled to social security or pensions.[13]

Both the increased police powers of the Rangers and the protection contracts negotiated with industrialists via their 'private' security company have undoubtedly favoured the involvement of paramilitaries in labour disputes. Not to be outdone, the police have in turn used the Karachi Operation to get back into the game—though not without some friction with their new economic partners.

The return of the police?

As Sindh Police Chief A. D. Khawaja lamented during an address to the Karachi Chamber of Commerce and Industry (KCCI) in 2017, the Rangers have served as 'crutches' for the local police since the 1990s.[14] During the 2000s, the targeted killings of officers involved in the anti-MQM operations of the previous decade further delegitimized and demoralized the police force, which appeared unable to ensure the safety of its own personnel—let alone that of ordinary citizens.[15]

The Karachi Operation provided police with an opportunity to regain at least some of the ground they had lost in terms of the maintenance of public and economic order. The return of relative calm to the city in the mid-2010s opened up new perspectives for civilian law enforcement, even more than the operation itself, which was de facto led by the Rangers. While SITE's industrialists decided (despite a certain amount of dissent) to call on the Rangers' private company to secure the area, their counterparts in Korangi made a different choice. The application of pressure from the Rangers' management, which tried to convince the Korangi industrial association to sign a similar contract with the RSGs, was unsuccessful. The cost of such a service was considered exorbitant, and a number of industrialists saw it as a Rangers racketeering scheme.[16] Korangi's business elites decided instead to strengthen their cooperation with the police—albeit with mixed results.

In 2014, an official partnership between police and industry was established in the area. Under the Police Patrolling Partnership Project (PPPP), the Korangi Association of Trade and Industry (KATI) provided both vehicles and funds for additional patrols. Industrialists had expected these police patrols to dismantle roadside canteens (thought to serve as observation posts for the informers of criminal groups).[17] Through these police operations, the aim was to deprive extortionists of their surveillance capacities—even if that meant depriving the working-class population of its main place of relaxation and sustenance.

This collaboration project was, however, suspended after just a few months. According to a senior police officer involved in the project, tensions soon arose between the police and their clients. In violation of the terms of the original contract (which called only for increased motorized patrols around industrial facilities), some Korangi industrialists sought to use the police to secure cash or cargo shipments. Top police officials in District East, while not necessarily averse to their men becoming involved in such activities, did insist on being paid extra for them.[18]

As the ups and downs of this project show, the interests of industrialists and the police do not always converge. Beyond the aforementioned officer's feeling of having been duped by his industrial partners, his resentment towards them reflects a more general feeling of exasperation in the face of repeated illegalities on the part of employers: 'Nothing is documented [in the activities of the industrialists], which considerably disturbs our investigations. And then they systematically violate labour law and fire regulations. There are also frequent cases of insurance fraud. All this has created tensions in the relationship between the police and industrialists'.[19] This is a perception shared by many police officers. A senior official of the Intelligence Bureau (IB), the intelligence service of the Interior ministry, puts it this way:

> When you don't have to follow the rules, doing business becomes easier. In theory [industrialists] are obliged to declare their activities and income, to respect the law. But how do you enforce when there is lawlessness? Nobody is going to go and check that their electrical installations are up to standard. [...] I always wonder why it's so easy to do business here. Anyone can open a factory anywhere, in a slum or anywhere. Where else in the world is it so easy to do business? One morning you decide to produce this or that product, you buy second-

hand equipment, possibly scrapped equipment. And the next day you start working. There are no restrictions... no effective restrictions at least.[20]

Industrial illegalisms are not only an attack on the authority and dignity of the police; they are also seen by some senior officers as a factor of public disorder, and thus an additional burden on a chronically overburdened institution. Whether they result from the casualization of employment or the grievances of permanent workers, labour disputes are said to pose a threat to public safety. One former Karachi police chief said:

> They [industrialists] have a lot of issues with their workers. They want to save money, so they use contract workers. But after a while, contract workers demand to be made permanent. And when they get permanent jobs, they ask [for] health insurance, pensions... So there is lot of unrest. The bosses resort to lockouts and the workers organize protest actions in the factories or outside the factory area, where the goods are being transported. So the business comes to a standstill and it becomes a police problem, though we are not responsible for it: it's between the industrialists and workers.[21]

These relationships are further complicated by the industrialists' connections in the political class, which expose overzealous officers to reprimands from their superiors, or even a transfer. For this reason, neighbourhood police officers and their superiors at district level generally tend to avoid registering a complaint against a prominent industrialist. However, some situations make it unavoidable—such as in cases of fraud between two parties of equal status, or when police officials are subject to injunctions from the judiciary. Because such situations result in contradictory pressures that are potentially costly in terms of their careers, they are feared by senior officers.[22]

As we will see later, the involvement of the police in the dirty work of employer domination can largely be explained by their structural insecurity relative to economic elites with a high level of social capital. At this stage, suffice it to say, the police institution has once again become a central actor in the maintenance of industrial order. In this respect, the tightening of the anti-terrorist arsenal has given both the police and the Rangers a free hand. In recent years, the Anti-Terrorism Act adopted by Nawaz Sharif's government in 1997 has served to silence the scattered components of a social movement no longer worthy of the name. One prime example of this empowerment of industrial capital by the security state is the case of the textile workers of Ettehad Town.

Criminalizing social struggles

Ettehad Town is one of the main centres of the garment industry in Karachi and is renowned for its spinning mills and towel factories, which are particularly lax on labour laws. Most are not even registered with the provincial authorities as required by the Factory Act. Located in residential areas, these factories are known to divert electricity from the local population by tapping into pirate power installations (known as *kunda*, or 'hook').

In protest against their deplorable working conditions, some workers at Chawla Tex Industries organized under the banner of the Al-Ettehad Power Loom Workers Union, which was duly registered with Sindh's Labour Department in January 2012. The fact that these workers have managed to organize at all is already an achievement, given that in order to avoid the tax regime affecting larger garment factories, the looms are divided between production units, each of which employs no more than a dozen people. Since the Industrial and Commercial Employment (Standing Orders) Ordinance of 1968 imposes a number of constraints (in terms of recruitment and dismissal) on companies employing more than twenty people, labour law can be circumvented.

Over the next few months, union members mobilized to register illegal factories, obtain higher wages, and ensure that medical expenses were covered for workers who suffered accidents. These actions were strongly resisted by the employers, who both resorted to dismissals and lock-outs, and used the police to intimidate unionized workers. While this crackdown may have fuelled workers' sense of being oppressed, they do not necessarily use the confrontational language of resistance in recounting their struggle. The story I was told by one of them—let's call him Gul Bahadur*—depicts people being shunted from pillar to post by a 'system' (*chakar*, lit. a circle) over which they no longer have any control.

Having spent about fifteen years employed as a machine operator in one of these sweatshops, Gul Bahadur did not hold back in his criticism of his former employer, whom he described as a 'thug' (*badmash*) and a 'tyrant' (*zalim*). Yet in the course of our discussion, he recalled with nostalgia that the same employer used to share his meal with the workers, sitting among them and treating them with 'respect and honesty' (*achha ikhlaq, hisab kitab*). Gul Bahadur also repeatedly referred to the ambivalent attitude of the security forces in the months leading up to and during the 22 March raid. But even though they had told union members that they were convinced of their innocence, and sympathized with their cause, both police and paramilitaries went on to zealously comply with orders to drag men out of bed, push women around, and ransack houses.

Having survived an activist adventure gone wrong, Gul Bahadur would rather present the initiative as a desperate gesture than cast himself as a heroic figure:

> It's only when the workers are in a bind that they decide to form a union. Why would they attack the capitalists? What can the poor do? Frankly, when they don't even have enough to buy dates [to celebrate the breaking of the fast during Ramadan], how can they fight?

Gul Bahadur refuses to reduce the battle fought by himself and his comrades to its material dimensions, and insists that they had rejected attempts by the factory owner to buy their docility: 'It was not about money. Money can't do everything (*paise ka kya karna hai*). They disrespected us. They broke down the doors of our houses'.[23]

While Gul Bahadur's testimony is always nuanced in terms of the moral judgements cast on his oppressors (which suggests that the episode might have taken quite a different course), it is nonetheless strongly influenced by the dramatic conclusion to these events. As the situation became increasingly tense, the seven Chawla Tex Industries employees were arrested, then brutally tortured by the Rangers. Following union reports that alerted the media to their 'disappearance', the suspects were handed over to the police, who, after torturing each in turn, tried (unsuccessfully) to coerce confessions of their participation in racketeering activities. Faced with this resistance, the police registered a case of extortion against twelve workers at the factory—all members of the Al-Ettehad Power Loom Workers Union. The complainant, Samiullah, was a factory manager with close ties to the owner. He was also a member of the ANP—a Pashtun nationalist party which, as we saw earlier, maintains close links with the underworld. The police report presents his version of events:

Your Honour,

I wish to inform you that on 18/03/2012, the complainant Samiullah went to the police station to lodge a complaint. Chawla Textiles Industries is a factory manufacturing towels. [...] A trade union called Ettehad Union has been formed in this factory in Ettehad Town but it has no relationship with the workers. The union's sole objective is to harm the factory so that the owners succumb to the extortion demands made by union members. On 26/01/2012, at 3:30 pm, the accused Saifur Rehman, alias Khaista, Muhammad Room, alias Shoukat, Khan Zareen, Nizamuddin Afridi and Umer Gul entered the [administration] office and found the following employees there: Habib-ur-Rehman (son of Abdullah) and Chunzeb (son of Abdul Manan). The defendants then asked the complainant to inform the owner that they would not allow the factory to operate unless the owner paid them 710,000 rupees [7,500 US dollars at the current conversion rate] every month.

After making these threats, the accused withdrew. The owner was informed by the complainant. The factories remained in operation; there are six workshops in five buildings.

On 01/02/2012, at 2pm, Nek Mohammad, alias Bachawali, Irshad, Azam, Akhtar Ali, Sanaullah, Muhammad Amin and Abdul Muhammad barged into the office and reiterated the demand for *bhatta* made on 26/01/2012. They threatened to close down the factories. The complainant informed the accused that he had already conveyed their demands to the owner and that the owner had responded by saying he would rather shift the factories than pay the exorbitant amount demanded by the accused. The defendants stated that they would oppose such a move and withdrew. Dr. Ahsan and Hayat Ali are the other witnesses to this incident. On 02/02/2012, the factories were operational. The complainant was in his office when, at about 15:30, the accused entered with firearms and closed the factory by force. The complainant was dragged out of the office and the factories were locked down. The defendants threatened him, saying that the factories would not be allowed to operate until the money was paid. At this stage, the complainant preferred not to press charges against these *goonda*s for fear of damage to the company's reputation, and instead sought the help of prominent members of the community, which led to the factories being reopened.

On 14/03/2012, at 3pm, the accused entered with firearms and forced the complainant out of the office, before seizing the account books and locking the office. The accused also threatened to kill the owner and set fire to the factory unless their demands were met. The factories have remained closed since the day the complaint was filed. They can no longer obtain supplies, the owner can no longer pay his bills and is suffering significant financial damage [...].[24]

The police officer registering the complaint invoked Section 7 of the ATA, on the grounds that the accused were suspected of extortion (*bhatta*)—an offence which (since the introduction of a series of amendments to the ATA) has been equated with a 'terrorist act' on account of its contribution to the promotion of 'civil commotion'. This charge first appeared in the Pakistan Armed Forces (Acting in Aid of Civil Power) Ordinance, 1998, which gave extensive judicial powers to the army to restore law and order in Sindh province, particularly in Karachi. This ordinance not only allowed the army to set up parallel courts in which civilians could be tried by military personnel, but also introduced the offence of 'civil commotion'—punishable by seven years' imprisonment. This offence was defined as follows:

'Civil commotion' means creation of internal disturbances in violation of law or intended to violate law, commencement or continuation of illegal strikes, go-slows, lock-outs, vehicle snatching/lifting, damage to or destruction of State or private property, random firing to create panic, charging Bhatha [*sic*], acts of criminal trespass (illegal qabza), distributing, publishing or pasting of a handbill or making graffiti or wall-chalking intended to create unrest or fear or create a threat to the security of law and order.[25]

The military tribunals project was supported by Prime Minister Nawaz Sharif, who, in 1991, introduced an amendment to the Constitution providing for the creation of special tribunals responsible for judging 'heinous crimes'. Contrary to its usual practice, the Supreme Court (which has, since the 1950s, tended to legitimize military coups) firmly opposed this project, which it described in a landmark judgement as unconstitutional (Mehram Ali & others vs. Federation of Pakistan - PLD 1998 SC 1445). This did not however prevent the offence of 'creating civil commotion' from being introduced into the anti-terrorism legislation via an amendment to the ATA. This legislation (which was amended no fewer than fifteen times in the following years) sought to respond to the intensification of Pakistan's internal conflicts with an ever-expanding definition of terrorism in which any event disruptive to the economic interests of traders and industrialists came under increasing scrutiny.

The ATA was first used against trade union activists in 2010, when thirty-five of them were charged with terrorism after organizing a strike at the Pakistan Telecommunication Company Ltd (PTCL), a telecoms operator that had been privatized a few years earlier.[26] And while the offence of 'creating civil commotion' introduced in 1999 had initially targeted workers' 'terrorist' practices as much as it did those of employers (by equating go-slow tactics with lock-outs), a new set of amendments, adopted in 2010, mentioned for the first time the protection of the 'business community', in the face of attempts at intimidation. This amendment came in response to the concerns of Karachi's business elites, who were particularly alarmed by the explosion of racketeering.

The charging of Ettehad Town's workers with terrorism was part of an urban pacification project that had economic undertones;

its aim was to prevent capital flight and (as far as possible) attract new investments to the country's economic and financial capital. Top Rangers officials readily admitted this in front of me; they had no difficulty in conceding that the so-called Karachi Operation primarily served the interests of the wealthiest fringes of Karachi's population—described by General Mohammed Saeed, Director General of the Sindh Rangers from 2016 to 2019, as the '20–25% of elite-areas people, who are culturally superior compared to the slum population.'[27]

During interviews conducted in 2016 and 2017, both General Saeed and his predecessor, General Bilal Akbar (Director General of the Sindh Rangers, 2014–2016) were keen to take credit for putting the local economy back in order, especially for the benefit of industrialists. Thus, for General Saeed:

> Many industries were moving out of Karachi. Alhamdulilah, there has been no such thing in the last few years. For the last one year and a half, 100 major industrial units have been revived. The price of real estate has increased by 300%. Construction is now booming. The industrial section is doing well. There is no more fear among the business community.[28]

The Rangers' (ultimately, the army's) leadership of the Karachi Operation went far beyond the mere neutralization of criminal groups, or even the revitalization of the local economy for the benefit of private interests. The state of disorder into which Karachi seemed to be descending in the early 2010s provided an opportunity for the paramilitaries and their military patrons to recover their ability to have a say in the country's economic policies. The army and its supporters claimed that normalizing the situation in Karachi was the first step towards stabilizing the country as a whole. And although Pakistan's macro-economic situation remained in a dire state even after a semblance of normalcy had returned to the city, the army's leadership of the Karachi Operation certainly paved the way for its return to the helm of economic affairs. Marketed as an unmitigated success by the military top brass and a complacent media, the operation served to rejuvenate the development-security equation that has structured Pakistan's economic policies ever since the country's early years—while also projecting an image of the army as the candidate most likely to deliver on this dual promise. During the following years, the army tightened its grip on economic affairs, especially after the establishment in 2023 of the Special Investment Facilitation Council (SIC)—a so-called 'hybrid civil-military forum' designed to facilitate foreign direct investment in the country, but which has in fact served to institutionalize the army's increased role in economic decision-making.[29]

For Pakistan's 'Military Inc.' (the conglomerate of business ventures formed around the country's security forces),[30] restoring order in the country's financial hub and largest seaport was also central to securing its own economic interests, at a time when massive Chinese investment was on the horizon as part of the China-Pakistan Economic Corridor (CPEC). However, as was shown by both the case of the Al-Ettehad Power Loom Workers Union and by more frontal attacks against the 'milbus' (military business), attempts by both the army and the Rangers to use anti-terrorism legislation to defend either their own economic interests or those of their protégés were met with resistance from the judiciary.[31]

Five years before the arrest of the Ettehad Town trade unionists (following the removal of Chief Justice Iftikhar Muhammad Chaudhry), General Musharraf had found himself confronted with an unprecedented revolt by Pakistani judges and lawyers. This mobilization of the legal profession left lasting traces within the judiciary, and these were manifested in particular through *suo motu* procedures and a jurisprudence that was oriented towards the defence of the fundamental rights of the population as much as towards matters of 'public importance'.[32]

The judiciary's assertiveness in the face of attempts to criminalize social struggles cannot be explained solely by the judicial activism of certain judges who, in the context of the so-called 'lawyers' movement' of 2007–2008, had often formed ties of friendship and solidarity with the country's most prominent lawyers. While this judicial activism mainly concerned the higher echelons of the judiciary (the Supreme Court and the regional High Courts), some lower-level judges (such as the District and Sessions judges) also sounded a discordant note, despite having lesser discretionary power.

This is reflected in the outcome of the trial of the Al-Ettehad Power Loom Workers Union activists. In his judgement of 29 August 2014, in which he acquitted all the accused, Judge Irfan Ahmad Meo Rajput invoked the principle of 'prudent mind' to cast doubt on the plaintiff's accusations. At the same time, he stopped short of calling into question the charge of terrorism brought against the defendants, even though the defence counsel had invited him to do so.[33] More cautiously, Judge Meo settled for pointing out the inconsistencies in the prosecution's account and the problematic profiles of the witnesses. In the end, on the basis of documents provided by the defence (starting with the union registration certificate), the judge was persuaded that the defendants had been punished for their trade union activities, and that these activities had been in the interests of the workers' welfare.

There is nothing revolutionary about this judgement. It neither takes a side in the debate over the misuses of the ATA, nor at any point mentions the role played by the Alkaram group and its owners, despite the fact that the illegal activity of these 'business tycoons' (from systematic labour law violations to corrupt practices towards law enforcement officers and witnesses) were thoroughly documented by the defence counsel. The judgement is significant precisely because of its middle-ground legal position: it shows the relative (though nonetheless significant) room for manoeuvre available to all lower-tier judges in seeking to adjudicate asymmetrical conflicts between ever-weakening progressive forces and a vast coalition of coercive actors, economic interests, and middlemen bridging these social worlds. These judges reaffirmed the autonomy of the judiciary in the face of security injunctions and the demands of development by opposing the inclusion of exceptional measures in ordinary law, rejecting the indictment of trade unionists or environmental activists for terrorism,[34] or demonstrating a procedural zeal that consigned the majority of cases brought under the ATA to failure.[35]

Yet, we must take care not to overstate the scope of these legal interventions, which have scarcely scratched the surface of structural power relations in Pakistan, and whose forms and justifications are too diverse to be collectively qualified as forms of 'resistance'. Moreover, as the legacy of the 2007–2008 lawyers' movement faded, and anti-terrorism emerged as a new hegemonic political discourse in the wake of the attack on a military school in Peshawar in December 2014, the Pakistani judiciary seemed less willing to clarify the boundaries between war and peace. And Supreme Court judges, by endorsing the creation of military tribunals to try civilians accused of terrorism, then failing to engage with the criticism of the procedural flaws attributed to these courts by many Pakistani and foreign lawyers, have actually rekindled this confusion.[36] And as emergency laws once again became the order of the day, it has become increasingly common in recent years to see terrorism charges being brought against progressive activists—some of whom are handed heavy sentences.[37]

Extrajudicial extensions of legal violence

The multi-faceted effects of the fight against terrorism are not only manifested in the judicial arena, through the criminalization of protest movements; in a more discreet way, they extend to extrajudicial violence which—in Karachi as in other conflict zones across Pakistan—is an integral part of the security forces' repressive repertoire. Indeed, since the 1960s, the use of extrajudicial violence has become routine in operations against banditry and designated terrorist groups.

Breaking the law to maintain order: this uninhibited use of public force is a legacy of the country's first military regime and its condition of nervousness. The end of Ayub Khan's reign (1958–1969) was marked by a rise in opposition, especially after the 1965 military defeat by India. These political and social tensions worried the General/President, who was convinced that he was the target of an assassination plot. In this poisonous climate, (retired) General Muhammad Musa, the newly appointed Governor of West Pakistan, launched a vast anti-crime operation in Punjab, the country's richest and most populous province.

As a former regional police chief testifies in his memoirs, the police were given carte blanche to get rid of notorious criminals. Under the mandate of General Musa (1967–1969), fake encounters (summary executions disguised as shootings) increased, and, according to the same former police official, hundreds of suspected criminals were arrested and shot in cold blood.[38] In the following decades, the use of enforced disappearances and summary executions became widespread among the police and paramilitary forces deployed throughout the country to defeat separatist and Islamist movements.[39]

In Karachi, law enforcement agencies made extensive use of these extrajudicial methods against MQM militants during the 1990s and, more recently, against members of the Pashtun Mehsud tribe, whose members were suspected of supporting the Pakistani Taliban.[40] With the COVID-19 pandemic and the resurgence of worker mobilizations against unfair dismissal and other employer illegalisms, these extrajudicial practices have been extended from counter-insurgency to the containment of social struggles.

In September 2020, lawyer Mohib Azad, a founding member of the Sindh Sujagi Mazdur Federation (Workers' Federation for the Rebirth of Sindh), was arrested and illegally detained for thirty-seven days for defending the 'disappeared' of his village, most of whom were industrial workers and farmers suspected of sympathizing with Sindhi nationalists.[41] Another member of the group, human rights activist Sarang Joyo, was also arrested illegally and held incommunicado for seven days. During his detention, his jailers accused him of defaming the country and dividing workers along ethnic lines. Their efforts to intimidate him included threatening to eliminate him in the course of an 'encounter'.[42] In April 2021, a third member of the group, Yaseen Jhulan, was arrested while participating in a demonstration against the illegal practices of the Korangi-based Denim Clothing Company. The police accused him of destabilizing the national economy by defaming local businesses in an attempt to encourage their foreign customers to turn to India and Bangladesh—historical adversaries now turned economic competitors.[43]

No doubt the profile of these activists explains the vindictiveness of law enforcement agencies. While members of the Sindh Sujagi Mazdur Federation are at pains to stress their commitment to the working class across all communities, they are, by their own admission, 'nationalists' (*qawm parast*) defending indigenous Sindhis.[44] Since Sindhi nationalism has long had a troubled relationship with the central Pakistani state and has consistently denounced its oppression, this knowledge is essential to understanding the said episode of state repression.[45] The organization's mobilization around the issue of enforced disappearances has served to fuel intelligence and police hostility towards its activists, who have learned to expect a police raid on the eve of each of their gatherings.[3]

The resurgence of armed Sindhi groups, which have stepped up attacks in Karachi in recent years, makes it all the easier to equate these activists with terrorists. However, the group's ideological allegiance alone cannot explain the sheer relentlessness of the police response; it is also meeting a demand that is coming from certain companies. In particular, the management of the Denim Clothing Company is behind a series of repressive actions taken against the organization's activists.

Founded in 2005 and attached to the Machiyara family conglomerate, this company employs 8,500 people at four production units, all of which are based in the Korangi industrial zone.[46] Producing jeans for major international brands (H&M, C&A, Zara, Mango, Walmart, etc.), the company is very image-conscious and boasts of its ethical and environmental commitments, and its state-of-the-art equipment.[47] By contrast, the workers interviewed describe a stifling work environment in which human resources management has been entrusted to former army officers who rely on brutal and unruly thugs to enforce their concept of factory discipline.[48] These hardened criminals (reputedly rapists and murderers) are said to have made the factory their 'den' (adda), in which they would indulge in the worst debaucheries. Workers also accused some managers of orchestrating a vast traffic in hashish within the workshops, thus, in the words of one young machine operator, turning the whole company into a 'mafia'.

Moral considerations and professional grievances, as well as fiction and reality, are inextricably intertwined here. One worker who had been particularly vocal about the misdeeds of his employers and their henchmen self-identified with the captives in *K.G.F.*—a recent Indian blockbuster in which a ruthless gang, adept at human sacrifice, uses kidnap victims as slaves in a gold mine. By framing their social critique around local anti-mafia tropes and references to popular cinema, these workers have managed to transform their professional grievances into an inspiring struggle for justice and morality, while at the same time turning the accusation of gangsterism against their employers: the real thugs here are the factory owners, who have corrupted the workplace by striking deals with the forces of disorder.

Such collusions do occasionally come to light. In April 2021, Faiza,* a seamstress in her thirties, was beaten with an anti-theft chain after demanding payment of the annual bonus traditionally allocated to their employees by the more profitable companies. Among her attackers, she recognized several bullies recently recruited by her employer. After their crime, the thugs continued to wander around the workshops without hindrance.[49] Yet the company's repressive tactics do not, by any stretch of the imagination, stop at beatings like this one. Troublemakers are also exposed to both criminal prosecution and the summary justice of the police.

As was demonstrated in 2021 by the dismantling of a group of so-called 'agitators' within the company, the line between legal and extra-legal action in these corporate policing operations is becoming blurred. Arshad Khashkheli,* a fellow member of the Sindh Sujagi Mazdur Federation, had been a machine operator at Denim Clothing for several years. During this time he and a group of friends had constantly demanded improvements to working conditions and denounced the drug trafficking in which some managers were allegedly involved. These activities brought him and his colleagues to the attention of Colonel Waheed,* head of security—and they soon found themselves under police scrutiny. Several of Arshad's colleagues were silenced after having their national identity cards confiscated by police, returned to them only in exchange for a letter of resignation.

After several months of strained relations with his hierarchical superiors, Arshad was himself subjected to intimidation. He recounts being stopped by armed thugs (employed by Colonel Waheed) and having his mobile phone confiscated before being handcuffed and transferred to another production unit, where he was placed in solitary confinement. For Arshad, this experience felt more like a typical forced disappearance scenario than a mock arrest. His captors did release him after a few hours, though not before claiming to have struck a deal with the army intelligence services and threatening to make him secretly disappear if he challenged his dismissal from employment in court.[50] As confirmed by several corroborating testimonies, the trivialization of such threats shows that the culture of terror fostered by anti-terrorism has penetrated even the most innocuous labour disputes.[51]

The use of legal tools alongside threats of extrajudicial violence can give rise to its own set of arbitrary practices. Shortly after Arshad's abduction by Colonel Waheed's thugs, his cousin Sajid* discovered that a police report had been filed against him. In it, he was accused—along with another Denim Clothing employee and four 'unidentified persons'—of having ambushed a company director as he left the factory. These 'assailants' were reported to have used their motorbikes to block the director's path as he returned home with two other executives, including the group's 'Admin', who filed the complaint.[52] According to the director, Sajid had beaten up the passengers in the vehicle and drawn a pistol before being scared off by the arrival of armed company guards—an account staunchly denied by the main defendant, who claimed that the accusations were fabricated.[53]

First Information Reports are more than mere coercive instruments designed to push outspoken workers out. As Sajid points out, the filing of such reports serves to both 'ruin the reputation' and 'destroy the life' of any worker who dares challenge corporate order by depriving them of future employment prospects; such stigma will not escape the attention of a meticulous recruiter. By keeping the identity of suspects unclear, the police also afford themselves the opportunity to put pressure on their target by striking those close to them. The 'unidentified persons' mentioned in FIRs may be a brother or cousin, who will be arrested as a way of forcing the targeted individual to surrender or comply. The legal costs involved in these proceedings are both an additional punishment and a gag order. Sajid was forced to go into debt to escape arrest (by paying pre-arrest bail), and then to free his younger brother, who had been taken hostage by the police.

When such targeted pressure proves inadequate (for example, in the case of collective mobilizations), the police presence in and around factories is increased. Often, the presence of police vehicles on company premises is enough to deter protesters. However, footage shot in 2021 by Denim Clothing workers shows police officers charging and beating workers inside one of the group's factories, proving that police sometimes intervene both directly, and brutally, on production sites.[54]

The workers interviewed believe that police loyalty towards the *malik*s (owners) is bought through bribes. Sajid is absolutely convinced that the management of Denim Clothing pays a million rupees a month to the two main police stations in the neighbourhood. Such accusations are unverifiable and, other than the occasional air-conditioning unit installed at the neighbourhood station, police officials are generally reluctant to discuss 'gifts' received from industrialists. When asked about his relationship with local employers, one senior police officer based in Korangi downplayed the material dimension of this relationship, preferring to stress the structural vulnerability of the police to the demands of the ruling classes. To politicians, these industrialists (who contribute to both the state coffers and export revenues) are 'blue-eyed boys', and very little can be denied them. By dint of scarce resources, police are also encouraged to delegate ordinary policing tasks to the private security providers hired by companies. Police interventions can then be limited (often at the request of the manufacturers themselves) to major incidents of unrest in factories or on public roads.[55] Cautious as this analysis is, it is probably not completely out of touch with reality, and does confirm the confusion that has developed in Karachi's industrial zones between the defence of corporate interests and the maintenance of public order—to the benefit of the former.

* * *

Karachi's urban conflicts have fostered discreet arrangements between industrialists and a vast array of specialists in coercion, particularly in the field of factory policing. The existence of such a plethora of coercive services is the embarrassing (though potentially fruitful) legacy of decades of political and criminal violence. While

ANTI-TERRORISM TO THE RESCUE

such deregulation of the market of protection tends to empower private enforcers, state authorities are not passive observers of these discreet repressions.

In his study of a Guatemalan *maquila* where employer domination has been reproduced through the everyday violence of street gangs, Quentin Delpech shows how the response of state authorities can be decisive in its effects on both the form and intensity of trade union repression.[56] In Karachi, this response developed through regular (more or less formalized) contacts between business and security actors. The public events that often bring the heads of the army and the police together with representatives of the 'business community' constitute only the most formal (and most publicized) aspect of these exchanges. Interdependencies between law enforcement agencies and business elites have also been strengthened in recent years through private security agencies that allow industrialists to draw on public security: a logic which confirms that among Pakistani economic elites, access to the state continues to be perceived as a powerful multiplier of wealth.

State arbitration in labour disputes is also negotiated through personalized relationships between certain industrialists and law enforcement professionals (senior army officers or senior police officers, approached via the school, family, or social network), as well as through the mediation of retired military personnel who now manage security or (more rarely) human resources in large industrial companies. In the event of labour conflicts, the relational network of these retired soldiers is brought into play. Both the workers who try to organize and the union activists who support them are thus exposed to the vindictiveness of the police and the paramilitaries. This is a threat that has only intensified since the launch of the Karachi Operation in 2013.

The repression of social struggles has been fuelled by anti-terrorism. In Pakistan as elsewhere, this repressive repertoire is conducive to role confusion and has many different effects; without necessarily having been intended for this purpose by its designers, it easily lends itself to anti-union ends. While this tendency is evident in the Pakistani case, similar observations have been made about Colombia, Sri Lanka, and Algeria.[57] In August 2023, after they demanded wage increases, six trade union activists were convicted of conspiracy and criminal association, and subsequently sentenced to 16 years in prison in Venezuela. This trend is not limited to the Global South. For example, in France, anti-terrorism laws and units are increasingly being deployed against trade unionists and other activists.[58]

As the fight against terrorism has played out on a global scale since the end of the Cold War, interventions framed by law have also extended to extrajudicial practices of intimidation and repression.[59] Across Pakistan, such practices have become routine in the course of 'clean-up' campaigns against criminal gangs, nationalist movements, and jihadi groups. In Karachi, where summary executions and enforced disappearances (or at least the threat of them) now figure prominently in the repressive arsenal of those enforcing industrial order, the genealogy of these extrajudicial practices is more than just a history of state terror. Far from being reduced to the excesses of an unbridled security apparatus engaged in mimetic rivalry with its adversaries,[60] these extrajudicial acts of violence are also the result of a public-private partnership. This is demonstrated by the latest aspect of local industrialists' defence policy, which involves mobilizing the instruments of so-called 'citizen' security in the service of capital.

7

COMMITTED CITIZENS OR
CORPORATE VIGILANTES?

*You know, our justice system doesn't work. If you arrest them [the
kidnappers], you're going to have them on your hands. And the
judicial process is such a mess. I'm not in favour of extrajudicial
killings. But... [laughs].*

Ali Shah,* SITE factory owner and
former senior CPLC official (2016).[1]

The Citizens-Police Liaison Committee (CPLC) is an anti-crime
organization funded and run by Karachi's business community. As
part of an investigation into it, in July 2017 I visited Amir Jalal,*
who oversees the organization's activities in the Korangi industrial
area. Over the previous weeks, I had made a habit of dropping
by to greet this small, outspoken entrepreneur whenever I was
in the neighbourhood. Sometimes, long conversations ensued—
occasionally interrupted by the arrival of other visitors.

On that day, one such visitor really caught my eye. He was living in
one of Korangi's few residential areas, and a conversation that began
with him complaining about persistent insecurity in the locality led
to him asking about how to go about launching a Neighbourhood
Care project. Amir Jalal explained the broad outlines of these security

arrangements to him. Using a well-oiled argument, he insisted on the CPLC's commitment to installing barriers at the neighbourhood's various access points. Assuming that his interlocutor would be aware of the current regulations applicable to these structures (i.e. their illegality), he was at pains to reassure him that this security plan had the approval of the Rangers—implying in so doing that the paramilitaries were allowing the CPLC (and its protégés) to circumvent the law for the sake of the security of 'honest citizens'.

The visitor looked interested, but had obviously been mandated to cut costs. He found the monthly salary (about 120 dollars) for CPLC-certified guards excessive, and asked about whether owners could hire security guards independently. Amir Jalal replied in the affirmative, but warned him that if such a guard were to injure or kill a suspect, complications with the police were to be expected. Using a private security company certified by the CPLC, explained Amir Jalal, was insurance in case of an incident.

Probably for financial reasons, Amir Jalal's offer was declined by the visitor—despite its attractiveness. After all, what was on offer to 'honest citizens' willing to pay for security was a free pass on the use of force. The CPLC was originally mandated to bridge the gap between the police and the citizens of Karachi as a whole—but has it now morphed into a private police force for the benefit of the 'haves'? Or even into a provider of rough justice? Beyond its innovations in the field of citizen security, to what extent has this industrialist-founded and -driven organization been part of a larger urban transformation project?

In response to these questions, this chapter will track the successive mutations of this 'twilight institution' whose authority is deployed not only at the interface of the public and the private, but also at that of the legal and the extra-legal, both imitating and opposing the state in one fell swoop.[2]

My concerns here are in line with those of the sociologists and anthropologists of policing, who are attentive both to the pluralization of police functions and to the rise, over the past few decades, of security mobilizations led by citizen groups acting in collaboration with law enforcement agencies (or at their margins).[3] The CPLC's involvement in securing Karachi (both in partnership *with* and as a substitute *for* the police) has also led me to engage with the literature on contemporary urban pacification. The CPLC's recent initiatives in the field of industrial security echo this literature and confirm that these dynamics of 'pacification', far from being the sole responsibility of the state, involve a multitude of competing authorities around a single issue: the management of urban margins, understood in the sense of populations as well as territories kept at bay from the rest of the city.[4]

Blurring the boundaries of war and peace, this programme of pacification is not only manifested through demonstrations of force that take the shape of more or less militarized police operations. As theorists of the 'new military urbanism' have shown, it also extends to spatial and architectural transformations—an insidious militarization of urban life, the effects of which are felt far beyond the zones of open conflict and the peaks of tension generated by police or military operations.[5] In its preoccupation with the malignant circulations (of people, goods, or germs) deemed to originate in the urban margins, this project meant to keep cities under control returns to the founding principles of modern security, claiming to tame flows and isolate those deemed harmful, while multiplying others.[6] More novel is the way in which this project replaces a regime of universal rights with citizenship by permit, reserved for the most honest and deserving.[7]

This emerging body of work finds particular resonance in Karachi, whose landscape and habitat have been profoundly reshaped in recent decades both by the security forces' 'clean-up operations' and by the population's collective self-defence strategies.[8] These transformations are manifested in particular in the dynamics of residential clustering—which primarily concern economic elites but also affect some lower-income communities determined to ensure their own security.[9] On the other hand, the new forms of control that have appeared in recent years in the territories reserved for industrial activity remain neglected by researchers. This omission is not specific to Karachi: from the pioneering work of Mike Davis on Los Angeles to that of Teresa Caldeira on São Paulo, the securitization of contemporary metropolises has thus far been studied mainly through the prism of the enclosure dynamics that

are specific to residential neighbourhoods and the places where the
upper classes work and relax.[10]

This chapter also intends to contribute to the ongoing debate
about the transformation of urban citizenship under a regime of
securitization that is conducive to ever-greater interdependencies
between capital and coercion, but it does so from a contested space
of production and circulation. By focusing on corporate uses of the
information and know-how acquired by the CPLC in the context of
citizen participation in policing, I also aim to prolong the discussion
about the productive effects of urban disorder for Karachi's industrial
capitalism and its modes of control.

*'Let's beat crime together': when businessmen come to the rescue of the
police*

The Citizens-Police Liaison Committee (CPLC) was formed in 1990,
following a reception held in honour of Sindh Governor Fakhruddin
Ebrahim by a group of industrialists, editorialists, and philanthropists
concerned about the deteriorating security situation in Karachi and
its economic fallout. Among these self-described 'engaged citizens',
the historical merchant groups were over-represented. Maher Alvi,
for instance, was a businessman and philanthropist from an old Bohra
family (his grandfather, Hatim Ali Alvi, had been the first Muslim
mayor of Karachi in 1938–1939).[11] Nazim Haji and Majyd Aziz also
hailed from merchant communities tracing their roots to Gujarat.
Another founding member of the CPLC, Ardeshir Cowasjee,
belonged to a family of Parsi ship-owners.

Over the years, this relative sociological diversity has given way
to greater uniformity—at least in terms of professional identity. In
1995, all 50 statutory members of the CPLC were industrialists or
businessmen.[12] While the CPLC's first leader, Nazim Haji, owned a
plastic box factory based in SITE (and was simultaneously President
of the SITE Association of Trade and Industry), his right-hand man,
Jameel Yusuf (who belonged to the Khoja community), ran a small
textile company in the same industrial area.

Under the patronage of the Governor of Sindh (who offered
to host the organization in his office) the CPLC was tasked with

addressing the grievances of 'ordinary citizens' lamenting law enforcement apathy, arbitrariness, and corruption. Because the CPLC had the ability to write its own FIRs, police discretion in this area was significantly limited—police officers tend to refuse to register a complaint in situations where the respondent has political protections or the complainant belongs to a disadvantaged group. In addition to these police powers, the CPLC has developed widely recognized expertise in the field of preventing kidnapping and vehicle theft.

This recognition can be attributed to intensive data collection in close cooperation with the police: the CPLC continues to manage the largest criminal database in the city, which was extracted from FIRs written by the police since 1987. Containing more than a million names, it can be consulted by law enforcement agencies and, under certain conditions, by private individuals—mainly the administrative and security managers of private firms, who wish to check that new recruits do not have a criminal background. These files are updated on the basis of police reports sent to the District Reporting Cell (DRC) of the CPLC in each district, housed in the offices of the local Superintendent of Police (SP). FIRs are often handwritten, but their main content (including the names of suspects and the nature of the facts alleged) is extracted and digitized at each DRC before being transmitted to the organization's central office.

This database is complemented by a series of datasets, including information on unidentified bodies deposited in the Edhi Foundation morgue since the 1990s, a record of all vehicles and mobile phones stolen across the city during the same period, and above all, records of all prisoners having passed through Karachi's prisons since 2009, along with their fingerprints and identifying photographs. This last file forms the backbone of the CPLC's most recent projects for both the general public and industry.

Much of this data comes from police sources. Nonetheless, its digitization, compilation, and archiving has endowed the CPLC with unique 'information capital'.[13] The fact that the Sindh police have only been digitizing criminal records since 2015 means that the CPLC has a significant advantage in this area. Over and above these resources, it is the fact that CPLC staff are able to decipher and serialize this information that earns them expert status among law enforcement professionals. What other actors in the security sector (police officers, Rangers, military personnel, and corporate security officials) are acknowledging in according CPLC staff this expert status is the value of the CPLC's explanatory and predictive models—a variant of the 'coding systems' that constitute a primary attribute of police organizations.[14]

Recognition of this expertise is materialized in the frequent participation of CPLC staff in law enforcement agency raids on criminal gangs. Prior to these operations, police officers often consult the CPLC databases, using them in collaboration with CPLC staff. It is also commonplace for some of these staff to be present alongside police intervention teams during raids on gangs of kidnappers, burglars, or car thieves.[15]

The CPLC trade-off between mobility and security

Coupled with the spatial crime analysis tools developed by its members during the 1990s, the CPLC's informational capital has enabled it to reintroduce legibility to an urban landscape disfigured by violence, by combining the authority of statistics with cartographic reason. CPLC maps and graphs, massively disseminated within the police and the media, have both framed representations of urban disorder and designated certain neighbourhoods and communities as threats to the city's political and economic integrity.[16] I have already discussed this aspect of the organization's work and its contribution to a form of policing that amounts to risk management.[17] Here, I focus on how the resources and skills accumulated by CPLC members in their fight against crime are being redeployed to defend industrial order.

Knowledge for action: the formation of expertise in geocriminology within the CPLC

Rashid Memon* is a resident of the Defence Housing Authority (DHA)—a very high-end, upmarket area of southern Karachi—and the owner of a bed linen company based in SITE. He is also Director of the SITE Association of Trade and Industry's security department, and it was to meet him in this capacity that I first visited his factory in July 2016.

Due to traffic jams on the congested roads leading to SITE, and the dilapidated road infrastructure within the industrial zone, I found myself significantly delayed. This provided the young *seth* with an opportunity to express his anguish over commuting routines:

> As you can see, the road you came along is very much poor and you will see water falling here and there everywhere, the *nalas* [open sewers] are not clean. It needs to be improved because crime is directly related to infrastructure. Whenever your car gets stuck anywhere, two men on a bike come and they will snatch you. The same goes for traffic flows: if you go from SITE to Defence, or any other area in the city, around 6 to 7 PM, you will [get] stuck in the traffic, and when you get stuck in the traffic, they come and they snatch you.[18]

Rashid Memon's case is far from isolated. The owners and managers of industrial firms tend to live in Karachi's high-end southern neighbourhoods (Clifton, DHA) and thus have long daily commutes to and from work. These journeys take them through working-class neighbourhoods reputed for their political and criminal violence. This experience of commuting goes a long way to explaining the sense of insecurity that has developed among Karachi's industrialists since the late 1980s. Their sense of vulnerability is rooted in a worrisome 'phenomenology of density': a cognitive and sensory engagement with the chaotic and congested space of the city, where the regulatory pretensions of urban planning are constantly subverted by the interventions of the multitude.[19]

This sense of being ill at ease while travelling is exacerbated by the malignant forces supposedly lurking in the informal settlements (*katchi abadi*s) along or through which industrialists must pass on their way to and from work.[20] Widely considered 'no-go areas', these urban margins are thought to provide sanctuary for thieves, racketeers, kidnappers, and other forces menacing life and property—as well as industrial order more broadly.

Convinced that the state has abandoned them to their fate, these fearful commuters have drawn on the resources and expertise of the CPLC to ensure the safe movement of people and goods. The organization's expertise in geocriminology was developed in the late 1990s through a cooperative agreement with the United Nations Development Programme (UNDP). The technologies resulting from this international collaboration have since spread to the police, but it is in the industrial sector that they have had the most notable influence. Promoted by business leaders like Rashid Memon (who became familiar with security technologies through his involvement with the CPLC), these tools initially helped industrialists bring legibility to a chaotic urban landscape. Later on, these tools for the study and prevention of crime provided the blueprint for new security architecture in industrial areas, enabling factory owners to act on their troubled environment. This security scheme thus became part of a larger social control project that (echoing other contemporary urban pacification programmes) merged economic and military objectives into the taming of urban margins.[21]

From hot-spot policing to military-industrial zones

The involvement of Karachi's business community in securing industrial zones is not a new idea; indeed, such participation was first discussed between police officials and employer representatives as far back as the early 1970s. In January 1970, the Deputy Inspector General (DIG) in charge of security at SITE organized a meeting to inform the industry that too few personnel and resources were being allocated to 'watch and ward' tasks in the area. Noting the inadequacy of government funds likely to be earmarked for additional staff, the DIG appealed to the generosity of industrialists and, without waiting for their formal agreement, issued a statement acknowledging their financial participation. This statement resulted in consternation, then anger, within the employer community. Hashim B. Sayeed, President of the Manghopir Association of Trade and Industry (the predecessor of the SITE Association of Trade and Industry), contradicted the DIG's claim, stating that meeting participants had categorically refused to help fund law enforcement operations in the area. SITE industrialists preferred to commit themselves to funding charity work in the surrounding working-class localities.[22]

However, these positions changed as a result of the rise in crime in SITE from the late 1980s onwards; as attacks on property and people increased against a backdrop of partisan rivalries and inter-communal clashes, self-defence found more and more support in business circles. In 1995, Siraj Kassam Teli, heir to a large Memon family and a leading figure in local business circles, lamented in an interview with *The Herald* magazine that industrialists were constrained by Section 144 of the Criminal Procedure Code, which prohibits the carrying of weapons in public.[23] Over the following decades, the easing of these restrictions led to spectacular development of the private security market.

In addition to these individual investments in self-defence, the CPLC was, for a number of industrialists, both a rallying point and a training ground. As we have seen above, the initial mobilization carried out by the CPLC primarily concerned SME owners hailing from the historical merchant groups, though rarely those from the most prominent families.

The sociology of this organization likens it to other corporate mobilizations for security that, rather than simply putting forward a 'demand for police',[24] develop their own solutions to the problem of crime. In contrast to more plebeian forms of rough justice, these mobilizations are led by entrepreneurs in possession of a high level of economic and social capital. This is reflected in their bureaucratization and use of more or less sophisticated statistical, graphic, and IT tools.

As a laboratory for 'anti-crime social movements', Latin America has seen a proliferation of collective business interventions in the security field in recent years.[25] In Peru, artisans, shopkeepers, and small businessmen have set up urban patrols to maintain order in markets and 're-educate' thieves and prostitutes by whipping.[26] In Mexico, the business community has responded to the rise in kidnappings (of which its members were the main victims) by joining forces with law enforcement agencies against kidnapping gangs. Some entrepreneurs involved in these operations—such as the Minerva 1997 collective in Guadalajara, whose members use phone taps—operate on the very edge of legality, while other initiatives are more in tune with the original model of citizen participation in policing that was developed by the CPLC in the early 1990s.[27]

One example of this is the Centro de Integración Ciudadana (CIC) in Monterrey. Launched in 2011 by the CEO of cement multinational Cemex, this is a platform that allows people to report offences, accidents, or poor urban services online, with the option of anonymity. The information reported is then passed on to the relevant authorities, on the assumption that ordinary citizens' requests are more likely to succeed when they have the support of the economic elites (which tends to be confirmed by the clearance rate of crimes reported via the platform[28]). The information transmitted to the CIC is geo-located and automatically inserted into cartographic representations that are accessible via a mobile phone application.[29] However, the CPLC's gradual evolution towards the provision of security and surveillance services to industry contrasts with this view of citizen participation in policing, where industry merely mediates between ordinary citizens and public authorities.

Despite the over-representation of industrialists in the CPLC, it was not until the 2010s that they explicitly mobilized for the protection of their property and people. For the young *seth* Rashid Memon, the increase in kidnappings and the proliferation of racketeering convinced the members of the SITE employers' association to 'develop their own security system, in parallel with the protection provided by the police and the Rangers'. This pro-security project feeds on a geography of fear, focusing on the neighbourhoods in which factory workers are being recruited. Collectively assimilated to the repulsive category of *katchi abadi*s (squatter settlements)— even though a large proportion of them were legalized in the early 1970s—these neighbourhoods are perceived as lawless areas in which terrorists and criminals can find refuge without fear of being questioned.

The geographical distribution of working-class neighbourhoods on the outskirts of SITE feeds a siege mentality among the area's industrialists, convinced that they are surrounded by a ring of 'no-go areas' rife with plots against industrial order and the owning class. This fear of crime extends to private occupations of public space within the industrial zone itself. This 'quiet encroachment of the ordinary' (to borrow Asif Bayat's expression in reference to the tactics of working-class urban resistance in the cities of the Global South)[30] covers illegal dumping sites as well as small roadside shops and workers' canteens that encroach onto the main roads (*chappra hotels*). These encroachments are seen as threats to industrial order and the security of corporate actors, since in SITE (as in Korangi), these small businesses are considered a vantage point for the informants of racketeers and kidnappers who monitor the movements of factory owners and their managers.

In the eyes of industrialists, these encroachments are a concentrate of the disorder, defilement, and dangers associated with the working classes—as evidenced by this post by Majyd Aziz, an ex-member of the CPLC and former president of the SITE Association, published in one of the city's leading English-language daily newspapers in 2013:

> SITE is blatantly encroached on by whoever pays the piper. Makeshift huts are found on every corner: these shops sell food, betel leaves, oil, and just about everything else. Even the drains are encroached. Janitorial staff is seldom seen in the area. The whole estate is filled with unpicked garbage that, at times, spills over onto the roads and lanes. Political slogans, threats from ethno-religious political elements, remedies for male impotence and haemorrhoids and advertisements for educational institutions can be found sprayed rudely on nearly every wall in the area: even obelisks, billboards and curb stones have not been spared by aspiring graffiti artists.
>
> Things become all the more difficult and frustrating when petty criminals start staking out the dilapidated roads to hunt the vehicles which slow down. They snatch cell phones and wallets conveniently, confidently and shamelessly.[31]

To eradicate the threat of these encroachments, the SITE Association (like its counterpart in Korangi) ordered the systematic demolition of *chappra hotels*—food stalls that, given the absence of proper canteen facilities at many factories, used to provide cheap meals to workers. The security project led by Rashid Memon extended this sanitation work by proposing to create a sanitary cordon between the industrial zone and the surrounding working-class neighbourhoods. This task was complicated both by the daily circulation of the working-class population and by the entanglement of the productive space with the surrounding 'labour colonies'.

As a statutory member of the CPLC, whose operations he oversaw within the Western District of Karachi, Rashid Memon approached the organization in 2013 with a view to preparing a series of street crime maps in and around SITE. These maps would serve two purposes: in addition to providing SITE's industrialists with a full picture of the public problem of insecurity (which would help raise funds in the future), they would identify priority areas for intervention (as a way of rationalizing expenditure).

The technical aspects of the project were supervised by the head of the CPLC IT department. Heir to a family of Gujarati industrialists, Umar Shah* heads up an export-oriented food gum company that is associated with an American firm. This strong international outlook has encouraged Umar Shah to regularly update not only his company's operating and control systems, but also his own knowledge. To that end, he trained as a programmer, which sparked a lifelong interest in open-source software. To meet the food safety requirements of his American partners and foreign customers, he also learned about risk management. Although these skills were initially developed to improve the performance and competitiveness of his company on the international market, they went on to shape his approach to the fight against crime.

Within the CPLC, then, Umar Shah has championed a risk management approach to security that rests on a belief that uncertainty can be tamed if it is organized into quantifiable risks.[32] Early leaders of the CPLC had prided themselves on being self-taught security experts, drawing inspiration from crime novels and films, but Umar Shah advocates continuous upgrading. Using the open-source software model he is so fond of, he sees his knowledge as a programme in need of frequent updates. And while this requirement undoubtedly owes much to his corporate responsibilities, his involvement in the CPLC has enabled him to acquire new technical skills. It was through a collaboration with South African specialists posted to the CPLC by the UNDP and supervised by Roman

Pryjomko (a former British police officer turned geocriminologist) that Umar Shah became familiar with GIS software.[33] A few years later, these were the skills he was able to put to use for the security of SITE's industrial companies.[34]

The first contribution made by this computer enthusiast to SITE security was the production of 'knowledge maps' showing the distribution of crime in each police jurisdiction. This descriptive work identified hotspots—a prerequisite for the production of more tactical maps—which went beyond description to formulate a response to the problem of insecurity by allocating resources via a situational prevention logic.[35] Using these maps, Rashid Memon and successive presidents of the SITE Association sought to convince local employers that they should help finance an ambitious security system comprising three elements: fortifications, video surveillance, and motorized patrols.

The cost of the operation was relatively high, in part because its designers planned to use the services of the Rangers Security Guards (RSGs). Newcomers to a highly competitive security market, the RSGs had quickly built up a prestigious clientele that was attracted by their proximity to the Rangers and access to certain paramilitary resources—be these logistical (second-hand vehicles and weapons), informational (military intelligence), or human (most RSG recruits have served in the Rangers or the army).[36] In contracting the services of the RSGs, their clients were attracted not only by the reputational capital of these 'private' security agents, but also by the privileged access they granted to the Rangers themselves—a guarantee of resources and impunity in the event of complications related to the use of force by guards.

In 2014, having managed to build a consensus among its members by playing on the local industrialists' sense of insecurity (itself fuelled by CPLC maps), the SITE Association set out to give shape to the 'SITE Self-Security System'—better known as the 'Double S, Double S'. Plans for this security system were designed by the CPLC on the basis of tactical maps prepared the previous year. These plans included: the construction of 19 perimeter walls separating the industrial area from the working-class neighbourhoods reputed to be most 'sensitive'; the opening of 40 checkpoints (*chowkis*) guarded by the RSGs, and the installation of 143 cameras (covering about 40% of the total SITE area). These cameras were funded by the Governor of Sindh, the historical patron of the CPLC, which has accommodated the CPLC offices in Governor House since the 1990s. The control room for this video surveillance system is located in the SITE Association office, yet those monitoring the screens for any incidents are Rangers personnel. The job is not without difficulty, as the cameras regularly break down because of the faulty power supply.[37]

Far from being part of a process of privatization of the state, the 'Double S, Double S' is emblematic of contemporary security assemblages in which agents, components, and logics of action become entangled—despite the fact that they belong to seemingly distinct social worlds.[38] And in this 'mixed economy of protection',[39] the state—or at least its security apparatus—retains a central role. Via the mediation of the Rangers' security company, the intention of those within the SITE Association responsible for designing the project was to consolidate a privileged relationship with the most powerful force in Karachi.

For the Rangers, these investments both offered employment prospects for their veterans and provided access to new surveillance tools, while outsourcing their cost to the private sector and civilian authorities. In addition, as we will see below, the increased involvement of paramilitaries in industrial security has granted them a say in the management of manufacturing companies—particularly in terms of recruitment policies.

Controlling worker mobility for industrial security

This coercive architecture simultaneously mobilizes the resources of the state, the private sector, and a myriad of security actors of hybrid status (employers turned security experts, violent entrepreneurs at the interface of public force and private security).

This architecture is partaking in a form of 'power over movement' in its bid to decide who goes where, and at what pace.[40] Employer domination is thus re-enacted on the asphalt, via the production of a mobility differential. In order to restrict the right to freedom of

A Rangers Security Guards checkpoint at the 'border' between SITE industrial area and the Bawani Chali working-class neighbourhood.

L. Gayer, 2017

movement to honest citizens, the 'Double S, Double S' modulated the movement of the dangerous classes by controlling its speed. This production of inertia primarily targets the dreaded figure of the motorized robber who appears unexpectedly then disappears into the flow of traffic or the labyrinth of working-class districts. The turnstiles installed at each gate to filter comings and goings between SITE and neighbouring labour colonies are aimed more broadly at young people on motorbikes, whose stealth feeds the anxiety of factory owners.

By attempting to regulate the flow of traffic, Karachi's industrialists have seized upon a tried-and-tested repertoire of public action and authority. Ever since Bushra Zaidi's death in a traffic accident in 1985,[41] urban conflicts have most commonly been sparked by disagreements as to who was in charge of roads and traffic.[42] Yet the intervention of industrialists in such vehicular politics is in response to specific concerns; it is an attempt at resolving a dilemma that is as old as industrial capitalism itself—because if 'to produce is to move', as John Stuart Mill's famous formula had it, then 'the liberation of flows cannot take place without the counterweight of the principle of security'.[43] The removal of barriers to the movement of people and goods opens up new opportunities—but also gives rise to new perils, particularly in terms of health and crime risks. For security, in the modern sense of the term, it thus becomes a question of 'maximizing the positive elements, for which one provides the best possible circulation, and of minimizing what is risky and inconvenient, like theft and disease, while knowing that they will never be completely suppressed'.[44]

City planning, as the primary object of this science of traffic, is devoted to the organization of multifunctional elements. As Michel Foucault asks, 'What is a good street?'. From the perspective of security,

> A good street is one in which there is, of course, a circulation of what are called miasmas, and so diseases, and the street will have to be managed according to this necessary, although hardly desirable role. Merchandise will be taken down the street, in which there will also be shops. Thieves and possibly rioters will also be able to move down the street. Therefore all these different functions of the town, some positive and others negative, will have to be built into the plan.[45]

Such dilemmas resurface in the regulatory 'Double S, Double S' project, which aims to grapple with the street's multi-functionality as both an essential economic infrastructure for the smooth running of industry and a vector of disturbances that threaten the productive order. Having relied on probabilistic reasoning, cartographic representations, and cost calculations to constitute street crime as a manageable phenomenon, this security system then demanded difficult trade-offs between the controlled production of inertia and the maximization of urban vitality. SITE's industrialists agreed to sacrifice some of their mobility for their own safety by, for example, declaring a curfew for heavy goods vehicles across the entire area. However, the designers of the 'Double S, Double S' project were forced to adjust the original plan to accommodate certain traffic requirements. As Rashid Memon explains, the construction of walls and checkpoints at certain identified hotspots had to be abandoned, to avoid interfering too much with the flow of goods through the industrial estate: 'Heavy goods vehicles used to pass through there regularly and we didn't want to disrupt the traffic, it's important for the industries'.[46]

This concern with avoiding traffic disruption is, to say the least, somewhat selective. It concerns only the flow of goods, for the sake of protecting supply chains. Yet this security system is much less respectful of the freedom of movement of working-class people—whose journeys, modes of transport, and velocity it claims to control. It is in this asymmetry that the 'Double S, Double S' reveals itself as an architecture of domination. The violence of this power over movement (which produces inertia for some and freedom of movement for others) has not escaped the attention of those most directly concerned. During a series of exchanges with residents of the working-class neighbourhoods of Bawani Chali and Pathan Colony in August 2018, a consensus emerged on the legitimacy of the fight against street crime, including in their own neighbourhood. Most of the people I spoke to worked for SITE-based industries and approved of the principle of increased security in the area. However, the 'Double S, Double S' has served only to 'ensure the safety of the bosses', deplored a resident of Pathan Colony I met at the office of a local lawyer specializing in labour disputes. For him—as for the other workers present in the office that day—the walls and gates installed by industrialists have only displaced petty crime to their neighbourhood, where recurrent power outages are a godsend for robbers.

Because they deprive residents of these neighbourhoods of their right to free movement, lengthen their daily commute to work, and, in emergency situations, endanger those who are sick or injured, these walls are widely considered a 'calamity' (taklif). Referring to the recent case of a patient with severe breathing difficulties, whose transfer to hospital was disrupted by these traffic restrictions, one person pointed to the new vulnerabilities created by this demonstration of corporate power. This denial of mobility has sharpened the sense of subjugation within the working-class population. In a city facing a permanent state of emergency (especially in its poorest neighbourhoods), restrictions on movement

213

are seen as an existential threat. They endanger the lives of sick or injured people in need of urgent care, and increase the vulnerability of entire neighbourhoods in the event of fire or flooding. In 2016, a residential building in Bawani Chali was completely gutted by fire before the fire brigade managed to get there.[47]

The hostility of the population towards this security architecture has further increased in subsequent years. In August 2022, I went to Zia Colony—a working-class Pashtun neighbourhood on the edge of SITE, whose main access is blocked by a series of walls supposedly protecting an adjacent steel factory. As I interviewed a shopkeeper, a group of residents soon gathered around us and each person began complaining about the nuisance caused by these reviled walls. Once again, the lengthening of daily journeys and the risks incurred in emergency situations were primary concerns. Local residents also mentioned the difficulty of access for the tankers brought in to alleviate the neighbourhood's water supply problems and the inconvenience of turnstiles for women carrying groceries or small children—as well as the opportunities offered to drug addicts to indulge their vice away from the police gaze (but before the eyes of local youths). This hostility was exacerbated by a deep sense of animosity towards the neighbouring factory, whose effects on air pollution and the stability of the houses (evidenced by cracks caused by its vibrations) were vociferously denounced by residents.

This resentment was aggravated by the fact that it has now been some years since the factory in question has employed any inhabitants from the locality, preferring workers from the rural areas of Sindh, who are reputed to be more docile.

The effects of this security architecture are thus also visible in the loosening of economic ties between working-class neighbourhoods and their industrial environment, reinforcing perceptions of a predatory capitalism lacking any sense of social responsibility. Enraged by the alliance of capital and coercion materialized in these obstacles to movement, the residents of Zia Colony twice tried to tear them down. The most recent attempt was in the spring of 2022, and industrialists have since gone to great lengths to rebuild the walls using concrete renowned for its durability. As one local elder told me, defeatedly: 'Now these walls are here for eternity.'

From fighting crime to workforce profiling

Alongside its materialization in the form of buildings, this security scheme extended its reach by applying intense profiling practices to the working population. Unlike discipline, which 'proceeds by direct control in complete transparency and requires the individual to work on himself to adapt to the norms', profiling 'is carried out without the person's knowledge or participation'.[48] As noted above (Chapter 2), these practices of using in-depth knowledge of each person to maintain control have a long history in Karachi's industry. In the early years of the industrialization process, they were meant to make the working population more legible to the newly formed entrepreneurial class, while simultaneously providing the management with information about the ethnic power balance on the shop floor.

With the rise of civil strife in the city, the purpose of this profiling changed; it was now aiming to track criminal or political antecedents. Like the 'workers' logbook' in nineteenth-century France, these profiling practices are based on 'multi-level control'.[49] Every applicant for a job in the industry is now expected, after presenting various identification documents and providing fingerprints, to produce a character certificate issued by their local police authority as well as their biometric CNIC national identity card issued by NADRA, the National Database & Registration Authority. Some employers also require contractors and security managers to conduct additional background checks, while some contractors require employees to provide written certification that they have no political background.

Relying on a variety of information sources (including police, NADRA officials, recruiters, and applicants' families), this profiling system works by accumulating certifications, rather than systematically cross-checking information, and it was in these terms that Umar Shah presented his latest project. Having been involved in building the largest criminal database in Sindh, he is now working within the CPLC on the creation of a biometric database covering everyone working at SITE—workers, employees, and executives alike. Following the 'Double S, Double S' example, this dataset—which should be operational in the course of 2024—will be based on information extracted from FIRs and the biometric data (both collected by the CPLC) from Karachi's prisons.

Once the system is up and running, entering the fingerprints of a new recruit will immediately reveal whether they have ever been the subject of a criminal complaint, or spent time in prison in Karachi— thereby neutralizing the risk of identity fraud. According to Umar Shah, this database will provide 'added value to the character certificates issued by the police'. In other words, it will provide an additional, forgery-proof level of certification. Because it draws on highly reputed CPLC information resources, this certification would have a critical edge over that of any competitors.

The creation of this database would thus make it possible to streamline the profiling process, using this enhanced capability to meet the increasingly stringent requirements of foreign buyers. As someone who is partnered to an American firm and thus highly dependent on access to the American market for his business, Umar Shah's specific goal is CTPAT certification, which is essential to continuing to work with groups like Walmart, Kmart, etc.[50] The systematic monitoring of SITE employees will rely on fingerprinting—achieved either with the consent of those concerned, or with neither their consent nor their knowledge—via the biometric punch clocks installed at the entrance to each factory. And in the event that any of the few remaining unions at SITE move against these methods, their silence can always be purchased, believes Umar Shah.[51]

This contingency plan shows the extent to which the requirements of industrial safety have quashed the legalistic citizenship originally promoted by the CPLC. This new surveillance tool will indeed allow SITE industrialists to streamline profiling of their employees with a view to obtaining international certification. But it will also be used to compile a blacklist of troublemakers that will be available online to employers—thus formalizing practices already well underway in the city's industrial estates, where company security managers have been known to share information on unruly workers as a way of preventing them from finding employment at another company following their dismissal for professional misconduct or union activism. Umar Shah's frank description of this plan to neutralize potential trade union resistance also shows how CPLC monitoring projects are helping bring Karachi closer to those risk societies in which due process is being eroded to make way for the 'system rights' allocated to surveillance systems.[52]

The CPLC—agent of the new military urbanism

The 'Double S, Double S' and its extension to the profiling of SITE workers are part of a larger project designed to pacify the urban margins of Karachi, which places both the control of workers' mobility and the defence of industrial order at the heart of fresh struggles for the city. Beyond the case of Karachi, this provides an opportunity to more broadly interrogate the issues raised by contemporary security policies for practices of citizenship. As critical geographer Stephen Graham suggests, this invasion of urban life by tracking and profiling technologies threatens to 're-engineer ideas of citizenship'. To him, emerging security politics, 'instead of legal or human rights and legal systems based on universal citizenship, [...] are founded on the profiling of individuals, places, behaviours, associations and groups'. Far from being automatic, access to rights would increasingly be modulated according to the risk level assigned to each group on the basis of its perceived potential for violence and disruption of the liberal economic order.[53] The culture of risk introduced by the CPLC in the fight against crime—in the city at large, in industrial areas, and finally within production units—echoes these transformations.

Backed by the state security apparatus, Karachi's industrialists are dedicated to ever-stricter profiling of workers as 'risk objects'[54] requiring constant surveillance. And alongside the registration of all SITE employees, Umar Shah has been working on new biometric databases and profiling tools for security guards and domestic staff. In 2022, the CPLC helped launch a new profiling app developed by the NGO Safe Pakistan Welfare Trust.[55] Called 'Tasdeeq' (Attestation/Verification), it offers users the possibility of verifying the backgrounds of domestic workers and company employees.

Users have two options: after scanning the employee's computerized ID card, certification can be obtained from the police (via access to the Sindh, Punjab, and Khyber Pakhtunkhwa police files) and/or from the CPLC (via its prison database, registering present or former detainees of Karachi's prisons). Users do not have access to employees' criminal records, and are simply told whether the employee has 'passed' or 'failed' the test.[56] The target audience for this application is residents of affluent neighbourhoods who want to ensure the reliability of their household staff, including guards. The Tasdeeq app also offers companies the opportunity to check their employees' criminal record by uploading a simple CSV file. Back in August 2022, the application was still in the running-in phase and was experiencing some technical glitches, but this procedure could eventually make it possible to 'certify' hundreds (or even thousands) of employees simultaneously.[57]

This compulsive profiling (which targets segments of the working classes that serve and interact with economic elites) partially overlaps with the categories of risk produced by the Pakistani security state in the context of its 'war on terror'.[58] By indexing deviance and subversion on ethnic affiliation, it singles out Pashtuns. This is in line with a general trend in contemporary urban pacification projects, namely their focus on an enemy located 'at the margin, or more precisely at the frontier—in the sense of the *frontier* of colonial conquest'.[59] Karachi's Pashtuns originally came from the mountainous region bordering Afghanistan (a region once known as the North West Frontier Province, abbreviated to 'Frontier', from 1901 to 2010) and are consubstantially defined by their marginality—which is reinforced by the fact that they are geographically concentrated in peripheral neighbourhoods.

This marginalization does not, however, preclude forms of intimacy with the upper classes of all communities. Until recently, then, Pashtuns formed the largest contingent of factory workers, security guards, and service personnel (drivers, cooks, cleaners) employed by Karachi's economic elites. State propaganda and media hype around the over-representation of Pashtuns in the Pakistani Taliban movement have however transformed perceptions of this population by projecting an image of it as being compromised by crime and terrorism—and thus as a triple threat to productive order, domestic tranquillity, and national security.[60]

This population thus ends up bearing the brunt of the new 'citizenship by permit', leaving each person's entitlement to rights conditional on the level of risk assigned to his/her peer group.

Evidence of this can be found in the increased surveillance and police violence to which Pashtuns in Karachi have been subjected over the past 15 years, as well as in their restricted access to the labour market, the attacks on their mobility (all of the neighbourhoods affected by the 'Double S, Double S' are predominantly Pashtun), and obstacles to the voting rights of Internally Displaced Persons (IDPs) driven out of the north-west by the fighting between the Taliban and the army. In response to this disenfranchisement, the Pashtun Tahafuz Movement (PTM), which calls for full citizen status for all Pashtuns in Pakistan, first emerged in Karachi in 2018, before spreading to the rest of the country.[61]

This security urbanism reserves the benefits of citizenship for those who are most compliant and most deserving, and is accompanied by an increased militarization of urban space. In contrast to the model proposed by Stephen Graham, however, this is implemented less through the 'extension of military ideas of tracking, identification and targeting into the quotidian spaces and circulations of everyday life' than it is through the appropriation by (para-)military forces of surveillance technologies financed and developed by the private sector.[62] Thus, the 'Double S, Double S' has equipped the Rangers with a new instrument with which to control the flow of traffic in a strategic area—by means of both the deployment of RSGs in the area, and the presence of paramilitaries in the SITE Association's control room.

By calling attention to those employers daring to transgress the security norms imposed by the Rangers since the start of the Karachi Operation, the plan to build a comprehensive database of SITE employees extends the surveillance net as far as the industrialists themselves. These security norms include a ban on the recruitment of undocumented migrant workers (be they foreigners or Pakistanis); this has long been a bone of contention between the Rangers and a section of employers. Here, the logic of profit maximization clashes with the grand designs of the security state in seeking to impose a 'paper citizenship'[63] that is materialized by the possession of (theoretically) forgery-proof identification documents (in this case, computerized identity cards). This project aims to extend the outreach of the state through the production of legibility, and has (according to the bureaucratic terminology in use in Pakistan) resulted in the merging of the 'illegal alien' category (and, by extension, that of the 'undocumented worker') with the dreaded figure of the terrorist.[64] As General Bilal Akbar, Director General of the Rangers, explained to me in 2016:

> There are two categories of labour: labourers with documents, and then there is a cheaper option—labourers without documents, Burmese, Bengalis, Afghans, Tadjiks, Uzbeks... So we talked to people [factory owners] and said, 'Don't do this: I can provide you an outer perimeter of security. My force can patrol your streets, but criminals are working in your factories, you have to behave in a more responsible manner. Your margins of profit will go down but you will be more secure. I don't want to get into a factory and at every corner there's a terrorist who's run away from Bajaur [a former Pakistani Taliban stronghold on the border with Afghanistan] and working there. I don't want to do that. You have to throw them out and we'll apprehend them'.[65]

In proposing generalized and automated profiling of SITE employees, Umar Shah and his supporters within the SITE Association were serving the paramilitaries' security agenda, which was calling for the normalization of a notoriously unlawful brand of capitalism. However, this demand did not get very far, because even as they called for the regularization of recruitment policies in large-scale industry, the Rangers were proving themselves very accommodating to other industrial illegalisms (see Chapter 8). The paramilitaries, then, were—both by action and by omission—participating in the establishment of security arrangements that showed as little regard for the law as it did for the public monopoly on the use of force.

Negotiating industrial 'permissive spaces'

The reallocation of the CPLC's informational capital and coercive resources to the defence of employer domination led to the formation of zones of industrial autonomy, which are left in the hands of capital's agents of violence. Borrowing from anthropologist Sarah Cooper-Knock, whose work addresses the pluralization of policing in South Africa, it is apt to speak here of 'permissive spaces', in which groups of citizens engaged in policing activities negotiate their own ability to use extra-legal violence with impunity.[66]

Rooted in a critique of the legalism and statocentrism of Agamben's work on the state of exception, this contribution focuses on the pluralization of police functions and the proliferation of authorities empowered to use force in contemporary societies. At the same time, it emphasizes the fragility of unofficial 'police formations'(that is, vigilante groups, people's courts, lynch mobs, etc.) whose capacity to use violence outside the framework of the law has to be continually (re)negotiated with the state and society, on pain of criminal or extrajudicial sanctions.[67] Or, to put it another, more Foucauldian way, private enforcers are seeking to secure for themselves the '*droit de glaive*'—that is, the right to kill, historically reserved for sovereign powers.[68]

Echoing the literature on vigilantism and de facto sovereignties,[69] Cooper-Knock reminds us that 'street justice' tends to be exercised within a defined perimeter—a spatial framework that endows it with an 'intimate' character while exposing it to particular contingencies.[70] This work does not, however, escape a subalternist bias common in the literature on vigilantism, which tends to perceive rough justice as a cheap and popular solution to the insecurities generated by neoliberal-inspired reforms.[71]

Yet the 'permissive spaces' that have sprung up in Karachi's industrial areas in recent years show that the working classes brutalized by neoliberalism have no such monopoly on vigilante justice. Prevailing favourable conditions for the exercise of rough justice by the dominant classes include: knowledge and mastery of the legal rules, the protections they enjoy within the state apparatus, and the sense of impunity that arises out of their everyday illegalisms. Private security schemes, with their fortifications and armed guards filtering access to a secure perimeter, also create a spatial environment that, sheltered as it is from outside scrutiny, is conducive to the unleashing of extra-legal violence—even if this violence, as we shall see, does not entirely get around the need for legitimation.

At SITE, the rules that govern the use of force by security guards deployed in the 'Double S, Double S' context speak volumes about capital owners' ability to negotiate state leniency regarding their use of violence. As Rashid Memon pointed out, 'guards were directly arresting the criminals, they injured the criminals and then they directly handed them to police or Rangers'. When I asked under what conditions the guards were entitled to use force in such situations, he explained that they simply shoot suspects in the legs to immobilize them. He added,

> Criminals were free to roam around in the SITE area and they were just snatching every second man who is crossing by, so Rangers, police and us, SITE Association, we allowed these guards to fire if there is a need and then police and Rangers will come up and they will take over that person, then pursue the case.[72]

Coupled with Rashid Memon's discourse, these rules of engagement show a persistent commitment (at least on the surface) to legalism and the principle of subsidiarity between private security guards and law enforcement professionals. In the Korangi industrial area, where the CPLC has implemented security arrangements that are both more circumscribed spatially and less inhibited in their use of force, this is not the case.

Each CPLC Neighbourhood Care (NC) project in Korangi covers one 'sector' of the industrial area (comprising a few dozen factories at most). The collective fee payable by factory owners covers implementation and maintenance of the project, as well as the construction of checkpoints and gates and the salaries of the guards recruited by the CPLC. In 2018, when I carried out my investigation of this scheme, eight sectors of the Korangi Industrial Estate had such arrangements, adjusted to a territorial organizational mode that bears the hallmark of the most ambitious urban planning programme undertaken in Karachi since Partition. Overseen by Greek architect Constantinos Doxiadis, the development of Korangi was originally organized on a grid pattern, which survives in the industrial part of the area.[73] The estate thus comprises rectangular blocks known as 'sectors', bounded by straight avenues and crossed by a central axis, along which the production units are arranged.

The Neighbourhood Care project is based on this grid: each end of the area has checkpoints and traffic flows are filtered by manually operated barriers. Smaller checkpoints are located along the central road, at the intersection of secondary roads. In some cases, a watch tower provides additional surveillance. Armed guards recruited by the CPLC are stationed at each checkpoint, and patrol the central axis. The whole system is supervised from the office of the 'controller' (a CPLC employee, often retired from the police or army), which is generally located at the centre of the sector. Sometimes, a few police officers are assigned to this office (which tends to reinforce the analogy with a police station) but this is not systematic.

While the private guards' positioning and movements undoubtedly play an essential role in the formation of these securitized enclaves, their autonomy is also evident in the architecture of roadside checks.

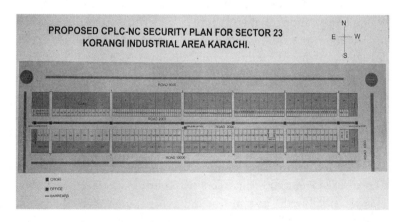

Plan prepared by the CPLC for the Neighbourhood Care Project in Korangi's Sector 23 and displayed on the wall of the local controller's office.

L. Gayer, 2017

223

We have already seen how these obstacles to traffic have served to crystallize working-class hostility towards the 'Double S, Double S' and the apparatus it uses to impose power over movement. Yet these obstacles can also be decisive in negotiation with the state around permissive spaces. Barriers and palisades hold a special place in Karachi's recent history. Each anti-terrorist operation carried out since the 1990s has offered the state an opportunity to reassert its sovereignty through shows of force that often featured the dismantling of the fortifications and roadblocks obstructing traffic in contested districts.

In the very first days of Operation Clean-up (1992–1994), which targeted the MQM political-military apparatus, the army opened up Mohajir neighbourhoods to traffic by destroying the walls and gates the party had erected—in part via the diversion of steel bars produced at the Pakistan Steel Mills (PSM), where the party had a strong presence.[74] The Karachi Operation (launched in 2013 and Rangers-led) resulted in the dismantling of the barriers installed at the entrances to the strongholds of the various groups fighting for control of the city. This action followed an injunction from the Supreme Court—which, as we saw in the previous chapter, was concerned about the deteriorating security situation in the country's economic and financial capital.

Implementation of this directive, which theoretically covered any traffic obstruction installed by non-state actors, was left to the discretion of the paramilitaries. Determined to restore their road supremacy and make the whole of Karachi an open city in which state authority would cease to be undermined by the existence of 'no-go areas', the Rangers systematically tore down the defences erected by gangs and political parties (barriers, concrete blocks, sentry boxes, sandbags, etc.). They were however much more accommodating of industrialists—who were granted exemption from the Supreme Court directives, allowing them to control access to factories. This was notably the case in Korangi, where paramilitaries allowed the CPLC to install barriers not only on main roads, but also on secondary roads in areas within Neighbourhood Care projects.

In addition, law enforcement agencies have shown tolerance of the use of force by private security guards—as long as they were employed by the CPLC. Charged with guarding factories and preventing crime on the roads, these sentinels of industrial order are, in theory, only authorized to use force in self-defence. In practice, CPLC members seem unconcerned by either the seriousness of allegations against presumed offenders or the principles of necessity and proportionality that supposedly govern the right of self-defence.[75] This much was evident throughout my exchanges with Amir Jalal,* the CPLC member in charge of the Neighbourhood Care programme in Korangi. Jalal joined the CPLC in 2008 and, though he belongs to the Memon merchant community, he comes from a humble background, having started his career as a factory clerk.

His involvement with the CPLC seems to have helped him to climb the social ladder. A year after joining the organization, he was elected General Secretary of the Korangi Industrial & Trading Estate Development and Management Company (KITE)—which is responsible for the development and maintenance of Korangi's infrastructure and also oversees the distribution of water and electricity to factories in the area. While it is impossible to establish this link with certainty, it seems that his administrative CPLC responsibilities helped him obtain a number of contracts. In any case, the fact that he was awarded several important contracts in Korangi allowed him to turn his company, in his own words, into a 'multimillion business.'[76]

As architect of the Neighbourhood Care programme in Korangi, Jalal has introduced a new style of policing to the area, involving the use of 'desperate measures'—in his own words. In a series of interviews with myself and Sophie Russo between 2016 and 2018, Jalal showed us his 'trophies'—in the form of photographs of alleged thieves caught or shot by CPLC guards, which he proudly keeps in his phone and in a dedicated photo album. Some of these alleged offenders were subjected to the '*half-fry*' (a bullet in the thigh or knee), while those less fortunate were given the '*full-fry*' (a euphemism for summary execution).

These expressions, which originated in police jargon, are now common parlance across Sindh province,[77] and (although he never explicitly used them in our discussions) Amir Jalal seemed familiar with the rules and application of this rough justice. The violence exhibited by this corporate enforcer bears striking similarities to punishments administered by the Sindh police, which are adjusted in line with the seriousness of the allegations brought against the alleged offender, and/or his criminal record. Jalal claims that, most of the time, 'his' guards simply shoot suspects in the leg. This type of wounding suggests some restraint on the part of the guards, but remains very much a form of punishment—reminiscent of the Northern Irish practice of kneecapping[78]—and can result in permanent disability.

Jalal's contacts in the local police also seem to recognize this private justice as a reflection (even an extension) of their own punitive practices. Sharing his photo album with Sophie Russo in 2016, Jalal focused on a photograph of the corpse of a suspected thief, shot by a CPLC guard after attempting to steal a passer-by's mobile phone. As in many similar cases, the victim was taken to the nearest police station, where the Station House Officer was quick to justify this use of force (however disproportionate it might seem) as self-defence. 'The police know that our cause is just. To be honest, this kind of incident does not really pose a problem. That's how it works', Jalal told his French visitor, aware that he was being slightly provocative.[79] CPLC members do not seem overly concerned with the bureaucratic framing of private security work; on the contrary, the ability to use force with impunity is one of the organization's main promotional arguments.[80]

This propensity for ostentatious, extra-legal violence among CPLC's current members is consistent with the expedient methods promoted by the CPLC's founders. In the early 1990s, these self-taught security experts managed to become key partners to army commandos, and later police units, specializing in anti-kidnapping operations. During these operations, the CPLC leadership approved (even encouraged) a policy of summary executions designed to maintain secrecy about the stratagems used to trap kidnappers. In a joint interview with Sophie Russo, one former member of the organization involved in these operations confided to us, confident that he had acted within his rights:

I was always for the victim, never for the criminals, so I don't care what any human rights... My rights are for the people who suffer—so my condition with the police was, I brought in these expensive gadgets, when we raid the house [the kidnappers' hideout with the beacon hidden in the suitcase containing the ransom money], detecting with the beacon, whoever has the briefcase should be killed, shot, so that he doesn't go to jail and tell them that I'm using this equipment and this is how I reached there. Now, the sad part is, they did it once, twice, three, four times. After that, some other corrupt police officers, they refused to do it. [...] Because a dead man can't give a bribe [laughs].[81]

Nicholas Rush Smith has observed a similar rejection of the liberal regime of rights in post-apartheid South Africa, where a range of vigilante groups propose to respond to its failings by violent means.[82] But perhaps the most obvious parallel to be drawn is with Brazil. Since democracy was restored there in the 1980s, human rights have been accused of protecting criminals at the expense of 'honest citizens'. This criticism takes a particularly virulent form among the upper strata of the population, calling the normative basis of the liberal regime of rights into question and accusing the judiciary of inertia, inefficiency, and corruption.[83]

Karachi's industrialists have always had a tense, distrustful relationship with the law that has certainly predisposed them to turn to rough justice. As in Brazil, fear of the working classes has fuelled the vigilante proclivities of these economic elites—a feeling sharpened, in Karachi, by the political protections that criminal actors supposedly enjoy. In contrast to more ordinary forms of vigilantism, whose initial impetus comes from security mobilizations beyond the control of the state,[84] it is in the context of collaborations with the army and police that Karachi's corporate enforcers have become accustomed to breaking the law as a way of maintaining order. And it is partly through working in partnership with these self-taught security experts that the habit of taking no prisoners has gained such a foothold among law enforcement professionals.

* * *

GUNPOINT CAPITALISM

The escalation of political and criminal violence in Karachi that
began in the 1990s has had profound repercussions in terms of both
the geography imagined by members of the industrial elite and their
relationship to the city's troubled peripheries. This geography of fear,
understood as much as a representation as a practice of the city,[85] has
been structured by the supposedly malignant movements of people
from working-class neighbourhoods. Some industrialists, drawing
on the resources and know-how arising out of their partnership
with law enforcement agencies, have turned to cartographical and
statistical tools in a bid to reduce the uncertainties of this chaotic
urban landscape—an operation founded on a conviction that
calculable space must necessarily be more navigable. Through the
visualization and spatial distribution of risks, the cartographic tools
used by the CPLC sought to render legible certain urban spaces
that had always remained unfamiliar to industrialists, despite their
proximity to production units.

This cartographic work, and the geo-criminological world view
that supported it, provided the foundations for complex security
assemblages and the establishment of new police territories. Rather
than a coming together of 'public' and 'private' (two categories that
tend to dissolve into an infinite variety of nuances), this was more
a meeting of the calculating management of risk and the violence
of vigilantes. This convergence of probabilistic reason and punitive
spectacle contradicts the assumption (defended by authors such
as Richard Ericson and Kevin Haggerty) that in risk societies the
logic of surveillance renders coercion superfluous.[86] The coercive
practices of the armed guards of the CPLC and the RSGs also show
the limitations of the opposition between the preventive logic
commonly attributed to private security (with its specific concern for
the prevention of property damage) and the repressive logic assigned
to public security—a dichotomy popularized by criminologists
Clifford Shearing and Philip Stenning[87] and now undermined by the
punitive practices of certain actors in commercial security.

The foregoing chapters have shown that Karachi's industrialists
have, throughout their history, relied on the coercive resources of
specialists in extra-legal violence. Building on this experience, and
following in the footsteps of other economic actors fighting the

liberal regime of rights, these industrialists could have outsourced their security plan to vigilantes (or armed militias) in the service of capital.[88] Indeed, it was this very configuration that began to emerge in the 2000s, with political parties acting as enforcers of industrial order. However, midway through the following decade, the parties' offer of protection became less effective, and industrial employers were forced to reconsider their self-defence strategy. After approaching law enforcement agencies, they negotiated privileged access to their resources, while making their own surveillance technologies available to national security services. Employer domination has emerged from these security assemblages rejuvenated, in terms of controlling both labour and traffic flows.

Denying working-class people the right to free movement, this kinetic power is exercised through a mobility differential that re-signifies the subaltern condition as a state of inertia. This vehicular art of domination is materialized through an architecture of control that is more concerned with the distribution of conditional and temporary passes than it is with blocking flows. It has also established new urban territories in which the security state has farmed out the right to kill to the holders of capital. In these 'permissive spaces', the owners of capital and the professionals of coercion each agree that the law may be violated in defence of their respective conceptions of order.

This security configuration, like all of its predecessors, is fraught with internal tensions. Now that security guards constitute the factory world's first line of defence in the face of urban disorder, they embody the paradox of an industrial security system in search of professionalization. Even though they are poorly trained and weakly integrated into the business world (where they sustain deep-seated tensions), they have become indispensable cogs in the corporate security wheel.

This paradox serves as a reminder that, while vulnerability is always unevenly distributed, the powerful also have their Achilles' heel.[89] In the next chapter, we will see that the sense of fragility that has now emerged among Karachi's industrialists has arisen primarily as a result of their own security arrangements.

8

WHO WILL WATCH THE WATCHMEN?

Quis custodiet ipsos custodes?

Juvenal, Satire VI

Najam Kathiawari* owns a textile factory in the heart of the Sindh Industrial Trading Estate (SITE), which has long been known for its high crime rate. Both his own security and that of his company are entrusted to armed guards, 24/7. Yet underlying mistrust means that his relationship to these people is fraught with tension: 'You can never be completely sure that it won't be your guards who come to rob you', he says. This problem of loyalty and probity aside, Kathiawari also worries that the city lights might turn the heads of these armed guards, who are often fresh migrants from the country's rural north: 'Like the soldiers, the guards are generally from Punjab and the Frontier, not Karachi. They are used to living in small villages or hamlets. When they arrive in Karachi and see all these "bungalows" [luxury villas], it disturbs them psychologically'.

As proof of this, Najam Kathiawari points to a recent tragedy. One morning he found one of his guards prostrate on the steps leading to his office: 'He had shot himself in the head. He must have had health problems, mental problems or family problems. That's why psychological tests are essential'.[1]

231

This story pushes to the point of paroxysm the angst-ridden relationship between Karachi's economic elites and their armed guards. In so doing, it alerts us to a blind spot in contemporary security arrangements—namely, their endogenous production of uncertainty. In Karachi, the tensions generated by a teeming security apparatus have given rise to an anxiety-driven domination that is much less secure than first appears. While the forces of urban disorder always made uneasy bedfellows in the defence of industrial order, a relationship of distrustful intimacy now binds the entrepreneurial class to its armed security guards, who are both heirs to the *chowkidars* of the past and the embodiment of a new surveillance precariat.

These armed guards have now become a central component of Karachi's security landscape. Private security guards were already outnumbering police officers in the mid-2000s, and by 2013–2014 (with more than 50,000 guards in the employ of 231 companies), they were almost twice as numerous as the police.[2] Yet because those employing these new guardians of industrial peace remain suspicious that those they hire may prove disloyal, unstable, or simply incompetent, they must maintain constant vigilance. And, for employers and senior management, Juvenal's classic question— 'Who will watch the watchmen?'—is taking on a haunting character.[3]

As anthropologist Jamie Cross shows in his ethnography of a British manager employed in an Indian free-trade zone, fear has not, by any stretch of the imagination, disappeared. Indeed, it continues to loom large in the global factory—and is by no means confined to the least qualified sections of the workforce. On the basis of his observations, Cross concludes that 'the same social relations and technical systems that are designed to assert control over a labour force also generate an anxiety that control cannot be guaranteed', so that 'for companies that remain competitive by keeping labour casual, insecure and precarious, this fear becomes inseparable from production processes.'[4] The purpose of the following pages is to extend this line of thought, focusing on the production of new risks by security mechanisms that are themselves highly precarious.[5]

Private security and neoliberal concerns

The first researcher to focus on the private security sector in South Asia was the historian and sociologist Nandini Gooptu, whose ethnography of a group of security guards in Calcutta opened the debate. As a specialist in the working classes and worlds of labour in India, she believes that contemporary developments in private security are based on a fundamental paradox: while the new surveillance precariat is the product of the 'flexploitation' process denounced by Pierre Bourdieu,[6] it has nonetheless assumed the role of sentinel in the neoliberal city.[7] As Bourdieu saw, 'strategies of casualization' proceed by means of the 'rational management of insecurity', which, in both North and South, reaches its peak in the private security sector. Based on 'the institution of a generalized and permanent state of insecurity', its aim is to 'force workers into submission, into the acceptance of exploitation'.[8]

In the industrial security sector, this quest for flexibility is based on the relaxation of labour law along with a whole series of illegalities (failure to comply with the statutory duration of working hours, refusal or violation of collective agreements, etc.), that are in no way specific to security companies of the Global South. World leader in the sector is the British multinational G4S—internationally denounced by trade union campaigns demanding the company be banned from tendering for the 2010 Football World Cup and the 2012 Olympic Games.[9]

It is important that we take account not only of the professional insecurities inherent to 'flexible management' of the workforce, but also a feeling of physical vulnerability; private security guards tend to see themselves as expendable pawns in the battle against disorder—whatever the level of violence in the urban environment they operate in.[10] As one French team leader at a record shop confided in an interview with sociologist Frédéric Péroumal, 'When you work in private security, you are not safe because anything can happen, at any time'.[11]

Even though these casual workers may be underpaid, ill-equipped, and poorly trained, in addition to being subjected to gruelling work schedules and confronted with a multitude of perils, they have nonetheless acquired a primary role in the maintenance of urban order in most latitudes. The uncertainty surrounding the remit of these workers (who oscillate between domestic help, care, and policing) is at the heart of their subaltern condition.[12] However, their primary vocation, in South Asia as elsewhere, remains the control of flows—more specifically, regulation of the movement of poor people across the city. Both indispensable and interchangeable, these casual workers filter urban traffic flows to keep out populations deemed undesirable—even though, absent their uniforms, these security workers would soon be identified as belonging to the very populations they are employed to exclude.[13]

To date, the contribution made by private security agents to the defence of industrial order remains little studied, and in this respect, Karachi's manufacturing sector is a privileged observation site. Armed guards recruited from private security companies have been omnipresent since the 2000s. Taking on duties that go way beyond straightforward guarding, they are often responsible for monitoring workers all the way into the workshops. The versatility of these security guards prompts strong reservations regarding the emergence of a new disciplinary formula of capitalism in which the endorsement of 'just-in-time' would (allegedly) render coercion superfluous.[14]

The new methods of maintaining order that we will be examining in the following pages certainly owe much to the recent global changes in commercial security, which manifest as readily in the development of managerial tools as they do in the casualization of labour by most corporate security managers. However—in this field as in so many others—we must be careful not to make neo-liberalism the birthplace of (all) history. Thus, I seek to go beyond explanations based on the triumph of the market and its immanent rationalities, which in this case risk leading us astray to two distinct illusions. The first is that the progress of security privatization comes at the expense of state power and knowledge; the reality is that these continue to play a key role in contemporary corporate security. The second illusion is that the steamroller of neo-liberal bureaucratization will render corporate violence and outward forms of coercion redundant.[15]

234

The new surveillance precariat

Karachi's private security market first emerged back in the 1980s. As elsewhere in Pakistan, it developed around security firms founded by retired army officers. Although the military has played a central role in drawing up Pakistani development policy since the 1950s, with former officers turning to the private sector early on, their hold on the economy was considerably extended under the dictatorship of General Zia-ul-Haq (1977–1988). As the 'milbus' (military business) developed around the private foundations managed by the armed forces, many retired military personnel found positions in the administration, in the public sector, and in private companies. For Zia's military regime, this was both a way of consolidating its control over society and of rewarding deserving officers.[16] From the late 1990s on, the outsourcing of a growing number of public service missions to the private sector gave fresh impetus to this privatization of the state, resulting in the development of business-like behaviour among professionals of violence and increased army influence across all sectors of activity.

The security contractor profile has changed little since then. Most private security companies are run by former officers who ended their careers holding the rank of major. Majors also predominate among corporate security managers—although there is also a handful of ex-captains (and even ex-colonels) among them. This coincidence can be explained by the rather limited options available to middle-ranking officers post-retirement. Officers who have completed their careers at a higher rank than major (lieutenant-colonel and above) can aspire to more prestigious positions in the administration or the private sector—or having been given agricultural land, instead reinvent themselves as landowners.

The continued predominance of ex-officers in the private security industry does not detract from the fact that the sector is becoming increasingly competitive, especially among law enforcement professionals.[17] Furthermore, we are now seeing the emergence of civilian security experts, who mainly offer their services to the more internationalized Pakistani companies and multinational firms based in the country's major cities.

Although both kidnappings (of businessmen) and extortion practices increased significantly during the 1990s, the spectacular growth of the security market was not perfectly in sync with the rise in criminal violence.[18] The security market only really took off at the end of the decade, in a context of state-driven externalization of security tasks.

One former army major who founded his own private security company during this period is quite explicit about this:

> Some say that private security has developed because of the deteriorating law and order situation. I do not share this view. I think it's more because of the development of outsourcing. Because previously in Pakistan, outsourcing was not an option. It started after the government itself started outsourcing its security, labour or whatever... Once they started outsourcing, they found it was a good option. Two things. One: no union. Second, we are service providers, contractors. So the company which is hiring us, people are our employees, not their employees, so they're saving bonus and so many things...

The combined forces of weak regulation of the sector, competition between providers, and cost pressure from clients have contributed to the emergence of a surveillance precariat:

> If I really wanted to pay my guards properly, they should get around 18–19,000 rupees [$185–196/month]. The clients would like to be provided with six-foot giants with two X-rays for eyes... They ask for impossible things. But when it comes to payment... they would like us to provide them with guards for 13,000 rupees... There are certain social responsibilities that we are supposed to fulfil, but we rarely do... You know, I opened a shop, well now it has to be run... For my children... If I start playing the hero, committing to do the right thing... There is a centrifugal force and I would soon be out... I would be out of the system...[19]

Here, as elsewhere, it is important to guard against making sweeping generalizations about the 'new' global precariat, as these tend to both minimize the local historicities of labour casualization (especially in the Global South) and neglect the great diversity of experiences subsumed by the notion of 'informal labour'.[20] Thus, in Karachi, the generic 'security guard' status covers a multitude of work practices and pay scales. At the top of the pyramid are former army commandos (veterans of the Special Services Group, SSG), who provide close protection security for top corporate executives and can be paid up to 50,000 or 60,000 rupees a month (around 500 USD). Next come former *jawan*s (soldiers) and constables (police officers), who, if they are authorized to bear arms, are paid up to 30,000 or 35,000 rupees (around 300 USD) a month. Guards without police or (para-)military experience are paid significantly less (between 15,000 and 20,000 rupees, or 140–200 USD)—even though they perform the same tasks (protecting warehouses and factory premises, searching staff entering and leaving factories, and watching workers in the workplace to prevent theft, drug use, and sleepiness).

Alongside these private armed guards (provided by security companies and commonly referred to as 'security'), companies also continue to recruit *chowkidar*s for guarding duties. These guards do not carry weapons, and tend to receive lower salaries (around 12,000 rupees, or 120 USD) although they are sometimes also entitled to a share in the company's profits. The salaries of these guards, like those of armed guards deployed by private companies, are reduced by the commissions taken by their employers. In addition, they are very regularly required to work gruelling shifts, often lasting up to 12 or even 14 hours—and are rarely paid for more than eight.

Equipped with semi-automatic weapons, the guards provided by security companies often receive only rudimentary training when they are recruited—although in recent years some companies have promoted their professionalism by showcasing the training offered to their employees.[21] Security companies used to prioritize the recruitment of former military and police officers, but the boom in Karachi's security market has forced them to be less stringent. In 2016, out of Pakistan's 600 registered security companies, 278 were in Karachi—although only 150 of those were reported to be operating within the rules.[22]

The continued growth of the Chinese presence and capital in Karachi under the China Pakistan Economic Corridor (CPEC) is adding to the dynamism of the security sector. It has also resulted in a shortage of ex-soldiers and ex-police officers available for deployment in the industrial sector, which highly sought-after security guards find unappealing. They prefer to work either as bodyguards to businessmen, diplomats, or politicians, or in the protection of consular premises or the offices of multinational firms—all of which offer significantly higher pay. Former police and military personnel also have the option of selling their services to Gulf security forces (in the UAE and Bahrain, for instance), where they can earn three times what they would get for protecting industrial sites in Karachi. Coupled with employers' growing distrust of Pashtuns (who formerly provided the bulk of factory guards), this shortage of ex-security professionals has opened up fresh employment opportunities for such populations as the Sindhis and the Seraikis of South Punjab, who have historically been under-represented on the security market.

In 2014, one agricultural worker—we'll call him Zulfikar*— left his village in northern Sindh to settle in Karachi. His trajectory is emblematic of the precarious condition of the new guardians of industrial peace. In making this move, he was following in the footsteps of hundreds of thousands of Sindhis who have, since the early 2000s, fled the poverty and climate change affecting the province's rural areas. At the time, Zulfikar had no experience of security work, and it was one of his new neighbours—himself employed in a security company—who steered him towards the sector. He recalls the conditions in which he entered the profession, and his first—and only—weapons training session:

> Zulfikar: They have an office, I went there, they checked my identity card and I got a job.
>
> L.G: Did they train you?
>
> Zulfikar: Yes, they took us there. They have their own [training] ground.
>
> L.G.: Where?

Zulfikar: They took us in a van. I don't really know where. Then they brought us back.

L.G: How many were you?

Zulfikar: There were quite a few of us. There were people from another company. There were people from all communities (*har zaat*). There were Punjabis, Pathans, Mohajirs, Balochs. There were really guys from all over (*har bande*). But well, I didn't stay long, ten–fifteen minutes, not more, and after that I was brought back.

Now assigned to protect a warehouse in the Korangi industrial area, in the south-east of the city, Zulfikar works a twelve-hour shift six days a week, stopping only for a ten- to fifteen-minute break to eat a meal provided by the company.

Every morning and evening, he has to cope with Karachi's chaotic traffic to travel across the city; he lives in Orangi, about 20 kilometres from his workstation, and his transport costs eat into his meagre salary. He earns 14,000 rupees (80 dollars) a month, has no insurance, and knows he would be no match for a group of thieves determined to take the *maal*—the goods stored in the warehouse before being transported to the docks or wholesale markets in the old city. 'From morning to evening, I stand in the den of death. God forbid, anything can happen. If thieves come, the first thing they will do is shoot the guard. Every life is in God's hands', he says with a tired smile.[23]

This feeling of insecurity is increased tenfold by a deep-seated feeling of being ill at ease in the urban environment. However, this uneasiness differs from that referred to by Najam Kathiawari in the vignette opening this chapter. For many migrant workers, the city of Karachi is both disturbing and disquieting, a place of protean and elusive violence that is often incomprehensible to new arrivals from southern Punjab or the rural areas of Sindh. These workers have come from rural areas in which custom and honour are still the dominant tropes for the interpretation and justification of violence,[24] and to them, Karachi's urban conflicts—in which partisan, ethnic, sectarian, and criminal rivalries are intertwined—appear as illegible as they are unpredictable.

To these security agents who feel insecure, the pacification of the city—which the civilian and military authorities have been boasting about since the 2013 launch of the 'Karachi Operation'—remains a pipedream. Zulfikar tells me that 'the *goondas* (thugs) are everywhere. How could they ever desert Karachi? They will never leave'. This anxiety is sustained by the topographical confusion Zulfikar refers to in the interview excerpt quoted above: in this indecipherable city, newcomers find themselves bereft of landmarks; the threat is omnipresent, and danger seems to lurk everywhere.

The way these security guards are perceived by the city's longer-established working-class population only adds to their sense of vulnerability. Unlike the *chowkidars* of the past, most of whom were recruited from communities renowned for the martial skills of their male members (such as the Pashtuns and Punjabis), the new guardians of industrial peace come from populations (the Sindhis, the Seraikis) more renowned for their docility—according to the social representations consolidated by colonial theories of 'martial races', and reinforced by Pakistani army recruitment policies.[25] Several of my Punjabi and Pashtun contacts, employed as workers or shop floor managers in local factories, scoffed at the feebleness of these security guards, describing them as 'weaklings' (*duble patle*) or 'sickly' (*murde*).[26] Not only do they endure appalling working conditions, they are poorly integrated into the local working class and lack the resources necessary for coercion (namely, professional skills and identity capital) that would allow them to negotiate their place in a hostile urban environment. All of this only adds to the precariousness of their condition.

Living and working in insecurity, this surveillance precariat is in turn a source of concern to the industrialists they are meant to be providing protection for at a lower cost. What feeds these new elite insecurities (and compels factory owners to keep a watchful eye over their own watchmen) is precisely the 'cheap' nature of the provision. This is characteristic of the hybrid forms of policing associated with neoliberal globalization.[27]

The cascading effect of surveillance

In July 2016, Ashraf Siddiqui,* Director of Administration and Security ('admin') at Hamid Textiles,* a large textile and garment company based in Korangi (mentioned earlier, see Chapter 4), invited me to visit the control room overseeing the group's video surveillance system. The eyes of three young employees were glued to their screens, monitoring access points to the various production units and their perimeter walls as well as the workshops in which goods are cut, stitched, cleaned, pressed, and packaged. The movements of all workers and guards were carefully monitored. Some cameras were positioned to cover the guards' own deployment area. Noting my curiosity, faced with a screen specifically tracking the movements of a group of armed guards, Ashraf Siddiqui smiled as he pointed to a camera mounted above the young controllers, exclaiming, 'Oh, but I'm watching them too!'

This kind of panoptic apparatus is common in Karachi, where security guards assigned to protect banks and elite residences are often kept under surveillance.[28] But industrial companies have proved particularly imaginative in this domain.

Referring to two fairly dissimilar case studies, I examine different initiatives implemented by industrial companies in a bid to protect themselves from their own security guards. It should be noted that both of the cases discussed in the following pages concern only the most institutionalized of security measures—this is by no means an exhaustive account of the range of disciplinary practices available to industrial companies. The 'Karachi Operation' may have demonized the figure of the political thug, but as the Denim Clothing Company case (Chapter 6) case shows, the underworld plays a persistent role in ordinary surveillance and control tasks within certain companies—including those that are most technologically innovative. Such security arrangements are of course less open to investigation.[29] In any case, I wanted to draw attention to the logics of professionalization at work in corporate security, which have not resolved the paradox of an anxiety-inducing security. Besides, even the most corporate of security departments have often adopted defensive mechanisms strikingly similar to those relying upon thugs and henchmen.[30]

Manufacturing consent at Hamid Textiles*

Hamid Textiles is a clothing company founded in 1973 by a family of Memon entrepreneurs. The company employs 14,000 people and specializes in producing jeans, chinos, and sportswear for the international market. Its customers include groups such as Zara, Kmart, Walmart, Mango, and Carrefour. The vertical integration of the various tasks carried out by the company is typical of the evolution of large Pakistani textile companies, which have gradually diversified their activities in order to control the entire production process, including weaving, packaging—and even distribution through their own sales outlets (though this is not the case for Hamid Textiles).

As in most large companies in Karachi, the security department at Hamid Textiles is under the authority of the 'admin'. Ashraf Siddiqui was born into a middle-class Mohajir family and grew up in the Burns Road area, where Urdu-speaking refugees from India settled in large numbers after Partition. After studying at a local university, he completed an apprenticeship with a small factory owner before going into business for himself, setting up a clothing company. Alongside his business responsibilities, he became involved in 'citizen' security, first as a Civil Defence volunteer, and then with the CPLC. It was within this organization—of which he was a member for 20 years—that Ashraf Siddiqui trained in security and risk management.

Ashraf Siddiqui's involvement with the CPLC has profoundly shaped his relationship with the city and its people. In order to find their way around peripheral neighbourhoods, most industrialists in Karachi will use factories as landmarks; for them, the *basti*s (working-class neighbourhoods, generally developed by means of illegal occupation of public land) and the *goth*s (predominantly Baloch or Sindhi urban villages) surrounding the factories constitute a *terra incognita*, collectively included in the abhorrent category of *katchi abadi*s. Ashraf Siddiqui, however, boasts that he knows 'every nook and cranny of Karachi' as a result of his participation in CPLC anti-kidnapping operations (which always involve intense upstream reconnaissance activities) and his contribution to the development of GIS mapping tools dedicated to researching the spatial and temporal properties of urban crime. His participation in CPLC activities—both in the field and in the organization's offices—would also have made him aware of the importance of 'discipline'.

This commitment to law and order has been constantly put to the test since Ashraf Siddiqui joined Hamid Textiles in the 1990s. The company's offices and production facilities are located in the Korangi Industrial Area, which is plagued by recurrent unrest. The area was central to the turf wars waged by the various MQM factions from 1992 to 2002,[31] and local industries also bore the brunt of an increasingly competitive protection market during the following decade, which was marked by the rise of the Baloch gangs gathered within the People's Amn Committee (PAC).[32] Korangi was also at the forefront of the riots that broke out across Sindh after the assassination of Benazir Bhutto on 27 December 2007. Dozens of trucks and their cargoes were set on fire, and several factories vandalized in the days that followed. Rioters even set fire to a local towel factory—the Fazal Sardar Textile Mills.

As one resident of the nearby Sharafi Goth neighbourhood testifies, these riots prompted Korangi's industrialists to review their security arrangements. This social worker remembers, as a child, regularly stepping over the low wall of a pharmaceutical company located on the route to school to pick roses in its garden—a practice which, he says, carried only a limited amount of risk due to the benevolence of the guards. After the 2007 riots, this was no longer possible; factory walls were raised so high that they became impenetrable. This explosion of violence reinforced local employers' perception of the surrounding neighbourhoods as hotbeds of trouble and threats to industrial order. Residents of these Sindhi and Baloch neighbourhoods had defended some factories against rioters (particularly those employing locals), but their efforts were soon overshadowed by rumours of PAC-linked Baloch gangs moving into the area's semi-rural communities from 2009 onwards.[33]

Alongside other entrepreneurs of Karachi, Ashraf Siddiqui embraces an ethos of confrontation that is intertwined with the art of negotiation.[34] He is convinced that criminal actors must be 'confronted'. As a result, he had no hesitation in negotiating with gang leaders seeking to monetize protection. The bureaucratization of the Hamid Textiles security department did, however, allow its 'admin' to put his own body on the line less frequently—a process that was accelerated by the recruitment of a former military officer, Major Qasim Balkhi,* who had turned to industrial security after twenty-seven years of service in the army. After two years as Head of Administration & Security in a group active in the clothing sector and ship dismantling, he joined Hamid Textiles in 2010, as Senior Manager, Administration & Security—reporting to Ashraf Siddiqui.

Originally from Balochistan and a member of the Hazara ethnic minority (which is very weakly represented in Karachi), Major Balkhi is free of ethnic ties both to the company's workers and to the working-class population of Korangi more generally. His appointment is far from an isolated case, reflecting the changing profile of security managers in large industrial companies. Indeed, since the 2000s, these corporate security executives are recruited mainly from among security or management professionals with few connections to surrounding labour colonies. This disembedding contrasts with the approach taken to security by family businesses that are organized around the *seth* and his coercive intermediaries. Based as it is on more impersonal hierarchical relationships and more bureaucratic management, this corporate approach to security has not entirely eliminated violent brokers—but it has demoted them, as shown by the recent undoing of Riaz Ali, one of the most emblematic political thugs of the 2000s.[35]

The new generation of security managers has little in common with the violent entrepreneurs of that time. Major Balkhi wears civilian clothing, and access to his office is restricted to authorized personnel only. He receives few visitors, conducting most of his business by phone or email. Any incident involving a company employee (guard or worker) is reported to him in real time, either (in the most serious cases) through screenshots sent by video surveillance agents, or through the log book (updated daily by these same agents), or through reports written by his subordinates. On the basis of these reports, and depending on the status of the accused staff and the nature of the violation of company rules and regulations (which follow the Standing Orders Ordinance of 1968), Major

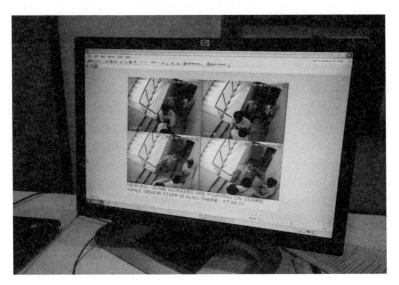

Images transmitted to Major Balkhi by video surveillance agents, reporting an incident between two Hamid Textiles employees. The two men managed to exonerate themselves by claiming that they were 'joking'.

L. Gayer, 2017

Balkhi can, in consultation with his superior, initiate a disciplinary procedure.

The guards employed by Hamid Textiles—some 170 of them, deployed across a dozen sites—have a special status that must be kept in mind in order to understand the nature of the proceedings in cases of alleged misconduct. Unlike most industrial companies in Karachi, Hamid Textiles recruits its own security guards and grants them permanent worker status, which allows them to access health insurance, pensions, and annual bonuses—and protects them against arbitrary dismissal. While their salary is in the lower range (160 USD, in 2016), which is equivalent to that of low-skilled workers employed by the company, they are still in a comparatively privileged position, since most of the low-skilled employees are contract workers.

This strategy of 'manufacturing consent'[36] is the brainchild of Ashraf Siddiqui; it aims to persuade guards to cooperate in their own subordination as well as that of the working population. He

245

sees this as a way of securing the loyalty of potentially disruptive employees, while minimizing the risks associated with them. Guards are only awarded permanent worker status at the end of a rigorous selection process; like most Pakistani companies, Hamid Textiles favours ex-police and *faujis* as security guards, so retired army and law enforcement personnel account for almost half of the workforce. To be eligible, 'civilians' must have at least four years' experience in private security.

Applicants are then subjected to a screening procedure that is based on both a practical skills check and a thorough character investigation (involving the police, the administration, and the applicant's neighbours). This process is ethnically oriented. Following a general shift in the recruitment demographics of security guards, only 30% of the guards at Hamid Textiles are Pashtuns. Here, Major Balkhi explains both the reasons for this marginalization and the specific procedures that are in place for Pashtun candidates:

> Major Balkhi: With Pashtuns we prefer to recruit only former army or FC people, not normal Pashtuns. Because Pashtuns are a bit doubtful, you know, if they are totally civilian, they are doubtful. If they are retired (from the army/paramilitary units) we can track their records, and we can handle them.
>
> L.G : Do you take people from FATA [the former 'tribal areas']?
>
> Major Balkhi: We only take retired FC or army personnel, not civilians. Because they have a record, they have a discharge book, they have a number. We have contacts with their record offices, so they're clear, that's why we take them.
>
> L.G: Is it because the verification process is impossible in FATA?
>
> Major Balkhi: No. the verification process is very much possible. It's because the members of Mehsud or Wazir tribes [from which the Pakistani Taliban recruited many of its fighters from 2007 onwards], maybe they're involved in some criminal activities, plus maybe in [religious] extremism also.[37]

Candidates recruited and eventually appointed through this highly selective procedure are subjected to strict control measures designed to prevent guards from organizing and showing solidarity with the working-class population while also preventing deviant behaviour and punishing offenders. The guards are assembled in 'units' of six, and Major Balkhi ensures that a certain ethnic diversity prevails within these units. Ideally, each unit is supposed to be made up of two Pashtuns, two Sindhis, and two Balochs—a model that is reflective of the ethnic diversification of security recruitment in recent years. The prescribed balance is not always complied with, but certainly each unit has some level of ethnic diversity, which is supposed to encourage mutual surveillance:

> You can't have six people from the same community in the same unit. If we keep it mixed, it encourages [members of other communities] to report to us that 'those dirty Punjabis are up to something'. It gives us an inside view. And then, if one group dominates in a unit, it is to be expected that the unit will do favours to members of its community and turn a blind eye to drug smuggling and fabric theft. In this way, it maintains surveillance within the group.

Both the organization of daily rotations from one post to another, and the circulation of guards through the group's various production units (to which they cannot be posted for more than two consecutive years) are also aimed at preventing the development of collusion with the working population. Thus, according to Major Balkhi,

> If you keep a guard in the same production unit for too long, he starts having *gup shup* (small talk) and develops friendships [among the workers]. And if security guards develop some affairs, relations, friendships with workers, then you know the result. That's why they're moved. We keep getting reports from security and workers as to any abnormal activity. So if we get to know that a guard has developed some links with people, we immediately transfer him to another unit.[38]

These rotations are also intended to thwart actions disruptive of industrial order via the introduction of an element of unpredictability to the security system. Major Balkhi was drawing on his experience in the army, where he had organized the security perimeter of certain installations: 'The basic principle of security is: do not present a definite pattern to security. Keep the other person confused'. In other words, the frequent transfer of guards from one post to another, coupled with the varying intensity of checks at each site, is a way of countering those forces that are subversive of industrial order with organized uncertainty. In this way, security can cultivate unpredictability—admittedly at the risk of increasing feelings of insecurity among the guards, who are thus denied the comfort of routine.

Video surveillance also plays a central role in this disciplinary apparatus, which is oriented towards the control of security agents. However, those in charge of the Hamid Textiles security department have contrasting perceptions of the purpose of CCTV cameras.

According to Ashraf Siddiqui, the primary purpose of the cameras deployed inside factories and administrative buildings is to act as a deterrent, while serving a panoptic logic: 'It serves to remind people that someone is watching them. That's all'. Major Balkhi, who was present during the interview, begged to differ: 'At times there is some abnormal activity... It allows us to observe them. In fact, a large proportion of incidents involving guards or workers are reported to the management staff by the CCTV officers'. Managers of the various units or shifts can also send a report to the Assistant Manager In-Charge of Security, who passes it on to Major Balkhi.

The head of security then sorts out the incidents and (depending on their seriousness) may order an investigation by the relevant production unit. The resulting report is then forwarded to Ashraf Siddiqui, who may, in consultation with Major Balkhi, decide to initiate disciplinary proceedings. Between ten and fifteen minor incidents are recorded every day. Serious incidents are much less frequent—one or two per month—and revolve around three main types of offence: (1) the introduction or use of drugs (hashish, opium, or heroin) in the workplace; (2) the theft of goods; and (3) brawls between employees. Regardless of the seriousness of these incidents, the industrial relations (IR) department (which corresponds to a human resources department) is responsible for drawing up a charge sheet (indictment) against the employee suspected of the offence. The employee is then required to explain him/herself before a disciplinary committee, in the presence of any witnesses. At the end of its investigation, the committee may decide to issue a simple warning or initiate dismissal proceedings. The accused has the right to appeal a dismissal decision in the Labour Courts.

These disciplinary commissions almost always result in a decision hostile to the accused—which is hardly surprising, given that the 'Investigation Officer' appointed by the company is always a manager from the industrial relations department. Procedural flaws can sometimes be enough to scupper a case in court, so the managers of Hamid Textiles are careful to respect procedure. Few disputes end up in court, however. Since there are no worker representatives at Hamid Textiles, there is nobody to relay worker grievances, so that the possibility of appeal at the Labour Courts remains fairly theoretical. Nevertheless, these legal standards do retain some validity insofar as they guide the conduct of employers—at least with regard to their permanent employees.[39] It is however almost impossible (in the absence of any employment contract or other proof of employment) for contract workers to contest a possible dismissal—so much so that companies rarely bother to formalize such cases.

With the cooperation of Ashraf Siddiqui and Major Balkhi, I was able to obtain the charge sheets prepared against some 15 guards who had been accused of misconduct between 2015 and 2017. The circumstances and nature of the offences they were charged with are shown in the table below.

The majority of these breaches of company discipline—especially those relating to absenteeism—are not specific to security guards.[40] Similarly, brawls and exchanges of insults are common on the shop floor. However, the number of incidents involving the 'aggressive' and disrespectful behaviour of some guards towards their superiors is of particular concern where such acts are carried out by armed guards, who are constantly suspected of having mutinous tendencies. These flare-ups also mark the limitations of Ashraf Siddiqui's strategy of manufacturing consent—though the rate of dismissals in this armed corps does not exceed 5% of the workforce per year.

This preoccupation with respect for hierarchy is a hallmark of security officials with military backgrounds. Commenting on incident I.1, Major Balkhi tells me that 'there has to be a chain of command. No institution or factory can run without a proper chain

Misconduct by guards at Hamid Textiles, October 2015–August 2017

Reference of the incident (I)	Date of incident	Nature of alleged misconduct	Security guard role	Nature of sanction
I.1	01.10.2015	Absenteeism; refusal to obey an order from a superior; aggressiveness	Guard in the group washing unit	Dismissal
I.2	29.10.2015	Absenteeism; insults and threats to superior (to whom he reportedly said '*factory ke bahar se uthwa lunga*'—'once you are out I will get rid of you')	Guard in a group production unit	Dismissal
I.3	30.10.2015	Abandoning post at Head Office gate; trespassing in group CEO dining room	Guard at the group Head Office	Warning
I.4	03.11.2015	Taking part in a brawl	Female guard in charge of worker body search at a group production unit	Dismissal
I.5	6.01.2016	Absenteeism; disrespect/ insults to a superior demanding explanations	Custodian at group Head Office	Dismissal
I.6	22.04.2016	Failure to challenge a group of individuals writing graffiti on a company wall	Guard at a group production unit	Warning
I.7	22.06.2016	'Unruly' and 'aggressive' conduct; refusal to obey a superior, followed by insults	Custodian at group Head Office	Dismissal

Reference of the incident (I)	Date of incident	Nature of alleged misconduct	Security guard role	Nature of sanction
I.8	15.07.2016	Absenteeism (failure to report for work for more than ten consecutive days)	Guard at a group production unit	Dismissal
I.9	03.03.2017	Theft (discovery of pair of trousers in her bag during body search prior to leaving factory)	Female guard in charge of body search of workers at a group production unit	Dismissal
I.10	05.04.2015	Responsible for accidental shooting while cleaning his rifle	Guard at a group production unit	Warning
I.11	07.04.2017	Absenteeism; disrespect/insults to a superior demanding explanations	Guard at a group production unit	Dismissal
I.12	09.06.2017	Insults to superior	Fire Officer assigned to group Head Office	Dismissal
I.13	19.06.2017	Absenteeism (failure to report for work for more than ten consecutive days)	Guard at group Head Office	Dismissal
I.14	03.08.2017	Caught raping (*badfeli*) a worker in sewing department	Guard at a group production unit	Dismissal

of command… without a proper reporting line… There has to be a discipline, norms, SOPs [Standard Operating Procedures] for security to work'. Accidental shootings (I.10), or the unauthorized movement of certain guards within secure areas frequented by management staff (I.3), are evidence of specific anxieties around these armed subordinates.

The rape of a worker mentioned in incident I.14 was initially described by Major Balkhi as a breach of the company's moral order: 'Sodomy is definitely not allowed in our establishments', he told me during an initial discussion of the case. Because the Urdu term *badfeli* used in the indictment is ambiguous (it usually means rape but can also refer to an 'unnatural' sexual act), I initially thought it referred to a consensual homosexual act in the workplace. However, in a subsequent interview, Major Balkhi explained that it was indeed a rape case—though he later changed his mind, downplaying the incident as a mere instance of 'sexual harassment'.

Only one of these incidents (I.6) involved a guard who, from the point of view of his superiors, had failed in his responsibilities by not reacting to an offence. Compared to the type of misconduct commonly attributed to guards, this may seem a relatively minor offence, but it does merit further consideration. Although the offender was given only a warning, I was left to wonder what problem the company had with these people leaving their mark on the wall of its production unit. Asked about this, Major Balkhi explained that 'if they can write [graffiti] on the walls of our factories, they can also come inside… they can do anything'. So this was really more of a sovereignty dispute than a security issue.

The practice of 'wall-chalking' in Karachi has long been associated with militants from political parties or religious groups using more or less inflammatory slogans to mark their territory. Preservation of the integrity of the perimeter walls of company headquarters or factories is therefore powerfully symbolic; it is a question of reaffirming the autonomy of the productive world against the turbulence of the city. More prosaically, defence of perimeter wall integrity sends out a signal to potential racketeers who might, through these apparently benign transgressions, be seeking to test the company's defences.

This border conflict is conceived of as a war of the worlds, pitting industrial order against urban disorder—and the guards are on its front line. This social prophylaxis may be based on a fiction— if only because these same companies have long had recourse to representatives of political parties, religious organizations, and gangs, the better to repress worker mobilizations and maintain factory discipline. Yet it continues to inspire the control strategies of corporate security managers, further confusing the mandate of security guards—who serve both as border guards (securing the outer perimeter of factories) and enforcers of factory discipline (tracking down workers who are slacking at their machines, or taking advantage of the relative privacy of the toilets to share a joint).[41]

Managing security at Shahbaz Pharma*

My second case study concerns a large pharmaceutical group founded in 1995 and specializing in the production of generic drugs. Shahbaz Pharma* employs more than 5,000 people and (like most companies in this sector) has set up a workplace organization that is very different from that which prevails in the textile and garment industry.

The use of contract workers has also become widespread in the pharmaceutical industry, but here, casual labour coexists alongside informal forms of employee retention. This is an industry that requires a more qualified workforce and (under draconian international standards) is subject to more restrictive health and safety rules. In return, it offers more attractive working conditions and remuneration than textiles—a fact that was identified by every worker I met, regardless of their own sector of activity. These companies are committed to retaining their workforce in order to avoid the endemic problem of high workforce turnover. The extremely strict disciplinary rules prevailing at Shahbaz Pharma, coupled with its managers' strong attachment to employment flexibility (thus preserving the freedom to dismiss any offender and preventing the formation of unions within the its workforce), thus coexist with a policy of profit-sharing and social assistance measures that are without equal in the textile sector.

Alongside the structural characteristics of the Pakistani pharmaceutical industry and its distinctive patterns of labour organization, the security arrangements at Shahbaz Pharma owe much to the social and political background of its CEO, Mehmood Hussain.* Like many entrepreneurs in the pharmaceutical sector, he belongs to the Punjabi Saudagaran merchant community. This is an Urdu-speaking group that was, until Partition, based in Delhi. Its

253

position in Karachi business circles was strengthened following the
(relative) decline of the Memons in the wake of Zulfikar Ali Bhutto's
nationalizations of the 1970s.

Mehmood Hussain, for his part, grew up and was educated in
the United States, where his contact with progressive groups during
the 1970s led him to develop a left-leaning political orientation.
This political socialization left Mehmood Hussain with a lasting
hostility towards the military—though not enough to deter him
from recruiting a retired officer to revamp his company's security
department. This confirms the widespread belief among Karachi's
business elites that corporate security is a matter best left to the
professionals of violence. In this case, however, the relation soon
soured, and Mehmood Hussain found himself having to explore
other solutions:

> In this company, when we first started, in 1995, things were
> just heating up, in terms of MQM. So what we did was we
> had one guy [retired] from the army. He was a guy who was
> a non-commissioned officer in my childhood friend's unit
> [his friend was a colonel]. When I used to live in the US and
> whenever I came back to Pakistan, I used to visit him wherever
> he [his friend] was. He was in 54 Baloch. And whenever I met
> my friend I saw him [the major]. I was very impressed by his
> sense of judgement, I would sit with him, have a cup of chai
> or something... In 1995, at age 40, he took retirement. At that
> time, the company was a big mess. The financial controller was
> stealing, the operation manager as well... There was sexual
> harassment to the point that it was an open secret that there
> were five or ten women in the production who they would call
> to their rooms, and did whatever they want... I had to break that
> gang in the management that I inherited here. So I recruited him
> and I expected that he would... [...] I expected him to break
> that gang... And it was the same guy who was fired for sexual
> harassment, twenty years later! [...]
> He was the first and last [military officer to head the security
> department]. One day, when the security situation got really
> bad, I hired a captain, but within one month I fired him because
> he started scheming, he thought that everyone, including his

manager, was his platoon… He would stand at the gate and when somebody was walking in without his entry card, he would tell them—even senior persons—'Why did you forget it? Are you a school kid?'. That's not how you address people. He would also call the guy in charge of the fleet to say, 'I want you to send this car from this workshop to that workshop'. And when the manager asked him 'Why?', he replied 'How dare you ask me why?' And in front of former customers, with whom we had been in business for years, he would say things like 'We don't owe you anything'…[42]

The strained relationship between this CEO and his director of security cannot be explained by the CEO's personal backstory and ideological orientations alone. The tension is indicative of a more structural problem, namely the complex relationship between these business leaders and their security managers, which rarely results in a harmonious alliance of capital and coercion. Prior to joining Hamid Textiles (where, by his own admission, he maintains a relationship of mutual respect with his superior), Major Balkhi sometimes felt alienated in the corporate world. He has bitter memories of his first professional experience in the civilian sector, in the course of which his employer first pushed him to the front line to contain a strike, only to withdraw his support when the protest escalated. This betrayal was completely at odds with his own (still very military) conception of authority, in which a true leader does not abandon his troops under fire.

While it is true that labour conflicts can put relations between the holders of capital and the professionals of coercion to the test, their relations in more ordinary times can also be marked by tensions. It is in such everyday interactions that we see both the professional habitus of these former military men and the discrepancy between that habitus and what these retired *faujis* view as a corporate culture that is entirely profit-oriented. During one interview, a former non-commissioned officer occupying a mid-ranking position in the security department of the KFG* textile group expressed feeling ill at ease in a professional environment in which he felt that his contribution was not recognized:

Working in [corporate] security means that you restrict yourself from eating while preventing others from gorging themselves. I'm like a snake sitting on a pile of gold, restricting myself from drawing on it while preventing others from accessing it. If you have the trust of your employer, after four o'clock in the afternoon, the soldiers are the bosses (*fauji malik hain*). At four o'clock, the *seth*s close their offices, climb into their cars and leave the factory. After that, Security is in charge of the factory. [...] But in the eyes of the bosses, Security does nothing. It just eats the money. We don't make money and we don't produce anything for the bosses. All we do is to get money out of them.[43]

The discomfort described by this ex-military man highlights a major challenge facing everyone involved in corporate security, namely 'knowing how to transform an apparently unproductive constraint into a longer-term resource.'[44] In most of the industrial firms based in Karachi, exploitation of the relational resources of former military personnel was more effective in addressing this problem than the use of cost optimization rationalization techniques (as in the case of the French security managers studied by Frédéric Ocqueteau).[45] Given an urban context in which the army has regained a leading role following the launch of the Karachi Operation in 2013, the interpersonal skills of retired servicemen are now valued more highly than ever by civilian management.

In the case of Shahbaz Pharma, the CEO's progressive beliefs undermined such pragmatic arrangements. However, the breakdown of the relationship between this top businessman and his director of security had more to do with managerial rationality than it did with ideological considerations. Every industrial firm follows written and unwritten rules that govern both hierarchical relationships within the company and its interactions with suppliers and customers. It was primarily because of his poor performance and failure to comply with these rules that Shahbaz Sharma's first head of security was sacked. His dismissal, in turn, prompted a reassessment of the company's security system.

Following this experience, Mehmood Hussain decided to turn away from reliance on former military men, and towards a new type of civilian security expert, then on the rise in Pakistan. In the aftermath of an incident in which Riaz Chenoy (head of the IIL Group) was kidnapped by a group of Islamist militants, deeply shocking the industrialists based in Korangi, Hussain called in a security consultant who had been recommended by a close friend.[46] His own political orientation notwithstanding, recruiting a civilian for this task remained a challenging task—which shows just how deeply embedded and normalized the use of ex-military personnel for these roles is:

> When he sent me his name, his name was Abdul Karim,* he didn't have 'Colonel' or anything written in front of his name, and I thought, 'This guy is not even in the army, how is he taking care of this ?' So I met him. He had lived in the Netherlands for 20 years, and was in the Netherlands police commandos, in charge of protecting high-target diplomats: Palestinians, Israelis... The security business was thriving [in Pakistan] and he moved back here and set up a company. He went to the Corps Commander [the head of the V Corps in Karachi] and said, 'Sir, I want to tell you about gaps in your security'. It's like someone who has the balls to go to the Pope and tell him how to pray correctly, right... [laughs]. [...]
>
> After that, he set up a large security firm. Then I gave him a very large security assignment. He came here and did a complete audit. And, oh my god, we had zero security... zero... Not a single guy knew how to fire. They were all tailors or something before [becoming guards]. So he asked them if they had already fired a gun before and they said, 'Yes, when we were hired by the security agency'. 'So how did you do it?', and they said, 'we were given a pistol and we fired four shots in the air'. That's all the training they were having. [...] That was in 2011, after Riaz Chenoy's kidnapping... I was very concerned at that time because they had my name, my children's names... It was like the Italian mafiosi... The subedar major was still there at the time—he was fired a year later—and he was very insecure. He thought that he was the best. Actually, he was a good manager but very bad at security... [...] So we gave him [Abdul Karim] a consulting and we did a complete revamp. We fired just about

everybody, we just kept the best. Then he recruited new guys, gave them training, got them new weapons. But more than anything, he promoted the idea that security is in the head, not in the gun.

The security model in place at Shahbaz Pharma is therefore quite distinct from that of Hamid Textiles; it is closer to the forms of corporate security that prevail in transnational firms operating in Karachi.[47] It relies on new security experts, who have a more managerial culture. Presenting themselves as consultants and resorting to regular audits aimed at rationalization, what these actors have imported into corporate security is the language and practices of the advanced capitalist firm, rather than violent know-how.

Within Shahbaz Pharma, this managerialization of corporate security extends to choosing civilians to supervise security matters. The group's 'admin', Omer Shirazi,* was born into an upper-class Mohajir family. His father was a diplomat, posted to Paris in the late 1960s. He went to school there and developed a taste for French New Wave cinema and jazz that has never left him— for a few years, he even hosted a music programme on a local FM station. Unlike Ashraf Siddiqui, he has no experience in either civil security or citizen participation in law enforcement, and prior to joining Shahbaz Pharma, he had worked mainly in airline marketing departments. Since he has no security-specific background at all, in everyday matters he has to rely on the expertise of the group's head of security, Ameer Hasan.*

Hasan joined the CPLC as office assistant in 1991, emerging as Head Controller for the whole of Sindh in 2014. He was involved in the development of the organization's databases through the digitization of FIRs and prison registers. He continues to use the databases he is so familiar with to satisfy himself that no group employee (including guards) has any criminal history. The outsourcing of guard recruitment has not rendered this profiling work completely obsolete. As Ameer Hasan explains:

> Generally speaking, we have recruited former military or police officers. Because I worked for the CPLC for a long time, I know how to check their background. First of all, we check their name

and ancestry through the CPLC databases. They are very useful databases, really excellent. Secondly, before we recruit someone, we ask two guarantors to commit themselves by presenting their identity cards. They can be parents, but in the case of guards we prefer to ask neighbours because the applicant's parents can sometimes be biased. We then check this information with NADRA. We also check with senior army officers for former military personnel. We send them for interviews. Because they can ask them questions and check. Our security consultant employs a [former] colonel, who interviews them. About 50% of our guards are ex-military, we have very few ex-police.[48]

We can see here that the development of a managerial culture of corporate security is not necessarily synonymous with a distancing from the knowledge and agents of public security—and therefore cannot be reduced to a dynamic of security privatization. The databases Hasan relies on for his profiling operations were set up through a partnership between the Karachi police and an organization founded and managed by businessmen. The police remain central to this arrangement, if only insofar as they collect and redistribute the FIRs registered at the city's police stations, from which the CPLC extracts its data. This echoes the literature (discussed in the previous chapter) on police officers as 'knowledge workers' feeding the risk management systems of public and private actors via institutionalized communication formats such as databases.[49]

This heavy reliance on police knowledge and institutionalized information systems does not preclude a certain scepticism towards these resources. The risks of fraud and corruption, technical glitches, or the long-limited interconnectivity of police files explain why Karachi's industrialists and their security managers continue to be so attached to the individual level of risk analysis—which Ericson and Haggerty had predicted would give way to a 'systematization' process associated with computerized databases.

Ultimately, for Karachi's more security-conscious industrialists, it is the interpretative skills of their security managers that make it possible for them to see through this troubled world in which the true nature of both people and things seems to be constantly slipping away.

The CEO of Shahbaz Pharma says that Ameer Hasan 'knows all about security, about political parties, the undercurrents... He is almost like a psychiatrist [in his ability to see through people's natures]'. Indeed, like Waseem Dehlvi (the contractor we met in Chapter 4), Ameer Hasan takes pride in his ability to spot potential activists through their body language as job applicants. This ability to make bodies speak also extends to an ability to read the city, reintroducing legibility to the opaque world of intertwined partisan affiliations and criminal connections that must be kept at arm's length from the business world.

Several decades of armed conflict have undoubtedly led every Karachi inhabitant to develop a 'hermeneutic of danger', by which I mean an ability to anticipate danger by deciphering the moods of the city.[50] The skills of specialists in detection are less commonly found, and entail identifying signs of duplicity in individuals; they can be forged only through a combination of professional experience and access to certain reserved knowledge. Because this know-how is unevenly distributed through society, it is a producer of expertise. Nonetheless, it is as much a part of the economy of suspicion as are more ordinary ways of deciphering the urban environment. It is based on the same frenzy of interpretation alongside divination skills that, like the culture of risk, are fundamentally pessimistic: the worst is always possible (if not probable).

Beside this multi-level profiling, which combines individual and institutional sources of knowledge, Shahbaz Pharma's risk reduction system is based on a continuous training programme for security guards. The consultant hired by the company organizes annual training sessions, in the course of which the guards perfect their shooting skills and familiarize themselves with crisis management. As Nandini Gooptu points out,[51] this kind of training process is as much about imparting practical knowledge as it is about instilling a dynamic of self-control that is essential to the 'emotional labour' expected of these guards—that is, their ability to control their own emotions while on the job, as well as those of others.[52] In emphasizing the importance of self-control for security guards, these training programmes aim both to improve the performance and reshape the personalities of these precarious service sector workers—while also ensuring their continued condition of servility. Some authors have even described these workers as an 'emotional proletariat' whose employers control their physical labour, their behaviour, their attitudes, and their feelings.[53]

This combination of intensive profiling and emotional shaping is seen as a success by both security managers and the CEO at Shahbaz Pharma. And while the problem of absenteeism does persist, only one guard has reportedly been dismissed for severe misconduct since 2014, and that was in the wake of a complaint of sexual harassment by a female employee, where the guilt of the accused was established with the help of video surveillance. The sense of security provided by this 'success' remains extremely relative, however. The fact that the company guards, as a result of the training they have received, now have improved technical mastery of their weapons and improved self-control is proving to raise risk levels by encouraging more aggressive responses in crisis situations. This can be seen in one guard's reaction to a recent attempted armed robbery of company employees that happened while they were travelling to a nearby mosque:

> They had gone to [Friday] prayer, and then some armed men came in and tried to rob them and take the weapons from the guards. So one of our guards, his name is Ashraf,* he had been trained by Abdul and our people, opened fire. At this point he was trained, so he didn't shoot blindly. He adjusted his shot to scare them without hitting them. It was risky, but I guess he did his job. When he came back, we took care of him. I told him it really wasn't worth it for a couple of mobile phones. But they were armed, and he was afraid they would attack our employees. So when he came back, we offered him a reward.[54]

This testimony (gathered from Omer Shirazi) reveals security managers' uneasiness in the face of a new type of risky security behaviour, identified by them as the result of the successive training sessions they had imposed on guards. This training has, by controlling the risks associated with unskilled guards, inadvertently created a new threat—posed this time by armed guards who are more confident and thus more likely to resort to violence in a crisis—even at the risk of a deadly escalation. Mentioned in passing by Omer Shirazi, the company reaction—to reward the guard involved while urging him to show more restraint in the future—is indicative of this uneasiness. But it also speaks of a new kind of risk arising not out of the guards' deviation from the rules, but from their overzealous adherence to the behavioural model inculcated by the company and its security consultants. There is an ambivalence inherent to a security model that relies on the production of a new condition of servility, and in which the intensity certain security guards take on their role with leaves their employers in fear of fresh excesses. This ambivalence is perhaps summed up in the grudging satisfaction expressed by those employers: 'I suppose he has done his job'.

* * *

The relationship between the industrialists of Karachi and their guards is, then, one of uneasy, fragile domination. This fragility is due, first of all, to the social characteristics of the guards. Often recruited from the very same communities that are providing factory labour, these foot soldiers of the industrial order tend to have divided loyalties that can soon become problematic in the event of labour conflict. The emergence of a security market has given rise to new security manager and security guard profiles, and members of both groups now maintain a more distant relationship with the working population. In turn, these transformations of the industrial security apparatus have created fresh uncertainties, both by handing over security departments to former military personnel (whose professional ethos is often very different from that of civilian managers) and by producing poorly trained, poorly motivated security guards who are little inclined to defend the interests of employers in crisis situations.

Faced with the inevitable dilemmas of cheap policing, each company has experimented with its own forms of 'organised informality',[55] in line with its own managerial model and—above all—with the professional background of its security managers. Yet these differences do not preclude the use of similar profiling practices, which show how societies confronted with the trauma and uncertainty of chronic civil strife are prone to compulsively check on things and people.[56] While profiling practices do take on a particular intensity in this troubled urban context, they also have a more general dimension—as evidenced by the fact that they have held a central position in the technologies of control of industrial capitalism ever since the nineteenth century.[57] These days, they rely as much on institutional databases as they do on the informal networks of risk experts such as security managers.

The importance of interpersonal relations and unofficial practices in these profiling operations points to the limitations of the bureaucratization of corporate security—a trend that, again, is not confined to the industrial circles of Karachi—as the recent scandal surrounding the spying practices of IKEA France has shown.[58] The hypothesis of a global privatization of security also needs to be qualified in the light of evidence emerging from Karachi, since police knowledge and military expertise remain central to these verification mechanisms—even though they are subject to multiple reservations and suspicions. What we are dealing with here is more of a mixed economy of domination, one that is susceptible both to various forms of irregularity and to generating its own uncertainties.

In addition to these compulsive profiling practices, training programmes and various strategies for manufacturing consent have been designed to ensure the active participation of guards in their own domination and that of an increasingly precarious working population. These strategies of control have in turn created new vulnerabilities—one of which is the threat of new types of screw-ups by more confident guards, which could potentially draw their employers into engagement with a spiral of violence involving criminal groups active in the industrial estates. These companies' desire to exist as an autonomous, pacified world is thus once again thwarted. Because its chosen modes of domination are as coercive as they are driven by anxiety, Karachi's industrial capitalism can only confirm Robert Castel's insight that insecurity is, for two reasons, 'consubstantial with societies that are built around the search for security'—first, because security programmes, swimming in a sea of uncertainties, produce disappointment and resentment, and second, because 'their success, even if it is relative, in controlling certain risks, gives rise to others'.[59]

Challenged as it is by the tensions and contradictions of their own security apparatus, the domination exercised by Karachi's industrial elites is always somewhat shaky. But what about their management of those risks that emanate from the production processes themselves? Are these industrial firms, now free of the constraints imposed by trade unions, political parties, and—to a large extent— state regulation on their way to achieving the neo-liberal ideal of corporate freedom? The tragedy of Ali Enterprises, with which my investigation began, adds nuance to this hypothesis. However, what this ordeal by fire has revealed is an overheated capitalism, whose self-limiting factors are difficult to perceive.

TRIAL BY FIRE

This anarchy of the law, it's wrong to say that only the powerful take advantage of it. It is people who are organized that take advantage of it.

Advocate Faisal Siddiqi.[1]

At first glance, the image shows a mountain of discarded clothing—it looks like jeans. Half-lying in shadow, they seem freshly washed, the still wet denim crumpled. Exposed to the harsh midday light, however, stains of ash and soot are revealed on those areas not reduced to charred shreds. Bits of straw have been scattered across the heap of blackened rags—no doubt by the force of the water jet. Untitled, the photograph gives the lie to Walter Benjamin's famous assertion that, without a caption, 'photographic construction would remain stuck in the approximate'.[2] First shown to the Karachi public in February 2013 as part of a series of photographs soberly entitled 'Koi Din Aur' (Another Day), it is the accompanying images that make sense of it: a sign bearing the Ali Enterprises address and motto ('Striving to Contribute to & Promote Pakistan's Economy'), overlooked by a general view of the factory after the tragedy of 11 September 2012.[3]

The remains of jeans originally destined for the German company KiK, burned in the Ali Enterprises fire of 11 September 2012.

Naila Mahmood/Vasl Artists' Association, 2012, reproduced with her kind permission

Presented just a few months after this industrial disaster of unprecedented scale in Pakistan, as part of a group exhibition at Karachi's Arts Council, Naila Mahmood's photograph spoke volumes to visitors still in shock. Everyone would have recognized that this image was using a poignant metonymic effect between the workers and their production to reference the more than 250 lives lost that day.

As a well-known artist acclaimed in particular for her work on shared kitchens in Karachi's working-class neighbourhoods, Naila Mahmood recalls both the difficult circumstances in which she captured this image and its equally trying aftermath:

> Before I took this picture, I had been working in [the] Mohajir camp/Baldia area for my kitchens project. I personally knew a couple of affected Katchi families in Baldia and one Bengali family in Orangi Town when the fire happened. I did not take many pictures then, but later brought in my camera. This picture

was taken on one of those trips. A friend of mine and I were asked by PILAR to put together a book. For this project, I started recording interviews [with] the survivors, victims' families and witnesses. I was careful about photography but slowly took photos of them as well. These were the initial days, when most of them narrated stories of psychological trauma and nightmares. Then came the lawyers and the prospect of money and things got messy. People started confronting me about my motives for being there and once I got a serious threat about what would happen unless I stayed away and stayed out. We had to abandon that project, which was more poetic than documentary, and addressed the human condition and social injustice.[4]

The conditions governing the production and circulation of this image are indicative of far-reaching transformations in the critique of industrial capitalism in Karachi, which has been taken over by actors from outside the working class. The organization that commissioned Mahmood's book project (PILER) is a progressive think tank conducting research, training, and advocacy work. PILER has long resorted to using the law to achieve activist ends, by means of running awareness programmes among workers, offering legal aid to victims of accidents or abuse in the workplace, and filing Public Interest Litigations (PILs) in the Sindh High Court and the Supreme Court in various public interest cases (the right to electricity, environmental protection, water quality, working conditions, etc.). Founded in the early 1980s by former trade unionists and academics with backgrounds in various leftist movements, this organization bears witness to the way in which trade unionism in Karachi has given way to an expert activism that is eager to turn the weapon of law against those who hold power.

The exhibition in which Naila Mahmood's photography was shown to the public for the first time was curated by one of Pakistan's most highly regarded contemporary artists, Adeela Suleman, who happens to be the wife of the activist lawyer who has been a major supporter of PILER's causes (there will be more about him at the end of this chapter). Dedicated to the Ali Enterprises fire, this event at the Arts Council in Karachi in 2013 was called *Awaaz* (the voice/ cry); its aim was to publicize the disaster to raise public awareness and compel provincial and federal authorities to enact structural reforms. This campaign (which included Naila Mahmood's aborted book project) was, for its promoters, complementary to the legal proceedings against the owners of Ali Enterprises. The same coalition of committed artists, cause lawyers, progressive businessmen, and trade unionists converted to advocacy work was involved in both the cultural and legal aspects of this mobilization.

This group was less disparate than it seemed. Most of its members came from the upper (or upper middle) class and had been politicized in left-wing student movements in Pakistan and the US. The PILER leadership came from more modest backgrounds, yet have had a long-standing relationship with these affluent progressives. The friendship between Naila Mahmood and Karamat Ali (the late director of PILER) thus dates back to their student days, when both were members of the left-leaning National Students Federation (NSF), collaborating on the staging of several plays by Bertolt Brecht.[5]

These friendly relations and political affinities helped this small group of activists devise a common strategy, and from the outset, the weapon of the law seemed to be a key instrument in obtaining justice for the victims of the Baldia factory fire and their families.

However, as Naila Mahmood soon realized in the face of hostility to her photographic project, turning to the law brought its own share of turmoil. Because the civil proceedings were focused on financial compensation for the families of the victims, they sowed doubt and discord. At the same time, the interference of law enforcement agencies in the criminal proceedings, coupled with the growing credibility of the arson theory, changed both the course and the political significance of the controversy, which progressive circles had hoped to turn into a reformist cause.

Concluding my exploration of Karachi's industrial capitalism with a return to the catastrophic event that originally prompted my questioning, this final chapter takes stock; in terms of defending themselves against the predatory tendencies of their employers and global value chains, are Pakistani workers left with any tools at their disposal? The Ali Enterprises industrial disaster was unprecedented in both its scale and its media impact—did it help bring about change?

As the sociology of public controversies has shown, a scandal calls into question the order of things by giving rise to 'organizational reworkings, the production of new legal provisions, and the collective validation of new practices'.[6] For industrial cities, a literal trial by fire such as the Ali Enterprises tragedy marks a critical moment in which both the role of capitalist institutions in the making of the city, and their ability to reform themselves, are put to the test.[7] The question of fire constitutes a laboratory for the transformation of the world of work, around which new modes of organizing productive spaces and labour relations are invented.[8] In the context of the industrialization of European societies, then, factory fires (especially within the textile industry) have been 'one of the characteristic and yet largely neglected witnesses of capitalist rationalisation'.[9] For its part, the Baldia fire's ability to rewrite the rules of the game came up against its limits as soon as the industrial scandal turned into a political matter—to the benefit of a coalition of conservative elites.

However, we must be wary of falling prey to retrospective illusions: this outcome was not a foregone conclusion, and, in a society where the law of the jungle seems to reign supreme, it is worth noting that each stage of the legal proceedings confirmed that the judicial realm did retain a measure of autonomy. This autonomy is a prerequisite to the effectiveness of the law as an instrument of domination in the service of the powerful. Indeed, as E. P. Thompson argued, such effectiveness rests on the law's propensity to respect its own criteria of equity—and thus, on occasion, to actually *be* just.[10] Because the legal register is characterized by a reversibility of its offensive and repressive uses, it would also be wrong to downplay the ability of activists to twist the law towards subversive ends.[11]

Beyond this reflection on the double-edged sword of the law and its ambivalent place in the reproduction of Karachi's industrial capitalism, this chapter intends to close the investigation with a kind of theatrical recap. The analysis of the Baldia factory fire case provides an opportunity to bring together, in the concrete situation of a shared ordeal, the most enduring players in this industrial capitalism, namely the *seth* (the factory owner, who has little regard for the law), the *badmash* (the henchman, who may take the form of either the neighbourhood kingpin [*dada*] or the unscrupulous *lumpen* [*goonda*]), the *contractor* (the recruiting agent, who oscillates between community 'boss' and shameless exploiter), and the *fauji* (the para/ military man, referee of the political game and ultimate guarantor of 'industrial peace'). By summoning this cast of characters and submitting them collectively to trial by fire, the controversies raised by the Ali Enterprises disaster attest not only to the longevity of these figures of authority but also to their sudden reversals of fortune. Their tribulations bear the imprint of a volatile urban environment, whose disorder they claimed to organize, even as they fuelled it.

Karachi's industrial capitalism in the dock

Ali Enterprises was owned by Abdul Aziz Bhaila and his two sons, Shahid and Arshad. The Bhailas are a 'caste' affiliated with the Memon *jama'at* (community) of Kutiyana (in present-day Gujarat). Like Memon communities from Bantva, Dhoraji, and Jeptur, the Kutiyana *jama'at* has a long-standing affinity with merchant and industrial capitalism. Its merchant ethos is rooted in a long history of transoceanic connections and was consolidated during the colonial period, when Memon traders and financiers played a key role in the new circulatory flows that accompanied the expansion of the *Pax Britannica* in the Indian Ocean.[12] The Bhailas were particularly prominent in the textile trade in Sri Lanka, where their community has established a lasting presence and continues to play a major role in both economic and political life.[13] After Partition, some of these Memon merchants relocated to Karachi. Like the more prestigious *jama'ats*, such as those of Bantva and Dhoraji (from which most of the major Memon industrialists have hailed since the 1950s), the Memons of Kutiyana cultivate a strong attachment to their locality of origin. This is reflected in philanthropic projects that are systematically stamped with the name of their locality of origin (such as the Kutiyana Memon Hospital in Kharadar, founded in 1993).

Having followed in the footsteps of these traders-turned-industrialists, Abdul Aziz Bhaila and his two sons prove the resilience of the entrepreneurial figure of the *seth* and the management model with which he continues to be associated, despite competition from a more bureaucratic model. Ali Enterprises was thus a family business with little bureaucracy, in which the recruitment of managers was dictated less by the educational capital of applicants than their skills as mediators and navigators in troubled waters. In working environments such as these, managers were meant to interface with workers and their political representatives while showing a strong sense of initiative in ensuring the smooth running of factories; this would often entail a somewhat creative engagement with the law. For peace of mind, the *seths* depended on the ability of these heavy-duty characters to take on the dirty work of employer domination, no questions asked. At Ali Enterprises, this role was filled by two shady figures: Mansoor Ahmed, who was the company's contractor and Production Manager, and Muhammad Zubair, an MQM-affiliated henchman in charge of supervising the finishing department.

While they run through the history of Karachi's industrial capitalism, these interrelated figures of the *seth*, the contractor, and the *badmash* have evolved with the political environment and regulations of the time. Throughout Karachi, the grip of political parties on productive activity has demanded new skills among the aspiring brokers of industrial order—starting with an intimate knowledge of each party and its militant apparatus, which has proved crucial to negotiating their repeated demands.

On a more global scale, the supply chains and regulatory regime Ali Enterprises was embedded in were very different from those of the early days of Pakistani industrial capitalism. In this context, circumventing (or neutralizing) the rules of the game was no longer a simple matter of mastering the domestic legal framework. Now, it entailed the acquisition of more internationalized know-how and relays, which became essential to the certification of globalized companies. Just three weeks before the fire, Ali Enterprises had been awarded the prestigious SA8000 certificate—a label created by (US-based) Social Accountability International to identify companies meeting a number of basic requirements in eight areas, including health and safety, wages, working hours, and child labour.

Over the years, this certification system, which was designed to compensate for the negligence of state control services, has been overtaken by the very logics of subcontracting that it claimed to regulate. The SA8000 certificate was awarded to Ali Enterprises by the Italian company RINA, itself commissioned by Social Accountability International to carry out social audit activities.[14] However, RINA's experts had never set foot in Pakistan, preferring to subcontract the inspection work to the Pakistani firm RI&CA. This company had already been viewed with suspicion for several years because of its particularly high rate of approval; between 2007 and 2012, reports submitted by its inspectors led to 118 companies being awarded the SA8000 label. In contrast, auditing firm Bureau Veritas awarded only 46 certificates in Pakistan, over a period twice as long.[15]

The Bhailas were informed of these visits and ensured compliance with the auditors' (minimal) requirements. A former supervisor of the company's sewing department recalls that prior to each audit, the factory was cleaned, and emergency kits hung up in all the buildings—only to be removed as soon as the visitors were gone (supposedly to deter workers from stealing their contents).[16] One more rigorous auditor, who came to inspect the factory for a potential foreign-based client, recalls that the Bhailas presented him with documents signed by employees, stating that they had received safety and emergency evacuation training. However, the workers interviewed by these auditors denied having received any such training, or having signed any such documents.[17]

The Bhailas proved themselves masters in this game of deception (in which auditing firms are sometimes accomplices) and attempted to exonerate themselves from any responsibility for the fire by hiding behind this certification. As their lawyer, Amer Raza Naqvi, explained a few months after the disaster, 'This was a state-of-the-art factory that met international standards. The SA8000 is accepted all over the world. They have very strict rules before issuing any certificate'.[18]

While such a pledge of good conduct may be enough to convince the least discerning foreign customers, its limits soon come to the fore in the event of an accident. In the aftermath of the disaster of 11 September 2012, the national and international press, followed by various teams of Pakistani investigators, demonstrated not only that the certificate had been obtained under dubious conditions, but also that the factory had accumulated numerous violations of both Pakistani legislation and the international standards associated with the SA8000 label. The extent of these violations earned the owners of Ali Enterprises much condemnation from progressive Pakistanis and global labour rights groups. Yet the Bhailas were not outliers. On the contrary, they were well integrated into Karachi's business community and seem to have been fairly well respected by their peers. At the time of the fire, for example, Abdul Aziz Bhaila was a member of both the Karachi Chamber of Commerce and Industry (KCCI) and the Pakistan Readymade Garments Manufacturers and Exporters Association (PRGMEA). Nor were the Bhailas' illegal practices anything out of the ordinary. The various legal proceedings initiated against them attest to the banality of these illegal practices, as well as to the extent of collusion between local industrialists and provincial officials; more than commonplace, these violations of labour and safety regulations were systemic.

At the instigation of the Sindh provincial authorities, the Bhailas were initially charged with murder under Section 302 of the Pakistan Penal Code, while two of the company's managers, and three of its security guards, were charged with criminal negligence. The criminal proceedings, which were conducted by the District and Sessions Judge of Karachi West, were supported by a series of simultaneous investigations by different police and judicial authorities. Alongside the police investigation, headed by a Superintendent of Police (SP),[19] two other teams conducted their own investigations—a commission of enquiry constituted at the request of the Sindh Home Ministry and headed by a retired provincial High Court Judge, and a Federal Investigation Agency (FIA) team.[20] The 'Alavi tribunal' (named after the magistrate chairing the enquiry commission) was limited to interviewing representatives of provincial departments and law enforcement agencies, but the FIA team interviewed witnesses and searched the disaster site for physical evidence.

Both investigations came to a convergent conclusion, suggesting a short circuit as the most likely cause of the fire—a theory that was all the more credible, given that the plant was operating at overload at the time of the incident, consuming 318 KW of electricity for a maximum planned electrical load of 210 KW.[21] Though a criminal act was ruled out, the various investigators were unable to establish the cause of the fire with certainty. The margin of doubt that remained in their conclusions fuelled much speculation, contributing to a dramatic turnaround in the legal proceedings.

In the early stages of the investigation, various public institutions were called to the stand. Their representatives exposed a thick network of collusion between industrialists and the provincial bureaucracy. The Labour Department fired the opening shot by informing the Alavi tribunal that Ali Enterprises had never registered with it, and that in any case violations of the Factory Act (1934) carried a maximum fine of 500 rupees (five dollars)—an amount that has remained unchanged since this colonial legislation came into force.

The Sindh Employees' Social Security Institution (SESSI) and the Employees' Old-Age Benefits Institution (EOBI) hammered the point home by revealing that most Ali Enterprises employees were not registered with them either (just 200 of the company's 3,000 employees were registered with the EOBI, and 268 with the SESSI). Like most textile and garment companies, Ali Enterprises used a contractor to source cheap labour. As we have seen, it is particularly difficult for these precarious workers, who lack social protection and employment contracts, to organize and form a union. Unsurprisingly, there was no union at Ali Enterprises, though a handful of workers were members of the Sindh Hosiery, Garment and General Workers Union (for textile workers).

The officials of SITE Ltd, the body that oversees land use planning and factory development in the area, defended themselves by stating that they were not responsible for ensuring compliance with health and safety regulations. The Director and Chief Engineer of this administrative body did however acknowledge that any violation of the construction plan of a given factory (such as the addition of an extra floor, or the absence of a fire escape) could be rectified at little cost. Civil defence officials, who are responsible for ensuring the safety of factories in the country, admitted that they had never visited Ali Enterprises—because it was not registered with the Labour Department.

Taking advantage of the systematic failures of these state agencies, the Bhailas had not bothered to equip their factory with even the most basic back-up facilities. Survivors' accounts suggested that the alarm was faulty, that almost all fire exits were blocked from the outside, and that no fire extinguishers were in working order even though a fire had broken out in the same building just a few months earlier.[22] For the Bhailas, controlling workers (whether to prevent theft or to force them to work overtime) clearly took priority over their safety. Both the Investigation Officer (IO) from the local police and the FIA investigators pointed out that several doors in the building where the fire occurred were locked (especially those on the second floor), mainly to prevent theft of goods. The few functioning CCTV cameras in the building were focused on the workers, rather than on potential safety hazards.[23] Brigadier Jehanzaib Khan, the second officer in charge of the judicial investigation, went so far as to compare this intensely coercive factory environment to a prison.[24]

The preliminary investigation also revealed the deplorable state of the inspection regime in Sindh (hardly surprising, given that there are over 100,000 factories in the country and just 541 labour inspectors).[25] EOBI officials claimed to have made several attempts to inspect the factory, but had been denied access by management.[26] Labour inspections were suspended in Sindh from 2003 to 2017, but even before this, the scarce human and financial resources for inspection services severely limited their capacity to act, and all criticism could be stifled by a bribe. In the unlikely event of a visit from inspectors, workers were encouraged to lie about their wages and working conditions—a systematic practice when faced with foreign auditors.[27]

Karachi, the mother of all evils?

The Alavi tribunal report went beyond blaming an out-of-control production system; to a large extent, it attributed responsibility for the disaster to the system of governance in Karachi. Here, the city was more than a mere context; it was a party to the crime, and as such directly implicated by the investigators. In this megacity of 25 million people that still lacks a public transport system, and where traffic accidents have been at the heart of urban struggles since the 1980s, the chaotic state of traffic and road infrastructure was presented as a powerful amplifier of the disaster.

According to the FIA report, the dispatch of rescue vehicles by the fire brigade was delayed by the poor state of the road network in SITE: 'The dilapidated condition of roads in SITE might be a contributing factor. Due to the road condition it takes a long time for vehicles to reach from one point to another'.[28] The Alavi tribunal report suggested that the 'pathetic traffic conditions' in the city contributed to the late arrival of firefighters at the scene of the fire. For the authors of the report, this was an opportunity to indict the political and economic elites whose convoys regularly disrupt road traffic: 'It would not be out of place to mention here that traffic jams created due to VIP movements on the main arteries of Karachi have repeatedly resulted in precious loss of lives [sic]'.[29]

As in several other parts of the report, here Justice Alavi speaks out for the people of Karachi, who have been brutally oppressed by corrupt and uncaring elites. This critical attitude towards the political class echoes the judicial activism that had emerged in previous years around the Chief Justice, Iftikhar Muhammad Chaudhry.[30] The general tone of the Alavi tribunal report, and its lamentations for a city betrayed by its elites, bear the imprint of this singular moment in the history of Pakistan's judiciary and its relationship to political authorities.

These accusations had repercussions for the controversy surrounding the role of the firefighters during the disaster. During the fire itself, 'there was a tremendous altercation between the public and fire engine personnel as there was not enough water in the fire engines', notes the Alavi tribunal.[31] These criticisms only escalated after the disaster. The Bhailas tried to exonerate themselves by accusing the fire brigade of having taken more than an hour to arrive at the scene, even though they were allegedly contacted at the first sign of the fire. In addition, the fire brigade was said to have deployed an inadequate number of fire engines, which had to then waste time refilling their water tanks, once their supply was exhausted.

At the Alavi tribunal, the Karachi Fire Chief defended the performance of his men, claiming that the first responders arrived at the scene within 10 to 15 minutes of the first report. Television footage from the scene shows that the fire engines arrived less than half an hour after the Lyari fire station was informed of the incident.[32] However, the fire brigade's lack of preparedness for a disaster of this magnitude was obvious. Only two fire engines equipped with fire hoses were initially dispatched to the scene, and their water supply quickly ran out. Over the next few hours, almost every available fire engine in the city (45) converged on the site, drawing on the resources of the navy, the Karachi Port Trust, and the Defence Housing Authority (DHA).[33]

Nor was the forensic division of the Karachi police spared criticism. Justice Alavi complained about the lack of cooperation from this department, going so far as to suggest that, 'in the absence of and lack of any competent facility and persons available to carry out complete modern forensic investigation which is available throughout the world perhaps this Division might as well close down as no tangible purpose is being served'.[34] Even the highly respected Edhi Foundation was accused of adding to the confusion. As is usual in Karachi, the bodies of the victims were taken over by the foundation and stored in its morgue pending identification—a process both delayed and complicated by the condition of some of the bodies. In a report written three months after the disaster, the police surgeon deplored the fact that the staff of the Edhi Foundation were not qualified to carry out such an arduous task, and this considerably disrupted the work of forensic experts. In its conclusion, the report notes that:

   i. Dead bodies identified after DNA test with same Tags/PM numbers are found in Edhi Cold Storage.

   ii. On one stretcher two or more than two dead bodies were lying leading to mixing of papers & body fragments due to large number of dead bodies and the short space of the cold storage.

   iii. As information obtained that some dead bodies taken away by relatives without legal formalities and buried by them. But after DNA test identification another dead bodies [sic] were received by claimants.

iv. As staff working at Edhi Cold Storage is not educated that's why mixing of Tags and PM numbers incorrect disposal of bodies had happened.[35]

The lack of coordination between the institutions in charge of urban policy—a feature of Karachi's governance often decried by politicians and urban planners alike—was also said to have complicated both the rescue operations and the subsequent investigations. This criticism is explicit in the Alavi tribunal report, which suggests that 'too many agencies have jumped in to investigate the cause of fire and the loss of lives. To our mind there has been a great tampering of evidence'.[36] Finally, the lack of technical expertise in both the fire service and the forensic division of the Sindh police is said to have hampered the work of the investigators while preventing them from reaching a definitive conclusion on the cause of the fire. According to the FIA report,

> It must also be mentioned here that no expert opinion in this regard was available from the fire department or the Sindh Police Forensic division. It appears that there is lack of expertise on fire and arson investigation. [...] Absence of expert opinion in the relevant fields made reaching a definite conclusion extremely difficult.[37]

Implicating the city at large in the tragedy did have important legal consequences, and (especially in the case of the Alavi tribunal) may not have been devoid of ulterior motives.

Critical though it may seem of the powers that be, the Alavi tribunal report was not perceived as a threat to political and economic elites. Within the legal fraternity, Justice Alavi was reputed for his docility, especially when handling cases involving members of the business community. Perhaps this leniency might be explained by the elitist background of this retired judge from the Sindh High Court: born into the prominent Bohra family that gave Karachi its first Muslim mayor, Hatim Alvi, in 1941, he hailed from Karachi's old patrician elite. Over the years, he headed numerous government-appointed commissions, and this earned him a reputation for being pro-establishment. Within the legal fraternity, his reputation was also tainted by his chairmanship of a regulatory body reputed to be one of the most corrupt in the province, namely the Sindh Land Committee, which oversaw the process of bringing illegally occupied land under control.

According to Faisal Siddiqi (legal counsel for the civil society organizations acting on behalf of the victims), the Alavi tribunal report was consistent with its chairman's past record. By 'dividing the anger all over the place' and introducing contradictory evidence regarding the responsibilities of the Bhailas in the fire—in particular by questioning the assumption that most of the factory exits had been blocked at the behest of the management—he would have both helped them secure bail and paved the way for their gradual exoneration of all charges.[38] The main twist in the judicial process came, however, from another direction.

From industrial scandal to political affair

Muhammad Rizwan Qureshi, 55, was suspected of leading a double life: a sanitary sub-inspector at the Saddar town branch of the Karachi Municipal Corporation (KMC), he allegedly confessed to his involvement, as the head of an MQM 'death squad', in dozens of murders and kidnappings dating from the mid-1990s onwards.[39] In 2013, he was arrested by the police in Karachi's southern district and, in view of the high profile of the case, was interrogated by a Joint Investigation Team (JIT) comprising representatives of the Karachi police, the Inter-Services Intelligence (ISI), the Intelligence Bureau (IB, the main civilian intelligence agency), the Rangers, and the FIA.

During his interrogation, this alleged 'target killer' (hit man) confirmed his involvement in a considerable number of murders—a confession to be treated with caution, as there is no way of knowing that it was not obtained under duress (which is why such confessions have no legal value). In any case, chilling though these 'revelations' may have been, it was a different point in the JIT report that caused a major uproar once it was made public.

In a section of the report devoted to the Baldia factory fire, Qureshi relays information (allegedly from the former MQM

Sector-in-charge in Baldia Town) that senior party official Hammad Siddiqui attempted to extort Rs 200 million from the owners of Ali Enterprises through his front man Rehman Bhola (appointed MQM Sector-in-charge of Baldia in 2012). According to this account, it was after the Bhailas had refused to comply that Bhola's accomplices set fire to the factory, using chemicals. Although the JIT met on 22 June 2013 under the supervision of the Senior Superintendent of Police (SSP) for Karachi's District South, its report was not submitted to the judges until 6 February 2015. In the meantime, the political scene in Karachi had undergone profound changes.

In September 2013, Prime Minister Nawaz Sharif announced a crackdown on the militant and criminal groups that stood accused of bleeding the city dry. The Rangers were put in charge of field operations, paving the way for the army's re-engagement in local politics. This repressive strategy relied heavily on the testimony of Rizwan Qureshi. Though the army had supported the MQM under Pervez Musharraf (who was from Karachi's Urdu-speaking community), it was now determined to reduce MQM's influence on political life in Karachi, primarily by dismantling its coercive apparatus. And while previous investigations had ruled out the possibility of foul play, this testimony from within the MQM helped shift blame onto the party—particularly for its notorious extortion practices.

On the basis of this 'confession', the Sindh Home Minister constituted a new JIT under the supervision of the Deputy Inspector General (DIG) of the Central Investigating Agency (CIA).[40] The team included representatives from the Karachi Police, ISI, Military Intelligence (MI), IB, and FIA. On 29 March 2015, Sajid Ameer Sadozai (SITE's Superintendent of Police (SP)), was mandated to reopen the investigation. He did so under considerable pressure from his superiors (the army and its intelligence services), eventually concluding that 'This kind of fire cannot be caused by an electric short circuit'.[41]

The JIT's report, which sets out the case for the prosecution, was presented to the District and Sessions Judge of Karachi West, Maqbool Memon, in March 2016. The evidence it is based on came from both the new Investigation Officer and the hearings and site visits conducted by JIT members and the various experts they commissioned. This counter-investigation, which claimed to be more rigorous than any of its predecessors, resulted in a 25-page document intended to demonstrate that Rehman Bhola and his accomplices had indeed set light to the factory after the Bhailas had refused to pay the 200 (or perhaps 250) million rupees demanded by the MQM.[42]

The factory owners confirmed to the JIT investigators who interviewed them at the Pakistani Consulate in Dubai in 2019 that they had been prepared to pay the MQM 10 million rupees (though such an arrangement would have been declined by Hammad Siddiqui). The Finishing Manager at Ali Enterprises (an MQM member with close ties to Rehman Bhola) is reported to have retaliated by setting fire to the warehouse and possibly other parts of the building, including the upper floors. This contradicts all previous investigations, none of which had ever raised the possibility of multiple simultaneous fires. The report adds that, even after the fire, there was no let-up in the pressure exerted on the factory owners by senior MQM officials, with party cadres continuing to 'terrorize' them. Under pressure, the Bhailas reportedly agreed to transfer 59 million rupees to an MQM account in Hyderabad, where the money would be used to acquire a piece of land.[43]

By identifying new culprits and exposing their criminal motives, the disaster was reclassified as a 'terrorist' act (in the extensive sense that Pakistani law accords to the term).[44] And by accusing those who supported the 'accident' theory of protecting the MQM, the report discredits the way in which the facts had initially been interpreted. This is reminiscent of a process described by the sociology of controversies in which the accused and their allies are able to transform a 'scandal' into an 'affair' by shifting blame onto the denunciator.[45] One way in which this undermining can be achieved is by 'putting to the test a certain "state of the world" and the capacities of that world to order political assertions in a coordinated way'.[46]

In their report, Pakistan's security agencies show that there was more to the Ali Enterprises fire than just unbridled capitalism, or a city rendered ungovernable by its institutional failures. It reveals a world in which a key sector of the economy, one that is vital to the nation's survival, could be held hostage by violent racketeers. A world dominated by mafia interests dressed up as a political project, where the police and the judiciary are themselves at the behest of the criminals—so much so that their agents systematically resort to lies and malicious fabrications to protect their powerful bosses by accusing the innocent. This is another characteristic of the 'affair', in which protagonists are concerned with 'showing that one version was based on a lie, a lie conceived and imagined to support particular interests, while the other, one's own, was the truth of the facts obtained by direct investigation and a disinterested love of the truth'.[3]

However, insofar as this particular 'affair' involved turning a *cause* (criticism of a certain brand of capitalism and its administrative protections, with a view to institutional reform) into an *accusation* (denunciation of the criminal practices of the MQM), it worked in the opposite way to the classic cases studied by pragmatic sociology. Moreover, this reversal was achieved by means of the intrusion of a repressive state body into the judicial process, rather than through political interventions or popular mobilization. Here, the indictment of the MQM and its extortion practices is hiding a project designed to liberate corporate interests through anti-terrorism: companies generating jobs and wealth would have become trapped in an economy of violence that they had long accepted—but which, by losing all sense of proportion, was now threatening their very survival.

Both to support the argument and to render visible this alternative world (in which the industrial firm ceases to be seen as a place of alienation and becomes the target of oppression from outside), the JIT report dwells on the collusion, over the years, between the Bhailas' company and the forces of urban disorder. The picture painted by the report is riddled with inconsistencies and based on testimonies rendered unreliable by the relations (of collusion or subordination) between the witnesses and the factory owners. However, this key piece in turning the prosecution against the dominant party fought hard to remain credible by making points that were plausible, if not proven. It seems more fruitful, then, to see it as a reflection of social reality filtered through a notoriously partisan brand of anti-terrorism, rather than to reject it outright as a tool of manipulation.

The issue of extortion is central to this narrative. In order to secure the goodwill of the MQM, the owners of Ali Enterprises would have been paying the *bhatta* regularly—in the form of religious alms (*zakat/fitrana*), or more occasional donations. As confirmed by several witnesses cited in the report, the contract for the recovery of industrial waste (mainly cotton scrap) was in turn awarded to a local MQM member. The party also allegedly monitored the human resources policy at Ali Enterprises, sometimes requiring the recruitment of its protégés; several party members appear to have been hired over the years. Their arrogance and notorious lack of discipline is said to have been a constant source of concern for the company management—a plausible claim, given the chronic tensions between factory owners and their henchmen.

Throughout the report, the tense relationship between urban turmoil and the defence of industrial order is embodied in a series of more or less dubious characters who echo the figures of violent brokers we have already met in preceding chapters.

One such case is that of Muhammad Zubair (one of the main defendants), who embodies the 'political thug' figure to the point of caricature.[47] Zubair, who also went by the name of '*chariya*' (the madman), was known to be an MQM member—not least because he apparently boasted about it in a bid to enhance his own stature within the company. According to the Production Manager, he was regularly tasked with 'solving the worker-related problems' (in other words, intimidating troublemakers).[48]

According to Muhammad Arshad, a former mechanical worker at Ali Enterprises, it was Zubair and his accomplices who set fire to the factory. Arshad's testimony states that, at around 6pm on 11 September 2012, he went to the factory's warehouse and ran into Zubair, who asked him to escort a group of unknown people to the washroom, before joining them, and passing around cigarettes stuffed with a mix of tobacco and hashish. Arshad claims to have distanced himself from the group at this point, since smoking (let alone drug use) was strictly forbidden in the factory. Nevertheless, he says he saw Zubair handing out black objects to his cronies, which they promptly threw into various parts of the warehouse, causing an instant and intense fire. This strange conspiracy scene shrouded in narcotic vapours, in which the conspirators seem to care little about prying eyes, is central to the JIT evidence—so much so that it is twice recounted in the report, almost word for word.

The other prosecution witness against Zubair is Mansoor—also a troubled character, and visibly in charge of the company's dirty work. Presenting as a trusted employee of the Bhailas, his loyalty had been rewarded with the post of Production Manager in 2004. The report also explains that Mansoor was the company's main contractor, and as such played a key role in his employers' illegal activities, particularly regarding the circumvention of labour laws. He would also have managed the complex relationship with the MQM (regarding 'donations', the recovery of fabric scrap and the recruitment of party protégés), as was confirmed by other witnesses cited in the report, who had themselves been involved in some of these transactions. It is mainly the testimony of this 'dirty work' specialist,[49] who was vulnerable to all kinds of pressure both from his former employers and from the investigators, that is used to establish the extortion claim made by Rehman Bhola on behalf of the MQM.[50] It should be noted that there had been no mention of any such request in any of the previous investigation reports. Speaking to the FIA investigators, Mansoor even denied that the company had been the subject of extortion attempts in the past.[51]

These testimonies incriminating Rehman Bhola and Zubair followed a move to rehabilitate the Bhailas. Muhammad Arshad mentions the exemplary attitude of his former employers during the fire. According to this testimony, the Bhailas encouraged their employees to sacrifice the '*maal*' (goods) to save the workers trapped in the upper floors—a heroic picture contradicted by many converging testimonies about the Bhailas' eagerness to save their property and their own lives at the expense of their employees.[52]

The conclusion of the Punjab Forensic Science Agency (PFSA) experts recruited by the JIT—namely, that the fire was a clear case of arson—further supported the thesis of a 'terrorist' attack.[53] This conclusion was based on a flimsy body of evidence that—given the fire brigade's tampering with the alleged crime scene and the passage of time—was more a matter of speculation than one of rigorous demonstration. However, despite the technical shortcomings mentioned by previous investigation teams, the summoning of these experts was enough to enshrine the JIT report in a new regime of truth. Because the PFSA was known to have the most advanced forensic technologies in the country, it guaranteed the JIT the stamp of scientific authenticity by bringing its re-investigation closer to so-called 'international standards', in contrast to the failings of earlier Pakistani investigators.

A meticulous judge would have noted the inconsistencies, blatant untruths, and elisions scattered through the report, yet they were not so implausible as to entirely strip it of credibility.[54] This credibility rested on more than just its claim to scientificity; it also validated the predominant interpretation of the events held by the public. In the weeks that followed the fire, many observers of Karachi's political and economic life suggested that it was the result of foul play. Just three days after the disaster, a close friend of mine who is a member of the Urdu-speaking middle class was already echoing this rumour in a post on his blog:

> There are reports of threats received by the owners of this factory from the so-called 'Bhatta Mafia'—the extortion mafia—which extorts industrialists and traders on pain of retaliation. The hypothesis put forward by a number of observers is not without merit: this fire could be a criminal act of the most heinous kind, sending a warning to industrialists who refuse to comply with the demands of this mafia. And this happened on payday to claim as many victims as possible.[55]

This widely held conviction was based more on a 'public judgement' dictated by the past abuses of the former hegemonic party than it was on any tangible elements.[56] Across class lines, attempts to cast doubt on the party's culpability in this matter were met with consternation from my interlocutors—as if I were incapable of grasping the *logic* of this guilt, in the face of the party's long record of violence and extortion.

This broad consensus was then based on a 'given' so evident that it did not need to be specified, and it would be wrong to conclude that the JIT members were cynically trying to manipulate public opinion; most were probably already convinced of this interpretation of the facts, as evidenced by the tensions between them and their more sceptical colleagues.[57] Ironically, one of the police officers involved in the JIT was later assigned to the same department as some of the members of the investigation team of the FIA, who had suggested in their report that the fire was probably accidental. The officer was quick to take his colleagues to task, asking them if they felt no shame in exonerating mass murderers. 'I was really angry. How can you tolerate the murder of 260 people? How can you be a police officer and be so indecent?' this officer asked me in an interview in 2017, his voice trembling with anger.[58]

This revised version of the facts, which was widely reported in the media without any doubt being cast as to its veracity, favoured, of course, the Bhailas. On this point, the interests of the owners (and their supporters in the Karachi business community) converged with those of the military authorities. However, connivance does not necessarily imply coherence; here, the military intervention— officially intended to restore state sovereignty in the face of criminal actors—coexisted alongside the mobilization of the delinquent elites blocking the resurgence of the regulatory state. Paradoxical as it may seem (at least from the point of view of a unitary conception of state power) this alliance of circumstances was nonetheless a force to be reckoned with. On the basis of the new 'evidence' presented before the judicial system and the court of public opinion, JIT members urged the Sindh government to withdraw the original complaint (on the basis of which the Bhailas had been charged with murder) and register a new FIR against Rehman Bhola and his accomplices under anti-terrorism legislation (ATA).

Sindh police chief A.D. Khawaja, who was reputed to be close to the army, was appointed to supervise a new team of investigators, despite protests from the legal counsel of civil society organizations representing the families of the victims.[59] In August 2016, a new charge sheet was presented to the judge. Both the owners (who had left the country after being released on bail) and some factory employees who had initially been charged with murder and criminal negligence were now called as prosecution witnesses after the charges against them had been dropped.[60] And two MQM cadres, Rehman Bhola and Hammad Siddiqui, along with '3-4 other unidentified accused', were charged under the 1997 anti-terrorism law.[61]

On 27 August 2016, the District and Sessions Judge hearing the criminal case against the Bhailas and their alleged accomplices decided to transfer the case to an Anti-Terrorism Court (ATC), in accordance with the new charge sheet. On 5 September, the case was transferred to the ATC-II for a first hearing. Against all expectations, the President of the ATC-II refused to accept the charges brought by the police. He challenged the stay of proceedings against the Bhailas, pointing out that 'serious allegations are leveled against the factory owners that they had locked emergency gates which resulted in the deaths of 259 workers'.[62] Three months later, the same judge had to stand down; one of the main suspects, Rehman Bhola, had been arrested by Interpol in Bangkok and extradited to Pakistan—where he reportedly confessed to setting fire to the factory at Hammad Siddiqui's instigation. This new 'confession' paved the way for the MQM to be charged, and the Bhailas exonerated.

Over the next few years, this politically charged trial slowly but surely took shape. The transfer of the case to an anti-terrorism court allowed the Rangers to represent the prosecution, and lawyer Sajib Mehboob Sheikh, who headed the paramilitary prosecution team, was appointed as Special Public Prosecutor (SPP).[63] The long-awaited trial began in 2018, in a court specially set up within Karachi Central Prison. This was a decision justified on security grounds, but which conveniently kept the public out of the hearings. On 22 September 2020, two of the accused—Rehman Bhola and his alleged accomplice Muhammad Zubair—were sentenced to death after being found guilty of charges of terrorism, extortion, and arson.

It was difficult to imagine that the judge would not have accepted the theory of a 'terrorist' act, given the weight of the prosecution's case, the army's increasing control over the country's political and judicial affairs, and the general consensus that the MQM was guilty. By confirming the downfall of Karachi's former sovereign, the verdict also exonerated the production system that, even if it did not cause the disaster, had greatly increased its human toll. And while this victory for industrialists may have been primarily

287

due to intervention by the security state, the business community's demonstration of unity also played a major role in this outcome.

Survival of the fittest?

The mobilization of the business community had, then, played a key part in exonerating the Bhailas. On 29 December 2012, the Karachi Chamber of Commerce and Industry requested that Prime Minister Raja Pervez Ashraf intervene on behalf of the 'wrongly accused' owners of Ali Enterprises. For KCCI officials, the implication of the Bhailas in a murder case was clear example of 'misuse of state power', which carried the risk of 'scaring away new investment'. Thus, it was now the 'duty' of the state to revoke the FIR and absolve these entrepreneurs of the murder charges, allowing them to both resume their activities and send a reassuring message to the business community.[64] To this, the Prime Minister replied, in his speech, that 'Authorities should reinvestigate the case and provide justice to the employers of Ali Enterprises if a wrong case has been registered against the factory owners under section 302'. Shortly thereafter, the Federal Finance Minister announced, on behalf of the Prime Minister, that the murder charge against the Bhailas had been dropped. This resulted in an outcry from civil society organizations and a section of the media, leading the Prime Minister to backtrack and announce that the case was only being reinvestigated. In February 2013, however, the murder charges against the Bhailas were suspended and the owners of Ali Enterprises were charged only with 'negligence'.

The success of this corporate mobilization was largely due to the common front presented by the business community throughout the controversy—a solidarity that was reinforced both by the Bhailas' affiliation to the powerful Memon community and by their membership of various business organizations. As already mentioned, A. A. Bhaila was a member of the KCCI and the PRGMEA, and even though he had never held a leadership position in these organizations, the affiliations alone were enough to make him a respected member of Karachi's business community—membership in trade associations, multi-sectoral bodies, and chambers of commerce is an important marker of status among Karachi's entrepreneurs. In addition to its symbolic value, membership in these organizations ensures privileged access to state regulators because these institutions (and this is especially true of the KCCI and the business associations representing each of the city's industrial zones) are the main interlocutors of the provincial and federal authorities (both civilian and military) in their dealings with Karachi's business community.

The demonstration of unity around the Bhailas extended well beyond their individual case. Local entrepreneurs (especially those in the textile and garment sector) were aware that the fate of the Bhailas was not the only issue at hand—their own autonomy from the law, and from state regulators, was also at stake. In expressing solidarity with the Bhailas and mobilizing all their resources to put pressure on the executive, they were also voicing a collective sense of belonging and seeking to immunize themselves against government interference in their affairs (which might, for instance, take the form of a resumption of inspections). Bailing out the Bhailas, then, was essential to the business community at large.

As James Galbraith points out in relation to the US case, economic predators tend to be reluctant to openly target the regulatory power of the state, for fear of appearing to be opponents of the public good.[65] The mobilization around the Bhailas solved this dilemma by allowing those who opposed regulation to advance their reactionary agenda under the guise of a more legitimate cause, namely the defence of entrepreneurs victimized by political parties and criminal groups. On the day the court finally succumbed to pressure, this victory was celebrated—as advocate Faisal Siddiqi recalls:

> On the day they were granted bail in court, the entire... I mean, what was amazing was that... 255 people have been burnt alive so you would imagine that the court would be full with victims and their families. But the entire court room... There were about 50, 60 people in the courtroom, and they were all industrialists and supporters of these people. And they were clapping...[66]

Though their causes are difficult to disentangle, the successive bifurcations of the legal proceedings initiated in the aftermath of the Ali Enterprises disaster are nonetheless instructive about the place of the law in political and social struggles in Pakistan.

Far from heralding the arrival of a neutral third party to provide arbitration to the parties in conflict, the fact that the fire at the Baldia factory was brought before the courts has paved the way for a re-engagement of security agencies in the political and social life of the country. The army saw an opportunity to subdue a troublemaker who had been challenging its authority in the country's economic and financial capital. This is supported by the testimony of one union leader involved in the court case against the Bhailas, who says he was approached by Inter-Services Intelligence (ISI) agents who were determined to turn him against the MQM.[67]

Political struggles mediated by the law are not confined to the judicial arena; they extend to truth-making mechanisms whose legal status is ambiguous. Thus, the series of JIT reports had no legal value, though this did not prevent them from making a major contribution—both to the public debate, and to the successive about-turns of the criminal case. It is hard to resist drawing a comparison with the 'memoirs' or 'factums' of the Ancien Régime in France studied by Elisabeth Claverie, which, despite their unofficial nature (they could not be presented publicly before the judges), did strongly constrain the course of judicial proceedings.[68]

Whether through formal procedures, or the more informal practices that it generates, the judicialization of social conflicts is undoubtedly a privileged place of rapprochement between holders of capital (embodied in this case by delinquent elites) and specialists in coercion (represented in this case by the repressive bodies deploying the weapon of the law in the service of a political agenda). However, the contingencies that accompanied (and occasionally disrupted) the Baldia factory fire case serve as a reminder that, far from being a foregone conclusion, such convergence can always be subject to unforeseen tensions and reversals. Despite all the evidence pointing in this direction, the law can never be reduced to a symbolic and strategic weapon in the hands of the dominant. But can this instability offer any comfort to those subjected to its authority, especially among the most vulnerable sections of society?

'The Wild West form of public litigation'

Alongside the criminal case, civil compensation proceedings were initiated by a collective of workers' rights organizations and civil society representatives; this coalition included PILER and the National Trade Union Federation.[69] These organizations sought compensation for the victims' families and enforcement of labour laws in the industrial sector through a constitutional petition to the Sindh High Court.[70]

The fact that these labour organizations and their legal advisers were unable to persuade the family of any of the victims to file a claim for compensation speaks volumes about industrialist intimidation of workers. Faced with this reluctance, PILER, NTUF, and other self-described civil society organizations have taken it upon themselves to represent the families of victims and seek compensation on their behalf—a project that has proven fraught with tension and misunderstandings on both sides.

Since Pakistani law allows only victims and their families to sue for compensation or tort damages, this reluctance among victims' families to sue for damages should have benefited the owners of Ali Enterprises.[71] However, with the goodwill of some High Court judges, reinforced by the solidarity built during the 2007–2008 Lawyers' Movement, advocate Faisal Siddiqi was able to get around this obstacle.[72] As a partner in MCAS & W Law Associates (one of Karachi's most prestigious law firms), Siddiqi is an atypical cause lawyer, since these legal activists generally tend to accept a certain level of professional marginality as the price to be paid for their political commitments.[73] Siddiqi's legal activism has more to do with the causes he brings to the courtroom (the defence of workers' rights, the protection of the environment, the fight against state violence, etc.), and the way he uses the law than with his (dominant) position within the profession. He himself used the word 'eccentric' to describe the legal strategy he had adopted in order to overcome the obstacles facing him in the Baldia factory fire case:[74]

> Nobody files compensation cases through constitutional jurisdictions. According to [Pakistani] law, every victim has to

come to court and prove his claim. There's a very elaborate structure of private law which guarantees that no victim [ever] gets compensation. Nobody can really check whether [petitioners] have received their pensions, whether government compensation has been dispersed… Very early on, we realized that we could not mobilize 255 people, filing their individual claims. So we took the gambling route. It was really a gamble: if you get a good judge, [then] you get good orders … It's really the Wild West form of public litigation… So we have been able to achieve about 18,000 dollars per victim, within a period of two years, whereas a normal civil claim would have lasted between fifteen to twenty years.[75]

The intertwining of these civil proceedings with the criminal case certainly did play into the hands of the victims' families. Brief though it was, the Bhailas' incarceration in Karachi Central Jail left the owners of Ali Enterprises vulnerable. As the petitioners had hoped, it forced them to agree to compensate the victims of the disaster before their criminal liability had even been established, in hope that this gesture of goodwill would stand them in good stead for release on bail.[76] However, this tactic came at a cost:

We made a strategic mistake. We got bogged down in money matters. By trying to get this compensation, we really didn't concentrate on other things [e.g. the passing of a new safety law or on the resumption of inspections in factories]. The monetization of the entire struggle was a big mistake. It had a very bad effect on the victims, also. It really limited their consciousness to the sole issue of money. Really, we played on the wicket of the enemy. They were willing to give us money if we gave up all other rights—the right to accountability, the right to labour rights enforcement… That was the deal. I think we fell into that trap.

This self-criticism echoes the frustrations of other legal activists engaged in similar causes, both in South Asia and beyond. In Bangladesh, for instance, the Activist Anthropologist group filed a Public Interest Litigation in the country's High Court to seek justice for the 117 victims of the November 2012 fire at the Tazreen

Fashions factory. The damages solution has proved so inexpensive, politically, that it has gained consensus among the judiciary and the industry—so much so that these activists have been forced to admit (not without frustration) that 'public recognition of suffering and the rights of compensation that it entails remains a largely ad hoc affair and generates a political program for compensation that keeps particular demands for structural change at bay'.[77] This chapter began with the testimony of Naila Mahmood, which points out that this focus on compensation (which always comes at the expense of identifying causes and convicting the guilty parties) can also lead to discord and mutual suspicion. Moreover, it should be noted that few of the judgements in the public litigation system are made on the merits of the case; most frequently, they result in simple injunctions.[78]

For the advocacy networks that have, to a large extent, taken over from trade unions in Karachi, the decisions of the Pakistani courts and the agreement reached with German company KiK on compensation for the victims and their families represent great success, and offer a model for the transnational workers' rights movement.[79] Yet this 'victory' was far from consensual.

Numerous conflicts were generated by the modalities for transferring funds, which mainly benefited male members and elders in the victims' entourage.[80] At a more structural level, the initial results of the tragedy were mixed, to say the least. The agreement negotiated with KiK, under the aegis of the International Labour Organization (ILO), was strictly voluntary and did not commit global value chains as a whole.

Both in our discussions and in his public interventions, Faisal Siddiqi repeatedly lamented the limited effect the tragedy had on the practices of Pakistani industry. The comparison with the Triangle Shirtwaist Factory fire of 1911 (recurrent in the national and international press) served as a historical basis for this criticism. This tragedy claimed 146 lives and marked world labour history, leading to far-reaching reforms in the United States. Under pressure from New York firefighters and workers' rights advocates, US legislators imposed an unprecedented regulatory framework on industry for workplace safety.[81] It was also a mobilization of trade unions in the wake of this disaster that led to the adoption of 'jobbers' agreements' during the 1920s and 1930s; these were tripartite agreements between unions, suppliers, and buyers that allowed for an upward harmonization of working conditions and put an end to the 'social dumping' practices that had been in force until then.[82] Lastly, this tragic event left a lasting imprint on American collective memory, as evidenced by the considerable number of books devoted to it— including children's books and comics.[83]

The Ali Enterprises fire inspired the adoption of the Sindh Occupational Safety and Health Act, 2017, which PILER made a significant contribution to. However, without increased inspection capacity and tougher penalties for non-compliance with existing regulations, the impact of the legislation is likely to remain limited. An effective industrial accident protection regime has thus yet to emerge in Pakistan.[84] Nor does this unprecedented disaster seem likely to leave a lasting mark on Pakistani popular culture, despite the contributions of a handful of local artists (painters, sculptors, video makers, and singers), who were mentioned in the introduction.

The impact of the Ali Enterprises disaster thus appears to be limited—even if we narrow the scope of comparison by, for example, contrasting this response with the reactions to the 2013 Rana Plaza disaster in Bangladesh, which killed 1,134 people. Sohel Rana, owner of the Rana Plaza, was arrested and jailed four days after the event, and an agreement on fire and building safety in Bangladesh was adopted in the wake of the accident. This had been initiated by international trade unions, multinational companies, and civil society organizations, with the support of the ILO. Known as the Bangladesh Accord, it was ratified by 200 companies (most of whom were based in Europe). It led to renovation work being carried out at 1,600 companies employing 2.5 million workers, and has probably saved hundreds of lives. A more binding agreement has followed: the International Accord for Health and Safety in the Garment and Textile Industry, whose reach is intended to extend beyond Bangladesh. It came into force on 1 September 2021 and, as of February 2024, had been ratified by 176 international brands and their suppliers.[85]

In January 2003, this international accord was extended to Pakistan, and within a year, 100 global brands and retailers had ratified the new 'Pakistan Accord'. Yet there is no doubt that an opportunity for reform was lost after the Baldia factory fire. As a result of the activist collective's focus on the issue of financial compensation and the way in which the industrial scandal turned into a political affair, the more structural demands coming from some sections of the Pakistani workers' rights movement were left unattended to. By making the judicial arena the preferred site of social struggle, workers' rights advocates have fallen prey to a form of legal reductionism that has severely constrained their demands.

This effect of depoliticization (in the sense of reducing collective causes to specific problems that demand technical solutions and/or financial compensation) is not inherent to legal activism. In Pakistan, these developments within social movements are largely due to the fact that collective action has all but disappeared from the public sphere—as evidenced by the absence of any large-scale protests in the aftermath of the Ali Enterprises disaster in Karachi or indeed anywhere else in the country. In the absence of strong organizations rooted in industrial firms and in working-class neighbourhoods, the casualization of labour and the severity of coercive measures combine to discourage expressions of working class solidarity, so much so that, as PILER's late director Karamat Ali deplored, 'at the time of the fire, even the workers in the neighbouring factory did not leave their posts'.[86]

* * *

The Baldia factory fire case demonstrates how the law, along with the production system it was designed to regulate, has been caught up in the spiral of conflict that engulfed the whole of Karachi from the mid-1980s onwards. In this troubled situation, it was no longer possible to establish certainties, not even at the level of language; the charges, culprits, and very nature of the disaster were constantly shifting as the proceedings progressed. Unlike other industrial scandals—such as the matter of asbestos in public buildings that rocked France during the late 1990s[87]—in this case the judiciary had no power to certify (to name and define things). This prevented the media from both relaying the scandal and raising the profile of the cause in support of demands for reform. In Karachi, the activists who had wanted to turn the Baldia disaster into an industrial scandal had to resign themselves to the fact that—at the initiative of a circumstantial but nonetheless powerful coalition of capital and coercion—it had become a political affair.

Karachi's industrial capitalism was not put on trial, and the various civil and criminal proceedings generated by the disaster did not set a precedent, since the owners of Ali Enterprises were gradually rehabilitated through 'restorative rituals' that compensated for the stigmatizing impact of judicial proceedings, minimized their responsibility, and ruled out any intentional wrongdoing.[88] This process of restoration generally does protect delinquent elites against the forms of degradation reserved for less privileged offenders. Not just the Bhailas, but all the predatory elites of Karachi have been exonerated, their sense of impunity reasserted. It stands to reason that in Karachi's factories, we have seen such deadly accidents repeated in recent years.[89] How could it be otherwise when, ten years after the Baldia Town disaster, barely 15% of garment workers had access to a fire escape?[90]

For all its circumventions, abuses, and informalization, Pakistani law remains a battleground for the state institutions, social forces, and various coalitions that transcend the (largely imaginary) boundary between state and society. This centrality of the law in Pakistan's political and economic conflicts stems from their early judicialization. The military first seized the weapon of law back in the 1950s, in a bid to both legitimize its domination and stifle labour protest (by means of bureaucratization). Yet, despite its weaponization in the hands of the powerful, the law has continued to offer common ground and language (Thompson would say a shared 'ideology') to various social forces, whether they aspire to power, wealth, or simply dignity.

The law's ability to mediate social conflicts is particularly evident in the controversies surrounding workers' rights—a cause that largely disappeared from the public arena following the repression of the great social struggles of the 1960s and 1970s. As both the prospect of collective mobilization and the visibility of workers in the media waned, social conflicts retreated to the courts. This was achieved at the cost of recoding labour conflicts into a technical language that was largely inaccessible to laypeople, which in turn elevated the new figure of the expert activist—who, despite being more internationalized, was cut from the same cloth as the unionist lawyers of the 1950s and 1960s.

This process of judicialization has not, however, entirely stifled more spontaneous forms of protest, nor the ability of the working classes to organize themselves on their own terms.[91] In this respect, the empowerment of the Ali Enterprises Victims' Families Association is exemplary. As they gradually gained confidence and legitimacy, its members entered into direct negotiations with Pakistani bureaucratic institutions for part of the compensation they were owed.[92]

The families' quest for recognition on the international stage has, however, faced resistance from the German judicial system. The association's chairwoman and most prominent figure, Saeeda Khatoon, travelled to Dortmund in November 2018 to attend the first public hearing in the case. This had been brought against KiK by four association members, with the assistance of a Berlin-based NGO—the European Centre for Constitutional and Human Rights (ECCHR). Rejecting a request from Saeeda Khatoon's lawyer, the judges refused to meet with her and denied her the right to take the stand. During the hearing, one of the judges doubted—in German—that this mother of a victim might bring any new evidence to the case file.[93] Hiding behind its alleged 'complexity', the two judges also postponed their decision on the merits of the case—i.e. on KiK's co-responsibility for the disaster.

On 10 January 2019, the verdict was finally handed down: in the absence of a provision on the duty of care of companies in German law, the complaint against KiK was deemed inadmissible. This was a serious setback—both for the families of the victims and workers' organizations around the world. However, by exposing the flaws in existing legislation, this setback did provide impetus for an ambitious reform movement in Germany. The case of Ali Enterprises seems settled, but the struggle against global predatory chains is set to continue.

CONCLUSION

Over the past few decades, Karachi's economy has demonstrated astonishing resilience. Despite civil unrest of a frequency and intensity unmatched by any other city in the region (with the notable exception of Afghanistan's war zones), this port city continues to be the cornerstone of Pakistan's economy. In 2018, it generated between 11% and 20% of GDP (depending on the methodology used),[1] and 55% of federal revenue.[2] Karachi remains the country's main financial centre, and 95% of the country's international trade is said to pass through its deep-water ports.[3] The regional capital of Sindh also retains a unique position in the manufacturing sector, contributing about 30% of national industrial output.[4]

During the COVID-19 pandemic, Karachi's business community, toughened up by three decades of armed conflict, proved adaptable. This was particularly true of the textile industry, as the backbone of the city's industrial sector—and still its biggest employer. As the domestic and international market for personal protective equipment opened up, both large groups and SMEs seized the opportunity and threw themselves into the massive production of masks and medical gowns.[5] As an income source, this venture was relatively modest, but it did allow many companies to negotiate exemptions from sanitary restrictions—even though textiles were not classified as 'essential services'.[6]

Under pressure from industrialists, these restrictions were soon relaxed, and by opting for a policy of 'smart' lockdowns (limited in time and space), Imran Khan's government enabled textile and clothing companies to gain market share over their Indian, Chinese, and Bangladeshi competitors—all of whom faced prolonged lockdown measures. This economically driven health policy impacted export volume in the textile sector, taking it to an all-time high in 2021–2022 ($19 billion).

The textile and clothing industry also benefited from the refinancing facilities offered by the Central Bank in response to the health crisis. These subsidized loans were intended to be used for modernization projects and to pay salaries—on the condition that beneficiary companies refrained from laying off staff for a period of three months after receiving the funds. Taking full advantage of the precarious employment status of the majority of their workers (only 26% of Pakistani workers currently have an employment contract),[7] a number of companies in the sector seem to have used these loans to replenish their cash flow, even as they laid off large numbers of workers.[8]

The wave of redundancies seen in 2020–2021 ('justified' by the health crisis) was expected to accelerate both the re-organization of production lines and the feminization of the workforce. In what has long been a male-dominated sector, the few vacancies in the textile and garments industry are now reserved for women. In large companies, this sex-based recruitment preference is increasingly explicit[9] and is now publicly announced—for instance, in recruitment adverts on the back of buses carrying female workers to and from work.[10] Like the casualization of the workforce, this policy of increasing the number of female employees is driven by a desire for control and cost reduction; the men in charge of the sector deem women to be more conscientious as well as more docile—and more likely to accept lower wages (than their male colleagues) for equivalent work.[11]

Having faced repeated crises since the 1970s, Karachi's industrialists have become highly skilled at navigating troubled waters. And despite factory owners' attempts to shield their companies from the turbulence of a city in which armed conflict has become a defining feature, these conflicts have not only spilled over into the world of production, but also reshaped it in their own image.

Over the years, industrialists have (like everyone else) had to adapt to social and political turmoil. But they have also taken advantage of a violent social order to gain access to certain illicit economic rents and to impose new labour relations that leave workers more vulnerable to exploitation. The social imprint left by these conflicts seems to have outlived them—whether in terms of how work is organized, of control mechanisms, or of solidarities within the working classes (severely eroded by decades of ethnic and sectarian tensions fuelled by political groups). The intensity of these struggles for the city may have diminished since 2015—nonetheless, they have set the terms of economic domination for years to come.

By intruding into the factory world, Karachi's conflicts have opened up cracks in the employers' defences. However, the benefits offered to industrial workers by this troubled situation have been limited. As evidenced by the trajectories of a handful of working-class contractors and managers, partisan affiliations may have served social mobility strategies, while allowing some workers to negotiate room to manoeuvre with their employers. Setting aside the fact that such benefits have been confined to the individual level, these attempts to use political parties (as much in their potential for influence as in their power to cause harm) have also played into the hands of employers by making it easier to equate any mobilization for better working conditions with an opportunistic approach, or even a criminal enterprise.

Defenders of the workers themselves are finding it increasingly difficult to distinguish between genuine social struggles worthy of support and the extortionate endeavours of venal contractors.[12] Despite the cost of urban disorder to productive activities, those who have benefited most from the long-running civil unrest are the industrialists. The specialists in violence, coupled with the legal arsenal inherited from this troubled period, have bolstered the immune system of an intensely coercive brand of capitalism. And while the main protagonists of these conflicts have (in recent years) been demilitarized, Karachi's industrialists have not been disarmed.

* * *

Each and every variant of capitalism has specific characteristics as a result of how it is anchored in politics and society.[13] Before becoming entangled with the struggles for the city, Karachi's battle-hardened economy was thus shaped by the bellicose spirit that permeated the process of state formation and wealth creation in Pakistan—a strategic mindset in which the lines between war and peace became blurred early on, against a backdrop of existential concerns about the survival of the nation-state.

This omnipresence of the strategic register, founded on the all-encompassing imperative of 'national security', provides the framework for a repressive configuration that defines disruptors of industrial order as enemies of the state. Thus, in the event of labour conflicts, it can be used to justify recourse to the legal instruments and coercion specialists initially assigned to (para-)military operations (the defence of borders, the fight against terrorism, etc.).

Karachi's industrialists became part of this repressive configuration by conjuring up the spectre of chaos to gag workers and negotiate margins of impunity. More controversially, these frightened elites have at the same time been fighting fire with fire, forging short-lived alliances with specialists in violence handpicked from the multitude that the city has mass-produced. These apparently contradictory engagements with the forces of disorder—calling for them to be tamed while simultaneously colluding with them—have become integral to Karachi's industrial capitalism and its modes of control.

By tying its destiny to both the convulsions of a volatile city and to the security projects of a praetorian state that is itself suffering from chronic nervousness,[14] this heteroclite coalition has produced a distinctive brand of gunpoint capitalism. This productive configuration (which has proved remarkably durable in comparison with the more ephemeral arrangements of capital and coercion discussed throughout the book) is neither an aberration nor a deviant form. And while it is true that I have stressed both the structural irregularity and the predatory tendencies of this regime of production, as well as the propensity of its dominant actors to make order out of disorder, my aim was not to exceptionalize, and still less to pathologize, a variant of capitalism whose exotic nature could be reassuring.

There is a more general significance to the ability of Karachi's industrialists not only to overcome political, social, and health crises—but also to find windfall opportunities amid the turmoil. While most schools of thought in economic sociology agree that capitalism needs both regularity and predictability to ensure its reproduction,[15] Karachi's productive disorders suggest that another, less pacified and less rationalized path to capital accumulation is also possible.

More specifically, both the historical review of capital's henchmen in Gilded Age America and post-1968 France (Chapter 1) and the discussion of Latin American and Philippine experiences of armed neoliberalism (Chapter 5) have helped us to spot 'family resemblances' between these situations—despite their distance in time and space. Beyond their irreducible singularities, these productive arrangements share the characteristic of being repressive configurations, inextricably linked as such. Without being indifferent to the nature of the goods produced or extracted (since the figures of authority characteristic of each regime of accumulation are rooted in specific labour relations), these entanglements of capital and coercion transcend the boundaries of capitalism (be it industrial, agrarian, or extractive) and seem destined for a bright future, in the age of so-called 'green' capitalism.

The key common denominator of this organization of labour and its related forms of life is the plethoric nature of its coercive apparatus, which is both overabundant and widely dispersed. Its primary protector is always the state (providing both legal and extra-legal violence), yet it is also a major consumer of private force. However, the state/society dichotomy runs up against the propensity of these violent arrangements to shatter the division between public and private via the circulation of specialists in coercion and the chains of interdependence that surround them.

This commodification of the use of force is particularly acute in societies that are facing long-term conflicts or are under military rule—both of which offer fertile soil for violent entrepreneurship. Yet, far from mechanically reinforcing the domination of those in power, the accumulation of coercive means obeys its own law of diminishing returns. With the increase and diversification of protectors comes uncertainty as to their effectiveness and loyalty. And cost-cutting efforts, from which security services are not exempt, exacerbate this dilemma by producing policing that is 'cheap' in both senses of the word: low-cost *and* low-performance. This in turn generates new forms of anxiety among the holders of capital. The result is an anxious domination that echoes Brecht's lines: 'Fear rules not only those who are ruled, but the rulers too'.[16]

* * *

Global supply chains also come with their share of contingencies. The Ali Enterprises disaster is emblematic of a predatory system that serves both to dismantle the institutions of industrial citizenship and to neutralize regulatory mechanisms; this is true in the North as well as the South. But the work of those in favour of regulation is still in progress, and the legacy of this disaster may prove to be less settled than I myself believed throughout the writing of this book.

While German courts have refused to recognize KiK's responsibility for the disaster, the 2021 Act on Corporate Due Diligence Obligations in Supply Chains (in German: Liefferkettensorgfaltspflichtengesetz, abbreviated to LkSG), which came into force on 1 January 2023, suggests the possibility of greater control over suppliers of major European brands. The scope of the law is currently limited to companies based in Germany and their suppliers, but could be extended through the adoption of similar legislation at European level.[17]

It was the tragedy of the Rana Plaza in Bangladesh that provided the main impetus for these laws, but the LkSG also came in response to judicial meanderings in the proceedings against KiK in the Baldia factory fire case. In this respect, it represents a delayed victory for the transnational coalition that formed around families of victims of the disaster.[18]

This coalition of activist lawyers, trade union actors, and representatives of victims' families sought to establish that KiK had a legal responsibility (duty of care) towards the employees of Ali Enterprises, and was thus liable for their safety—a claim repeatedly denied by KiK. It claimed to have acted in compliance with its own code of conduct, and that Ali Enterprises was responsible for the safety of its own employees.[19] The legal strategy came from the European Center for Constitutional and Human Rights (ECCHR), which initiated litigation against KiK on behalf of the Ali Enterprises Factory Fire Affectees Association (AEFFAA), echoing a larger, EU-wide mobilization for 'due diligence'. This mobilization (led by trade unions and human rights or environmental NGOs) aimed to move away from the 'soft law' norms of corporate social responsibility (CSR) and towards legally binding obligations for foreign buyers under the principle of due diligence. Such legal obligations were already recognized by the 2017 French Duty of Vigilance law, which requires larger French firms to both identify and prevent harm to workers and the environment caused by themselves as well as by their subsidiaries and subcontractors. This transition from 'soft' to 'hard' law implies the possibility of legal remedies and sanctions. The 2017 French law thus introduces the possibility, for 'any person with a legitimate interest to do so', to turn to the courts in a bid to establish whether a given company has failed to meet its obligations and is therefore liable to pay compensation for the harm caused. However, while the Paris judicial tribunal is competent to examine alleged violations of the French Duty of Vigilance law, no similar judicial remedy is provided for in the LkSG; its implementation is to be monitored by an administrative authority attached to the Federal Office for Economic Affairs and Export Control (BAFA). Yet the German law does provide for the creation of a strong control apparatus, which should be able to check company reports, identify violations, and impose hefty financial penalties (fines of up to eight million euros or 2% of the group's annual turnover)—to which exclusion from public contracts may be added. Moreover, this supervisory authority will be open both to complaints from victims of human rights violations and to those from third parties representing workers living abroad (e.g. NGOs or German trade unions). This clause should make these procedures both easier, and cheaper, for workers in the South.

As law, the LkSG is thus far more binding than the International Accord adopted in the wake of the Rana Plaza disaster in Bangladesh. Its implementation could have significant consequences for global value chains—especially in Karachi, since the human rights violations covered by the law include restrictions on freedom of association enacted by public or private security agents.[20] This particular clause in the LkSG Act seems designed to call the specialists in violence to order—starting with the retired military personnel who are active in the security departments of Karachi companies.

It is much too soon to consider the consequences of this law as a whole and each of its provisions—but it certainly opens up a new horizon of possibilities. Not just for workers and trade union activists in the South, but also for the convergence of social and environmental struggles on a transnational scale. The ripples of the social shockwave caused by the Baldia Town disaster clearly continue to spread.

GEOGRAPHIES OF CAPITAL

The origin story for Karachi's industrialization features a small number of visionary entrepreneurs backed by a handful of high-ranking government officials, who served as demiurge. It was this meeting of the entrepreneurial spirit of the nascent industrial bourgeoisie with the ambitious vision of senior civil servants that resulted in the development of peripheral areas hitherto destined to remain on the fringes of history—or so the epic story goes. Wiping out all traces of the rural and pastoral populations formerly established on these lands, the enormity of this story is proportionate to the physical and social upheaval brought about by industrialization.

The photographic essay that follows gives voice to the landscapes and architecture shaped by industrial capitalism, offering a counterpoint to this heroic narrative. It tracks the transformative and disruptive effects of 'development' (an ongoing project that is still a work in progress) through its imprint not only on the natural environment, but also on the topography of industrial estates, on popular housing, on funerary monuments, on workers' canteens, on heavily policed roads, and on barricaded factory buildings.

Although this visual narrative follows the chronology of the main text, the commentary allows itself to meander slightly as it reads the sedimentation of time in industrial landscapes. And while it more or less follows the line of the book's main arguments, this photographic series highlights cases of dissonance, acts of resistance, and dysfunctions of the apparatus of control. This editorial choice reveals that employer domination—no matter how coercive it may be—does not appear to be without flaws. By deliberately maintaining ambiguity, this photo essay resists the temptation (inherent to such a pictorial narrative) to freeze the city in a series of tableaux, depicting a 'panorama-city' that—as Michel de Certeau warns us—only seems to be more legible due to being seen both from above and from afar, lifted out of 'the murky intertwining daily behaviours'.

Washdil Baloch was born in 1950 and lives in Sharafi Goth. He recalls, 'In my childhood, there were only gardens and fields here'. As an urban village on the fringes of the Korangi industrial estate, Sharafi Goth—where trees and streams have long served as topographical landmarks—has preserved a semi-rural way of life. Trees were also used to delineate properties:

> Sometimes, torrential rains washed away the low walls demarcating plots of land, but the trees held firm. Each tree took the name of the person who had planted it. And when his grandson made a claim to the property, all he had to do was say: 'This date tree was planted by my grandfather, this plot of land is mine'.

Sharafi Goth, Korangi, 2022

308

In the early 1960s, orchards and pastures gave way to textile mills and silos, and a new geography, shaped by the forces of capital, was born. It left its mark on place names and spatial orientation practices. The Korangi industrial estate is organized around a grid plan (bequeathed by Greek architect Constantinos Doxiadis), which has official 'sectors' designated by a letter. In practice, however, people tend to use the roundabout names to find their way, and these bear the names of the predominant local industry (e.g. tanneries) or company (e.g. Brookes Pharma, Singer, Shan Foods, etc.).

Korangi Industrial Area, 2022

In the working-class neighbourhoods that developed unofficially around industrial estates, factories can literally be a stone's throw from workers' homes. In the newest part of Sharafi Goth, the Sunlight Wood Products plant has had to raise its corrugated iron walls to protect itself from stones cast at it by residents in protest against the air pollution caused by the plant.

Sharafi Goth, Korangi, 2022

310

K2 is one of the highest hills in Orangi, and those who climb it are rewarded with a panoramic view of the biggest informal settlement in Pakistan (and perhaps in all Asia). They will also walk through a place of memory that is haunted by past tragedies. In the mid-1980s, when inter-community clashes were on the rise in Orangi, K2 was a favourite firing point for the Pashtun militiamen who were targeting Urdu-speaking residents living further down.

Fareed Colony, Orangi, 2018

On 8 June 1972, a huge crowd gathered at Banaras Chowk, on the edge of SITE industrial area, to attend the funeral of Muhammad Shoaib—a trade union leader shot dead by the police the previous day. Protesters were determined to carry the coffin to the Governor's residence and clashed with the police, who opened fire on the crowd, killing at least a dozen people. This massacre brought the biggest worker mobilization in Pakistan's history to a halt. The graves of the 1972 'martyred workers' are painted red and occupy a specific section of the Frontier Colony cemetery, not far from Banaras Chowk. In 2012, PILER (an organization for the defence of workers' rights) erected a memorial in their honour.

Shuhada-e-Mazdoor Qabristan, Frontier Colony, 2017

312

نشہ کی حالت میں   سیاسی گفتگو سے پرہیز کریں

'Abstain from political discussions.' In the roadside restaurants where Karachi's workers can find a cheap meal and get some rest, this injunction has survived the dictatorship of General Zia-ul-Haq (1977–1988), who saw workers' canteens as hotbeds of subversion. Amid the ethnic and sectarian rivalries of the following decades, it has taken on fresh significance, and now represents an attempt to insulate these establishments from the turbulent unrest of the city.

Landhi Industrial Area, 2015

Green Park City is a gated community located on the outskirts of Landhi
Industrial Area. Seeking to replicate the features of elite housing, it is a
showcase for the self-made men of local industry. Most of its residents
are contractors and managers from working-class backgrounds and their
families. Although the neighbourhood's infrastructure does not always
match up to its ambitions (the power grid is just as unreliable as that of the
surrounding working-class localities), its upstart prosperity testifies to the
upward social mobility that the manufacturing sector has opened up to a
hitherto marginalized group of workers.

Green Park City, Landhi, 2016

'We have three parks here. One for families, and two reserved for men', boasts Ataullah Masood,* a transport contractor for the surrounding industries. In a city where green spaces are found only in the most affluent neighbourhoods, these parks signal collective distinction—but they also serve as a battleground in a culture war. This emerging middle class is determined to rise above the working class and to set itself apart from the morally dissolute elite—yet these parks, by opening up opportunities for 'inappropriate' contact between men and women, form a focal point for the very risks of acculturation from which it seeks to protect itself.

Green Park City, Landhi, 2016

The security architecture that has flourished in Karachi's industrial zones over the last few decades is a reflection of the companies that implement it. The most tech-savvy firms have invested in relatively sophisticated surveillance systems, but garment factories often rely on makeshift solutions—a few breezeblocks, possibly covered with a sheet or two of corrugated iron. As such hastily cobbled together security architecture shows, maintaining industrial order can be a decidedly cheap affair.

Korangi Industrial Area, 2015

The alliance between capital and coercion is also negotiated at the aesthetic level. Ubiquitous in industrial areas, the crenellated towers erected by the paramilitary Rangers are decorated with a camouflage pattern that reveals more than it hides. Ostensibly conferring paramilitary protection on the surrounding factories (here, on the Liberty Mills textile factory), these structures, visible from afar, also serve as billboards. Urban pacification is no stranger to the concept of branding, and the logos of its sponsors, both public and private, are displayed on every wall of these *chowkis*. Emblazoned alongside the Sindh Rangers' logo (a yellow palm tree on a red background) is the signature of the paint manufacturer in charge of the decoration work—which has itself become more sophisticated in recent years. The colour palette has been broadened (there is a growing craze for pink), and check-posts are being 'greenified'.

SITE, 2016

Above the gate (originally designed to filter traffic, and now reserved for pedestrians) between SITE's industrial area and the working-class locality of Bawani Chali, graffiti in Urdu salutes the 'greatness' of the Rangers. This is a reminder that the productive space extending beyond this gate is under paramilitary protection. This call to order is flanked by a slogan advertising the services of a telecommunications company. This advertising space has been allocated to the company by SITE's industrialists' association, to finance its security operations.

SITE/Bawani Chali, 2016

318

In Karachi as elsewhere, it is important to resist the 'charms' of surveillance: in particular, its tendency to subjugate us by suggesting that we are constantly caught in its web. In practice, the watchful gaze of the surveillance officers often gets lost. Anyone who zooms in on the SITE Self-Security System control screens will soon notice that several of them are frozen, displaying the message: 'The server has lost connection to the camera'. Not only do these Sindh Rangers paramilitaries fail to unravel the mysteries of the city, they often have to settle for an unedifying view of static white noise.

'Double S-Double S' control room, SITE Association of Trade and Industry, SITE, 2016

In Korangi, security architecture proclaims the sovereignty of capital. Stamped with the logos of both the local employers' association and the Citizens-Police Liaison Committee (CPLC), the surveillance buildings erected by industrialists are styled as 'police check-posts'. Although the CPLC logo sustains the official narrative of a public-private partnership in the realm of security, the routine tasks of maintaining order have in fact been delegated—in and around the factories, and even on certain roads— to employers.

Korangi Industrial Area, 2016

This guard is posing beautifully here—not for the camera, but primarily for the benefit of his superior, a CPLC inspector, who is looking on from outside the frame. My own (unintentional) contribution to industrial order was never more apparent than at a moment when I mistakenly believed I could photograph security installations autonomously from these chaperones. Having tried to take an unsolicited photo of a check-post, I was instantly held at gunpoint by one of the guards. Unwittingly, I had just confirmed the effectiveness of the employers' security arrangements. I have a vivid memory of the smile this put on the face of Rashid Memon,* the head of security at SITE.

Korangi Industrial Area, 2017

Corporate defences are not without flaws. While residents of working-class neighbourhoods sometimes claim to have demolished the fortifications that disrupt their movements, the saboteurs are not easily identifiable. In 2016, I investigated one such unauthorized breakthrough. It had occurred near Saif Industries, a steelworks factory in SITE. To some, this was the work of the residents from a nearby locality; others saw it as the work of factory guards eager to find a shortcut when sent on errands by their employers. One thing was certain: in the industrial zones of Karachi and the adjacent working-class neighbourhoods, there is no shortage of reasons to walk through walls.

SITE, 2016

NOTES

ACKNOWLEDGEMENTS

1. David Graeber, *Debt: The First 5,000 Years*, New York, Melville House, 2011, p. 99.

INTRODUCTION

1. This account is based on a series of interviews conducted in Karachi in July 2017 with officials of the Edhi Foundation, as well as on the investigation reports of the local police, the Federal Investigation Agency (FIA), and the judicial tribunal (officially known as the Alavi Commission) mandated by the Sindh authorities. See Charge Sheet No. 238 - A/2012, 12 November 2012; *Enquiry Report. Fire Incident at Ali Enterprises S.I.T.E Karachi On 11th September 2012, 3 October 2012 (subsequently FIA Report); Tribunal's Report for Ascertaining the Circumstances and Cause Leading to the Fire and Subsequent Deaths and Injuries in the Incident That Took Place on 11.09.2012 in the Factory of M/S Ali Enterprises Located at Plot No. F-67 SITE Karachi* (subsequently Alavi Tribunal Report). Reference can also be made to the remarkable work of reconstruction, using 3D modelling, by the Forensic Architecture collective: https://forensic-architecture.org/investigation/the-ali-enterprises-factory-fire
2. Developed in 1997 by Social Accountability International (SAI), SA 8000 certification builds on the ILO conventions, the Universal Declaration of Human Rights and various UN conventions to provide companies with a certificate of compliance with the principles of social responsibility, issued after an audit by accredited experts.

3. Sébastien Chauvin and Nicolas Jounin, 'L'externalisation des illégalités: ethnographie des usages du travail "temporaire" à Paris et Chicago', in Laurence Fontaine and Florence Weber (eds.), *Les Paradoxes de l'économie informelle. À qui profitent les règles?*, Paris, Karthala, 2011, p. 114.

4. Michel Naepels, *Dans la détresse. Une anthropologie de la vulnérabilité*, Paris, Éditions de l'EHESS, 2019, p. 25.

5. Thorstein Veblen, *The Theory of the Leisure Class*, New York, Oxford University Press, 2007 [1899], pp. 15, 242.

6. John Kenneth Galbraith, *The New Industrial State*, Boston, Houghton Mifflin, 1967.

7. James Galbraith, 'Predation from Veblen Until Now: Remarks to the Veblen Sesquicentennial Conference', in Erik S. Reinert and Francesca Viano (eds.), *Thorstein Veblen: Economics for an Age of Crises*, New York, Anthem Press, 2013, p. 326.

8. James Galbraith, *The Predator State: How Conservatives Abandoned the Free Market and Why Liberals Should Too*, New York, The Free Press, 2008.

9. Paul D. Hutchcroft, *Booty Capitalism: The Politics of Banking in the Philippines*, Ithaca, Cornell University Press, 1998.

10. David Harvey, 'Accumulation by Dispossession', *Socialist Register*, Vol. 40, 2004, pp. 63–87.

11. J. Galbraith, 'Predation from Veblen Until Now', op. cit., p. 326.

12. Pierre Bourdieu, 'Droit et passe-droit: le champ des pouvoirs territoriaux et la mise en œuvre des règlements', *Actes de la recherche en sciences sociales*, No. 81–82, 1990, p. 87.

13. J. Galbraith, 'Predation from Veblen Until Now', op. cit., p. 327.

14. J. Galbraith, *The Predator State*, op. cit., p. 130.

15. John Braithwaite, *Corporate Crime in the Pharmaceutical Industry*, New York, Routledge, 1984

16. Established in 1947, the All Pakistan Textile Mills Association (APTMA) is the most influential trade organization in Pakistan. Under pressure from its leaders, who come from the largest Memon and Chinioti families, successive governments have guaranteed the mills a supply of cotton that is at least 30% lower than the international price.

17. The 'terror attack' thesis has not met with the same response abroad and has had little impact on the legal proceedings against KiK in Germany or RINA in Italy. On these proceedings, see Miriam Saage-Maaß, Peer Zumbansen, Michael Bader, and Palvasha Shahab (eds.), *Transnational Legal Activism in Global Value Chains: The Ali Enterprises Factory Fire and the Struggle for Justice*, Cham, Springer, 2021.

18. The broad definition of terrorism that has prevailed in Pakistan since the late 1990s has made it possible to describe this alleged act of arson as a terrorist attack.

19. Laurent Gayer, *Karachi: Ordered Disorder and the Struggle for the City*, London, Hurst, 2014.

20. In 1989–1990, as the city settled into a state of chronic disorder, manufacturing growth was approaching 8%. See United Nations Industrial Development Organization, *Pakistan: Towards Industrial Liberalization and Revitalization*, Oxford, Basil Blackwell, 1990, p. xv.

21. World Bank, *Transforming Karachi into a Livable and Competitive Megacity: A City Diagnostic and Transformation Strategy*, Washington, World Bank, 2018, p. 16, fig. 2.1.

22. For more on the trajectory of this colourful character, who was a key figure in the revolutionary days of 1848, see Mark Traugott, 'The Limits of Protagonism: A Political Anthropology of 1848', *Politix*, No. 112, 2015, pp. 89–92.

23. Lesley Gill, 'The Parastate in Colombia: Political Violence and the Restructuring of Barrancabermeja', *Anthropologica*, Vol. 51, No. 2, 2009, pp. 313–325.

24. Alexander Dunlap, 'Counterinsurgency for Wind Energy: The Bíi Hixo Wind Park in Juchitán, Mexico', *The Journal of Peasant Studies*, Vol. 45, No. 3, 2018, pp. 630–652.

25. Alexander Dunlap and James Fairhead, 'The Militarisation and Marketisation of Nature: An Alternative Lens to "Climate Conflict"', *Geopolitics*, Vol. 19, No. 4, 2014, pp. 937–961.

26. All names followed by an asterisk have been changed to preserve respondent anonymity. I have chosen not to anonymize public figures who spoke on the record, or those people (often elderly) who had taken pride in testifying about their past involvement, or about other events relatively distant in time.

27. See Chapters 2 and 3 for more on this 'family entrepreneur' figure, associated with the merchant castes originating from the present-day Indian province of Gujarat.

28. Nationally, the textile and garment industry employs around 40% of Pakistan's manufacturing workers (10 to 15 million people) and contributes around 8% to the country's GDP. These figures are however contested, and the higher estimates (circulated by the textile lobby) tend to be picked up indiscriminately by the Pakistani media. In 2020–2021, the export earnings generated by this industry reached an all-time high of $19 billion—representing 76% of export earnings.

29. Geert de Neve and Rebecca Prentice (eds.), *Unmaking the Global Sweatshop: Health and Safety of the World's Garment Workers*, Philadelphia, Penn University Press, 2017.

30. The two textile companies in question are referred to in the text by the pseudonyms Hamid Textiles* and KFG Textile Mills,* while the two pharmaceutical companies studied appear as Qudrat Pharma* and Shahbaz Pharma.*

31. L. Gayer, *Karachi*, op. cit.

32. I worked on three main archival collections: (1)–(2) two British and American diplomatic archival collections (including both chancery telegrams and reports written by labour attachés), held at the National Archives in Kew (UK) and College Park (USA) respectively, covering developments in Pakistani industry and trade unionism from 1955 to 1975; (3) a collection of documents deposited at the British Library by the India, Pakistan and Burma Association, a private British business support agency founded in 1942, which had correspondents in the region up until the early 1970s.

33. These judgements are collected in the *Pakistan Labour Gazette*; I was able to consult an almost complete collection covering the period 1947–1990 at the Columbia Law School library. I have tried to fill in the gaps by consulting *Pakistan Labour Cases*—another official publication that publishes Labour Court judgements.

34. The only social science book on the Karachi textile industry makes no use of these legal sources. See Zafar Shaheed, *The Labour Movement in Pakistan: Organization and Leadership in the 1970s*, Karachi, Oxford University Press, 2007.

35. I had already adopted this perspective in my previous book, which focused on the conflictual configuration at work in the city as a whole since the second half of the 1980s. See L. Gayer, *Karachi*, op. cit.

36. Norbert Elias, *What is Sociology?*, New York, Columbia University Press, 1984, p. 131.

37. 'De près, de loin: des rapports de force en histoire' (Interview by Philippe Mangeot with Carlo Ginzburg), *Vacarme*, January 2002.

38. Ali Arqam, 'A family sport', *Newsline*, October 2017; Ali Arqam, 'How the vote was lost and won', *Newsline*, August 2018.

39. For an overview of the different ways in which field photography can be used by the social sciences, see Howard Becker (ed.), *Exploring Society Photographically*, Chicago, Chicago University Press, 1981; Douglas Harper, *Visual Sociology*, London-New York, Routledge, 2012.

40. Adam Baczko, Laurent Gayer and Élise Massicard, 'La monographie

comparative: embrasser la tension entre singularité et universalité',
Critique internationale, No. 100, 2023, pp. 101–117.

41. Paul Veyne, *L'Inventaire des différences*, Paris, Le Seuil, 1976, p. 19.

42. Karl Marx, 'The Usefulness of Crime', in D. F. Greenberg (ed.), *Crime and Capitalism: Readings in Marxist Criminology*, Philadelphia, Temple University Press, pp. 52–53.

43. Regina Bateson, 'The Politics of Vigilantism', *Comparative Political Studies*, Vol. 54, No. 6, 2021, p. 927.

44. Edward Palmer Thompson, *Whigs and Hunters: The Origin of the Black Act*, London, Penguin Books, 1975.

1. THE GUARDIANS OF INDUSTRIAL PEACE

1. Sub-committee of the Senate Committee on Education and Labor, *Violations of Free Speech and Rights of Labor, Hearings Pursuant to S. Res. 266* (later *La Follette Hearings*), 76th Congress, First Session on S. 70, 25 May 1939, p. 20.

2. See Alex Baskin, 'The Ford Hunger March—1932', *Labor History*, Vol. 13, No. 3, 1972, p. 338.

3. Stephen H. Norwood, *Strikebreaking and Intimidation: Mercenaries and Masculinity in Twentieth-Century America*, Chapel Hill, The University of North Carolina Press, 2003, p. 180.

4. Keith Sward, *The Legend of Henry Ford*, New York, Rinehart, 1948, p. 235.

5. Ibid., p. 237.

6. *Detroit Times*, 8 March 1932, quoted in S. H. Norwood, *Strikebreaking and Intimidation*, op. cit., p. 181.

7. Robert M. Weiss, 'Corporate Security at Ford Motor Company: From the Great War to the Cold War', in Kevin Walby and Randy K. Lippert (eds.), *Corporate Security in the 21st Century: Theory and Practice in International Perspective*, Basingstoke, Palgrave Macmillan, 2014, p. 25.

8. Stephen Meyer, *The Five Dollar Day: Labor Management and Social Control in the Ford Motor Company, 1908–1921*, New York, SUNY Press, 1981, Chapter 8.

9. James J. Flink, *The Automobile Age*, Cambridge-London, MIT Press, 1990, p. 221.

10. R. M. Weiss, 'Corporate Security at Ford Motor Company', op. cit.

11. S. P. O'Hara, *Inventing the Pinkertons, or Spies, Sleuths, Mercenaries, and Thugs: Being a Story of the Nation's Most Famous (and Infamous) Detective Agency*, Baltimore, Johns Hopkins University Press, 2016; Quentin

Delpech, *Mobilisations syndicales et violence au Sud. Protesting in the factories of international outsourcing in Guatemala*, Paris, Karthala, 2013; Lesley Gill, *A Century of Violence in a Red City: Popular Struggle, Counterinsurgency, and Human Rights in Colombia*, Durham, Duke University Press, 2016.

12. Pierre Bourdieu, 'La représentation politique: éléments pour une théorie du champ politique', *Actes de la recherche en sciences sociales*, No. 36–37, 1981, p. 4.

13. Charles Tilly, 'Theories and Realities', in Leopold H. Haimson and Charles Tilly (eds.), *Strikes, Wars and Revolutions in an International Perspective: Strike Waves in the Late Nineteenth and Early Twentieth Centuries*, Cambridge, Cambridge University Press, 1989, p. 11.

14. Romain Bonnet and Amerigo Caruso, 'Industrial Europe and Counter-Internationalism: The Yellow Movement in the Franco-German Area Before 1914', *Histoire@Politique*, No. 39, 2019; Amerigo Caruso and Claire Morelon, 'The Threat from Within Across Empires: Strikes, Labor Migration, and Violence in Central Europe, 1900–1914', *Central European History*, No. 54, 2021, pp. 86–111.

15. S. H. Norwood, *Strikebreaking and Intimidation*, op. cit.; Robert Michael Smith, *From Blackjacks to Briefcases: A History of Commercialized Strikebreaking and Unionbusting in the United States*, Athens, Ohio University Press, 2003; Chad E. Pearson, *Capital's Terrorists: Klansmen, Lawmen, and Employers in the Long Nineteenth-Century*, Chapel Hill, The University of North Carolina Press, 2022.

16. Matteo Millan and Alessandro Saluppo (eds.), *Corporate Policing, Yellow Unionism, and Strikebreaking, 1890–1930*, Milton Park, Routledge, 2021.

17. For an overview of this literature, see Teo Ballvé, *The Frontier Effect: State Formation and Violence in Colombia*, Ithaca, Cornell University Press, 2020; L. Gill, *A Century of Violence in a Red City*, op. cit.; Jacobo Grajales, *Agrarian Capitalism, War and Peace in Colombia: Beyond Dispossession*, London-New York, Routledge, 2021; Lucia Michelutti and Barbara Harris-White (eds.), *The Wild East: Criminal Political Economies in South Asia*, London, UCL Press, 2019; Tania Murray Li and Pujo Semedi, *Plantation Life: Corporate Occupation in Indonesia's Oil Palm Zone*, Durham, Duke University Press, 2021.

18. Etienne Penissat, 'À l'ombre du dialogue social', *Agone*, No. 50, 2013, p. 8.

19. Harry Bennett (as told to Paul Marcus), *Ford: We Never Called Him Henry*, New York, Gold Medal Books, 1951, Chapter 1.

20. See for example Amy Wilson, 'The rise and fall of Harry Bennett', *Autonews.com*, 2 June 2003.

21. The son of a poster painter, Bennett himself had trained as a painter before joining the navy.

22. David Lanier Lewis, *The Public Image of Henry Ford: An American Folk Hero and His Company*, Detroit, Wayne State University Press, 1976, p. 249.

23. Anton Blok, *The Mafia of a Sicilian Village, 1860–1960: A Study of Violent Peasant Entrepreneurs*, New York, Harper & Row, 1974; Carlos Miguel Ortiz Sarmiento, *La Violence en Colombie. Racines historiques et sociales*, Paris, L'Harmattan, 1990; Imdad Hussain Sahito, *Decade of the Dacoits*, Karachi, Oxford University Press, 2005.

24. For the United States, see S. H. Norwood, *Strikebreaking and Intimidation*, op. cit., Chapters 5 and 6. For France, see Juan Sebastian Carbonell and Vincent Gay, 'Violences et contre-violences dans les conflits du travail', *Tumultes*, No. 57, 2021, pp. 119–135.

25. Friedrich Engels, *The Peasant War in Germany*, trans. Moissaye J. Olgin, New York, International Publishers 1966 [1850].

26. Michel Foucault, *Discipline and Punish: The Birth of the Prison* (trans. Alan Sheridan), New York, Vintage Books, 1995 [1975], p. 285.

27. A. Blok, *The Mafia of a Sicilian Village*, op. cit.; Vadim Volkov, *Violent Entrepreneurs: The Use of Force in the Making of Russian Capitalism*, Ithaca, Cornell University Press, 2002.

28. A. Blok, *The Mafia of a Sicilian Village*, op. cit., p. 8.

29. V. Volkov, *Violent Entrepreneurs*, op. cit., p. 41.

30. Ibid., p. 19.

31. Marc Lenormand, Sabine Remanofsky, and Gilles Christoph (eds.), *Anti-syndicalisme. La vindicte des puissants*, Vulaines-sur-Seine, Éditions du Croquant, 2019; Gregor Gall and Tony Dundon (eds.), *Anti-Unionism: Nature, Dynamics, Trajectories and Outcomes*, Basingstoke, Palgrave MacMillan, 2013.

32. Q. Delpech, *Mobilisations syndicales et violence au Sud*, op. cit., p. 142. See also Sophie Russo, *The Arts of Order: Protecting Trade and Containing Violence in Karachi's Old City Bazars*, doctoral thesis (political science), Sciences Po, Paris, 2022, for whom the 'art' of domination refers to the spectacular dimension of power, its creativity in the face of the trials of social life, as well as its technical and artisanal dimension (domination as the acquisition and testing of know-how).

33. Dipesh Chakrabarty, *Rethinking Working Class History: Bengal 1890–1940*, Cambridge, Cambridge University Press, 1989; Rajnarayan Chandavarkar, *The Origins of Industrial Capitalism in India: Business Strategies and the Working Classes in Bombay, 1900–1940*, Cambridge, Cambridge University Press, 1994; Chitra Joshi, *Lost Worlds: Indian*

Labour and Its Forgotten Histories, London, Anthem Press, 2003; Patrick Joyce, *Work, Society and Politics: The Culture of the Factory in Later Victorian England*, London, The Harvester Press, 1980.

34. Bernard Mottez, 'Du marchandage au salaire au rendement', *Sociologie du travail*, No. 3, 1960, pp. 206–215.
35. Loren Ryter, 'Pemuda Pancasila: The Last Loyalist Free Men of Suharto's Order', in Benedict Anderson (ed.), *Violence and the State in Suharto's Indonesia*, Ithaca, Cornell University Press, 2001, pp. 129–130.
36. Robert Cribb, *Gangsters and Revolutionaries: The Jakarta People's Militia and the Indonesian Revolution 1945–1949*, Singapore, Equinox Publishing, 2009 [1991], pp. 14–15.
37. Arup Kumar Sen, 'Mode of Labour Control in Colonial India', *Economic & Political Weekly*, Vol. 37, No. 38, 2002, pp. 3956–3966.
38. Geert de Neve, 'Entrapped Entrepreneurship: Labour Contractors in the South Indian Garment Industry', *Modern Asian Studies*, Vol. 48, No. 5, 2014, pp. 1302–1333. On the place of the contractor in Indian economic history, see Tirthankar Roy, 'Sardars, Jobbers, Kanganies: The Labour Contractor and Indian Economic History', *Modern Asian Studies*, Vol. 42, No. 5, 2008, pp. 971–998.
39. R. Chandavarkar, *The Origins of Industrial Capitalism in India*, op. cit., Chapter 5.
40. Ibid., p. 206.
41. Ian Douglas Wilson, *The Politics of Protection Rackets in Post-New Order Indonesia: Coercive Capital, Authority and Street Politics*, London, Routledge, 2015.
42. Nicolaas Warouw, 'Community-Based Agencies as the Entrepreneur's Instruments of Control in Post Soeharto's Indonesia', *Asia Pacific Business Review*, Vol. 12, No. 2, 2006, pp. 193–207.
43. Daniel Warfman and Frédéric Ocqueteau, *La Sécurité privée en France*, Paris, PUF, 2011, p. 11.
44. Amerigo Caruso, "We Can Kill Striking Workers Without Being Prosecuted": Armed Bands of Strikebreakers in Late Imperial Germany', in M. Millan and A. Saluppo (eds.), *Corporate Policing…*, op. cit., p. 196.
45. S. P. O'Hara, *Inventing the Pinkertons*, op. cit., p. 2.
46. William Serrin, *Homestead: The Glory and Tragedy of an American Steel Town*, New York, Vintage Books, 1993, p. 76.
47. This legislation prohibited federal authorities from using the agency's services, and twenty-six states subsequently passed legislation prohibiting the use of private police. In the following decades, however, these measures were circumvented by large companies.

48. The term 'muckraker' was coined in the United States in the 1890s to describe writers or (photo)journalists who investigated social issues and exposed the dark side of the powerful.
49. R. M. Smith, *From Blackjacks to Briefcases*, op. cit., pp. 41, 44.
50. Ibid., p. 55.
51. Louis G. Silverberg, 'Citizens' Committees: Their Role in Industrial Conflict', *The Public Opinion Quarterly*, Vol. 5, No. 1, 1941, pp. 17–37; Michael Cohen, '"The Ku Klux Klan Government": Vigilantism, Lynching, and the Repression of the IWW', *Journal for the Study of Radicalism*, Vol. 1, No. 1, 2007, pp. 31–56; C.E. Pearson, *Capital's Terrorists*, op. cit.
52. Vilja Hulden and Chad Pearson, 'The Wild West of Employer Anti-unionism: The Glorification of Vigilantism and Individualism in the Early Twentieth-century United States', in M. Millan and A. Saluppo (eds.), *Corporate Policing…*, op. cit., pp. 205–221.
53. See in particular M. Cohen, '"The Ku Klux Klan Government"', op. cit., pp. 35 and 48 for the cases of 'Wobblies' tarred and feathered in San Diego in 1912, as well as the account of the lynching of Wesley Everest in Centralia, Pennsylvania in 1919. According to some accounts, Everest was emasculated, prior to being lynched, by one of the town's leading businessmen in a punitive ritual usually reserved for black men accused of rape.
54. S. H. Norwood, *Strikebreaking and Intimidation,* op. cit., p. 172.
55. L. G. Silverberg, 'Citizens' Committees', op. cit.
56. Gilles Favarel-Garrigues and Laurent Gayer, *Proud to Punish:The Global Landscape of Rough Justice*, Stanford, Stanford University Press, 2024, p. 13. On the links between vigilantism and the repression of social struggles in the United States, see also Valerio Evangelisti, *One Big Union*, Mondadori, 2012, an impressive historical novel tracing the career of an anti-union mercenary from 1877 to 1919.
57. *La Follette Hearings*, Report No. 46, 75 Cong. 2 Sess. pt. 3, *Industrial Espionage,* Washington, 1937, p. 46.
58. Ibid., Report No. 6, 76 Cong, 1 Sess, pt. 1, *Strikebreaking Services*, and pt. 2, *Private Police Systems,* Washington, 1939.
59. S. H. Norwood, *Strikebreaking and Intimidation*, op. cit., p. 216.
60. Stephen R. Couch, 'Selling and Reclaiming State Sovereignty: The Case of Coal and Iron Police', *Critical Sociology,* Vol. 11, No. 1, 1981, pp. 85–91.
61. *La Follette Hearings*, Report No. 6, 76 Cong, 1 Sess, pt. 2, *Private Police Systems*, op. cit., pp. 126–144.

331

pp. [32–35]

62. Wilbur R. Miller, *A History of Private Policing in the United States*, London-New York, Bloomsbury, 2019, p. 153.
63. *La Follette Hearings*, Report No. 6, 76 Cong, 1 Sess, pt. 3, *Industrial Munitions*.
64. Rick Fantasia, 'Dictature sur le prolétariat: stratégies de répression et travail aux États-Unis', *Actes de la recherche en sciences sociales*, No. 138, 2001, pp. 3–18.
65. Michael Burawoy, *Manufacturing Consent: Changes in the Labour Process Under Monopoly Capitalism*, Chicago, University of Chicago Press, 1979, Chapter 7.
66. R. Bonnet and A. Caruso, 'Industrial Europe and Counter-Internationalism', op. cit.
67. A. Caruso, 'We Can Kill Striking Workers Without Being Prosecuted', op. cit., p. 194.
68. Ibid., p. 188.
69. Alessandro Saluppo, 'Strikebreaking and Anti-Unionism on the Waterfront: The Shipping Federation, 1890–1914', *European History Quarterly*, Vol. 49, No. 4, 2019, p. 579.
70. Ibid., p. 581.
71. Alessandro Saluppo, 'Vigilant Citizens: The Case of the Volunteer Police Force', in M. Millan and A. Saluppo (eds.), *Corporate Policing...*, op. cit., pp. 222–241.
72. Arthur McIvor, 'A Crusade for Capitalism: The Economic League, 1918–39', *Journal of Contemporary History*, Vol. 23, No. 4, 1988, pp. 631–655.
73. A. Saluppo, 'Vigilant Citizens', op. cit.
74. Prerna Agarwal, 'In the Name of Constitutionalism and Islam: The Murky World of Labour Politics in Calcutta's Docklands', in M. Millan and A. Saluppo (eds.), *Corporate Policing...*, op. cit., pp. 134–152.
75. Rajnarayan Chandavarkar, *Imperial Power and Politics: Class, Resistance and the State in India*, Cambridge, Cambridge University Press, 1998, p. 118.
76. Arnaud-Dominique Houte, *Citoyens policiers. Une autre histoire de la sécurité publique en France, de la Garde nationale aux Voisins vigilants*, Paris, La Découverte, 2024.
77. Roger Marchandeau, 'La Bande à Patin (1888–1999): histoire de la police privée de la Compagnie des mines de Blanzy', *Revue 'La Physiophile'*, No. 95, 1981.
78. R. Bonnet and A. Caruso, 'Europe industrielle et contre-internationalisme', op. cit.; Christophe Maillard, *Un syndicalisme impossible. L'aventure oubliée des Jaunes*, Paris, Vendémiaire, 2017.

332

79. Robert Durand, *La Lutte des travailleurs de chez Renault racontée par eux-mêmes. 1912–1944*, Paris, Éditions sociales, 1971, p. 40.

80. Alfred McCoy, *Marseille sur héroïne. Les beaux jours de la French Connection (1945–1975)*, Paris, L'Esprit frappeur, 1999.

81. Benoît Collombat, 'Les noires méthodes des "syndicats jaunes"', in Benoît Collombat et al., *Histoire secrète du patronat de 1945 à nos jours*, Paris, La Découverte, 2014, pp. 246–253.

82. Xavier Vigna, 'Préserver l'ordre usinier en France à la fin des années 1968', *Agone*, No. 50, 2013, pp. 115–133. See also J. S. Carbonell and V. Gay, 'Violences et contre-violences dans les conflits du travail', op. cit.

83. Claude Fabert, 'Les bons ouvriers des milices patronales', *Le Monde*, 27 February 1976. See also Claude Angeli and Nicolas Brimo, *Une milice patronale: Peugeot*, Paris, François Maspéro, 1975.

84. Daniel Bouvet, *L'Usine de la peur*, Paris, Stock, 1975.

85. Marcel Caille, *Les Truands du patronat*, Paris, Éditions sociales, 1977; and *L'Assassin était chez Citroën*, Paris, Éditions sociales, 1978.

86. *Rapport de la Commission d'enquête sur les activités du Service d'action civique*, Vol. 1, Paris, Alain Moreau, 1982, pp. 216–219.

87. R. M. Smith, *From Blackjacks to Briefcases*, op. cit., p. xv.

88. R. Chandavarkar, *Imperial Power and Popular Politics*, op. cit., p. 81.

89. C. Angeli and N. Brimo, *Une milice patronale*, op. cit., p. 90.

90. See the testimony of one of these anti-union mercenaries in C. Angeli and N. Brimo, *Une milice patronale*, op. cit., p. 85.

91. Marianne Debouzy, *Le Capitalisme "sauvage" aux États-Unis, 1860–1900*, Paris, Le Seuil, 1972.

92. Karl Polanyi, *The Great Transformation: The Political and Economic Origins of Our Time*, Beacon Press, 2001 [1944], p. 147.

93. This is, for example, the perspective advocated in one of the first books on 'industrial peace', L. L. Price's *Industrial Peace: Its Advantages, Methods and Difficulties. A Report of an Inquiry Made for the Toynbee Trustees*, London-New York, Macmillan and Co, 1887, p. 6.

94. Andrew Carnegie, 'Industrial Peace', Address at the Annual Dinner of the National Civic Federation, New York, 15 December 1904.

95. L. L. Price, *Industrial Peace*, op. cit., p. 14.

96. Ibid., p. 12.

97. Rick Fantasia and Kim Voss, *Hard Work: Remaking the American Labor Movement*, Berkeley, University of California Press, 2004.

98. *Report of the Royal Commission on Labour in India*, Calcutta, Government of India Central Publication Branch, 1931, p. 468.

99. Ibid., pp. 468–469.

100. M. O. L. Azam, 'Perceptual Variation of Labour Problems among Workers', *Pakistan Labour Journal*, Vol. 5, No. 8, July 1978, p. 3.
101. R. M. Weiss, 'Corporate Security at Ford Motor Company 2014', op. cit.
102. Alexandre Rios-Bordes, *Les Savoirs de l'ombre. La surveillance militaire des populations aux États-Unis (1900–1941)*, Paris, Éditions de l'EHESS, 2018, p. 89.
103. Frank Browning and John Gerassi, *The American Way of Crime*, Putnam, 1980.
104. S. H. Norwood, *Strikebreaking and Intimidation*, op. cit., p. 185.
105. Ibid.
106. Adam Stefanick, *Personality and Power in the Ford Motor Company Hierarchy: The Story of Harry Bennett, 1916–1945*, BA thesis, University of Michigan, 2011, p. 44. On 26 May 1937, Walter Reuther and Richard Frankensteen, along with other union organizers, were beaten by men from the Service Department. The attack was documented by a photographer from the *Detroit News*. His pictures went round the world, and the incident became emblematic of capitalist violence in America.
107. Robert Weiss, 'The Emergence and Transformation of Private Detective Industrial Policing in the United States: 1850–1940', *Crime and Social Justice*, No. 9, 1978, p. 41.
108. S. P. O'Hara, *Inventing the Pinkertons*, op. cit., p. 9.
109. Christopher Capozzola, *Uncle Sam Wants You: World War I and the Making of the Modern American Citizen*, New York, Oxford University Press, 2008, pp. 125–131.
110. M. Cohen, 'The Ku Klux Klan Government', op. cit.
111. A. Caruso, 'We Can Kill Striking Workers Without Being Prosecuted', op. cit., p. 197.
112. On this point, see the Mediapart dossier on Ikea France's spying practices: https://www.mediapart.fr/journal/france/dossier/notre-dossier-espionnage-en-serie-chez-ikea.
113. R. Weiss, 'The Emergence and Transformation of Private Detective Industrial Policing…', op. cit.
114. Louis Althusser, 'L'État et son appareil', in *Sur la reproduction*, Paris, PUF, 2011, p. 106.
115. Béatrice Hibou (ed.), *Privatizing the State*, New York, Columbia University Press.
116. R. Weiss 'The Emergence and Transformation of Private Detective Industrial Policing…', op. cit.
117. Ibid., p. 43.

118. R. M. Weiss, 'Corporate Security at Ford Motor Company', op. cit., p. 32.

119. Mark Neocleous and George Rigakos, 'Anti-Security: A Declaration', in Mark Neocleous and George Rigakos (eds.), *Anti-Security*, Ottawa, Red Quill Books, 2011, p. 16.

120. N. Elias, *What is Sociology?*, op. cit., pp. 130–131.

121. David Conwill, 'John Bugas, the man who cleared Ford of its gangster element', *Hemmings Classic Car*, March 2020.

122. Ann Japenga, 'Hatchet Man: The desert exile of Harry Bennett', *California Desert Art*, n.d. (https://www.californiadesertart.com/hatchetman-the-desert-exile-of-harry-bennett/).

123. Gregory A. Fournier, 'Henry Ford's tough guy: Harry Bennett', *Fornology.com*, 1 December 2015.

124. Karl Marx, *Capital*, volume 1, in *Marx and Engels Collected Works*, Vol. 35: *Karl Marx*, London/New York, Lawrence & Wishart/International Publishers, 1996; Ellen Meiksins Wood, *The Origin of Capitalism: A Longer View*, London, Verso Books, 2002 [1999].

125. On these different forms of work organization in the industrial enterprise, see Michael Burawoy, *The Politics of Production: Factory Regimes Under Capitalism and Socialism*, London, Verso, 1985.

126. According to the formula used by Gilles Deleuze in his critique of Althusserian Marxism. See Gilles Deleuze, *Foucault*, Paris, Éditions de Minuit, 2004 [1986], p. 33.

2.   NATIONAL SECURITY TRUMPS SOCIAL SECURITY

1. Extract from Liaquat Ali Khan's inaugural speech at the First Pakistan Labour Conference on 6 February 1949, Press Information Department, Government of Pakistan, Karachi, 8 February 1949, p. 4.

2. Founded in 1952, PIDC's mission was to launch risky industrial projects and then sell them to the private sector at cost price. The main beneficiaries of this policy were the large industrial groups.

3. M. L. Qureshi (ed.), *Report of the Seminar on 'Industrialization and Labour-Management Relations', Held in January 1959 at the Institute of Development Economics of Karachi*, Karachi, Institute of Development Economics of Karachi, 1959, p. 19.

4. Ibid., p. 20.

5. Report No. Pak 1/55, J. J. Keane to the Secretary, Ministry of Labour, Pakistan Labour Review, 11 June 1955, p. 4; LAB 13/525, National Archives (UK), Kew.

6. Until Partition, jute (mostly grown in Bengal) was sent to Calcutta for processing, while cotton (mostly grown in Punjab and Sindh) was sent to Bombay for spinning and weaving.

7. Irvin J. Roth, 'Government and the Development of Industry in Pakistan—1947–1967', *Asian Survey*, Vol. 11, No. 6, June 1971, p. 570. This is a high estimate. For a lower estimate, suggesting that Pakistan would have inherited only 3.6% of India's factories and 2.6% of its factory workers, see S. M. Akhtar, *Economics of Pakistan*, Lahore, 1951, pp. 263–264, quoted in Taimur Rahman, *The Class Structure of Pakistan*, Karachi, Oxford University Press, 2014 [2012], p. 188.

8. Sarah Ansari, 'At the Crossroads? Exploring Sindh's Recent Past from a Spatial Perspective', *Contemporary South Asia*, Vol. 23, No. 1, 2015, pp. 7–25.

9. Noman Ahmed, *Planning and Development of Industrial Locations in Karachi During the Post-Independence Period: A Case Study of Landhi-Korangi Industrial Area*, Karachi, Dawood College of Engineering & Technology, 1994, p. 1.

10. Letter of Yusuf Abdoola Haroon to Mir Ghulam Ali, 29 Jan. 1947; 'Trading Estates Karachi', MSS EUR F235/116: Jan.–Feb. 1947, India Pakistan Burma Association Papers (IPBA), British Library.

11. Special Officer for Industrial Survey, Department of Industries Sindh, Karachi, to Sir Roger Thomas, 4 Feb. 1947, DO No 18149, MSS EUR F235/116: Jan.–Feb. 1947, IPBA, British Library.

12. S. M. Idris, *Industrial Estates Run by the Sindh Industrial Trading Estate Ltd. Sponsored and Financed by the Government of Sindh*, Karachi, 1954, p. 1.

13. Among the Muslims of the subcontinent, caste refers to an endogamous group whose legal position derives from lineage, date of conversion to Islam, and sometimes from occupational specialization (as in the case of mercantile groups). In Karachi, the particularity of these mercantile communities is reinforced by language (Memni, a dialect without its own script, in the case of the Memons) and/or sectarian affiliation (in the case of the Dawoodi Bohras and the Ismaili Khojas, who are Shiite). Among the Memons, the cornerstone of this 'caste' endogamy is the *jama'at*—an associational structure based on the locality of origin of the members in Gujarat (Bantva, Dhoraji, Jetpur, etc.), offering various social services within the group: organizing marriages, resolving disputes (excluding commercial or financial disputes) and helping the needy. See Hanna Papanek, 'Pakistan's New Industrialists and Businessmen: Focus on the Memons', in Milton Singer (ed.), *Entrepreneurship and Modernization of Occupational Cultures in South Asia*, Durham, Duke University Press, 1973, pp. 1–32.

14. Ministry of Labour and National Service/Overseas Department, Questionnaire on Labour Conditions in the Cotton Textile Industry in Pakistan, 1958, p. 5; LAB 13/1467, National Archives (UK), Kew.

15. Iftikhar Ahmed Mukhtar, *Industrial Labour in Pakistan*, PhD thesis, School of Political Science, Columbia University, 1958, pp. 124–125.

16. In a January 1958 report, the Assistant Labour Officer of the British High Commission in Karachi wrote that 'a discussion on labour matters with a member of the new employing class is like taking a step backward into Early Nineteenth Century England'; W. Turner (Assistant Labour Adviser) to Ministry of Labour, 'The Labour Situation in West Pakistan', 13 Jan. 1958, p. 2; LAB 13/1317 Pakistan, National Archives (UK), Kew.

17. For an overview of these proverbs, see Herbert Risley and William Crooke, *The People of India*, Delhi, Asian Educational Services, 1999 [1915], pp. 311–312.

18. The term *seth* is of Gujarati origin and refers to a 'boss'. In Karachi, it refers mainly to Memon industrialists.

19. Lyari, located in the city centre and close to the docks, is the oldest popular district in Karachi.

20. Qaroon is a mythical character from Arabian tales, whose fortune was inexhaustible.

21. I am grateful to Hidayat Hussain for bringing this poem to my attention and for assisting me in its translation.

22. Gustav F. Papanek, *Pakistan's Development: Social Goals and Private Incentives*, Cambridge, Harvard University Press, 1967.

23. Ehsan Masood, *The Great Invention: The Story of GDP and the Making and Unmaking of the Modern World*, Norton, Pegasus, 2014, Chapter 4.

24. Mahbub ul Haq, *The Strategy of Economic Planning: A Case Study of Pakistan*, Karachi, Oxford University Press, 1963.

25. In his later writings, Haq developed a much more critical view of development and planning. See Mahbub ul Haq, *The Poverty Curtain: Choices for the Thirld World,* New York, Columbia University Press, 1976, especially Chapter 1.

26. Gustav F. Papanek, 'The Development of Entrepreneurship', *The American Economic Review,* Vol. 52, No. 2, 1962, pp. 46–58.

27. The methodology and the results of this survey are discussed in ibid. and in G.F. Papanek, *Pakistan's Development,* op. cit., Chapter 2.

28. This Gujarati term refers mainly to spices, but also to copra, pulses, and edible oils.

29. Gustav F. Papanek, 'The Development of Entrepreneurship', art quoted, p. 50.

30. G. Papanek, *Pakistan's Development*, op. cit., p. 44.

31. Ibid., pp. 109–110.

32. Gustav F. Papanek, 'The Development of Entrepreneurship', *The American Economic Review*, Vol. 52, No. 2, 1962, p. 51.

33. H. Papanek, 'Pakistan's New Industrialists and Businessmen', op. cit.

34. On this point, see the criticism by a group of *Muhajir* leftist intellectuals of an Urdu speech by Ahmed Dawood, in 'Dawoods: Empire and the Terror', *Pakistan Forum*, Vol. 3, No. 3, 1972, p. 13.

35. Ahmed Dawood, Chairman of the eponymous group, who was known for his awkward Urdu, was appointed Treasurer of the association in May 1972. See 'Dawood becomes Urdu Anjuman treasurer', *Dawn*, 10 May 1972.

36. M. Burawoy, *The Politics of Production*, op. cit.

37. Anita M. Weiss, *Culture, Class, and Development in Pakistan: The Emergence of an Industrial Bourgeoisie in Punjab*, Boulder, Westview Press, 1991, p. 11.

38. Anushay Malik, 'Public Authority and Local Resistance: Abdur Rehman and the Industrial Workers of Lahore, 1969–1974', *Modern Asian Studies*, Vol. 52, No. 3, 2018, p. 826. One of the founders of the Ittefaq group was Mian Muhammad Sharif, father of future prime ministers Nawaz and Shahbaz Sharif.

39. International Labour Office. Expanded Programme of Technical Assistance, *Report to the Government of Pakistan on Productivity in the Textile Industry*, Geneva, ILO, 1959 (ILO/TAP/Pakistan/R.20), p. 32.

40. M. Ali Raza, *The Industrial Relations System of Pakistan*, Karachi, Bureau of Labour Publications, 1963, pp. 68, 69, and Table XVI p. 70.

41. Richard F. Doner, Bryan K. Ritchie and Dan Slater, 'Systemic Vulnerability and the Origins of Developmental States: Northeast and Southeast Asia in Comparative Perspective', *International Organization*, Vol. 59, No. 2, 2005, pp. 327–361.

42. Ibid.

43. Adnan Naseemullah, *Development After Statism: Industrial Firms and the Political Economy of South Asia*, Cambridge, Cambridge University Press, 2017, pp. 206–207.

44. Ayesha Jalal, *The State of Martial Rule: The Origins of Pakistan's Political Economy of Defence*, Lahore, Vanguard Books, 1991, p. 141.

45. Government of Pakistan, Press Information Department, Inaugural Address of Prime Minister Liaquat Ali Khan in front of the Pakistan Council of Industries, 8 September 1949; DO 142/46, National Archives (UK), Kew.

46. *Pakistan News*, 24 December 1949.

47. Extract from Weekly Report for Period Ending 17th Oct, 1948, from the UK Deputy High Commissioner in Pakistan, Dhaka; DO 142/46, National Archives (UK), Kew.

48. Government of Pakistan, 'Statement of Industrial Policy', 2 April 1948, p. 2. Emphasis added.

49. Stanley Kochanek, *Interest Groups and Development: Business and Politics in Pakistan*, Karachi, Oxford University Press, 1983, p. 198.

50. Lawrence J. White, 'Pakistan's Industrial Families: The Extent, Causes, and Effects of their Economic Power', *Journal of Development Studies*, Vol. 10, No. 3–4, 1974, pp. 273–304.

51. Ravi Ahuja, 'A Beveridge Plan for India? Social Insurance and the Making of the "Formal Sector"', *IRSH*, Vol. 64, No. 2, 2019, pp. 207–248. In India and Pakistan, the opposition of the so-called 'organized' sector to the 'informal' one is nuanced (though not completely invalidated) by the long-standing use of precarious work in part of the 'organized' sector. On the continuing relevance of this distinction, see Jonathan Parry, *Classes of Labour: Work and Life in a Central Indian Steel Town*, New York, Routledge, 2020, pp. 61–70.

52. On the social protection measures obtained by Karachi dockworkers in the early twenty-first century, see Minerwa Tahir's ongoing doctoral work.

53. Charles Tilly, *Coercion, Capital, and European States. AD 990–1992*, Cambridge-Oxford, Blackwell, 1992 [1990], Chapter 7.

54. Dominique Linhardt and Cédric Moreau de Bellaing, 'Ni guerre, ni paix: dislocations de l'ordre politique et décantonnements de la guerre', *Politix*, No. 104, 2014, pp. 7–23.

55. These laws (the Security of Pakistan Act of 1952, preceded by two Public Safety Ordinances) allow for the indefinite detention, without further trial, of anyone who undermines the security of the state and its sources of supply. However, the use of this legislation against Mirza Ibrahim and other left-wing activists in 1951 cannot be attributed to their activism alone, and appears to have been precipitated by their candidacy to the Punjab provincial assembly; see Anushay Malik, 'Alternative Politics and Dominant Narratives: Communists and the Pakistani State in the Early 1950s', *South Asian History and Culture*, Vol. 4, No. 4, 2013, p. 526.

56. Quoted in *Dawn*, 26 January 1975.

57. Kamran Asdar Ali, *Surkh Salam: Communist Politics and Class Activism in Pakistan 1947–1972*, Karachi, Oxford University Press, 2015, Chapter 6.

58. T. M. Hoskison (Labour Adviser, United Kingdom High Commission,

Karachi) to A. G. Wallis (Ministry of Labour, London), 9 November 1960; LAB 13/1435, National Archives (UK), Kew.

59. Basic Labor Report No. 4, 'Who's Who in Pakistan Labor—Biographies of APCOL affiliated trade union leaders of East and West Pakistan' (5 parts), 21 March–May 1961; RG 59 From 890 D.062-5-161 to 890D.10/10-460, Box 2852, National Archives (US), College Park.

60. K. Asdar Ali, *Surkh Salam*, op. cit., p. 243.

61. Interview with Shafi Malik, former president of the National Labour Federation (NLF—the trade union wing of the Jama'at-e-Islami), Karachi, July 2018. On the history of the NLF and the trade union activities of Pakistan's main Islamist party, see Shafi Malik, *Islami Mazdoor Tehrik ki Safar Kahani* (History of the Islamic Labour Movement), Lahore, Mansoorah, 2016.

62. Qurratulain Hyder, 'The Housing Society', in *A Season of Betrayals: A Short Story and Two Novellas*, translated from Urdu by Suzanne Schwartz Gilbert and C.M. Naim, Delhi, Kali for Women, 1999 [1963]. Qurratulain Hyder (1927–2007) is one of the great figures of Urdu literature of the twentieth century. After migrating to Pakistan after Partition, she decided to return to India a few years later. She is the author of *Aag ka Darya* (The River of Fire), considered a gem of Urdu literature.

63. Ibid., p. 244.

64. Ibid., p. 249.

65. These mundanities remain essential to the reproduction of the Pakistani power elite, as shown by Rosita Armytage, *Big Capital in an Unequal World: The Micropolitics of Wealth in Pakistan*, New York-Oxford, Berghahn, 2020.

66. Gustav F. Papanek, 'The Location of Industry', *Pakistan Development Review*, No. 10, 1970, p. 294.

67. On the financial illegalisms of Karachi's wholesale merchants, see S. Russo, *The Arts of Order*, op. cit.

68. W. Turner (Assistant Labour Adviser) to Ministry of Labour, 'The labour situation in West Pakistan', 16 January 1958, p. 2; LAB 13/1317, National Archives (UK), Kew.

69. M. Foucault, *Surveiller et punir. Naissance de la prison*, Paris, Gallimard, 1975. On the difference between 'illegalities' and the Foucauldian notion of 'illegalisms', see Alex Feldman, 'Foucault's Concept of Illegalisms', *European Journal of Philosophy*, Vol. 28, No. 2, 2020, pp. 1–18.

70. Alexis Spire, 'La délinquance en col blanc: études de cas', *Champ pénal*, Vol. X, 2013.

71. Marshall B. Clinard and Peter C. Yeager, *Corporate Crime*, New York, The Free Press, 1980, p. 129.

72. M. Foucault, *Surveiller et punir*, op. cit., p. 98.

73. See Ayub Khan's account in his memoir, *Friends Not Masters: A Political Autobiography*, Islamabad, Mister Books, 2006 [1967], p. 138.

74. Edward Dahl (Commercial Attache) to the Department of State, 'Pakistan's Industrial Development Corporation', Karachi, 2 February 1952; RG 59 890D.053/4-1250, National Archives (US), College Park.

75. Rashid Amjad, 'Industrial Concentration and Economic Power', in Hassan Gardezi and Jamil Rashid (eds.), *Pakistan. The Roots of Dictatorship: The Political Roots of a Praetorian State*, London, Zed Press, 1983, p. 236.

76. A. R. Shibli, *Bais Khanvade. Jin ke Tasarruf 80 Fisad Qaumi Paidawar aur Daulat Hai* (The 22 Families. In Whose Hands 80% of the National Production and Wealth Is Concentrated), Lahore, Maktabah Peepilz Pablisharz, 1972, p. 80.

77. With Bangladesh's independence came the closure of an important market and the loss of many industrial assets for West Pakistan-based groups, although the Pakistani army is said to have helped some of them (particularly the Dawoods) to repatriate their machinery. See 'Dawoods: Empire and the Terror', op. cit.

78. Foqia Sadiq Khan, *Political Economy and the Rule of Law in Pakistan, 1999–2004. Resistance to Implementation of Law and Caste Capitalism*, PhD thesis (development studies), SOAS, University of London, 2014, p. 186.

79. Originating from the Chiniot locality in western Punjab, this trading community built its fortune and reputation in Calcutta at the end of the nineteenth century, where it specialized in the trade of hides and skins—a sector abandoned by the Hindus for reasons of ritual taboos. After Partition, the Chiniotis relocated to the Lyallpur region and then to Lahore, where they contributed to the development of the Pakistani textile industry.

80. Quoted in 'Commission for Labour Soon—Zia', *Pakistan Labour Journal*, Vol. 5, No. 9–10, August–September 1978, p. 35.

81. Ali Cheema, 'State and Capital in Pakistan: The Changing Politics of Accumulation', in Ananya Mukherjee Reed (ed.), *Corporate Capitalism in Contemporary South Asia: Conventional Wisdoms and South Asian Realities*, Basingstoke, Palgrave Macmillan, 2003, p. 134–170.

82. The capital of the 548 companies listed on the Karachi Stock Exchange is systematically held by shareholders owning more than 50% of the company's shares. In the case of private companies, these are usually members of the founders' family. See Sadia Khan (ed.), *The Corporate Governance Landscape of Pakistan*, Karachi, Oxford University Press, 2017, pp. 134–170.

83. F. S. Khan, *Political Economy and the Rule of Law in Pakistan*, op. cit., p. 196. For an application of this principle in one of the major family-owned conglomerates founded by Karachi Memons (the Dawood Group), see Naveed Hasan, *Management Practices and Business Development in Pakistan, 1947–1988*, Aldershot, Avebury, 1997, pp. 275–279.

84. See in particular the dossier coordinated by Surinder S. Jodhka and Jules Naudet, 'Sociology of India's Economic Elites', *SAMAJ*, Vol. 15, 2017 (https://journals.openedition.org/samaj/4270).

3. CAPITAL'S HENCHMEN

1. Author's translation.

2. Interviews with residents of Huseini Chowrangi, Karachi, July 2017.

3. 'Textile mills in Pakistan', in F. M. Saqi (ed.), *Industrial Pakistan. History of the First Decade 1947–1957*, Karachi, Saghar, 1958, p. 105.

4. Stanley Kochanek, *Interest Groups and Development. Business and Politics in Pakistan,* Karachi, Oxford University Press, 1983, p. 135.

5. The North West Frontier Province (abbreviated to 'Frontier') was, along with the princely state of Swat (dissolved in 1969), the main centre of Pashtun migration to Karachi.

6. R. Chandavarkar, *Imperial Power and Popular Politics*, op. cit., p. 111 ff.

7. Ahmad Azhar, 'The Making of a "Genuine Trade Unionist": An Introduction to Bashir Ahmed Bakhtiar's Memoirs', in Ravi Ahuja (ed.), *Working Lives and Worker Militancy: The Politics of Labour in Colonial India*, Delhi, Tulika Books, 2013, pp. 256–273.

8. Lucia Michelutti, Ashraf Hoque, Nicolas Martin, David Picherit, Paul Rollier, Arild E. Ruud, and Clarinda Still, *Mafia Raj: The Rule of Bosses in South Asia*, Stanford, Stanford University Press, 2019.

9. Ibid., p. 9.

10. Adam Baczko and Gilles Dorronsoro, 'Pour une approche sociologique des guerres civiles', *Revue française de science politique*, Vol. 67, No. 2, 2017, p. 318.

11. L. Michelutti et al., *Mafia Raj,* op. cit.

12. John T. Sidel, *Capital, Coercion and Crime: Bossism in the Philippines*, Stanford, Stanford University Press, 1999.

13. Max Weber, 'The Meaning of Discipline', in H. H. Gerth and C. Wright Mills (eds.), *From Max Weber. Essays in Sociology*, New York, Oxford University Press, 1946, p. 253.

14. M. Foucault, *Surveiller et punir*, op. cit., pp. 168–169.

15. Interview with a former army major responsible for overseeing the security arrangements of a major textile company, Karachi, July 2016.

16. Patrick Joyce, *Work, Society and Politics: The Culture of the Factory in Later Victorian England*, London, The Harvester Press, 1980.

17. R. K. Newman, 'Social Factors in the Recruitment of the Bombay Millhands', in K. N. Chaudhuri and Clive J. Dewey (eds.), *Economy and Society: Essays in Indian Economic and Social History*, Delhi, Oxford University Press, 1979, p. 278.

18. Morris David Morris, *The Emergence of an Industrial Labor Force in India: A Study of the Bombay Cotton Mills, 1854–1947*, Berkeley, University of California Press, 1965,

19. D. Chakrabarty, *Rethinking Working-Class History*, op. cit., p. 114.

20. For an ideal-typical organizational chart of Karachi's textile companies, see Z. Shaheed, *The Labour Movement in Pakistan*, op. cit., fig. 1, p. 119.

21. It was common for workers from rural areas of the country to return to the village at harvest time, or during the period of cotton ginning.

22. R. Chandavarkar, *The Origins of Industrial Capitalism in India*, op. cit., p. 101.

23. R. Chandavarkar, *Imperial Power and Popular Politics*, op. cit., pp. 105–106. On the changing role of the jobber in Indian industrial capitalism, see also Rajnarayan Chandavarkar, 'The Decline and Fall of the Jobber System in the Bombay Cotton Textile Industry, 1870–1955', *Modern Asian Studies*, Vol. 42, No. 1, 2008, pp. 117–210.

24. Z. Shaheed, *The Labour Movement in Pakistan*, op. cit., p. 159.

25. Ibid., p. 111.

26. Laurent Gayer, *Le Capitalisme irrégulier. Ordre industriel et désordres urbains à Karachi*, Habilitation thesis, Université Paris 1-Panthéon Sorbonne, 2020.

27. Interview with Shah Zarin Khan, Karachi, July 2016.

28. L. Gayer, *Le Capitalisme irrégulier*, op. cit., Chapter 2.

29. Industrial dispute between Saifee Development Corporation Limited Workers Union and Saifee Development Corporation Ltd, 29 June 1963, *Pakistan Labour Gazette*, Vol. 11, No. 3, July–September 1963, pp. 576–580.

30. Interview with Shah Zarin Khan, Karachi, July 2016.

31. In the case of Delhi, see Narayani Gupta, *Delhi Between Two Empires 1803–1931. Society, Government and Urban Growth*, Delhi, Oxford University Press, 1981, pp. 11, 80.

32. Harish Doshi, 'Traditional Neighborhood in Modern Ahmedabad: The Pol', in M. S. A. Rao, Chandrashekar Bhat and Laxmi Narayan Kadekar (eds.), *A Reader in Urban Sociology*, Delhi, Orient Longman, 1991, p. 196.

33. The term 'Pathan' refers to Pashtuns from the north-western regions of present-day Pakistan (and thus excludes Pashtuns from Afghanistan). The term is now considered derogative by many Pakistani Pashtuns and I use it only to refer to Pashtuns in Bombay in the colonial period.

34. R. Chandavarkar, *The Origins of Industrial Capitalism in India*, op. cit., p. 193.

35. The *shalwar kamiz* is a unisex garment traditionally worn in Afghanistan and Pakistan. It consists of loose trousers and a long shirt.

36. While these epaulettes serve to reinforce the confusion with (para-) military uniforms, they do not correspond to any specific rank in the Pakistani security forces, which would probably have objected to such an abuse of authority.

37. Interview with Saifullah,* long-time resident of Landhi, Karachi, August 2018.

38. Some of the titles used are indicative of cross-influences. For example, the term *jamadar*, which designated the head of security in some factories until the 1980s, dates back to the Mughal period, when it referred to the henchmen in the service of big landowners (*zamindar*). The British later made it a military and police rank. Since the colonial period, the term has also been used to refer to recruiting agents, especially on the docks.

39. R. Chandavarkar, *Imperial Power and Popular Politics*, op. cit., pp. 112, 113.

40. Some *hadiths* suggest that Ali (fourth Caliph of Islam and first Imam of the Shi'a) wore four rings set with the following gems: opaline (*yaqut*), associated with beauty and dignity; turquoise (*feruz*), associated with God's grace and victory; hematite (*adid thin*), associated with strength; and carnelian (*aqiq*), protecting against evil. In Sindh, this tradition is maintained by certain Sufi movements.

41. In rural areas of the country, *deras* are rooms that are separate from the rest of the house and are used only to receive visitors. Among Pashtun migrant workers in Karachi, the term originally referred to a residence shared by several single men, who shared the costs of maintenance and housekeeping. In recent decades, the term has taken on a more sinister meaning because it has become associated

with activities that are deviant (drug and alcohol use) and even openly criminal (extortion, drug trafficking, etc.).

42. Katherine P. Ewing, 'Malangs of the Punjab: Intoxication or *Adab* as the Path to God', in Barbara Metcalf (ed.), *Moral Conduct and Authority: The Place of Adab in South Asian Islam*, Berkeley, University of California Press, 1984, p. 359.

43. Dalmia Cement Factory Workers' Union vs. Dalmia Cement Ltd, *Pakistan Labour Cases* 1960, Vol. 1, Lahore, pp. 1058–1061; Workers' Union vs. Pakistan Beverage Company, *Pakistan Labour Cases* 1968, Vol. 9, Lahore, pp. 360–361.

44. For an alternative interpretation that recognizes some *chowkidars* as workmen, see the details of the industrial dispute between the representatives of the Flour Mills Employees Union of Karachi and the Management of Messrs. Karachi Steam Roller Flour Mills, Lawrence Road, Karachi, in *Pakistan Labour Gazette*, Vol. 14, No. 3, July–September 1966, pp. 528–544.

45. Workers' Union vs. Pakistan Beverage Company, *Pakistan Labour Cases* 1968, Vol. 9, Lahore, 1968, pp. 360–361.

46. *Industrial Relations Ordinance, 1969*, ss. 2 and 3, reproduced in *Pakistan Labour Gazette*, Vol. 20, No. 1, January–March 1970, p. 61.

47. Interview with Ghulam Haji,* former *Hawaldar* at Husein Mills, Karachi, August 2018.

48. Karachi [American Consulate] to Secretary of State, No. 1688, 8 March 1963; RG 59 LAB Nigeria 2/1/63 to LAB Pan 2/1/63, Box 3589, National Archives (US), College Park.

49. Interview with Ghulam Haji,* former *Hawaldar* at Husein Mills, Karachi, August 2018.

50. In 1990, a group of workers at a jute factory in Karachi attacked the company's Personnel Manager and, having severely injured him, threatened to kill him and hang his body in the factory. However, after some scuffles, guards managed to free the hostage; see Israr Ahmad vs. Mehran Jute Mills Ltd, *Pakistan Labour Cases* 1994, Vol. 35, Lahore, 1994, pp. 713–716.

51. International Labour Office. Expanded Programme of Technical Assistance, *Report to the Government of Pakistan on Productivity in the Textile Industry*, Geneva, ILO, 1959 (ILO/TAP/Pakistan/R.20), p. 32.

52. National Textile Labour Union, Karachi vs. M/S Jubilee Spinning and Weaving Mills Ltd, Karachi, 1965 PLV 77, *Pakistan Labour Journal 1965*, Vol. 6, Lahore, PLC, 1965, pp. 77–91.

53. Industrial dispute between Maple Leaf Cement Factory Employees

Union and Maple Leaf factory, Daudkhel, 12 September 1961, *Pakistan Labour Gazette*, Vol. 9, No. 4, October–December 1961, p. 644.

54. Interview with Shah Zarin Khan, Karachi, July 2016.

55. Sher Shah is a popular area on the edge of SITE.

56. Nayab Naqvi, *Ekim March 1963 ki Mazdur Tehrik. Ek Pas Manzar* (The Movement of 1 March 1963. An Introduction), Karachi, PILER, 2003, p. 49.

57. British High Commission, Karachi to British Embassy Teheran, Bata shoe factory, 6 June 1968, LAB 13/2461; National Archives (UK), Kew.

58. On the '*dadagiri* of the state', in the context of police repression of Punjabi labour struggles during the colonial period, see A. Azhar, 'The Making of a "Genuine Trade Unionist"', op. cit.

59. The following account is based primarily on the oral testimony of Abdul Hakim Khan, a former weaver and trade unionist, whom I interviewed in Karachi in August 2018.

60. Born in 1928, Tufail Abbas joined Orient Airways in 1948 as an ordinary employee. He later joined the national airline Pakistan International Airways (PIA), where he headed the union for nearly four decades. He joined the Pakistan Communist Party (CPP) in the early 1950s. In the mid-1960s, he took over the leadership of the pro-Beijing faction of the CPP (which had been operating clandestinely since its ban in 1954) in Sindh. See Tufail Abbas, *Subah ki Lagan. Pakistan ki Siyasi Tarikh Mazdur Tehrik ke Aine mein* (Yearning for Dawn. Pakistan's Political History in the Mirror of the Labour Movement), Karachi, Shiri Printing Press, 2010.

61. In 1970, Ashraf Tabani was appointed honorary administrator of the FPCCI by the military government of Yahya Khan. He remained in this position until 1972.

62. C. Joshi, *Lost Worlds*, op. cit., p. 116.

63. Layli Uddin, *In the Land of Eternal Eid: Maulana Bhashani and the Political Mobilisation of Peasants and Lower-Class Urban Workers in East Pakistan, c. 1930s–1971*, PhD thesis (history), Royal Holloway, London, 2016.

64. C. Joshi, *Lost Worlds*, op. cit., p. 116.

65. Suranjan Das, 'The "Goondas": Towards a Reconstruction of the Calcutta Underworld through Police Records', *Economic & Political Weekly*, 29 Oct. 1994, p. 2877.

66. *The Punjab Control of Goondas Ordinance, 1959* (West Pakistan Ordinance XXXV of 1959).

67. Industrial dispute between United Textile Workers Union Karachi and

Mumtaz Ahmad Silk Mills, 6 November 1963, *Pakistan Labour Gazette*, Vol. 11, No. 4, October–December 1963, p. 782.

68. AmEmbassy, 'Labor agitations in local textile mills', Karachi, 2 June 1967; RG 59 LAB 3-3 ORIT to LAB 6-1 PAK, Box 1275, National Archives (US), College Park.

69. Kaniz Fatima was Vice President of the National Awami Party (NAP) in Karachi and became leader of the main faction of the Pakistan Trade Union Federation (PTUF) in Karachi following the split of this communist-oriented union in 1966. In the main, her supporters came from the shipyards, and she was elected President of the powerful Karachi Shipyard Workmen's Union before being banned from the city in 1968–1969.

70. AmEmbassy, 'Alleged CIA infiltration of Karachi labor department', Rawalpindi, 19 September 1968; RG 59 LAB 3-3 ORIT to LAB 6-1 PAK, Box 1276, National Archives (US), College Park.

71. One of these clashes broke out at the Pakistan Steel Mills (which at that time was still called People's Steel Mills) during the 1974 union elections. See 'Goonda attack on workers alleged', *Dawn*, 19 April 1974.

72. 'SITE mills closed as unionists clash: Police use teargas', *Dawn*, 11 February 1972.

73. National Industrial Relations Commission, Islamabad, Case No. 4 (483)/74 NIRC, reproduced in *Pakistan Labour Journal*, January 1975, p. 42.

74. S. M. Idris, *Industrial Estates Run by the Sindh Industrial Trading Estate Ltd. Sponsored and Financed by the Government of Sindh*, Karachi, 1954, p. 16.

75. N. Naqvi, *Ekim March 1963 ki Mazdur Tehrik*, op. cit., p. 27.

76. 'Dawoods: Empire and the Terror', op. cit., p. 16. On this journal, see Shozab Raza, 'Theorizing Pakistan in Diaspora: The Pakistan Forum', *Jamhoor*, 1 July 2019.

77. 1975 PLC 483, Messrs Dawood Cotton Mills Ltd, Karachi *versus* Labour Union, Application No. 10 of 1972, decided on 30th November 1972, reproduced in *Pakistan Labour Cases, 1975*, Vol. 16, Lahore 1975, p. 484.

78. 1975 PLC 485 [IIIrd Labour Court Sind] Messrs Gul Ahmed Textile Mills Ltd, Karachi versus Labour Union, Application No. 11 of 30th November 1972, decided on 30th November 1972, ibid. at 485.

79. 'Who Is Sabotaging Production?', *Pakistan Forum*, Vol. 3, No. 2, November 1972, p. 5.

80. Fabien Jobard, 'Comprendre l'habilitation à l'usage de la force policière', *Déviance et société*, Vol. 25, No. 3, 2001, p. 339.

81. National Industrial Relations Commission, Islamabad, Appeal No. 12(24)/78, 10 September 1978, reproduced in *Pakistan Labour Journal*, November–December 1978, pp. 54–58.

4. THE TREMORS OF THE CITY

1. Author's translation. This successful Pakistani comedy follows the adventures of two penniless young men and their landlord, who decide to take advantage of a general strike (*hartal*) to burn down the bank where they have opened an account and run an insurance scam.
2. Jean-Pierre Warnier, *Construire la culture matérielle. L'homme qui pensait avec ses doigts*, Paris, PUF, 1999.
3. The author refers here to two rigorist, and decidedly anti-Shiite, strands of Pakistani Hannafi Sunnism.
4. The Sipah-e-Sahaba Pakistan (SSP) is a Sunni sectarian (Deobandi) group. Its armed wing has carried out numerous attacks against the Shiite population. The Jaish-e-Muhammad is a jihadist organization, also affiliated to the Deobandi current of Hanafi Sunnism.
5. Michel de Certeau, *The Possession at Loudun*, trans. Michael B. Smith, Chicago, Chicago University Press, 2000 [1970], p. 2.
6. Michael Taussig, 'Terror as Usual: Walter Benjamin's Theory of History as State of Siege', *Social Text*, No. 23, 1989, p. 4.
7. Ibid., p. 8.
8. For more details on this literature and the debates that run through it, see Laurent Gayer, 'La normalité de l'anormal: recomposer le quotidien en situation de guerre civile', *Critique internationale*, No. 80, 2018, pp. 55–70.
9. Leïla Vignal, *War-Torn: The Unmaking of Syria 2011–2021*, London, Hurst, 2021, Chapter 7.
10. Teresa Koloma Beck, *The Normality of Civil War. Armed Groups and Everyday Life in Angola*, Frankfurt am Main, Campus Verlag, 2006, p. 137.
11. Roland Marchal, 'Terminer une guerre', in Roland Marchal and Christine Messiant (eds.), *Les Chemins de la guerre et de la paix. Fins de conflit en Afrique orientale et australe*, Paris, Karthala, 1997, pp. 5–48; Thierry Boissière and Laura Ruiz de Elvira (eds.), 'Le quotidien économique dans un Proche-Orient en guerre', *Critique internationale*, No. 80, 2018.
12. Lesley Potter, 'Colombia's Oil Palm Development in Times of War and "Peace": Myths, Enablers and the Disparate Realities of Land Control', *Journal of Rural Studies*, Vol. 78, 2020, pp. 491–502; Ricardo

Soares de Oliveira, *Magnificent and Beggar Land. Angola Since the Civil War*, London, Hurst, 2015.

13. On civil war as a factor of fragmentation and duplication of the political order, see G. Dorronsoro and A. Baczko, 'Pour une approche sociologique des guerres civiles', op. cit.

14. L. Potter, 'Colombia's Oil Palm Development', op. cit.; Jacobo Grajales, *Gouverner dans la violence. Le paramilitarisme en Colombie*, Paris, Karthala, 2016, pp. 161 ff.

15. Akmal Husain, 'The Karachi Riots of December 1986: Crisis of State and Civil Society in Pakistan', in Veena Das (ed.), *Mirrors of Violence: Communities, Riots and Survivors in South Asia*, Delhi, Oxford University Press, 1990, pp. 194–214.

16. The party was renamed the *Muttahida* Qaumi Movement (*United National Movement*) in 1997 to downplay its ethnic dimension.

17. Eric Hobsbawm, *Labouring Men: Studies in the History of Labour*, Garden City, Anchor Books, 1967 [1964], p. 9.

18. 'Strikes', *The Herald Annual*, January 1996, p. 52.

19. Zeeshan Sahil, 'Ghair mehfuz sarmayakari' (A Risky Investment), in *Karachi aur Dusri Nazmen* (Karachi and Other Poems), Karachi, Aaj, 1995, printed in Zeeshan Sahil, *Sari Nazmen* (Anthology), Karachi, Aaj, 2011, p. 341. I am here using the translation of G.A. Chaussée, *Annual of Urdu Studies*, Vol. 11, 1996, p. 95. Sahil's 1995 collection, from which this poem is taken, is part of a poetic genre that emerged in the late Mughal period, the *shehr-e-ashob* (lit. 'lament for the city'), focusing on the decay of urban societies in the region. See Frances W. Pritchett, 'The World Turned Upside Down: Sahr-Asob as a Genre', *Annual of Urdu Studies*, Vol. 4, 1984, pp. 37–41.

20. Azhar Abbas, 'Pulling down the shutters', *The Herald*, January 1995, p. 58.

21. Fahmida Riaz, 'Karachi', in Ajmal Kamal (ed.), *Karachi ki Kahani* (The History of Karachi), Karachi, Aaj, 2007 [1996], Vol. 2, p. 476.

22. Azhar Abbas, 'Your money or your life…', *The Herald*, March 1995, p. 40b.

23. Altaf Hussain, with Khalid Athar, *Safar-e-Zindagi. MQM ki Kahani Altaf Hussain ki Zabani* (The Journey of My Life. The Story of MQM in the Words of Altaf Hussain), Karachi, Jang Publications, 1988, p. 38.

24. A. Abbas, 'Your money or your life…', op. cit., p. 40a.

25. Mancur Olson, 'Dictatorship, Democracy, and Development', *American Political Science Review*, Vol. 87, No. 3, 1993, pp. 567–576.

26. E-mail from Abdul Aziz Bombaywala,* 25 August 2020.

27. Romain Le Cour Grandmaison, '*Vigilar y Limpiar*: Identification and Self-Justice in Mexican Michoacán', *Politix*, No. 115, 2016, p. 106.
28. R. Chandavarkar, 'The Decline and Fall of the Jobber System in the Bombay Cotton Textile Industry, 1870–1955', op. cit.; T. Roy, 'Sardars, Jobbers, Kanganies', op. cit.
29. M. D. Morris, *The Emergence of an Industrial Labor Force in India*, op. cit.
30. R. Chandavarkar, *The Origins of Industrial Capitalism in India*, op. cit., pp. 109, 113.
31. D. Chakrabarty, *Rethinking Working Class History*, op. cit., p. 107.
32. Government of Pakistan, Ministry of Labour, *Report of the I.L.O. Labour Survey Mission*, op. cit., p. 21.
33. Stephanie Barrientos, 'Contract Labour: The "Achilles Heel" of Corporate Codes in Commercial Value Chains', *Development and Change*, Vol. 39, No. 6, 2008, pp. 977–990.
34. Geert de Neve, 'Entrapped Entrepreneurship: Labour Contractors in the South Indian Garment Industry', *Modern Asian Studies*, Vol. 48, No. 5, 2014, p. 1303.
35. Ibid., p. 1305.
36. David Picherit, '"Workers Trust Us!" Labour Middlemen and the Rise of the Lower Castes in Andhra Pradesh', in Jan Breman, Isabelle Guérin and Aseem Prakash (eds.), *India's Unfree Workforce: Of Bondage, Old and New*, Delhi, Oxford University Press, 2008, pp. 259–283.
37. Aasim Sajjad Akhtar, 'Patronage and Class in Urban Pakistan', *Critical Asian Studies*, Vol. 43, No. 2, 2011, pp. 159–184.
38. Working conditions deteriorated in the small-scale mechanical weaving industry in the second half of the 2000s, after Memon *seths* handed over the management of their companies to their former Punjabi employees. The latter imposed significantly harsher working conditions, as well as lower and, above all, more erratic pay, on their Punjabi compatriots. See Arif Hasan and Mansoor Raza, 'Impacts of Economic Crises and Reform on the Informal Textile Industry in Karachi', Working Paper, IIED, London, 2015, p. 18.
39. The political connections of these aspirants to social mobility constitute their main resource. Contractors and managers from a working-class background with whom I met over the years were all affiliated to a political party or could claim privileged access to local politics through their network of friends and family. However, the political affiliations of these self-made men changed as quickly as the fortunes of the parties that opened their ranks to them.
40. Beyond contractors, this success concerns a small number of managers in charge of production and finishing in large clothing

companies. In addition to their political connections, the success of these former workers, who sometimes started at the bottom of the ladder, is due to their faculty of discernment (as evidenced by their ability to see through appearances when selecting and evaluating their subordinates) and their resistance to stress (the demands of delivery times and quality of goods are directly passed on to them and they will be held accountable for the slightest hitch in the preparation of orders); interviews with a group of managers employed in large garment companies based in Landhi/Korangi, Karachi, May and August 2022.

41. Interview with Ataullah Masood,* transport contractor, Green Park City, Karachi, August 2018.

42. *Paan, ghutka, chaliya, niswar* and *mainpuri* refer to different preparations of chewing tobacco, which are popular among Pakistani working classes.

43. I thank the management of Shahbaz Pharma* for sharing this document.

44. Interview with contractor Waseem Dehlvi,* Karachi, July 2016.

45. Idem.

46. Interview with Aijaz Malik,* head of personnel at Qudrat Pharma, Karachi, July 2016.

47. Laurent Gayer and Nida Kirmani, '"What You See Is What You Get": Local Journalism and the Search for Truth in Lyari, Karachi', *Modern Asian Studies*, vol.54, No. 5, 2020, pp. 1483–1525.

48. Profiling practices are not a monopoly of contractors, as security and administrative officials sometimes conduct their own investigations in conjunction with the police, the military, or anti-crime NGOs (see Chapter 7).

49. Interview with Waseem Dehlvi,* Karachi, July 2016.

50. Founded in 1985 by Azim Tariq, this sectarian group renamed itself Ahle Sunnat wal Jama'at in 2002 following its ban by the Pervez Musharraf regime. However, it is still frequently referred to by its historical acronym. On the violent history of this group, see Mariam Abou Zahab, 'The SSP, Herald of Militant Sunni Islam in Pakistan', in Laurent Gayer and Christophe Jaffrelot (eds.), *Armed Militias of South Asia*, London, Hurst, 2009.

51. Conversation with an MQM activist in Landhi, Karachi, 2014.

52. Personal observation, Landhi, July 2017.

53. On the SSP's history of violence and its relationship with the LeJ, see M. Abou Zahab, 'The SSP, Herald of Militant Sunni Islam in Pakistan', op. cit.

54. Interview with Mahmud Farooqi,* leader of the SSP Labour Committee, Karachi, July 2014.
55. Interview with Naeem Beg,* CEO of Qudrat Pharma, Karachi, July 2016.
56. Idem.
57. While the rest of the sentence is in Urdu, the term '*sada*' (band/ gang) is borrowed from Punjabi. As Waseem Dehlvi is Urdu-speaking, his use of this term reflects his sociability transcending community boundaries.
58. Interview with contractor Waseem Dehlvi,* Karachi, July 2016.
59. Interview with Ali Akbar,* General Manager at KFG Textile Mills* Karachi, April 2014.
60. Stanley Tambiah, *Leveling Crowds. Ethnonationalist Conflicts and Collective Violence in South Asia*, Berkeley, University of California Press, 1996, p. 257.
61. Ibid., p. 192.
62. Ibid., Chapter 6.
63. On the extensions of partisan rivalries at the Pakistan Steel Mills (PSM), see L. Gayer, *Le Capitalisme irrégulier*, op. cit., pp. 259–261.
64. Interview with Maqsood Ali,* Industrial Relations Officer at Hamid Textiles,* Karachi, July 2017.
65. The Seraikis are an ethno-linguistic group from the Rahimyar Khan and Rajanpur districts of southern Punjab. Their presence in Karachi has been increasing since the early 2000s due to limited employment opportunities in this deprived region. In Karachi, they are mainly employed as domestic workers, rickshaw drivers (an occupation long monopolized by Pashtuns from Buner and Torghar districts), and textile workers. See Zia Ur Rehman, 'What is driving Karachi's Seraiki Migration Wave', *The News*, 11 April 2016.
66. Interview with Masood Sheikh,* Director of Hajra Textiles,* Karachi, November 2013.
67. Jean-François Bayart, *L'État en Afrique. La politique du ventre*, Paris, Fayard, 1989, p. 84.
68. Interview with Naeem Beg,* CEO of Qudrat Pharma, Karachi, July 2016.
69. Email from Naeem Beg,* CEO of Qudrat Pharma, August 2019.
70. Alfred Schutz, *Reflections on the Problem of Relevance*, in A. Schutz and L. Embree (eds.), *Collected Papers V. Phenomenology and the Social Sciences*, Dordrecht, Springer Netherlands, 1970, pp. 113–118.
71. Interview with Ashraf Siddiqui,* '*admin*' of Hamid Textiles, Karachi, July 2017.

72. Interview with Maqsood Ali,* Industrial Relations Officer at Hamid Textiles,* Karachi, July 2017.
73. Interview with Naeem Beg,* CEO of Qudrat Pharma, Karachi, July 2016.
74. Interview with Umar Shah,* owner of a food gum factory in SITE, Karachi, August 2018.
75. Interview with Naim Beg,* CEO of Qudrat Pharma, Karachi, July 2016.
76. Interview with Major Qasim Balkhi,* General Manager Administration and Security at Hamid Textiles,* Karachi, July 2017.
77. Interview with Maqsood Ali,* Industrial Relations Officer at Hamid Textiles,* Karachi, July 2017.

5. 'THEY ATE OUR RIGHTS!'

1. Anwar Saeed* worked for forty years as a machine operator in one of the country's leading textile groups; interview, Karachi, 2016.
2. The English term *source* is frequently used by Karachi workers to refer to their relational network and contacts that can be mobilized in the search for a job.
3. Geert de Neve, 'The Economies of Love: Love Marriage, Kin Support, and Aspiration in a South Indian Garment City', *Modern Asian Studies*, Vol. 50, No. 4, 2016, pp. 1220–1249; Alpa Shah, 'The Labour of Love: Seasonal Migration from Jharkhand to the Brick Kilns of Other States in India', *Contributions to Indian Sociology*, Vol. 40, No. 1, 2006, pp. 91–118.
4. Howard Becker, *Outsiders: Studies in the Sociology of Deviance*, New York, The Free Press of Glencoe, 1963, Chapter 8.
5. The Asian Human Rights Commission is a human rights NGO founded in 1986 by lawyers and activists from various Asian countries. It is based in Hong Kong.
6. Asian Human Rights Commission, 'Pakistan: A Hindu worker is lynched for blasphemy as punishment for loving a Muslim girl', AHRC-STM-103-2008, 22 April 2008.
7. An FIR is a police report based on a complaint, which allows for the opening of a preliminary investigation.
8. Asian Human Rights Commission, 'Pakistan: A Hindu worker is lynched for blasphemy as punishment for loving a Muslim girl', op. cit.
9. This chapter focuses on the conditions of access to the parallel

water market for industrialists. The practices of electricity theft are discussed in the next chapter.

10. See L. Gayer, *Karachi*, op. cit., pp. 178–183.

11. Interviews with several Korangi factory managers, Karachi, 2017.

12. Asian Human Rights Commission, 'Pakistan: A Hindu worker is lynched for blasphemy as punishment for loving a Muslim girl', op. cit.

13. V. Volkov, *Violent Entrepreneurs*, op. cit., p. 41.

14. Interview with Ali Akbar,* General Manager at KFG Textile Mills,* Karachi, April 2014.

15. *Pakistan. Labor Market Study. Regulation, Job Creation, and Skills Formation in the Manufacturing Sector*, Report No. 38075-PK, Finance and Private Sector Development Unit, South Asia Region, The World Bank, September 2006.

16. In Sindh, these provisions have been confirmed by the Sindh Terms of Employment Standing Orders Act of 2015.

17. Mukhtar Sumar, 'The Textile Sector—An Employer's View', in Qutubuddin Aziz (ed.), *Working Conditions in the Textile Industry in Pakistan. Report of a National Workshop Held in Karachi from December 1 to 6 1990. Organised Jointly by the National Institute of Labour Administration Training, Karachi, and Friedrich Ebert Stiftung of Germany, Islamabad*, Karachi, Pakistan Media Corporation, 1992, p. 38. The author was at the time the director of a large Karachi-based textile company, Farooq Textile Mills.

18. Willis D. Weatherford, 'Pakistan', in Walter Galenson (ed.), *Labor in Developing Economies*, Berkeley, University of California Press, 1963, p. 26, note 17.

19. M. Shafi, *Pakistan Labour Year-Book, 1949–1950*, Karachi, Labour Publications, 1951, p. 7.

20. W. D. Weatherford, 'Pakistan', op. cit., Table 2, p. 23.

21. It increased significantly during the years 1982–1984; many industrialists closed their factories and laid off their employees, before reopening under a new name and with a greater number of contract workers. See World Bank, *Pakistan. Labor Market Study*, op. cit., p. 21.

22. Z. D. Faruqi, 'Contract Labour in Textile Mills', pp. 67–68.

23. In the Pakistani textile industry, as in its Indian and Bangladeshi competitors, labour costs represent barely 2/3% of production costs, compared to almost 40% in the US or Italy. See 'Tracing production costs in the textile industry', *Knitting Trade Journal*, 14 June 2022.

24. Sébastien Chauvin and Nicolas Jounin, 'L'externalisation des illégalités: ethnographie des usages du travail "temporaire" à Paris et à Chicago', in Laurence Fontaine and Florence Weber (eds.), *Les*

Paradoxes de l'économie informelle. À qui profitent les règles, Paris, Karthala, 2011, p. 130.

25. Ibid.
26. This is well beyond the statutory 12 hours (including overtime).
27. Overtime is theoretically paid at double the usual hourly rate.
28. Fawad Hasan, 'Khaadi ripping off workers of over Rs100 million every year', *The Express Tribune*, 11 August 2017.
29. S. Chauvin and N. Jounin, 'L'externalisation des illégalités', op. cit., p. 114.
30. In Pakistan, the regulation of factory inspections is the responsibility of provincial authorities. In Sindh, factory inspections were suspended in 2003, partly under pressure from SITE industrialist Zubair Motiwala, then an adviser to the provincial chief minister. See 'Chief minister directed me to stop the inspection of factories: Labour minister', *The Express Tribune*, 13 September 2012. These inspections resumed following the passage of the Sindh Occupational and Safety Act in December 2017.
31. In 2017, there were an estimated 547 labour inspectors in the whole country, for about 350,000 factories. Of these, there were only 17 women, despite the fact that women make up a significant proportion of the industrial workforce, particularly in textiles (where at least 30% of the workforce is reportedly female). In Karachi, there are only two women among the 30 or so labour inspectors. See Human Rights Watch, *No Room to Bargain: Unfair and Abusive Labor Practices in Pakistan*, New York, Human Rights Watch, 2019, p. 8.
32. Ibid., p. 26.
33. Interview with a garment industry executive based in Landhi, Karachi, May 2022.
34. Adam Baczko, Gilles Dorronsoro and Arthur Quesnay, *Syrie. Anatomie d'une guerre civile*, Paris, CNRS Éditions, 2016, p. 35.
35. Between 1988 and 2023, the MQM has won every municipal election in which it has run. In 2001, the party's decision to boycott the election made it possible for the Islamists of the Jama'at-e-Islami to win the mayor's office, but the MQM returned to power in the next election in 2005.
36. Guy Standing, *The Precariat: The New Dangerous Class*, London, Bloomsbury, 2011.
37. Judith Butler, *Frames of War: When Is Life Grievable?*, New York, Verso, 2009, pp. 14–15.
38. Dina Makram-Ebeid, 'Between God and the State: Class, Precarity, and Cosmology on the margins of an Egyptian Town', in Chris Hann

and Jonathan Parry (eds.), *Industrial Labor on the Margins of Capitalism. Precarity, Class, and the Neoliberal Subject*, New York-Oxford, Berghahn, 2018, pp. 180–196.

39. Edwar Palmer Thompson, 'Time, Work-Discipline, and Industrial Capitalism', *Past and Present*, Vol. 38, No. 1, 1967, pp. 56–97.

40. Jan Breman, *The Making and Unmaking of an Industrial Working Class: Sliding Down the Labour Hierarchy in Ahmedabad, India*, Delhi, Oxford University Press, 2004, p. 214.

41. Interview with Hasan,* employee of a large garment company, Karachi, July 2017.

42. Interview with Asif,* operator at Khaadi, Karachi, July 2017.

43. Jonathan Parry, 'Introduction: Precarity, Class, and the Neoliberal Subject', in C. Hann and J. Parry (eds.), *Industrial Labor on the Margins of Capitalism*, op. cit., p. 43.

44. Interview with Asim,* school teacher and former right-hand man of a PPP-affiliated Labour Officer, Karachi, 2014.

45. Interview with Kamran Husain,* Finishing Manager at a large textile group, Karachi, 2017.

46. Interview with a member of the ANP Labour Committee, Karachi, 2017.

47. Interview with Anwar Saeed,* former machine operator in the textile industry, Karachi, 2016.

48. Béatrice Hibou, *Anatomie politique de la domination*, Paris, La Découverte, 2011.

49. Interview with Kamran Husain,* Production Manager in a large garment group, Karachi, May 2022. K. Husain is referring to the ritual repudiation formula, which consists of repeating the word 'divorce' three times to break the bonds of marriage.

50. Idem.

51. J.-F. Bayart, *The State in Africa: The Politics of the Belly*, London/New York, Longman, 1993; Richard Banégas, '"Bouffer l'argent": politique du ventre, démocratie et clientélisme au Bénin', in Jean-Louis Briquet and Frédéric Sawicki (eds.), *Le Clientélisme politique dans les sociétés contemporaines*, Paris, PUF, 1998, pp. 75–109.

52. R. Banégas, 'Bouffer l'argent', op. cit., pp. 77–78.

53. As Richard Banégas points out, in Benin, the register of 'eating' can also serve as a vehicle for criticism of the voracity of the powerful, but with the democratization of the country, it has instead become 'the idiom of equity and social justice', ibid., p. 86.

54. Jacob Copeman and Giovanni da Col (eds.), *Fake*, Chicago, HAU Books, 2018.

55. D. Harvey, 'Accumulation by Dispossession', op. cit.; see also Lesley Gill, '"Right There with You": Coca-Cola, Labour Restructuring and Political Violence in Colombia', *Critique of Anthropology*, Vol. 27, No. 3, 2007, pp. 235–260.

56. Ayesha Tammy, 'Story of Jagdish Kumar's murder in Karachi', *The News*, 4 June 2008.

57. Maulana Abdul Hamid Khan Bhashani (1880–1976) was one of the founders of the National Awami Party (NAP). A graduate of the great *madrasa* of Deoband, he was an active participant in the Khilafat movement, though he later moved towards the communist, and then Maoist, left. After supporting Ayub Khan's military regime (because of its rapprochement with China), he took an active role in the 1968–1969 opposition movement, before trying (unsuccessfully) to rally Beijing to the Bengali cause during the 1971 civil war. On the trajectory of the 'Red Maulana' and his political legacy, see L. Uddin, *In the Land of Eternal Eid*, op. cit.

58. On these industrial riots, see Layli Uddin, '"Enemy Agents at Work": A Microhistory of the 1954 Adamjee and Karnaphuli Riots in East Pakistan', *Modern Asian Studies*, Vol. 55, No. 2, 2021, pp. 629–664.

59. Interview with Seema,* pharmaceutical worker at SITE, Karachi, 2014.

60. Women make up 25–35% of the workforce in the garment sector. See PILER / Ethical Trading Initiative, *Increasing Female Voices in the RMG Sector through Social Dialogue*, Karachi, PILER, 2020, p. 4.

61. For an overview of the gendered aspects of social control in the Pakistani garment sector, see Clean Clothes Campaign, *Workers' Lives at Risk: How Brands Profit from Unsafe Factory Work in Pakistan*, July 2022 (https://cleanclothes.org/news/2022/report-a-decade-after-deadly-ali-enterprises-fire-pakistans-garment-workers-report-shocking-lack-of-fire-exits).

62. Sandya Hewamanne, '"City of Whores": Nationalism, Development, and Global Garment Workers in Sri Lanka', *Social Text*, Vol. 26, No. 2, 2008, pp. 35–59; Lamia Karim, *Castoffs of Capital: Work and Love Among Garment Workers in Bangladesh*, Minneapolis, Minnesota University Press, 2022.

63. However, I would like to thank Ravia Mysorewala for her collaboration.

64. Interview with Ali Akbar,* General Manager in a large textile group, Karachi, April 2014.

65. Asif Noorani, 'Films of memory', *Newsline*, August 2017.

66. Interview with Ehsanullah Khan,* former executive of the Sindh Pakhtun Students Federation, Karachi, August 2016.

67. Asad Hashim, 'Parched for a price: Karachi's water crisis', *Al Jazeera*, 18 December 2017.

68. On the involvement of the Rangers in the parallel water market in Karachi during the 2000s, see Laurent Gayer, 'The Rangers of Pakistan: From Border Defence to Internal "Protection"', in Jean-Louis Briquet and Gilles Favarel-Garrigues (eds.), *Organized Crime and States: The Hidden Face of Politics*, New York, Palgrave Macmillan, 2010, pp. 15–39.

69. Naziha Syed Ali and Aslam Shah, 'Selling liquid gold: Karachi's tanker mafia', *Dawn*, 24 January 2023.

70. Perween Rahman, *Water Supply in Karachi*, Karachi, Orangi Pilot Project, 2008, p. 15.

71. 'Illegal water connections: KWSB turns its focus on bulk consumers', *The Express Tribune*, 22 March 2015.

72. 'Water board MD, others summoned over illegal connections', *The Nation*, 7 November 2018.

73. Interview with a police officer posted at SITE in 2017–2018, Karachi, 2018.

74. Laurent Gayer and Fawad Hasan, 'Pakistan coercive sweatshop capitalism', *Le Monde diplomatique* (English edition), December 2022.

75. L. Gill, *A Century of Violence in a Red City*, op. cit.

76. Kilusang Mayo Uno, *Right-Wing Vigilantes and Labor Repression*, Manila, KMU, 1987.

77. John T. Sidel, 'The Underside of Progress: Land, Labor, and Violence in Two Philippine Growth Zones, 1985–1995', *Bulletin of Concerned Asian Scholars*, Vol. 30, No. 1, 1998, pp. 3–12.

78. Q. Delpech, *Mobilisations syndicales et violence au Sud*, op. cit.

79. J. Grajales, *Governing by Violence*, op. cit., pp. 85–88; Lesley Gill, 'The Parastate in Colombia: Political Violence and the Restructuring of Barrancabermeja', *Anthropologica*, Vol. 51, No. 2, 2009, pp. 313–325; L. Gill, 'Right There With You', op. cit.

80. L. Gill, *A Century of Violence in a Red City*, op. cit., p. 28.

81. L. Gill, 'The Parastate in Colombia', op. cit.

82. L. Gill, 'Right There With You', op. cit.

83. J.T. Sidel, 'The Underside of Progress', op. cit., p. 4.

6. ANTI-TERRORISM TO THE RESCUE

1. Quoted in Fawad Hasan, 'Battered but not broken: The struggle of Karachi's workers', *The Friday Times*, 18 June 2021.

2. K. Marx, 'The Usefulness of Crime', in *Crime and Capitalism: Readings in Marxist Criminology*, pp. 52–53.
3. Karachi Suo Motu Case No. 16 of 2011, 6 October 2011.
4. Dominique Linhardt and Cédric Moreau de Bellaing, 'Épreuves d'État: une variation sur la définition wébérienne de l'État', *Quaderni*, No. 78, 2012, p. 9.
5. In 2007, Justice Chaudhry was arbitrarily dismissed by Pervez Musharraf. A year later, he was restored as Chief Justice following an intense mobilization of the legal profession. On the ins and outs of this movement, see Yasser Kureshi, *Seeking Supremacy: The Pursuit of Judicial Power in Pakistan*, Cambridge, Cambridge University Press, 2022, Chapter 5.
6. On the dynamics and the legacy of this operation, see Zia Ur Rehman, 'Ten years of the Karachi Operation', *Dawn*, 27 August 2023.
7. Zoha Waseem, *Insecure Guardians: Enforcement, Encounters and Everyday Policing in Karachi*, London, Hurst, 2022, p. 158.
8. Only the Commander of the V Corps based in Karachi is authorized (at the request of the provincial authorities) to relieve the Sindh Rangers of their border guard duties for internal security purposes. This protocol confirms that the Rangers are, in fact, under the command of the army.
9. In the summer of 2016, the provincial authorities initially refused to extend these special powers, then went on to restrict their scope.
10. Hussain Askari, 'Thirsty for more', *The Herald* (Karachi), August 2003, pp. 54–55.
11. L. Gayer, 'Pakistan's Rangers', op. cit.; 'Rangers "cementing" hold in Karachi', *Pakistan Today*, 17 June 2015; Z. Waseem, *Insecure Guardians*, op. cit., p. 239.
12. Group interview at the Employers Federation of Pakistan, Karachi, August 2017.
13. Interview with Abdur Rahman,* trade union activist, Karachi, August 2016.
14. 'Sindh Police chief questions presence of Rangers', *The News*, 7 February 2017.
15. Z. Waseem, *Insecure Guardians*, op. cit., p. 225.
16. Interview with a former official of the Korangi Association of Trade and Industry (KATI), Karachi, 2016.
17. 'Korangi industrial zone: Regular police patrolling to improve security', *The Express Tribune*, 7 May 2014.
18. Interview with a senior police officer stationed in the Eastern District, Karachi, August 2016.

19. Idem.
20. Interview with a police officer stationed at the IB Karachi office, Karachi, July 2016.
21. Interview with a former Karachi police chief, Karachi, July 2017.
22. Idem.
23. Interview with Gul Bahadur,* former machine operator for Chawla Tex Industries and member of the Al-Ettehad Power Looms Workers Union, Karachi, 2013.
24. FIR No. 95/2012, U/s 384/386/506-B/511 34 PPC R/W section 7 of ATA (translated from Urdu).
25. Pakistan Armed Forces (Acting in Aid of Civil Power) Ordinance, 1998, section 6.
26. The intention of this strike's organizers was to remind the company's new management (it had been bought by the Emirati group Etisalat in 2006) of its commitments regarding wage increases. See Asian Human Rights Commission, 'Pakistan: More than 26,000 employees of Pakistan Telecommunication were denied wages increases as announced by the government', 18 November 2010.
27. Interview with General Mohammed Saeed, Director General of Sindh Rangers, Karachi, July 2017.
28. Idem.
29. Eve Register, 'Pakistan's military extends its role in economic decision-making through the Special Investment Facilitation Council', *TGP*, 4 December 2023.
30. Ayesha Siddiqua, *Military Inc. Inside Pakistan's Military Economy*, London, Pluto Press, 2007.
31. The army is one of the country's main commercial enterprises and landowning entities. This status is conducive to land disputes, which tend to focus on army-run farms. Since the 1990s, the Okara region of Punjab has been the scene of violent conflicts between the army and small landowners. The latter have organized themselves into a protest movement, the Anjuman Mazarin Punjab (AMP), and its main leaders have all, in recent years, been charged with terrorism and imprisoned. See Mubbashir A. Rizvi, *The Ethics of Staying: Social Movements and Land Rights Politics in Pakistan*, Stanford, Stanford University Press, 2019.
32. For a discussion of this judicial activism by protagonists of the 2007–2008 lawyers' movement, see Moeen H. Cheema and Ijaz S. Gilani (eds.), *The Politics and Jurisprudence of the Chaudhry Court, 2005–2013*, Karachi, Oxford University Press, 2015. For a more general discussion on judicial activism in Pakistan, see Yasser Kureshi,

Seeking Supremacy: The Pursuit of Judicial Power in Pakistan, Cambridge, Cambridge University Press, 2022.

33. In the High Court of Sindh, CP No. 1129 of 2012 (Muhammad Ameen & others vs. Government of Sindh and Station House Officer, Mochko Police Station, Karachi).

34. In April 2012, the Chairman of the Pearl Continental Hotel Employees Union (PCHEU) in Lahore, Muhammad Nasir, was charged with terrorism following a PCHEU victory in the union elections. He was charged with attempted kidnapping for ransom and illegal possession of firearms, and faced a 20-year prison term. The charges were dismissed by the Punjab High Court, which a few weeks later instructed the police to withdraw the terrorism charge against Mr Nasir and his colleagues.

35. In Punjab, in 2014, the acquittal rate by Anti-Terrorism Courts (ATC) was estimated at 75%, and it can be assumed that a similar rate prevailed in Karachi. In addition, many cases are transferred from ATCs to ordinary criminal courts, on the grounds that they do not fall under the jurisdiction of the ATA (this was the case for 69.2% of cases going through the five Karachi ATCs in 2013). See Tariq Parvez and Mehwish Rani, *An Appraisal of Pakistan's Anti-Terrorism Act*, Washington D.C., United States Institute of Peace, 2015, pp. 2, 5.

36. Faisal Siddiqi, 'Miracles' of military justice', *Dawn*, 5 September 2016 (this author is one of the country's leading *cause lawyers*, discussed further in Chapter 9); International Commission of Jurists, 'Military injustice in Pakistan', briefing paper, June 2016.

37. In 2011, progressive activist Baba Jan was sentenced to life imprisonment by an anti-terrorism court in Gilgit Baltistan, for participating in a demonstration in support of villagers affected by a landslide. In 2016, several dozen participants in the movement against the Okara military farms were charged with terrorism and imprisoned. In 2017, villagers, poets, and environmental activists protesting against a proposed coalmine in Sindh suffered the same fate.

38. M. A. K. Chaudhry, *Of All Those Years*, Lahore, Classic, 2006, pp. 54–55.

39. On the evolution of such extrajudicial violence, see in particular Mahvish Ahmad, *Destruction as Rule. Containment, Censuring and Confusion in Pakistani Balochistan*, PhD thesis (anthropology), Cambridge University, 2015.

40. See G. Favarel-Garrigues and L. Gayer, *Proud to Punish*, op. cit., pp. 146–153 and Z. Waseem, *Insecure Guardians*, op. cit., Chapter 4.

41. The Sindh High Court made a decision to form a commission to look into accusations of illegal practices in the largest textile companies, giving rise to the formation of the Sindh Sujagi Mazdur Federation in 2019. However, the commission never saw the light of day.
42. F. Hasan, 'Battered but not broken', op. cit.
43. Interview with Yaseen Jhulan, Chief Organizer of the Sindh Sujagi Mazdur Federation, Karachi, May 2022.
44. Interview with Yaseen Jhulan, Chief Organizer of the Sindh Sujagi Mazdur Federation, Karachi, May 2022.
45. Julien Levesque, *Pour une autre idée du Pakistan. Nationalisme et construction identitaire dans le Sindh*, Rennes, PUR, 2022.
46. The Machiyara Group was founded in the 1970s by a Memon entrepreneur, Hanif Machiyara. Originally specialized in tourism and construction, it later expanded into textiles and telecommunications. Although I attempted to approach the management on several occasions, my requests for interviews remained unanswered.
47. Denim Clothing Company—Factory Tour April 2021 (https://www.youtube.com/ watch?v=47RoEm8lLjE).
48. A dozen workers from Denim Clothing were interviewed, in collaboration with journalist Fawad Hasan, over the course of two visits to Karachi in May and August 2022.
49. Interview with Faiza,* seamstress at Denim Clothing Company, Karachi, May 2022.
50. Interview with Arshad Khaskheli,* former machine operator at Denim Clothing Company, Karachi, May 2022.
51. These threats are recurrent in the testimonies of the Denim Clothing workers interviewed in May and August 2022, and are also mentioned in F. Hasan, 'Battered but not broken', op. cit.
52. First Information Report serial No. 2729. No. 741/21, Awami Colony Police Thana, 27 October 2021.
53. Interview with Sajid Mallah,* former machine operator at Denim Clothing Company, Karachi, May 2022.
54. Video shared by Denim Clothing workers during a group interview, Karachi, May 2022.
55. Interview with a senior police officer from Korangi, Karachi, May 2022.
56. Q. Delpech, *Mobilisations syndicales et violence au Sud*, op. cit., p. 156.
57. Comisión colombiana de juristas, 'Informe a la 91a Conferencia Internacional del Trabajo de las Centrales Sindicales Colombianas', 30 June 2003; IndustriAll, 'Les syndicats algériens confrontés à la répression sur fond de réformes controversées du droit du travail', 4

October 2023; Rathindra Kuruwita 'Sri Lanka's Proposed Anti-terror Law Makes Dissent an Act of Terror', *The Diplomat*, 28 April 2023.

58. Alonso Moleiro, 'Wage of outrage in Venezuela after six trade unionists convicted of conspiracy and terrorism', *El País* (international), 9 August 2023.

59. Naïm Sakhi, '17 dirigeants de la CGT poursuivis: la acistsg antisyndicale s'accentue', *L'Humanité*, 7 December 2023.

60. Begoña Aretxaga, 'Playing Terrorist: Ghastly Plots and the Ghostly State', *Journal of Spanish Cultural Studies*, Vol. 1, No. 1, 2000, pp. 43–58.

7. COMMITTED CITIZENS OR CORPORATE VIGILANTES?

1. Interview with Ali Shah,* (conducted with Sophie Russo), Karachi, 2016.

2. Christian Lund, 'Twilight Institutions: Public Authority and Local Politics in Africa', *Development and Change*, Vol. 37, No. 4, 2006, pp. 685–705.

3. Trevor Jones and Tim Newburn (eds.), *Plural Policing. A Comparative Perspective*, London-New York, Routledge, 2006; Atreyee Sen and David Pratten (eds.), *Global Vigilantes*, London, Hurst, 2007; Tessa Diphoorn and Erella Grassiani (eds.), *Security Blurs. The Politics of Plural Security Provision*, New York, Routledge, 2019.

4. Michel Agier and Martin Lamotte, 'Les pacifications dans la ville contemporaine: ethnographies et anthropologie', *L'Homme*, No. 219–220, 2016, pp. 7–29.

5. Stephen Graham, *Cities Under Siege. The New Military Urbanism*, London, Verso, 2011. See also Peter Marcuse, 'Security or Safety in Cities? The Threat of Terrorism after 9/11', *International Journal of Urban Regional Research*, Vol. 30, No. 4, 2006, p. 923.

6. Michel Foucault, *Security, Territory and Population: Lectures at the Collège de France, 1977–1978*, Houndmills/New York, 2009 [2004], lesson of 11 January 1978.

7. S. Graham, *Cities Under Siege*, op. cit.

8. Stephen Graham and Sobia Ahmed Kaker, 'Living the Security City: Karachi's Archipelago of Enclaves', *Harvard Design Magazine*, No. 37, 2014, pp. 12–16.

9. Sobia Ahmed Kaker, 'Enclaves, Insecurity and Violence in Karachi', *South Asian History and Culture*, Vol. 5, No. 1, 2014, pp. 93–107.

10. Mike Davis, *City of Quartz: Excavating the Future in Los Angeles*, London, Verso, 1990; Teresa Caldeira, *City of Walls: Crime, Segregation, and*

Citizenship in Sao Paulo, Berkeley, University of California Press, 2000. See also Setha Low, *Behind the Gates: Life, Security and the Pursuit of Happiness in Fortress America*, New York, Routledge, 2003.

11. Originally from Gujarat, the Shia Ismaili community of Bohras has, like the Memons, historically specialized in trade.

12. Majyd Aziz, 'Vilifying the guardians', *Dawn*, 1996.

13. Anthony Amicelle, 'Naissance d'une agence de renseignement: droits d'entrée dans les univers de la finance et de la sécurité', *Cultures & Conflits*, No. 114–115, 2019, p. 183.

14. Peter Manning, *Symbolic Communication. Signifying Calls and the Police Response*, Cambridge, MIT Press, 1988.

15. Sophie Russo, *Policer la police? Milieux d'affaires et participation citoyenne au maintien de l'ordre à Karachi*, Master's thesis, Sciences Po Paris, 2017, pp. 39–40.

16. Nausheen Anwar, 'Mapping Politics in/of the Modern City: Cartography as Representation', in Shahana Rajani and Zahra Malkani (eds.), *Exhausted Geographies*, Karachi, Exhausted Geographies, 2016.

17. Laurent Gayer and Sophie Russo, '"Let's Beat Crime Together": Corporate Mobilizations for Security in Karachi', *International Journal of Urban Regional Research*, Vol. 46, No. 4, 2022, pp. 594–613.

18. Interview with Rashid Memon,* director of a textile company and head of the security department at the SITE Association of Trade and Industry, Karachi, July 2016.

19. Vijayanthi Rao, 'Proximate Distances: The Phenomenology of Density in Mumbai', *Built Environment*, Vol. 33, No. 2, pp. 227–248.

20. In official terminology and common parlance, the term *katchi abadi*, which continues to refer to informal settlements, is difficult to translate but is clearly depreciative. *Abadi* refers both to a group of residents of a locality and to the locality itself. The term *katcha*, inherited from Hindi and the Hindu dichotomy of pure and impure, refers to something coarse, dirty, or unfinished (like raw food).

21. M. Agier and M. Lamotte, 'Les pacifications dans la ville contemporaine', op. cit.

22. 'Mill-owners decline to share Police cost', *Dawn*, 14 January 1970.

23. Azhar Abbas, 'Pulling down the shutters', *The Herald*, January 1995, p. 57.

24. Emmanuel Blanchard, 'Recours à la force et demandes de justice en situation (post)-coloniale', *Crime, histoire et société*, Vol. 21, No. 2, 2017, pp. 87–102.

25. Diane E. Davis and Graham Denyer Willis, 'Anti-Crime Social Movements in Latin America', in David A. Snow, Donatella Della

Porta, Bert Klandermans and Doug McAdam (eds.), *Blackwell Encyclopedia of Social and Political Movements*, Oxford, Blackwell Publishing, 2011.

26. Fernando Alberto Calderón Figueroa, *Rondas Urbanas Cajamarquina. Estrategia Comunitaria de Acceso a la Seguridad y la Justicia*, BA thesis in Sociology, Catholic University of Peru, 2013.

27. Maria Teresa Martinez Trujillo, *Businessmen and Protection Patterns in Dangerous Contexts: Putting the Case of Guadalajara, Mexico into Perspective*, PhD thesis (political science), Sciences Po, Paris, 2019, p. 487.

28. In total, 6,180 of the 6,343 incidents reported to the CIC between 2011 and 2016 were recorded as resolved. See Sandra Ley and Magdalena Guzmán, 'Doing Business amid Criminal Violence: Companies' Strategies in Monterrey, Nuevo León', Sié Center/ University of Denver, Policy Brief, February 2017, p. 4.

29. Lucy Conger, 'The Private Sector and Public Security: The Case of Ciudad Juárez and Monterrey', Working Paper on Civic Engagement and Public Security in Mexico, Wilson Center/University of San Diego, March 2014.

30. Asef Bayat, *Life as Politics. How Ordinary People Change the Middle East*, Amsterdam, Amsterdam University Press, 2010, Chapter 3.

31. Majyd Aziz, 'When industrialists are forced to work in a hell hole', *The Express Tribune*, 2013.

32. Michael Power, *Organized Uncertainty. Designing a World of Risk Management*, Oxford, Oxford University Press, 2007.

33. Pryjomko has published a fascinating account of his collaboration with the CPLC. See Roman Pryjomko, *Someone, Somewhere. Encounters with People and Places*, Victoria, Trafford Publishing, 2006, Chapter 20.

34. Interview with Umar Shah,* business leader and head of CPLC's IT department, Karachi, August 2018.

35. Claire Cunty, Fabrice Fussy and Pascale Perez, 'Géocriminologie: quand la cartographie permet aux géographes d'investir la criminologie', *Cybergéo*, document 378, published online, 8 June 2007.

36. Interview with an official of the law & order committee of the SITE Association of Trade and Industry and the director of a private security company, himself a former military officer, Karachi, July 2016.

37. Personal observation at the control room of SITE Association of Trade and Industry's anti-crime cell, Karachi, August 2017.

38. Rita Abrahamsen and Michael C. Williams, 'Security Beyond the State: Global Security Assemblages in International Politics', *International Political Sociology*, Vol. 3, No. 1, 2009, pp. 1–17; T. Diphoorn and E. Grassiani (eds.), *Security Blurs*, op. cit.

39. Ian Loader, 'Private Security and the Demand for Protection in Contemporary Britain', *Policing and Society*, Vol. 7, No. 3, 1997, p. 147.

40. Paul Virilio, *Speed and Politics*, Los Angeles, Semiotext, 2006 [1975].

41. The death of this Urdu-speaking student in a road accident on 15 April 1985 precipitated inter-communal clashes that sparked a long sequence of violence and urban transformation. See Noman Ahmed and Saba Imtiaz, 'Bushra Zaidi, the woman who changed Karachi forever, by dying', *The Express Tribune*, 7 March 2012.

42. Laurent Gayer, 'The Need for Speed: Traffic Regulation and the Violent Fabric of Karachi', *Theory, Culture & Society*, Vol. 33, No. 7–8, 2016, pp. 137–158.

43. Armand Mattelart and André Vitalis, *Le Profilage des populations. Du livret ouvrier au cybercontrôle*, Paris, La Découverte, 2014, p. 31.

44. M. Foucault, *Security, Territory, Population*, op. cit., p. 20.

45. Ibid.

46. Interview with Rashid Memon,* director of a textile company and head of the security department of SITE Association, Karachi, July 2016.

47. Interview with Akbar Shah Hashmi, UC Nazim of Bawani Chali, Karachi, August 2018.

48. A. Mattelart and A. Vitalis, *Le Profilage des populations*, op. cit., p. 15.

49. Ibid., p. 43.

50. The Customs Trade Partnership against Terrorism (CTPAT) is a programme to secure global supply chains and improve US border security. Companies applying for certification must meet strict security requirements whilst ensuring that their trading partners also comply with these recommendations throughout their supply chain.

51. Interview with Umar Shah,* business leader and head of CPLC's IT department, Karachi, August 2018.

52. Richard V. Ericson and Kevin D. Haggerty, *Policing the Risk Society*, Toronto, Toronto University Press, 1992, p.18.

53. S. Graham, *Cities Under Siege*, op. cit., p. xv.

54. M. Power, *Organized Uncertainty*, op. cit., p. 4.

55. The NGO Safe Pakistan Welfare Trust brings together members of the business community and retired military officers around a security and neoliberal agenda (including an anti-poverty programme intended to 'empower blue-collar workers'). See https://www.safepakistan.pk/#initiatives.

56. Interview with Umar Shah,* businessman and head of the CPLC's IT department, Karachi, August 2022.

57. To the extent that young *seth* Rashid Memon, who had initially been impressed by the app, quickly deleted it from his phone. Interview, Karachi, August 2022.

58. Daanis Mustafa, Nausheen Anwar and Amiera Sawas, 'Gender, Global Terror, and Everyday Violence in Urban Pakistan', *Political Geography*, Vol. 69, 2019, pp. 54–64.

59. M. Agier and M. Lamotte, 'Les pacifications dans la ville contemporaine', op. cit., p. 10.

60. The Pakistani Taliban movement came into being in 2007. In Karachi, the establishment of the Taliban in certain Pashtun neighbourhoods led to the equation between this population and Islamist terrorism. On the dynamics of this entrenchment, mixing coercion and mediation in economic and social conflicts, see L. Gayer, *Karachi*, op. cit., Chapter 5.

61. For an account of the movement's demands penned by the young activist who became its main spokesperson, see Manzoor Pashteen, 'The military says Pashtuns are traitors. We just want our rights', *The New York Times*, 11 February 2019.

62. S. Graham, *Cities Under Siege*, op. cit., p. xi.

63. Séverine Awenego Dalberto and Richard Banégas (eds.), 'Citoyens de papier en Afrique', *Genèses*, No. 112, 2018.

64. James Scott, *Seeing Like a State. How Certain Schemes to Improve the Human Condition Have Failed*, New Haven, Yale University Press, 1998.

65. Interview with General Bilal Akbar, Director General of the Rangers, Karachi, July 2016.

66. Sarah-Jane Cooper-Knock, 'Beyond Agamben: Sovereignty, Policing and "Permissive Space" in South Africa and Beyond', *Theoretical Criminology*, Vol. 22, No. 1, 2018, pp. 22–41.

67. On the distinction between (unofficial) 'policing formations' and (official) 'policing organizations', see Lars Buur and Stephen Jensen, 'Introduction: Vigilantism and the Policing of Everyday Life in South Africa', *African Studies*, Vol. 63, No. 2, 2004, pp. 139–152.

68. Michel Foucault, *'Il faut défendre la société'. Cours au Collège de France (1975–1976)*, Paris, Gallimard-Le Seuil, 1976, pp. 227–232.

69. G. Favarel-Garrigues and L. Gayer, *Proud to Punish*, op. cit., Chapter 1; Laurent Fourchard, 'Le vigilantisme contemporain: violence et légitimité d'une activité policière bon marché', *Critique Internationale*, No. 78, 2018, pp. 169–186; Thomas Blom Hansen and Finn Stepputat (eds.), *Sovereign Bodies: Citizens, Migrants, and States in the Colonial World*, Princeton, Princeton University Press, 2005.

70. Sarah-Jane Cooper-Knock, 'Policing in Intimate Crowds: Moving

Beyond "the Mob" in South Africa', *African Affairs*, Vol. 113, No. 453, 2014, pp. 563–582.

71. Daniel Goldstein, '"In Our Own Hands": Lynching, Justice, and the Law in Bolivia', *American Ethnologist*, Vol. 30, No. 1, 2003, pp. 22–43.

72. Interview with Rashid Memon,* director of a textile company and head of the security department of SITE Association, Karachi, July 2016.

73. Markus Daechsel, 'Sovereignty, Governmentality and Development in Ayub's Pakistan', *Modern Asian Studies*, Vol. 45, No. 1, 2011, pp. 131–157.

74. Interview with Amir Masood,* former trade unionist employed at SHP, Karachi, July 2017.

75. Vanessa Codaccioni, *La Légitime défense. Homicides sécuritaires, crimes racistes et violences policières*, Paris, CNRS Éditions, 2018. These same principles frame self-defence in Pakistani criminal law. See Ashraf Ali and Muhammad Saleem, 'Right of Self-Defense in Pakistan', *Journal of Applied Environmental and Biological Sciences*, Vol. 4, No. 12, 2014, pp. 213–217.

76. S. Russo, *Policing the Police*, op. cit.

77. Moosa Kaleem, 'Police "fry" suspects to fight crime', *The Herald*, September 2016.

78. Heather Hamill, *The Hoods. Crime and Punishment in Belfast*, Princeton, Princeton University Press, 2011, pp. 74–75.

79. S. Russo, *Policing the Police*, op. cit., pp. 73–74.

80. On the bureaucratization of private security work, see François Bonnet, 'Les effets pervers du partage de la sécurité: polices publiques et privées dans une gare et un centre commercial', *Sociologie du travail*, Vol. 50, No. 4, 2008.

81. Sophie Russo's interview with a former CPLC member involved in its anti-kidnapping operations, Karachi, August 2016.

82. Nicholas Rush Smith, 'Rejecting Rights: Vigilantism and Violence in Post-Apartheid South Africa', *African Affairs*, Vol. 114, No. 456, pp. 341–360.

83. T. P. R. Caldeira, *City of Walls*, op. cit., pp. 340–346.

84. G. Favarel-Garrigues and L. Gayer, *Proud to Punish*, op. cit., Chapter 1.

85. L. Gayer, *Karachi*, op. cit., Chapter 7.

86. R. V. Ericson and K. D. Haggerty, *Policing the Risk Society*, op. cit., p. 41.

87. Clifford Shearing and Philipp Stenning, 'Modern Private Security: Its Growth and Implications', *Crime and Justice*, Vol. 3, 1981, p. 212; Julie Berg, 'Seeing Like Private Security: Evolving Mentalities of Public

Space Protection in South Africa', *Criminology & Criminal Justice*, Vol. 10, No. 3, 2010, p. 295.

88. In addition to the historical examples discussed in Chapter 1, the case of the Bakassi Boys (a Nigerian vigilante group initially funded by traders in the Aba market in the south-east of the country) comes to mind. See Daniel Jordan Smith, 'The Bakassi Boys: Vigilantism, Violence and Political Imagination in Nigeria', *Cultural Anthropology*, Vol. 19, No. 3, 2004, pp. 429–455.

89. M. Naepels, *Dans la détresse*, op. cit., p. 17.

8.   WHO WILL WATCH THE WATCHMEN?

1. Interview with Najam Kathiawari,* factory owner and former president of the Karachi Chamber of Commerce and Industry (KCCI), Karachi, July 2017.

2. Zofeen Ebrahim, 'Karachi residents trapped between armed assassins and private bodyguards', *IPS News*, 20 August 2014.

3. Juvenal's formulation is used regularly in the Pakistani press to argue for greater regulation of the private security sector. For further information, see this contribution from a renowned risk management consultant, in which he shares advice on how to choose one's guards... safely; see Norbert Almeida, 'Watching your watchmen', *Dawn*, 8 June 2014.

4. Jamie Cross, 'Three Miles from Anarchy: Managerial Fear and the Affective Factory', *Sarai Reader*, 08, 2010, pp. 164–170.

5. This reflection on the endogenous production of insecurity by security systems owes much to Robert Castel, *L'Insécurité sociale. Qu'est-ce qu'être protégé*, Paris, Le Seuil, 2003.

6. Pierre Bourdieu, 'Job Insecurity is Everywhere Now', in *Acts of Resistance: Against the New Myths of Our Time*, Cambridge, Cambridge University Press, 1998, p. 85.

7. Nandini Gooptu, 'Servile Sentinels of the City: Private Security Guards, Organized Informality, and Labour in Interactive Services in Globalized India', *International Review of Social History*, Vol. 58, No. 1, 2013, pp. 9–38.

8. Pierre Bourdieu, 'Job Insecurity Is Everywhere Now', op. cit., p. 85.

9. Tony Roshan Samara, 'Order and Security in the City: Producing Race and Policing Neoliberal Spaces in South Africa', *Ethnic and Racial Studies*, Vol. 33, No. 4, 2010, pp. 642–643.

10. Nathan Dobson, 'Private Security in Nairobi, Kenya: Securitized

Landscapes, Crosscurrents, and New Forms of Sociality', *African Studies Review*, Vol. 62, No. 2, 2019, p. 7.

11. Frédéric Péroumal, 'Le monde précaire et illégitime des agents de sécurité', *Actes de la recherche en sciences sociales*, No. 175, 2008, p. 12.

12. Ilia Antenucci, 'Security and the City: Post-Colonial Accumulation, Securitization, and Urban Development in Kolkata', in Iman Kumar Mitra et al. (eds.), *Accumulation in Post-Colonial Capitalism*, Singapore, Springer, 2016, p. 85.

13. Damien Carrière, *Filtering Class Through Space: Security Guards and Urban Territories in Delhi, India*, PhD thesis (geography), University of Minnesota/Université Sorbonne Paris Cité, 2018, p. 1.

14. Jean-Pierre Durand, *La Chaîne invisible. Travailler aujourd'hui: flux tendu et servitude volontaire*, Paris, Le Seuil, 2004.

15. Béatrice Hibou, *La Bureaucratisation du monde à l'ère néolibérale*, Paris, La Découverte, 2012.

16. Ayesha Siddiqua, *Military Inc. Inside Pakistan's Military Economy*, London, Pluto Press, 2007; Amélie Blom, 'Qui a le bâton a le buffle: le corporatisme de l'armée pakistanaise', *Questions de recherche*, No. 16, 2005.

17. This competition manifests itself both in the proliferation of small, poorly regulated companies and in the emergence of prestigious firms, whose appeal lies in the close relationship they maintain with the official security forces.

18. This increase is not easily quantifiable. The CPLC records only homicides and street crime (car and mobile phone theft), while the Sindh police have only recently started to produce systematic statistical data on extortion demands and abductions.

19. Interview with a former army major, head of a private security company operating in Sindh and Punjab, Karachi, August 2016.

20. Shahram Azhar and Danish Khan, 'Rethinking Informal Labor in Peripheral Capitalism: The Dynamics of Surplus, Market, and Spatiality', *Labor History*, Vol. 61, No. 3–4, 2020, pp. 320–334.

21. More specifically, 12-bore shotgun repeaters, theoretically intended for bird hunting.

22. Interview with a former army major, head of a private security company operating in Sindh and Punjab, Karachi, August 2016.

23. Interview with Zulfikar,* security guard, Karachi, August 2018.

24. In addition to the fact that these interpretations are often used to justify criminal acts *ex-post*, the meanings of 'custom' and 'honour' are dynamic and have shifted significantly under the influence of criminal law. See Nafisa Shah, *Honour and Violence: Gender, Power and Law in Southern Pakistan*, New York-Oxford, Berghahn Books, 2016.

25. Historically, the Pakistani army has recruited most of its personnel from the Potohar plateau in northern Punjab and the surrounding districts of the North West Frontier Province, a tradition dating back to the colonial period. See Hasan Askari Rizvi, *Military, State and Society in Pakistan*, London, Palgrave Macmillan, 2000, p. 39.

26. Interviews with a foreman in a textile factory and with the former assistant labour officer of a large garment company, Karachi, August 2018.

27. Atreyee Sen and David Pratten, 'Global Vigilantes: Perspectives on Justice and Violence', in idem (ed.), *Global Vigilantes*, op. cit., p. 3. The term 'cheap' has a double meaning here: it applies not only to the lower costs of the policing practices under consideration, but also to their questionable quality.

28. S. A. Kaker, 'Enclaves, Insecurity and Violence in Karachi', op. cit.

29. Significantly, the management of Denim Clothing did not respond to my (numerous) requests for an interview—a rare reaction during my eight years of investigation.

30. These similarities are particularly striking in companies where security managers are drawn from the military. Regardless of whether those they are giving orders to are notorious criminals or security guards recruited from private security companies, these ex-military personnel are careful to maintain a certain level of ethnic pluralism among their subordinates. They do this as a way of ensuring the persistence of a level of distrust that is conducive to mutual surveillance among security guards.

31. From 1992 to 2002, Korangi was occupied by the MQM (Haqiqi), which imposed a reign of terror by torturing its opponents and extorting money from traders and industrialists alike. Following an agreement with President Musharraf's military regime, the MQM (Altaf) regained control of the area in 2002, though it faced competition from the Baloch criminal groups established in the surrounding districts.

32. The PAC was founded in 2008 by a gang leader from the Lyari neighbourhood, Abdur Rehman, alias Rehman '*Dakait*' (Rehman 'the bandit'). Bringing together criminal actors, social workers, and PPP defectors, this motley crew carried out extortion, political, and social activities simultaneously. See L. Gayer, *Karachi*, op. cit., Chapter 4.

33. Interview with Rafique Baloch,* a social worker living in Sharafi Goth, Korangi, August 2022.

34. On this common posture among business representatives in Karachi, see S. Russo, *The Arts of Order*, op. cit.

371

35. Riaz Ali (see Chapter 5) was fired from a prestigious position as 'Admin' at the Alkaram Group in 2016 after failing to prevent a strike. He was then hired by another garment giant, Gul Ahmed, though in the lowlier post of General Manager, Production. Interview with a Gul Ahmed manager, Karachi, May 2022.
36. M. Burawoy, *Manufacturing Consent*, op. cit.
37. Interview with Major Qasim Balkhi,* General Manager Administration and Security at Hamid Textiles,* Karachi, July 2017.
38. Idem.
39. In the Weberian sense of the term, the validity of a prescription lies less in compliance with it than in its ability to guide the behaviour of individuals, if only as a way of circumventing established norms. See Max Weber, *Economie et société*, Vol. 2, Paris, Pocket, 1995, p. 13.
40. In addition to the disciplinary proceedings against guards, I was able to consult about ten proceedings against both male and female workers during the same period. Absenteeism was also frequently cited, along with theft of finished products, drug use, and brawls.
41. As suggested on a charge sheet shared by Major Balkhi, in July 2017 a guard caught two workers sharing a joint at the entrance to the toilet of one of the group's production units. The two men went through disciplinary proceedings and were dismissed.
42. "Interview with Mehmood Hussain", CEO of Shahbaz Pharma, Karachi, July 2017.
43. Interview with a former subedar major employed in the security department of KFG Textile Mills,* Karachi, July 2016.
44. Frédéric Ocqueteau, 'Chefs d'orchestre de la sûreté des entreprises à l'ère de la sécurité globale', *Champ pénal*, Vol. VIII, 2011.
45. Ibid.
46. Riaz Chenoy was abducted by a group of jihadist militants in November 2011, while travelling from his factory (located in Landhi, a few kilometres east of Korangi) to his home in southern Karachi. He was released a few days later, as a result of a CPLC intervention.
47. Transnational firms active in Karachi use risk experts, often trained abroad, who believe that Pakistani company safety managers have an archaic view of industrial security; interview with one such expert, Karachi, July 2017.
48. "Interview with Ameer Hasan", Head of security at Shahbaz Pharma, Karachi, July 2017.
49. R. V. Ericson and K. D. Haggerty, *Policing the Risk Society*, op. cit.
50. L. Gayer, *Karachi*, op. cit., p. 246 ff.
51. N. Gooptu, 'Servile Sentinels of the City', op. cit.

52. Arlie Russell Hochschild, *The Managed Heart: Commercialization of Human Feeling*, Berkeley, University of California Press, 1983.

53. Cameron Lynne Macdonald and Carmen Sirianni, 'The Service Society and the Changing Experience of Work', in idem (ed.), *Working in the Service Society*, Philadelphia, Temple University Press, 1996, pp. 1–26.

54. "Interview with Omer Shirazi", Director of Administration at Shahbaz Pharma, Karachi, July 2017.

55. N. Gooptu, 'Servile Sentinels of the City', op. cit.

56. Q. Deluermoz and J. Foa (eds.), *Les Épreuves de la guerre civile*, Paris, Presses de la Sorbonne, 2022. See also Adèle Blazquez, *L'Aube s'est levée sur un mort. Violence armée et culture du pavot au Mexique*, Paris, CNRS Éditions, 2022.

57. A. Mattelart and A. Vitalis, *Le Profilage des populations*, op. cit.

58. For more information on these practices, see the file compiled by Mediapart since 2012. URL: https://www.mediapart.fr/journal/france/dossier/notre-dossier-espionnage-en-serie-chez-ikea.

59. R. Castel, *L'Insécurité sociale*, op. cit., p. 8.

9. TRIAL BY FIRE

1. Interview with Faisal Siddiqi, Karachi, July 2016. By 'anarchy of the law', Siddiqi is here referring to the wide disjunction that prevails in Pakistan between law in the books and law in action.

2. Walter Benjamin, 'A Short History of Photography', *Screen*, Vol. 13, No. 1, 1972 [1931], p. 25.

3. *Awaaz. Baldia Inferno: Artists Respond*, Arts Council of Pakistan, 8–15 February 2013, exhibition catalogue (1 CD-ROM).

4. Email from Naila Mahmood, 24 May 2020.

5. Interview (zoom) with Naila Mahmood, 25 August 2020.

6. Damien De Blic and Cyril Lemieux, 'The Scandal as Test: Elements of Pragmatic Sociology', *Politix*, No. 71, 2005, p. 71.

7. Greg Bankoff, Uwe Lübken and Jordan Sand (eds.), *Flammable Cities: Urban Conflagration and the Making of the Modern World*, Madison, The University of Wisconsin Press, 2012, p. 5.

8. François Jarrige, 'Les usines en feu: l'industrialisation au risque des incendies dans le textile (France, 1830–1870)', *Le Mouvement social*, No. 249, 2014, pp. 141–142.

9. Ibid., p. 162.

10. E. P. Thompson, *Whigs and Hunters: The Origin of the Black Act*, London, Penguin Books, 1977 [1975], p. 263.

11. Jérôme Pélisse, 'Judiciarisation ou juridicisation? Usages et

réappropriations du droit dans les conflits du travail', *Politix*, No. 86, 2009, p. 76.

12. Thomas Blom Hansen, 'A History of Distributed Sovereignty: Trade, Migration and Rule in the Global Indian Ocean', in Harry Verhoeven and Anatol Lieven (eds.), *Beyond Liberal Order: States, Societies and Markets in the Indian Ocean*, New York, Oxford University Press, 2022, pp. 41–66.

13. Asiff Hussein, 'The Memons: from simple merchants to business captains', *Roar Media*, 11 December 2017.

14. Founded in 1861, RINA originally specialized in ship inspection.

15. Declan Walsh and Steven Greenhouse, 'Certified safe, a factory in Karachi still quickly burned', *The New York Times*, 7 December 2012.

16. Ibid.

17. Ibid.

18. Ibid.

19. The first Investigation Officer (IO) of this team, Zafar Iqbal, was replaced on 20 September by Brigadier Jehanzaib.

20. Founded by Z. A. Bhutto in 1975, the FIA is a federal criminal investigation department under the Ministry of Interior. It is the main investigative agency of the Pakistani government, and its Director General holds the rank of Inspector General of Police (IGP).

21. Charge Sheet No. 238 - A/2012, 12 November 2012.

22. Statement U/s. 161 Cr. P.C., September 14, 2012, PS SITE-B (testimony of Muhammad Umer, machine operator at Ali Enterprises).

23. Charge Sheet No. 238 - A/2012, November 12, 2012; Federal Investigation Agency, Sindh Zone Karachi, *Enquiry Report. Fire Incident at Ali Enterprises S.I.T.E Karachi on 11th September 2012* , 3 October 2012 (FIA Report thereafter), pp. 8–9.

24. Charge Sheet No. 238 - A/2012, 12 November 2012; FIA Report, pp. 8–9.

25. Hasan Mansoor, 'Laws of the devil', *Dawn*, 1 May 2016.

26. Nudrat Kamal, 'Burning questions: The Karachi factory fire', *Newsline* (Karachi), October 2012.

27. Interview with Hasan Saeed,* supervisor at a large ready-made garment group based in Korangi, Karachi, July 2016.

28. FIA Report, op. cit., p. 10.

29. *Tribunal's Report for Ascertaining the Circumstances and Cause Leading to the Fire and Subsequent Deaths and Injuries in the Incident That Took Place on 11.09.2012 in the Factory of M/S Ali Enterprises Located at Plot No. F-67 SITE Karachi* (Alavi Tribunal Report thereafter), pp. 23–24.

30. See Chapter 6.

31. Alavi Tribunal Report, op. cit., p. 22.
32. FIA Report, op. cit., p. 10.
33. The Karachi Fire Department has only 22 working trucks, and most are more than 30 years old; interview with Faisal Edhi, head of Edhi Foundation, Karachi, July 2017.
34. Alavi Tribunal Report, op. cit., p. 16.
35. Office of the Police Surgeon Karachi, No. PSK/4305/6, 8 December 2012, p. 3.
36. Alavi Tribunal Report, op. cit., p. 17.
37. FIA Report, op. cit., p. 20.
38. Interview with lawyer Faisal Siddiqi, Karachi, August 2017.
39. In the High Court of Sindh at Karachi, C.P. N° D-3318/2012, Report of Pakistan Rangers (Sindh), 20 January 2015.
40. The CIA is a crime investigation department that assists the police officers supervising each district in the country.
41. Office of the SP, SITE Division, District West, Karachi, In the Court of Additional District and Sessions Judge—V, West Karachi, Progress Report, 2016, p. 5.
42. Two amounts are mentioned in the report, though the inconsistency is not noted.
43. JIT Report on Baldia Factory Fire Case (FIR N°: 343/2012 U/S 302/322/337/435/436/34 PPC) PS SITE-B District West Karachi, 2016, p. 20.
44. On the gradual extension of the criminal definition of terrorism in the Anti-Terrorism Act, see Chapter 6.
45. Elisabeth Claverie, 'Sainte indignation contre indignation éclairée: l'affaire du Chevalier de La Barre', Ethnologie française, Vol. 22, No. 3, 1992, p. 285.
46. Ibid., p. 85.
47. See Chapter 5.
48. JIT Report on Baldia Factory Fire Case, op. cit., p. 14.
49. Arshad Bhaila's testimony to the JIT is instructive in this regard: one evening in July 2012, after spotting Rehman Bola talking to Mansoor in the latter's office, he reportedly walked away, in line with his policy of 'avoiding interaction with them [MQM people]'; JIT Report on Baldia Factory Fire Case, op. cit., p. 16.
50. Ibid., pp. 13–14.
51. FIA Report, op. cit., p. 14.
52. JIT Report on Baldia Factory Fire Case, op. cit., p. 12.
53. The PFSA prides itself on being the most successful forensic department in Pakistan, reportedly solving 280,000 cases in 10 years! See Shafiq

Sharif, 'Assessing Forensic Science Landscape in Pakistan', *MIT Technology Review* (Pakistan), 4 May 2017. URL: http://www.technologyreview.pk/assessing-forensic-science-landscape-pakistan/.

54. For instance, during their hearing by videoconference from Dubai, the Bhaila brothers implicitly suggested that their contractor, Mansoor, may have been in cahoots with MQM racketeers. They further alleged that Muhammad Zubair, one of the main suspects, was recruited by Mansoor in 2005. See Nasir Butt, 'Baldia factory fire: owners narrate a harrowing tale of extortion, greed and carnage', *The Express Tribune*, 19 September 2019. These excerpts from the Bhailas' hearing have been removed from the JIT's final report, in which Mansoor is shown in a better light.

55. Hidayat Hussain, 'FIncendie dans une usine d'habillement à Karachi: l'œuvre de la *Bhatta Mafia*?', post on his blog hosted by Le *Monde* website (no longer accessible), 15 September 2012.

56. E. Claverie, 'Procès, affaire, cause', op. cit., p. 84.

57. On the role of this common sense in the accusatory mechanics of modern scandals, see E. Claverie, 'Sainte indignation contre indignation éclairée', op. cit., p. 280.

58. Interview with senior Karachi police officer, JIT member, Karachi, August 2017.

59. Z. Waseem, *Insecure Guardians*, op. cit., p. 219.

60. The Bhailas fled on the evening of 11 September 2012 and took refuge in Larkana, a town in Sindh. The police made no serious attempt to arrest them. They were subsequently granted bail by the Lahore High Court, which allowed them to move around Sindh without fear of arrest. They were later granted bail by the Sindh High Court (Sukkur) to appear before provincial courts pending their trial. Their provisional release was cancelled, and they were detained in October 2012, before being released a few months later.

61. Charge Sheet No. 238-C/2012, SITE-B Police Station, Karachi West, 19 August 2016.

62. In the Court of Judge, Anti-Terrorism Court No. II, Karachi Division, Order 16 September 2016.

63. Special Public Prosecutors (SPP) are lawyers appointed by the Sindh provincial authorities to represent Rangers before the ATC in cases of terrorism involving the paramilitaries. These judicial powers are indicative of the expansion of the Rangers' mandate over the years.

64. Chambers of Commerce, 'Prime Minister Visits Karachi Chamber of Commerce and Industry', 29 December 2012 (http://

pakistanpressreleases.com/prime-minister-visits-karachi-chamber-of-commerce-industry/).

65. James K. Galbraith, 'Predation from Veblen Until Now: Remarks to the Veblen Sesquicentennial Conference', in Erik S. Reinert and Francesca Viano (eds.), *Thorstein Veblen. Economics for an Age of Crises*, NewYork, Anthem Press, 2013, p. 326.

66. Interview with lawyer Faisal Siddiqi, Karachi, July 2017.

67. Interview with a union leader involved in the Baldia factory fire case, Karachi, August 2022.

68. E. Claverie, 'Sainte indignation contre indignation éclairée', op. cit., p. 273.

69. Founded in 1999, the NTUF is a trade union platform that provides legal assistance to workers involved in industrial disputes and engages in advocacy activities vis-à-vis political authorities and the media.

70. CP No. 3318 of 2012, PILER and Others Versus Federation of Pakistan and Others. Article 199 of the 1973 Constitution provides for any aggrieved person to apply to the High Courts of each province to enforce fundamental rights (such as the right to life and the right to justice). Case law has extended the definition of 'aggrieved persons' to include 'public-spirited' individuals and organizations, but there is no consensus within the judiciary on this broad interpretation.

71. The orthodox approach would have been to file individual suits for damages under the Fatal Accidents Act of 1855.

72. As a result of this mobilization, Faisal Siddiqi became close to Justice Maqbool Baqar, Chief Justice of Sindh province from 2013 to 2015.

73. Brigitte Gaïti and Liora Israël, 'On the engagement of law in the construction of causes', *Politix*, No. 62, 2003, p. 19.

74. Faisal Siddiqi, 'Paradoxes of Strategic Labour Rights Litigation', in Miriam Saage-Maaß, Peer Zumbansen, Michael Bader, and Palvasha Shahab (eds.), *TTransnational Legal Activism in GlobalValue Chains.The Ali Enterprises Factory Fire and the Struggle for Justice*, Cham, Springer, 2021, p. 62.

75. Interview with lawyer Faisal Siddiqi, Karachi, July 2017.

76. F. Siddiqi, 'Paradoxes of Strategic Labour Rights Litigation', op. cit.

77. Mahmudul H. Sumon, Nazneen Shifa, and Saydia Gulrukh, 'Discourses of Compensation and the Normalization of Negligence: The Experience of theTazreen Factory Fire', in Rebecca Prentice and Geert de Neve (eds.), *Unmaking the Global Sweatshop: Health and Safety of theWorld's GarmentWorkers*, Philadelphia, University of Pennsylvania Press, 2017, pp. 147–172.

78. A. Bhuwania, *Courting the People*, op. cit., p. 10.

79. Farhat Fatima, 'Baldia factory fire incident: 4 years of successful campaign for justice', PILER, Karachi, December 2016, p. 3. The Bhailas agreed to pay Rs 61.8 million (about $600,000) in emergency relief to the families of the victims, while KiK signed a memorandum with PILER for the payment of $1 million in immediate relief, to be supplemented by longer-term compensation of $5.18 million, to be paid to the families in the form of pensions.

80. F. Siddiqi, 'Paradoxes of Strategic Labour Rights Litigation', op. cit.

81. Katie Marisco, *The Triangle Shirtwaist Factory Fire: Its Legacy of Labor Rights*, New York, Marshall Cavendish Benchmark, 2010.

82. J. Bair, M. Anner, and J. Blasi, 'Sweatshops and the Search for Solutions', op. cit.

83. Holly Littlefield (with illustrations by Mary O'Keefe Young), *Fire at the Triangle Factory*, Minneapolis, Milbrook Press, 1995; Jessica Sarah Gunderson, illustrated by Phil Miller and Charles Barnet III, *The Triangle Shirtwaist Factory Fire*, Mankato (Minn.), Capstone Press, 2006.

84. On 'industrial hazard regimes', which include 'those arrangements, formal as well as informal, by which public bodies, private interests, and civic mobilizations handle the danger and damage associated with an industry', see Christopher Sellers and Joseph Melling (eds.), *Dangerous Trade: Histories of Industrial Hazard Across a Global World*, Philadelphia, Temple University Press, 2012, p. 4.

85. See https://internationalaccord.org/signatories. The promoters of this agreement are currently working on its extension to Pakistan.

86. Interview with Karamat Ali, Executive Director, PILER, Karachi, July 2016.

87. Emmanuel Henry, *Amiante. Un scandale improbable. Sociologie d'un problème public*, Rennes, PUR, 2007.

88. Pierre Lascoumes, 'Elites délinquantes et résistance au stigmate: Jacques Chirac et le syndrome Teflon', *Champ pénal*, Vol. X, 2013.

89. The deadliest of these accidents occurred on 27 August 2021 at a suitcase factory in Mehran Town, Korangi. The company, which had not been registered with the Labour Department, was operating illegally on residential land. These breaches of the relevant legislation on safety regulations violations have caused more than 100 deaths across Pakistan since the Ali Enterprises fire. See Sammar Abbas, 'Mehran Town: the cost of negligence', *The News*, 5 September 2021.

90. Clean Clothes Campaign, *Workers' Lives at Risk. How Brands Profit from Unsafe Factory Work in Pakistan*, July 2022 (https://cleanclothes. org/news/2022/report-a-decade-after-deadly-ali-enterprises-fire-

pakistans-garment-workers-report-shocking-lack-of-fire-exits). This study was conducted among 600 garment workers in Lahore, Karachi, and Faisalabad.

91. Whilst wildcat strikes remain rare in Karachi, they can take spectacular forms. For example, at the ADM Group's Korangi factory in 2016, hundreds of company employees set fire to several vehicles belonging to the group's managers, then erected barricades on the main road running through the industrial zone. In the end, they won their case, receiving their salaries plus an Eid bonus. Small-scale acts of sabotage are quite common in the workshops, as attested to by workers themselves; see L. Gayer, *Le Capitalisme irrégulier*, op. cit., p. 481.

92. Palvasha Shahab, 'Loss and Legibility: A Conversation with Saeeda Khatoon', in M. Saage-Maaß, P. Zumbansen, M. Bader, and P. Shahab (eds.), *Transnational Legal Activism in Global Value Chains*, op. cit., pp. 15–23.

93. Zubair Ashraf, 'Saeeda Khatoon's story remains untold in Dortmund court', *The News*, 28 December 2018.

CONCLUSION

1. World Bank, *Transforming Karachi into a Livable and Competitive Megacity. A City Diagnostic and Transformation Strategy*, Washington, World Bank, 2018, p. 10.

2. 'Federal tax revenue: Karachi's contribution', *Business Recorder*, 22 July 2018.

3. World Bank, Karachi Port Improvement Project, Project Information Document, Report No. AB5722, June 2010.

4. Huma Yusuf, *Conflict Dynamics in Karachi*, Washington, United States Institute of Peace, 2012, p. 4.

5. Interview with Bilal Khan,* Production Manager at KFG Textile Mills,* Karachi, May 2022.

6. Interview with Ibrar Swati,* small business owner (textiles), Karachi, May 2022.

7. Iftikhar Ahmad, 'Covid-19 and Labour Law: Pakistan', *Italian Labour Law e-journal*, Vol. 13, No. 1, 2020, p. 5.

8. Interview with a prominent business journalist, Karachi, August 2022.

9. In some large textile companies, managers are now instructed to recruit only women; interview with Kamran Husain,* Finishing Manager in a large textile company, Karachi, May 2022.

10. Personal observation in the Landhi industrial area, May 2022.

11. Interview with Bilal Khan,* Production Manager at KFG Textile Mills,* Karachi, May 2022.

12. Interview with a local trade union leader, Karachi, May 2022.

13. Tania Murray Li and Pujo Semedi, *Plantation Life: Corporate Occupation in Indonesia's Oil Palm Zone*, Durham, Duke University Press, 2021, p. 3.

14. Z. Waseem, *Insecure Guardians*, op. cit., 2022, pp. 12–15. On the 'nervousness' of states obsessed with the spectre of chaos, see also Jean and John Comaroff, 'Criminal Obsessions, After Foucault: Postcoloniality, Policing, and the Metaphysics of Disorder', *Critical Inquiry*, Vol. 30, No. 4, 2004, pp. 800–824.

15. On capitalism's relationship to law in Max Weber's works, see 'L'économie et les ordres', in *Concepts fondamentaux de sociologie*, Paris, Gallimard, 2016, pp. 225–264. For a Marxist perspective on capitalism's supposed need for 'legally defined stability, regularity and predictability in social arrangements', see Ellen Meiksins Wood, *The Origin of Capitalism: A Longer View*, London, Verso Books, 2002 [1999], p. 178.

16. Bertolt Brecht, 'Die Ängste des Regimes' (The Anxieties of the Regime), *Das Wort* (Moscow), January 1938, quoted in John J. White and Ann White, *Bertolt Brecht's Fucht Und Elend Des Dritten Reiches. A German Exile Drama in the Struggle Against Fascism*, Rochester, Camden House, 2010, pp. 50–51.

17. On 15 March 2024, European Union member states adopted the Corporate Sustainability Due Diligence Directive, which will make large companies based or operating in the EU legally accountable for environmental and human rights violations within their supply chain. The directive, which remains to be made into a law, was significantly watered down from the initial proposal following opposition from Germany and France—among others.

18. Interview with Faisal Siddiqi, lawyer for families of Ali Enterprises victims, Karachi, August 2022.

19. Miriam Saage-Maaß, 'Legal Interventions and Transnational Alliances in the Ali Enterprises Case: Struggles for Workers' Rights in Global Supply Chains', in M. Saage-Maaß, P. Zumbansen, M. Bader, and P. Shahab (eds.), *Transnational Legal Activism in Global Value Chains*, op. cit., pp. 41–42.

20. Act on Corporate Due Diligence in Supply Chains, Section 2, s. 11, p. 4.

INDEX

Abbas, Tufail, 94, 346n60
Activist Anthropologist, 292
Adamjees (family), 58, 72, 78, 160
Akbar, Bilal (General), 186, 220
Al-Ettehad Power Loom Workers
  Union, 181, 183, 187, 188
Alavi, Zahid Kurban (Justice), 277,
  278
Ali Enterprises, 1-7, 17, 71, 264,
  265-274, 280-283, 288, 289,
  292, 294-297, 304, 305
Ali, Karamat, 268, 295
Ali, Riaz, 154, 156, 157, 244,
  372n35
Alkaram (Textile group), 125,
  154, 171, 188, 372n35
All Pakistan Confederation of
  Labour (APCOL), 48, 66
American Protective League
  (APL), 42
ANP. See Awami National Party
Asian Human Rights Commission,
  142, 160, 353n5
Awami National Party (ANP),
  109, 115, 125, 128, 132, 137,
  151, 154, 163, 165, 183
Ayub, Muhammad, 48, 56, 72

Aziz, Majyd, 200, 207

Bakhtiar, Bashir Ahmed, 79
Bangladesh, 9, 96, 159, 160, 162,
  190, 292, 294, 300, 304, 305,
  341n77, 354n23,
Bantva, 57, 270, 336
Bawani Chali, 163, 211, 213, 214,
  318
Bennett, Harry, 20, 21, 23, 30, 35,
  37, 40-44, 88
Bergoff, Pearl Louis, 29
Bhaila, Abdul Aziz, 3, 270, 272,
  273, 275, 276, 279-292, 296,
  378n79
Bhaila, Arshad, 3, 270, 272, 275,
  276, 279-292, 296, 375n49,
  376n54, 376n60, 378n79
Bhaila, Shahid, 3, 270, 272, 275,
  276, 279-292, 296, 376n54,
  376n60, 378n79
Bhola, Rehman, 280, 281, 284,
  286, 287
Bhutto, Benazir, 119, 243
Bhutto, Zulfikar Ali, 11, 49, 63,
  67, 73, 83, 157, 238-240,
  254

381

Bohras, 54, 57, 336, 364n11
Bombay, 28, 34, 37, 52, 57, 77,
  78, 80, 82-85, 88, 92, 93, 114,
  117, 336n6, 344n3
Bush, George W., 5

Caille, Marcel, 36
Calcutta, 34, 117, 233, 336n6,
  341n79
Caussidière, Marc, 9
Chaudhry, Iftikhar Muhammad,
  173, 174, 187, 276
Chiniotis, 73, 85, 132, 141,
  324n16, 341n79
Citizens-Police Liaison Committee
  (CPLC), 17, 114, 197-210,
  215-228, 242, 243, 258, 259,
  320, 321, 365-372
Collison, William, 34
Colombia, 10, 21, 24, 107, 108,
  109, 169, 170, 195
Communist Party of Pakistan
  (CPP), 346n60
Confédération française du travail
  (CFT), 36
Confédération générale des
  syndicats indépendants (CGSI),
  35
Confédération générale du travail
  (CGT), 35, 36, 37
Cowasjee, Ardeshir, 200
CPLC. See Citizens-Police Liaison
  Committee

Dawoods (Family), 72, 78,
  338n34, 341n77
Dawood Mills, 99
Defence Housing Authority
  (DHA), 202, 203, 277
Denim Clothing, 190-194, 241,
  362n51

Detroit, 19, 20, 23, 41
Dhoraji, 270, 336

Ebrahim, Fakhruddin, 200
Economic League, 34
Edhi Foundation, 3, 201, 277, 278,
  323n1
Employees' Old-Age Benefits
  Institution (EOBI), 63, 147,
  149, 274, 275
Ettehad Town, 171, 175, 181, 183,
  185, 187

Farley, James, 29
Farooqi, Aurangzeb, 124, ,125
Fatima, Kaniz, 97, 347n69
Federally Administered Tribal Areas
  (FATA), 87, 246
Ford Foundation, 47, 56, 60
Ford, Henry, 20, 21, 37, 40, 41,
  44, 88
Ford Motor Company, 19, 20, 21,
  23, 24, 30, 32, 37, 40, 41, 44,
  45, 47, 56, 60, 88
France, 26, 33, 35, 42, 148, 196,
  215, 263, 290, 295, 303
Frontier Constabulary (FC), 86, 87

General Motors (GM), 31, 32
Girni Kamgar Union, 28, 37
Green Park City, 119, 314, 315
Guatemala, 21, 169, 195
Gujarat, 54, 85, 152, 200, 208,
  270
Gul Ahmed (Textile group), 73,
  99, 100

H&M, 191
Haji, Nazim, 200
Haqiqis (MQM-H), 114, 115
Husein Mills, 78, 85-88

Movement/Muttahida Qaumi
Movement
Mukhtar, Iftikhar Ahmed, 53, 55
Musharraf, Pervez, 74, 110, 115,
151, 154, 166, 187, 280

Naqvi, Nayab, 93, 99
National Awami Party (NAP), 109,
357n57
National Database and Registration
Authority (NADRA), 215, 259
National Trade Union Federation
(NTUF), 291, 377n69
NOVA (Tanneries), 141, 143, 144,
145, 159, 160
North West Frontier Province
(NWFP), 86, 95

Orangi, 12, 166, 167, 239, 266,
311
Overney, Pierre, 36

Pak Tobacco Company, 90, 93, 99
Pakistan Employees Cooperative
Housing Society (PECHS), 69
Pakistan Industrial Development
Corporation (PIDC), 48, 72,
335
Pakistan Institute of Labour
Education and Research
(PILER), 267, 268, 291, 294,
312
Pakistan International Airways
(PIA), 346n60
Pakistan Muslim League (Nawaz),
174
Pakistan People's Party (PPP), 91,
109, 111, 114, 128, 137, 151,
154, 371n32
Pakistan Readymade
Manufacturers and Exporters

Association (PRGMEA), 273,
288
Pakistan Steel Mills, 130, 224,
347n71
Papanek, Gustav, 56, 57, 58, 70,
74
Papanek, Hanna, 56
Pathan Colony, 213
People's Amn Committee (PAC),
109, 115, 151, 243, 371n32
Peru, 205
Peugeot, 36
Philippines, 168, 170
Pinkerton (Detective Agency), 21,
29, 31, 33, 34, 37, 42
PPP. *See* Pakistan People's Party
Punjab/Punjabis, 11, 52, 59, 60,
73, 79, 85, 91, 92, 96, 118,
128, 132, 150, 175, 189, 217,
231, 238, 239, 240, 247, 253,
284, 336n6

Qureshi, Muhammad Rizwan, 279,
280

Rana Plaza, 294, 304, 305
Rangers (Sindh), 100, 166, 171,
174-178, 181, 182, 186, 187,
198, 202, 206, 209, 210, 211,
219, 220, 222, 224, 279, 280,
287, 317, 318, 319, 358n68,
359n8
Rangers Security Guards (RSG),
176, 178, 209, 210, 219, 228
Renault, 35, 36
Riaz, Fahmida, 112
RINA, 3, 272
Russia, 26, 35, 145

Sadri, Saleem, 144
Saeed, Mohammed, 186